The Complete **ROYAL FAMILIES** of Ancient Egypt

The Complete ROYAL FAMILIES of Ancient Egypt

AIDAN DODSON

DYAN HILTON

With over 300 illustrations, 90 in color

 Thames & Hudson

To our family
and in memory of
Frances Lilian Price
(1903–1990)

Frontispiece: *Tutankhamun and his wife, Ankhesenamun, as shown on the lid of an inlaid box from the king's tomb (CM JE61477).*

First published in 2004 in hardcover in the United States of America by Thames & Hudson Inc., 500 Fifth Avenue, New York, New York 10110

thamesandhudsonusa.com

First paperback edition 2010

Library of Congress Catalog Card Number 2003110207
ISBN 978-0-500-28857-3

Printed and bound in Singapore by Star Standard Industries Pte Ltd

Contents

Preface

This book derives from a melding of our long-standing respective involvements in the study of the Egyptian royal family in particular[1] and genealogy in general. Egyptian royalty having become a mutual interest over the past few years, a late-night discussion of why there wasn't a book of Egyptian royal family trees concluded with a decision to write one!

Curiously, in spite of the long-posthumous celebrity of one or two of their number, nothing has been available to give the general reader or enthusiast a meaningful picture of the ramifications of the Egyptian royal families. Indeed, even for the specialist, sources are both limited and widely scattered. Accordingly this book is intended to fill a gap in the literature, aimed at the lay reader, but hopefully also of use to the serious student of Egyptology.[2]

Therefore, a very extensive bibliography is provided, together with selective endnotes, which try to capture the key sources used in the writing of the book. On the other hand, while it would have been desirable in an ideal world to provide individual references for every single person listed, this would have led to a situation where references threatened to occupy more space than normal text. We hope that we have reached a reasonable compromise, and that sufficient hooks have been provided for those who wish to delve more deeply into what is known about most of the people who are the subject of this volume, without bewildering the general reader.

Another tension concerns how to deal with areas of controversy – of which there are many. Appeals to 'academic consensus' are problematic, since such a thing does not generally exist – at least amongst the true specialists in a given area. Thus, our approach has been to base the historical and genealogical narrative on what seems to us the best interpretation of the evidence, but to provide some indication of contrary views (and references thereto) in endnotes.

This work thus attempts to meet the requirements of a wide range of readers: it is hoped in carrying out this straddling exercise, the book has not suffered too serious (or embarrassing) an injury! Likewise, we hope that the title of the book does not make too much of a rod for our own backs. If nothing else, we hope to have been able to aid the posthumous well-being of our subjects by making their names once again 'live in the mouths of the living', as the ancient mortuary wish had it.

As always, it is impossible to write a book without the help of many others; we are thus indebted to numerous persons for their help; although it is invidious to single out individuals, we must thank in particular the editorial, design and production staff at Thames and Hudson for giving us all their customary encouragement and aid; Chris Bennett, for notification of his new website (Bennett 2001–2002), which was invaluable in compiling the Ptolemaic portion of this book; Ted Brock and Lyla Brock for information on their current pieces of fieldwork; Marianne Eaton-Krauss; Rolf Krauss; Marek Lewcun; Bill Manley; and Kristin Thompson, for photography in the Sudan. Last and by no means least, we must acknowledge the support given over many years by our family – Don and Edna Dodson, and John, Anne and Sheila Hilton, the last also for her careful reading and commenting upon the manuscript.

Aidan Dodson and *Dyan Hilton*   Redland, Bristol

The royal family writ large: part of the façade of the Small Temple at Abu Simbel, showing Queen Nefertiry D, flanked by images of her husband, Ramesses II, and accompanied by some of their children, Meryatum A, Meryre A, Amenhirkopshef A, Prehirwenemef A, Meryetamun E and Henttawy A.

Introduction

The pharaohs loom large in our vision of ancient Egypt, and countless books and articles have been written on their lives and achievements – both real and alleged. However, the other members of the royal family – wives, sons and daughters – have received relatively little attention. A few, such as Queen Nefertiti, have achieved some degree of popular recognition, but the vast majority are little known, even within the academic community.

However, the role of individual members of the royal family, and the group as a whole, is important for our understanding of the workings of the pharaonic state. Not only was the king himself the divine incarnation of the falcon-god Horus, but the King's Great Wife also had a pivotal theological role that sometimes translated itself into political power. The Crown Prince – the 'Falcon in the Nest' as the Egyptians put it – was also an important figure as the pharaoh-in-waiting, and at certain periods with a particular state role. Lesser spouses and offspring generally had less overt status, but certainly must have had influence at the very least.

This book, therefore, aims to shed light on the lives of the queens, princes and princesses of ancient Egypt, unravelling their family relationships

The Second Pyramid of King Khafre and the Central Field at Giza. In the foreground is the curious tomb of Queen Khentkaues I (see pp. 62–64, 68), while the former quarry face in the middle distance houses the rock-cut tombs of a number of 4th Dynasty princes.

and exploring their roles in the politics, society, monuments and religion of the country. In doing so, we will range from the very dawn of Egyptian history, where only isolated glimpses are available of the royal family, through the vast progeny of Ramesses II, to the fiendishly complicated – and often blood-soaked – interconnections of the Ptolemies and Cleopatras.

The start of the volume provides a basic summary of the structure of the pharaonic state, including the nature of kingship itself and how its functions meshed with those of the bureaucracy. It also looks at the key members of the royal family, and tries to assess what we know of the implications of the major titles that define the 'royal family'.

The book then moves from the general to the particular, with a chronological survey of the royal family from the beginnings of history to Egypt's absorption into the Roman Empire, centring upon discussions of the evidence as to the relationships of the dynasties, genealogical trees derived from these, and notes upon the protagonists' lives. In some cases, these notes are little more than a statement of a person's appearance as a bit-player in a corner of a monument of one of their greater relations; but in some cases an individual may be better attested and better known than many pharaohs – and far longer remembered.

The Pharaonic State

The King

At the heart of Egyptian society sat the king. Surrounding him was an elite ruling class of royalty, priests, courtiers and administrators known collectively as the *p't*. The king was the head of the civil administration, the supreme warlord, and the chief priest of every god in the kingdom: all offerings were made in his name, by a priesthood acting in his stead.

In many accounts the king is viewed as an incarnation of Horus, a falcon-god and the posthumous son of Osiris, a divine king slain by his brother, Set. Horus fought his uncle for the return of the throne and carried out the last rites for Osiris, part of the accession process of a king being the proper burial of his predecessor. There are a number of cases whereby such an act may have been the legal basis for a commoner's ascent to the throne.

The title of 'pharaoh' has come to us from the Hebrew text of the Old Testament. It originates in the Egyptian *pr-'3* ('Great House'), a designation of the palace, which first came to be used as a label for the king during the 18th Dynasty and became common only some centuries later. For most of the time, the usual word for king was *nsw*, but a whole range of titles was applicable to any full statement of a king's names and titulary.

From the late Old Kingdom onwards, an Egyptian monarch had five names. The first was the Horus-name, written inside a frame surmounting a representation of the façade of a palace (*serekh*: ▥), the falcon of the god Horus, patron of the monarchy, perched atop it. The second, the *Nebty* (*nbty*, 'Two Ladies')-name, linked the king with the patron goddesses of Upper and Lower Egypt, while the third was the Golden Falcon (*bik-nbw*)-name, whose significance has been much debated. Apart from the Horus-name, which was the principal means of designating the king during the very first few centuries of Egyptian history, these first three names were used far less than the remaining two, one or other of which became the usual way to refer to a king in both formal and informal contexts.

The remaining two names were enclosed in what is today referred to as a 'cartouche', from the French for a gun-cartridge. Representing a double rope, encircling the dominions of the king, the oval enclosure (Ꝏ) was called by the Egyptians *šnw*. The first of the names contained within a cartouche is today referred to as the 'prenomen', and was usually preceded by the titles *nsw-bity* (conventionally 'King of Upper and Lower Egypt', but perhaps more accurately 'Two-Aspected King') or *nb-t3wy* ('Lord of the Two Lands', referring to the valley and delta areas of Egypt).[3] This, like the preceding three names, was composed on the king's accession, and almost invariably incorporated the name of the sun-god, Re.

The second cartouche name, the 'nomen' (pl. 'nomina'), was preceded by the titles *s3-R3* ('Son of Re') or *nb-h'w* ('Lord of Appearances', or possibly 'Crowns'). It usually represented the birth-name of the king, sometimes – particularly in later periods – with some form of additional epithet, such as 'beloved of Amun' (*mry-Imn*), or 'god and ruler of Thebes' (*ntr-hk3-w3st*). It is by their nomina that the ancient kings are referred to by modern historians, who distinguish like-named individuals by the addition of ordinals such as

A number of statues of King Khafre were found in his valley temple. This, the finest of them, has often been cited as epitomizing the divine confidence of an Old Kingdom pharaoh, calmly facing eternity; from Giza (CM JE10062=CG14).

'II' or 'VI'. In ancient times, kings of the same birth-name were distinguished by their distinctive prenomina, it being extremely rare to find precisely the same combination of cartouche names used by different pharaohs.

Since the ancient Egyptian scripts did not write vowels, vocalization of names presents some problems, although there are conventions that allow acceptable transcriptions to be made: for example, the king *'Imn-mss* is usually referred to as Amenmesse. However, for a number of kings, Greek transcriptions survive, and these are used in many books where they are tolerably close to the Egyptian skeleton. Thus, a king *dhwty-ms*, who might otherwise be transcribed 'Djhutmose' or 'Thutmose', becomes 'Tuthmosis'; *S-n-wsrt* ('Senusret'/'Senwosret') becomes 'Sesostris'; *hnmw-hw.f-wi* ('Khnum-khufu') becomes 'Cheops'; and, at the extreme of the technique, *Nsi-b3-nb-ddt* ('Nesibanebdjedet') becomes 'Smendes'. Here, however, we will use the 'Egyptian' forms.

Many of these Greek writings derive from a history of Egypt written in that language around 300 BC by an Egyptian priest named Manetho, excerpts of which survive in the works of later antique authors. In its text, Manetho divided up the royal succession into 30 'dynasties'. Although there are numerous problems with this system, it is retained by Egyptologists to this day as the most straightforward way of reckoning the progress of the ancient civilization. These dynasties are usually grouped into 'periods' and 'kingdoms', corresponding to distinct phases in the country's political or cultural evolution.

(opposite) Isis as a kite conceives Horus with the mummified body of Osiris; temple of Sety I, Abydos.

(opposite, below) Thutmose III, in many ways the archetypal pharaoh of the New Kingdom, whose conquests extended Egyptian power over an area stretching from northern Syria to the heart of Sudan; from Karnak (Luxor Museum J2).

(above) The temple of Amenhotep III at Soleb, Nubia. Of similar design to the king's great temple at Luxor, this structure formed part of a major building programme in the far south, in which the divinity of the royal family played an important role.

On the façade of the Soleb temple, Amenhotep IV/Akhenaten (on right, partly erased) offers to a divine aspect of his father and probable co-ruler.

The Egyptian monarchy lasted in a recognizable form for over 3,000 years. Although many changes occurred during that time, almost all of the fundamentals remained in place. A central concept was that of the king as a divine being, and the degree to which this was made explicit varies considerably. Some monarchs simply used the usual stereotyped phrases and motifs on their monuments. However, others took things much further and had one or more of their divine aspects set up as distinct gods, to which the king could make offerings: thus, we find scenes of such a king as Amenhotep (Amenophis) III apparently making offerings to himself!

The transmission of the divine essence provides the basis for one of the major issues concerning the Egyptian monarchy: the way in which the crown was passed down from one generation to the next. There is little explicit evidence for this, with two exceptions. The first are the 'divine birth' texts[4] known from at least three kings of the New Kingdom – Hatshepsut,[5] Amenhotep III[6] and Ramesses II,[7] not to mention various Ptolemaic contexts and in Papyrus Westcar,[8] a folk tale that enshrines similar ideas relating to kings of the 5th Dynasty (see p. 62).

The New Kingdom texts are predicated on the concept that the king was the physical son of Amun, who had melded with the person of his (or in the case of Hatshepsut, her) earthly father to impregnate the king's mother. The surviving New Kingdom inscriptions begin with a council of the principal gods, deciding on the need for the king's birth. There is a discussion between Amun and Thoth, to which (in one version of the sequence) Hathor, goddess of childbirth, and the queen who is to become the mother of the king, are parties. Following this, the gods proceed to this queen, who is then seen seated facing Amun, both of them supported in the heavens by two females. The captions explain that Amun had taken the form of (or become incarnated

The theory of divine birth lay behind the institution of pharaonic kingship. The key elements begin with the conception, shown rather coyly with Amun and the queen held aloft by the goddesses Selqet and Neith; the sign of life (ankh) held to the queen's nose signified the transfer of the divine essence. The fertilization is signified by the ram-god Khnum creating the child and its ka (spiritual double) on his potter's wheel, while Hathor offers them life. The first phase is concluded with the annunciation of the forthcoming birth by Thoth (here abstracted from the birth-sequence of Amenhotep III in the temple of Luxor).

The royal child could be conceived of as being born from a lily-flower. This example shows a king of the late 3rd Intermediate Period, perhaps Iuput II (RMS A.1956.1485).

in) the queen's husband and come to her while she lay sleeping in the palace. She awoke and the god, having had sexual intercourse with her, revealed his true identity, telling the queen that the child just conceived would one day 'exercise the excellent kingship in this whole land'.

Amun then goes to Khnum, the original creator of mankind, who is charged with the making of the king-to-be and his/her *ka*, or spirit double,[9] which are made on a potter's wheel: the figures are then given life by one of the goddesses of childbirth (Heket at Deir el-Bahari, Hathor at Luxor). Following on from this, Thoth gives the news to the queen, who is led to her confinement by Khnum and Heket, in a procession led by Amun and containing nine other divinities.

At the actual birth, four divine midwives and other gods of childbirth, including Isis, Nephthys, Meskhenet, Thouris and Bes, attend the queen. The child is then presented to Amun by Hathor, the final scenes emphasizing the care bestowed on it by the gods and its manifest destiny: to become pharaoh.

The second set of evidence is provided by the 'autobiographical' texts of Hatshepsut and Ramesses II,[10] which in many ways form a coda to the divine birth sequence, and tell of their (earthly) fathers presenting them as children to the assembled court and designating them as their successor.[11] The text of Ramesses II runs as follows:

> *I came forth from Re, as you say, while Menmaatre (Sety I) brought me up.*
> *The Lord of All himself made me great, while I was a child, before I reigned.*
> *He gave to me the land while I was in the egg; the great placed their noses*
> *on the earth before me, when I was installed as Eldest Son, as Executive on*
> *the throne of Geb, and reported as Head of Infantry and Chariotry. My*
> *father appeared to the people, I being a child in his arms, and he said*
> *concerning me 'Crown him as king, that I may see his beauty while I live*
> *with him ....'*

In this case, Ramesses was also being made co-regent; however, in the Hatshepsut text, it is clearly the status of intended successor (*sti*) that is being conferred:

> *My person (Thutmose I) caused that there be brought to him the*
> *dignitaries of the king, the nobles, the companions, the officers of the court*
> *and the chief of the people, that they may do homage, to set the person of the*
> *daughter of this Horus (i.e. the king) before him in this palace. There was a*
> *sitting of the king himself in the audience hall, while the people were on*
> *their bellies in the court. His majesty said before them: 'This is my daughter,*
> *Hatshepsut-Khnemetamun, who lives: I have appointed her as my successor*
> *upon my throne; assuredly it is she who will sit upon my wonderful seat.*
> *She will command the people in every place in the palace; she will*
> *command you and you will proclaim her word, you will be united at her*
> *command ....'*

In addition, Thutmose III gives the following account:[12]

> I was serving as an ìwn-mwt.f-Priest ... and was standing in the northern
> Hypostyle Hall (of the temple of Karnak) .... His person (Thutmose II)
> placed incense upon the fire and offered to [Amun] a great offering
> consisting of oxen, calves and goats ... [the image of the god] made a circuit
> of both parts of the Hypostyle Hall, the hearts of those in front of me not
> understanding his actions, while searching for my person in every place. On
> recognizing me he halted .... [I threw myself] on the ground, I placed myself
> on my belly in his presence. He set me before his person: I was stationed at
> the 'Station of the King' ... then they made known before the people the
> secrets in the hearts of the gods ... I flew to heaven as a divine hawk ... Re
> himself established me: I was dignified with the diadems that were upon his
> head ....

In this case it seems that the heir was recognized by the image of the god
Amun, carried in procession, during a festival. Although slightly different
from the ceremonies recounted by Ramesses II and Hatshepsut, the underly-
ing theme of the heir to the throne being formally proclaimed before an
assembly is maintained.

From the foregoing, it seems fairly clear that the 'qualifications' for being
Crown Prince during the New Kingdom were to be the son of the ruling
pharaoh, and to have undergone a formal public 'investiture'. Whether it was
always the eldest surviving offspring, or whether some other concepts of
seniority came into play, is not explicit – particularly where more than one
wife existed. Nevertheless, during the New Kingdom, it seems reasonable to
infer that the heir to the throne was the eldest son by the senior wife.

Now, the matter of the status of the mother of the heir to the throne led to
an erroneous theory that for years bedevilled the study of the Egyptian royal
family. This was linked into the fact that some – but very few – of the
pharaohs married sisters, some of whom became the mothers of the heir to
the throne. This phenomenon is found from at least the Old Kingdom, down
to the end of Ptolemaic times when Cleopatra VII may have espoused two of
her brothers successively. The exceptional nature of such marriages in the
context of ancient Egyptian society as a whole has long since been demonstrated, and any social justification must have lain with the mythological
couplings of sibling deities such as Osiris and Isis. However, this was taken
further by invoking a theory popular in anthropology in the late 19th century
that the earliest rulers of primitive societies were women ('primitive matri-
archy').[13] Thus a scheme was developed that stated that the actual right to the
throne passed down the female line, mother to daughter, and that the
pharaoh held office only by virtue of marrying the 'Great Heiress' – his full-
or half-sister. This theory rapidly gained uncritical acceptance within Egyptology and beyond, and until the last third of the 20th century was generally
regarded as established fact; indeed, it still raises its head in many popular
books, and occasionally in the writings of older generations of scholars.

Thus on the basis of this theory, kings have been claimed by modern scholars to have been 'illegitimate' because their mother had not been an 'Heiress'; for example, some researchers proposed that the execration of the 'heretic' New Kingdom pharaoh Akhenaten and his family was not because of their attacks on the gods of Egypt, but because Akhenaten's mother, Tiye (A), was a commoner. Taking things the other way round, royal wives who nowhere used the title of 'King's Daughter' were nevertheless named as such by historians on the basis that they were their husband's senior spouse, and therefore that they were *probably* his sister. So secure were these assumptions felt to be that an early-20th-century study into brother–sister marriages and their effect on offspring[14] relied heavily on the Egyptian 18th Dynasty, during which, in fact, most kings had mothers who were commoners!

However, in 1952, some of the problems with this theory were raised by Barbara Mertz in her Chicago PhD thesis,[15] with comprehensive demolition by Gay Robins following in 1983.[16] It was pointed out that if the Heiress was so important, there ought to have been an unequivocal means of identifying her – yet none of the titles applicable to a king's wife can be shown to have such an implication. Furthermore, the number of royal wives who were undoubtedly also royal daughters was lower than one would have expected for the theory to be true, and research had indicated that a remarkably high percentage of wives, and even Great Wives, were the offspring of commoners. Finally, it should be emphasized that the divine birth scenes are focused wholly on the divinity of the king-to-be as the basis for his right to the throne. No divine engendering of a sister or betrothal to such a sibling is involved: the clear message is that a pharaoh is pharaoh by virtue of his father, *not* his wife. This is also the case with the divine prototype of the pharaoh, Horus succeeding his father Osiris: Horus is clearly king by virtue of his paternity; indeed, Horus' wife is not even mentioned in his myth.

With the phantom of succession via a Great Heiress laid to rest, the far more straightforward model of father-to-son succession should clearly be regarded as the basis for the designation of the heir to the throne. However, it is likely that the heir's formal investiture was the key event, rather than the birth, particularly given high infant mortality rates in ancient times. Its significance would be further extended where no son existed: it was presumably through a 'presentation to the people' that such a man as Paramessu – soon to be Ramesses I – became heir to Horemheb. While doubts have been expressed as to the warmth of the latter's relationship with his predecessor, Ay, it is possible to read Horemheb's coronation inscription as referring to just such a ceremony.[17]

This finally brings us to what one might term 'irregular' successions – through civil war or other skulduggery. In most cases we have little knowledge of how a usurper justified his (or her) seizure of power, but on the basis of what little we have, an appeal to divine intervention seems to have been standard. We have already seen how Hatshepsut neatly reprised the conventional image of a father nominating his offspring to the throne; this fits in well with the 'civilized' way in which she assumed a place as co-regent along-side her nephew, Thutmose III.

At the other end of the spectrum, Setnakhte came to the throne by the overthrow of his predecessor, Tawosret. Together with her erstwhile ward, Siptah, Tawosret was written out of history and their reigns condemned as 'empty years'.[18] Somewhere in between lies the case of Thutmose IV: he seems to have removed one or more of his elder brothers from the reckoning, but then attributed his accession to the favour of the god incarnate in the Great Sphinx at Giza, as repayment for clearing away the sand which engulfed the sculpture.[19]

The Administrators of Egypt [20]

The king stood at the centre of a great network of officials, both civil and sac-erdotal, through which the state was run. His own personal staff would sometimes undertake specific duties, such as the running of commissions for specific purposes, but there was a clear administrative structure that is detectable for much of Egyptian history.

Except in the very earliest times, the senior official was the 'Vizier' (*t3ity s3b t3ty*, later simply *t3ty*), roughly equating to a modern Prime Minister. The office may go back as far as the Early Dynastic (also known as the Archaic) Period, but its first properly documented holder was Nefermaat A, son of Seneferu. From the beginning of the 4th Dynasty until around the time of Sahure, all Viziers held the title of 'King's Son'. The majority were actually

The temple of Luxor, built under Ramesses II and Amenhotep III, and fronted by an avenue of sphinxes of Nectanebo I.

princes of the blood (or at least sons of princes), although there were a few commoners who had been granted the title honorifically towards the end of the sequence. This clearly indicates that the post was regarded at this time as a royal one. Subsequently, however, the title of King's Son ceased to be held by Viziers, apart from a brief revival under Isesi. At no point in the remaining two-and-a-half millennia of Egyptian history was the title to be reclaimed by an explicit member of the royal family.[21] Indeed, it was not until the New Kingdom that royals would once again be found holding state positions.

As the Old Kingdom continued, the vizieral title began to be bestowed on provincial officials, and also as an honorific tag; perhaps coming under both headings was Nebet A, mother-in-law of Pepy I, and unique as a female Vizier. By the Middle Kingdom the office seems to have reverted to being purely that of a chief official of the state, one of whom apparently obtained the throne as Amenemhat I. The office seems to have split between Upper and Lower Egypt during the 13th Dynasty, a division revived during the second half of the 18th Dynasty.

A considerable amount of data exists on the vizierate during the New Kingdom; the key sources are the 'Duties' texts found in a number of the tombs of 18th Dynasty Viziers, in particular Rekhmire.[22] From these, it may be seen that the Vizier was effectively the king's deputy for administrative matters, as well as chief justice. His power seems to have diminished from late in the 20th Dynasty, although the office continued to exist, because the rule of southern Egypt became far more focused on the High Priest of Amun – an office which had enormous military, as well as religious, authority. Little is known about those who held the northern vizierate.

Below the Vizier the administration split into specialized departments, whose relative roles and ramifications varied over time, but broadly covered public works, finance, grain storage and agriculture. During the Old Kingdom the Overseer of Works was often also Vizier, but during the New Kingdom it was a distinct post, with subordinate posts covering specific areas or institutions. Similarly, the other departments had both national and local officials responsible for various sub-divisions of the field. Generally there is little evidence of royal involvement, although interestingly enough during the 18th Dynasty two royal princes, Amenemhat B and Khaemwaset A, were appointed Overseers of Cattle.

The administration of the provinces, known by the Greek term of 'nomes', varied with time. From the latter part of the Old Kingdom until the late 12th Dynasty the nomes were headed by 'Great Chieftains' (ḥry-tp ꜥꜣ), whose status is shown by the magnificent tomb-chapels constructed at the main centres. However, reforms under Senwosret III re-centralized much power and, although the nome structure remained intact, the great provincial noble cemeteries disappeared and little is known of the details. At communal level, local government was carried out by councils, the knbwt, comprising the more prominent individuals of the area, with functions both administrative and judicial. A key title in local administration throughout Egyptian history was ḥꜣty-ꜥ, variously translated as 'Governor' or 'Mayor', and varying in

Statue of Mentuemhat A, who combined the offices of Mayor of Thebes and Fourth Prophet of Amun during the last years of the 25th Dynasty and early years of the 26th Dynasty (CM JE36933=CG42236).

significance with time and place. Although also borne by many distinguished figures in an honorific manner, it seems only to have been held by members of the royal family who discharged a formal administrative office – e.g. some of the Viziers of the 4th Dynasty. The upheavals of the late 3rd Intermediate Period splintered at least the northern part of Egypt into polities that bore little relationship to the old administrative structure, although old nome-titles continued to exist.

In the Ptolemaic Period there was a comprehensive revision in the way Egypt was run, reflecting the Macedonian/Hellenic background of the kings.[23] Many of the highest officials were Greeks, but some Egyptians were to be found, particularly from the time of Ptolemy VIII.[24] Locally, administration continued much as before, although at provincial level the military commander, the 'strategos', rose to overall leadership under Ptolemy III. An 'epistrategos' was in overall control of Upper Egypt from the time of Ptolemy V onwards.

The Temples [25]

The great religious institutions formed an important part of the running of Egypt – as landlords of many agricultural estates, as well as many workshops and other 'industrial' installations. Their personnel could also play major roles, both by virtue of the economic power of their institution, and by any secondary office that an individual might hold: for example, during the 3rd Intermediate Period, the High Priest of Amun at Thebes was also military Commander-in-Chief of Upper Egypt.

During the Old Kingdom, a major role seems to have been resolved for the temples of the royal pyramids, although our view may well be skewed by the almost total loss of 'ordinary' temples and their archives. However, while the temples built by the New Kingdom pharaohs as their memorials were certainly important, they were eclipsed by the temples of the 'state' cults, such as Amun of Thebes, Ptah of Memphis and Re of Heliopolis. These temples were the principal beneficiaries of the donations of war booty by the conquering pharaohs of the New Kingdom, and with this wealth could further enhance their economic and administrative power.

Such foundations (and many others) had large full-time staffs – the far more numerous local deities often had their shrines manned on a part-time basis, whereby local people of a certain standing spent a number of months per year serving as their god's priesthood. Thus, a priest will frequently also have been a farmer, a scribe, a soldier or a craftsman: religion was just one of a person's civic duties, rather than a specific vocation.[26] The 'shifts' of such priests (and priestesses) are generally referred to as 'phyles'.

The basic grade of priest in a temple was the w^cb ('Pure one'), while the 'Lector Priest' (hry-hbt) was responsible for the ritual books of the temple and readings therefrom. The office had considerable status, and the title is found as a subsidiary for some of those further up the sacerdotal hierarchy. The main grade of priest was the 'Prophet' (hm-ntr), who is found from the earliest times and responsible for the basic administration and functioning of the temple.

View of the Birth Room of Amenhotep III in his Luxor temple, adorned with the sequence of reliefs demonstrating his paternity by Amun (pp. 14–15).

Above all of them was the 'High Priest'. In most cases he was designated First Prophet (*ḥm-nṯrtpy*) of the relevant god, but in some of the more ancient state cults other titles were used. For example, the High Priest of Re at Heliopolis was *wr m³³w* ('Greatest of Seers') and the High Priest of Ptah at Memphis was *wr ḥrp ḥmwt* ('Greatest of the Masters of Craftsmen'[27]). In the largest temples there were layers of authority between the High Priest and the main body of Prophets; in the temple of Amun at Karnak, they were the Second through to Fourth Prophets, but at Memphis the deputy position was that of Sem-Priest, occasionally held simultaneously with the High Priesthood.

In local cults, the High Priesthood would often be held by the local mayor or 'nomarch', but in the great temples, the High Priest and many of his subordinates would be full-time. It was in these contexts that members of the royal family began to take office during the 18th Dynasty, apparently having been excluded during the Old and Middle Kingdoms. The earliest seem to have been Queen Ahmes-Nefertiry as Second Prophet of Amun (a male title!) under Ahmose I, and Amenhotep C as Sem-Priest of Ptah at Memphis under Amenhotep II. Such appointments continued into the Ramesside Period, in particular within the Ptah cult, where both Thutmose B and Khaemwaset C attained the High Priesthood, and that of Re (Ahmose B, Meryatum A, Meryatum B and Nebmaatre). It is also notable that under Amenhotep III, Thutmose B was given the office of Overseer of the Prophets of Upper and Lower Egypt (*imy-r ḥmw-nṯr nw Šmˁw T³-mḥw*), suggesting particular interest in placing the cults of Egypt under tight royal control at this pivotal point in New Kingdom religious history.[28] As the New Kingdom began, a new and important religious post was created at Thebes, that of God's Wife (*ḥmt-nṯr*) of Amun. This office was a female counterpoint for the High Priest, and was always held by a princess of the blood. The earliest holders of the office were actual queens, but from the late New Kingdom onwards they were virgin princesses, with the succession based on adoption of a royal daughter from the next generation.[29]

During the 3rd Intermediate Period the appointment of members of the royal family to priestly posts became even more marked, the 21st Dynasty royal and Theban High Priestly lines being inextricably linked. In the 22nd Dynasty it appears to have been royal policy to place princes in the key High Priesthoods, the Ptah and Amun offices generally being held by sons or grandsons of the ruling king.

Indeed, the very last known High Priests of Amun were the son and grandson of the Kushite king, Shabaka, the post itself being subsumed into that of God's Wife early in the 26th Dynasty. Interestingly, the placing of royal sons in High Priestly posts seems also to die out at this time, not to be revived.

The Military

The importance of placing the High Priesthood of Amun in royal hands was probably more closely linked with the fact that it was combined during the

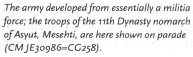
The army developed from essentially a militia force; the troops of the 11th Dynasty nomarch of Asyut, Mesehti, are here shown on parade (CM JE30986=CG258).

3rd Intermediate Period with the military position of Army Leader (ḥꜣwty), rather than any spiritual aspect. It is instructive to note that the majority of titles given to New Kingdom princes were military, with other close ties between the royal family and those employed in the army – for example, Amenhotep III's marriage with Tiye A, daughter of the Master of Horse, Yuya.

Until the New Kingdom there seems to have been little in the way of a standing army and, although a number of kings were militarily very active, our knowledge of the organization that underpinned their activities is very limited. However, with the New Kingdom, the pharaoh's status as warlord is greatly enhanced, and alongside this a definite military structure can be discerned.[30] Clearly as part of this process, royal princes are found in senior military positions from early in the New Kingdom. This begins with Amenmose A, son of Thutmose I, who held the title of 'Generalissimo' ('Great Overseer of Soldiers': imy-r mšꜥ wr, a title first found in the Middle Kingdom), which then appears frequently amongst the senior princes of the Ramesside Period. Some of these princes had the presumably even more senior title of 'First Generalissimo of His Person' (imy-r mšꜥ wr tpy); others were simply 'Generals' (imy-r mšꜥ). Yet other Ramesside princes were 'Masters of Horse' (imy-r ssmt), implying command over the chariotry rather than the infantry.

A major question is how far these military posts reflected active service, or whether they were merely sinecures. Certainly the sons of Ramesses II are depicted taking part in his campaigns, as are sons of Merenptah, and one suspects that the answer may well be ambiguous: that some pursued a genuine military career, while others merely enjoyed the trappings of

During the New Kingdom, a standing army was in existence and the military prowess of princes was emphasized; here, princes Khaemwaset C and Amenhirwenemef (later Amenhirkopshef) A fight in their chariots behind their father Ramesses II; temple of Beit el-Wali (plaster cast in BM).

military status. In any case, there is evidence that princes were given military training as part of their education, Amenhotep B (the future Amenhotep II) being shown under instruction in archery in the tomb of his tutor, Min (tomb TT109).

After the New Kingdom, princely holders of military titles generally held them in connection with other titles – in particular the High Priesthood of Amun, and later the High Priesthood at Herakleopolis. The military ethos continues into the Late Period, with soldier-princes known in the 26th and 30th Dynasties; indeed, the final scions of the native Egyptian royal family served as army commanders under the Ptolemies.

Also broadly classifiable under a military heading was the government of Nubia, varying proportions of which came under Egyptian control during the Old, Middle and New Kingdoms. At its greatest extent during the New Kingdom, the province extended some 500 km (300 miles) south of the conventional Egyptian border at Aswan, embracing amongst other things the goldfields that underpinned much of that period's prosperity. Its rule was under the responsibility of a Viceroy, given the title of 'King's Son of Kush' (*s3-nsw n Kš*), despite generally not being the blood son of the ruling king.[31] Subordinates controlled the two sub-provinces of Nubia, with another apparently running its military forces. The military and economic power controlled by the Viceroy was considerable, and seems to have been used at the end of the 20th Dynasty to try to wrest control of Upper Egypt, leading to a prolonged war with royal forces. This resulted in the definitive loss of Upper Nubia, which later developed into a distinct kingdom that was ultimately to conquer Egypt as the 25th Dynasty.

The Royal Family

Alongside the formal structure of the administrators and priests in the ancient Egyptian state was the king's family. After the Old Kingdom, in the structure of the palace and court, the government officals were distinguished – and usually kept apart – from the royal family. As we have seen, while there were civil titles that were on occasion held by a king's spouse or offspring, there were none (with the partial exception of the God's Wife of Amun) that were *necessarily* held by one of them. Rather, the royal family formed what might be seen as a parallel structure, intersecting with the plebeian world either through marriage or assuming a particular civil or sacerdotal function as the occasion arose.

For a large part of the Old, Middle and New Kingdoms, the royal family's visibility is low. While royal wives are seen not infrequently, the king's off-spring – and in particular his sons – are almost invisible. The evidence suggests that until the Ramesside Period the title of 'King's Son' was only used officially during the lifetime of the pharaoh to which it referred. The only time that this seems to have been waived is on the private monuments of royal tutors, whose own status depended on the parentage of their charges.[32] Significant in this connection is the lack of a title meaning 'King's Brother', except in the anomalous context of a set of 13th Dynasty court accounts, which enumerate the siblings of a king whose father had not been royal (and who were actually generally granted the *s3-nsw* title), and some Late/Ptolemaic contexts, where it generally has honorific meaning only.

Although a considerable range of titles could be accreted to them, five basic tags defined the categories of royal relation: 'King's Wife'; 'King's Mother'; 'King's Son'; 'King's Daughter'; and 'King's Sister', plus a unique example of 'King's Father'. A further tag is more problematic, but on occasion plays the same role of designating the commoner father of a king: 'God's Father'. Besides such titles, another distinction given to certain members of the royal family was the use of the cartouche, used by the king since the 3rd Dynasty, and his sole preserve until the late 12th Dynasty when a wife of Senwosret III received it, and then a daughter of Amenemhat III, Neferuptah (B), who was granted it late in life. Since it is uncertain whether Amenemhat IV was actually her brother, and since a sister (Sobkneferu) ultimately became king, it is possible that Neferuptah's cartouche went along with designation as heir to the throne. Certainly, the use of cartouches for royal children at any time was rare, and presumably must have been an honour specifically bestowed, but under what circumstances is wholly obscure. An early example is Iuhetibu B, daughter of Sobkhotep III, while a somewhat later one is Prince Wadjmose, apparently a younger son of Thutmose I but given a mortuary temple and a cartouche, probably after his death.

The granting of a cartouche to heirs is seen intermittently through the 18th Dynasty, beginning with Amenmose A under Thutmose I, and continuing with Amenhotep C, son of Amenhotep II. However, this subsequently died out, with only a few exceptions (e.g. Shoshenq Q, son of Osorkon I). On the other hand, cartouches are widely used for the senior wives of kings. The first female user was the very first holder of the King's Great Wife title,

King Akhenaten kisses his daughter. Such intimate scenes of the pharaoh are rare, and were an innovation of the heretical Amarna Period (Berlin 14145).

(right) Upper part of a limestone statuette of a queen of the early 18th Dynasty (MMA 16.10.224).

(below) From the late Middle Kingdom, the names of senior queens could, like those of the king, be enclosed in a cartouche. This is that of Ramesses II's favourite wife, Nefertiry D, the name expanded by the epithet 'Meryetmut', 'beloved of Mut', the consort of the great god Amun; from QV66 in the Valley of the Queens, Western Thebes.

Mertseger, in the reign of Senwosret III, the custom becoming universal after the beginning of the New Kingdom. However, for other spouses it is unclear as to precisely who was entitled and who was not, no patterns being obviously detectable. The mother of the king was also generally (but not always) provided with a cartouche, whether or not she had used one earlier in her career. A final category of user, from the 20th Dynasty onwards, was the God's Wife of Amun, the senior female member of the Amun clergy at Karnak, who from the next dynasty generally employed a prenomen cartouche as well, in keeping with the quasi-regal status of the office.

The King's Wife

It is clear that it was usual for a number of women to be the bed-partners of a king. It is also clear that these individuals ranged in status, although rather difficult to classify these states in modern relationship terms. At one end were those women who carried out official roles and would thus be what we would recognize as 'wives', but as for the rest the designations of 'mistress' or 'concubine' carry implications that may or may not reflect the reality of an ancient royal household. Any rationalization is made difficult by the fact that there is no consistency as to the designation of such females, generally only known from the memorials of their offspring. A particularly interesting

Glazed steatite statue of Queen Tiye A wearing twin-plumed crown, twin uraeus and feathered dress (Louvre E25493+N2312).

example is Maatkare B, mother of Shoshenq Q: although the daughter of King Pasebkhanut II, she is given no title to link her with Shoshenq's father, Osorkon I, merely being called 'his (Shoshenq Q's) mother', alongside her priestly titles and that of King's Daughter.

One of the very few 'sub-wives', to coin a phrase, known in her own right is Kiya, who held the unique title of 'Great Beloved Wife of the Dual King' (*ḥmt mrryt ˁ3t n nsw-bity*). However, in view of the novelty of many of the circumstances surrounding her husband, Akhenaten, her singular status is perhaps not surprising.

For most of Egyptian history, however, 'proper' wives were designated by the title *ḥmt-nsw*.[33] This translates directly as 'King's Wife', and thus does not carry the secondary meaning of 'ruling woman' that our word 'queen' does; for Egyptian female rulers, the usual titles of a male ruler were used, generally with female grammatical endings added.

'King's Wife' remains the core title used to designate a king's spouse for the vast majority of Egyptian history. The main exception is during the earliest times, when it is difficult to identify a specific title or set of titles to designate a royal spouse. However, the title 'Great of Sceptre' (*wrt ḥts*), which (like King's Wife) is the only queenly title that can be used alone, appears at the very end of the 3rd Dynasty and then becomes a key designation of a royal wife. It falls out of use in the Middle Kingdom, before experiencing a limited revival in Saite times, along with other ancient and obsolescent designations.

Other titles that may have been used during the Old Kingdom include 'She who sees Horus and Set' (*m33t Hr Sth*), 'Companion of Horus' (*tist Hr*), 'She who brings together the Two Ladies' (*sm3t nbty*) and 'Follower of Horus' (*ht Hr*). It is notable that most of these titles focus on Horus, the link between whom and the king was particularly close in Early Dynastic times, when the Horus-name was the almost universal way of referring to the king.

The characteristic Early Dynastic/Old Kingdom title-mix for the royal spouse undergoes changes in the Middle Kingdom. For example, Aat, wife of Amenemhat III is called 'Executrice (*iryt-p't*), King's Wife, whom he loves (*hmt-nsw mrt.f*), United with the White Crown (*hnmt nfr-hdt*)', in a fairly typical string of titles of that period. The first of these, *iryt-p't*, is initially found in queenly titles under Pepy II, and then used down to the Late Period. It has often been translated as 'Hereditary Princess' (and its male equivalent, *iry-p't*, as 'Hereditary Prince'), but it is clear that the title was neither necessarily hereditary nor a signifier of royal status. The Egyptian words used literally mean 'one belonging to the ruling elite'. Both male and female versions were bestowed on a wide range of individuals, and from the contexts in which they were found, it is quite clear that the implications of the title vary from time to time, and at best indicate a high degree of nobility and perhaps some kind of role as intermediary between the king and the population: 'Executive' may thus be a suitable short translation. However, little more can be read into it except at certain defined periods (see below, p.33, for one of the more significant of these).

The third title, 'United with the White Crown', on the other hand, is one essentially borne by royal wives, although a number of ladies use it who cannot be definitely shown to have been married to a king. It is found from the late 12th Dynasty until the earlier part of the 18th, and refers to the relationship of the lady with one of the two principal crowns of Egypt (or perhaps its wearer, the king). The White Crown is generally regarded as the crown of Upper Egypt, and another crown, the Red, that of Lower Egypt; but it is clear that north/south was not the only duality involved, and that in contexts such as this title it should not be regarded as geographical. Rather, the White Crown can signify the eternal aspect of Egyptian kingship, and the Red its earthly manifestations,[34] the *hnmt nfr-hdt* title thus linking the royal wife into overall 'mythic prototype' of the monarchy. Confusingly, it was also used as a personal name during the 12th Dynasty, and on occasion it is difficult to be certain whether a name or a title is meant.[35]

A second major new office introduced almost simultaneously with this title is that of 'King's Great Wife' (*hmt-nsw-wrt*). These two appellations are first found given separately to wives of Senwosret III.[36] The implications of the Great Wife title are fairly clear, in that it designates the first lady of the land, a status made particularly likely in view of the fact that the first Great Wife, Mertseger, is also the first royal wife to use a cartouche. She was the one who acted as the female counterpart of the pharaoh. This role may actually

Meryetamun E, who combined the status of royal daughter and queen of her father, Ramesses II; from a chapel north-west of the Ramesseum at Thebes (CM JE31413=CG600).

A 'marriage scarab' of Amenhotep III and Tiye (MFA 1985.420); the text reads as follows: 'Live the...(King) Amenhotep III, given life, and live the King's Great Wife Tiye, who lives! The name of her father is Yuya; the name of her mother is Tjuiu. She is the wife of a mighty king whose southern boundary is at Karoy (near Fourth Cataract) and whose northern boundary is at Naharin (northern Syria).'

have transcended her biological role, since there are instances where a king's daughter holds the title without a clear indication (i.e. unequivocal children) that she was also acting as her husband's sexual partner. It continued in use into the Ptolemaic Period.

This status of female counterpart of the king can be seen to link into various theoretical concepts that run throughout the conceptual underpinning of the Egyptian monarchy.[37] Sexual imagery is found throughout Egyptian theology, in particular through the duality that underlies much of it. With the exception of the self-generating creator, subsequent divine generation was sexual, with the ideal divine formation being the trinity: father–mother–child. The best-known example is that of Osiris, Isis and Horus, with the devoted wife rescuing her husband in time of need, and their son avenging his father's murder and taking his rightful place as his successor. The royal wife was thus an integral part of the monarchy, with some royal wives obtaining during their lifetimes a divine status not far short of the king himself.[38]

Although initially there was only one Great Wife at a time, from the latter part of the 18th Dynasty there are occasions when multiple holders of the title are to be found simultaneously, the most famous example being Nefertiry D and Isetneferet A under Ramesses II. After their deaths Ramesses elevated two daughters of Nefertiry and one of Isetneferet to the rank, as well as bestowing it on a wife who was a daughter of the Hittite king.

A particularly elaborate string of titles held by a Great Wife of the late 18th Dynasty (Nefertiti) runs as follows: 'Executrix; Great of Praise (*wrt ḥswt*); Lady of Favour (*nbt iᶜmt*); Great in the Palace (ᶜ*3t m 3ḥ*); Perfect of Face (*nfrt ḥr*); Beautiful with Plumes (ᶜ*n m šwty*); One whose voice one rejoices to hear (*ḥ3i.tw n sḏm ḥrw.s*); the King's Great Wife whom he loves (*ḥmt-nsw-wrt mrt.f*), Lady of

Two of the daughters of Amenhotep III shaking their systra, in a scene from the tomb of Kheruef at Thebes (TT192: Berlin 18526).

the Two Lands (*nbt-t³wy*).' This succession of titles does not by any means exhaust the list of those available to a New Kingdom queen, common additions being 'Mistress of the Two Lands' (*ḥnwt t³wy*) and 'Mistress of Upper and Lower Egypt' (*ḥnwt Šmᶜw T³-mḥw*), and many others are found on occasion. The exact length of such a list very much depended on the amount of space available on the document in question, but when this was limited, King's Great Wife had precedence, followed by Lady of the Two Lands, another new title that is simply a feminization of the kingly tag 'Lord of the Two Lands', used since the Old Kingdom. The key aim was clearly to ensure that whatever titles could be fitted in expressed the lady's relationship to the king.

The titular structure established during the New Kingdom remained broadly standard for the remainder of Egyptian dynastic history, although during the 26th Dynasty there was some revival of ancient titles such as Great of Sceptre, particularly by the God's Wives of Amun. This was in keeping with the archaism of the time, which is also to be seen in the simplified formulations of the kings' names of the period.[39] Final modifications to the scheme are to be seen under the Ptolemies, as the range of titles was rapidly reduced after Cleopatra I; the co-rulership held by many of these ladies is shown by the new title, '(Female) Ruler' (hk3t), used by Arsinoe II and most of her successors, down to Cleopatra VII herself.

The King's Mother

The title mwt-nsw, 'King's Mother', first appears at the very beginning of the Old Kingdom[40] and continues to be found until the end of the Late Period. Its use is generally straightforward, denoting a king's mother during his reign. However, there are occasional instances where it appears to have been used prior to any offspring's accession, in which case a co-regency between that king and his predecessor should probably be assumed.[41] The term may on occasion refer to the marriage of a lady's daughter to a king, although in this case it should be only part of a longer string, mwt-nsw n hmt-nsw(-wrt).

The title of King's Mother often appears alongside the principal wifely titles, where these were held prior to her son's accession. There are also situations where it is suspected that the woman in question may not actually have held certain titles under the king's father, but they were only granted by her son. This applies in particular to the status of King's Great Wife, given by Thutmose III to his mother Iset A, who may not even have been a hmt-nsw during Thutmose II's lifetime, when Hatshepsut seems to have been undisputed Great Wife.

King's Mother can also be found alone, either in cases where space is limited or for reasons of emphasis; an example of the latter is to be found in the tomb of Iset D in the Valley of the Queens, which was provided for her by her son, Ramesses VI. It was presumably to emphasize this role that he had omitted the wifely titles that linked her to Ramesses III, now long dead.[42] The other instance where the title is used on its own, of course, is where a king was not the son of a king: examples are Kemi, mother of Sobkhotep III and Neferhotep I, and Senisonbe, mother of Thutmose I.

An area of uncertainty is whether or not King's Mother alone could ever have the extended meaning of 'King's Mother-in-Law'. This has been claimed for certain individuals during the 21st Dynasty, but the evidence is equivocal at best, since there are reconstructions that would make the ladies in question the physical mothers of kings.[43]

A further area for query concerns the title 'God's Mother' (mwt-ntr), which is found essentially during the New Kingdom. Since the king was a god, it might appear likely that God's Mother and King's Mother could be equivalent. However, a number of God's Mothers did not have a king amongst their offspring, and indeed died before their royal husbands. The significance of this title thus remains obscure and may have been primarily priestly.

The King's Son

The first known *s3-nsw*, 'King's Son', appears at the beginning of the 2nd Dynasty. For much of that time it simply designates the male offspring of the king, but there are exceptions. At the very beginning of the New Kingdom, a (non-royal) viceregal post was established for the purpose of ruling the newly reconquered lands of Nubia. From the middle of the 18th Dynasty onwards, the Viceroy was designated *s3-nsw n Kš*, 'King's Son of Kush', and since the '*n Kš*' was from then on an invariable adjunct, there is little room for confusion with 'real' princes. However, prior to this time, the earliest Viceroys were simply called *s3-nsw*, with the termination merely implied, leaving room for possible confusion.

A procession of princes in the temple of Ramesses III at Medinet Habu. This relief was originally carved without names. However, when he came to the throne, Ramesses IV added his name and princely titles to the first figure, Ramesses VI following suit with the next two. He also added the names and titles of his other brothers to the images behind him, beginning with his only still-living brother, Sethirkopshef B. Finally, when the latter became king as Ramesses VIII, he added his cartouche alongside his princely figure (see pp. 188–89).

The other exception is (mainly) during the Old Kingdom, when King's Son could be bestowed upon people wholly unrelated to the king, as is shown by mentions of such an individual's real parents. It seems fairly clear that where the title is followed by 'of his body' (*n ḥt.f*), a 'real' royal son is often meant, but there are exceptions and examples of uncertainty even in this case. In addition, both during the Old Kingdom and very occasionally later, kings' grandsons also called themselves *s₃-nsw*. During the 13th Dynasty we also have the example of the brothers of Sobkhotep III holding the title. Although there were certainly still a few titular King's Sons in the Middle Kingdom,[44] and even in the very early years of the 18th Dynasty,[45] the phenomenon seems to have died out by Thutmosid times, although a few 'non-genealogical' uses of the string King's Son in unrelated titles are known.

The title of 'Eldest King's Son' (*s₃-nsw smsw*) is found as far back as the Old Kingdom and, although it may on occasion have designated the heir, there are many times where this was not the case. The latter are principally in the Old Kingdom where it was clearly bestowed honorifically, including upon those without royal blood (see above, p. 28, for such 'honorary' princes). However, by the New Kingdom it indeed seems to have become a 'political' appellation of the heir to the throne. As such, it was supplemented by 'First King's Son' (*s₃-nsw tpy*), apparently indicating the eldest son by a particular wife. While on occasion a person could be entitled to both, *s₃-nsw-tpy* seems normally to have been reserved for the head of a cadet branch, or a deceased elder brother of the Crown Prince.[46]

Another title that seems to have been generally synonymous with the heir to the throne during the latter part of the New Kingdom (but *not* before or after) was *iry-pᶜt*, the feminine form of which, as we have seen above, formed part of a royal wife's titulary. Perhaps best translated as 'Executive', its implication seems to be that its bearer is one acting for the king. Its re-definition into a designation of the heir to the throne seems to go hand-in-hand with the return to appointing royal princes to state posts from the middle of the 18th Dynasty onwards. The wide-ranging authority implicit in the title is shown by the expanded version used by a number of New Kingdom princes: 'Executive who is at the Head of the Two Lands' (*iry-pᶜt ḥry-tp t₃wy*).

One user of the title, apparently with its new meaning, was General Horemheb,[47] heir to Ay, who is given this title on a relief in Berlin, where he is shown leading a funeral procession with the two Viziers, normally first under the king, very definitely behind him. One might speculate that the situation at the end of the 18th Dynasty, with the succession of three non-royal kings, created a demand for a Crown Princely title that did not assume its bearer was the physical offspring of a monarch.

During the 3rd Intermediate Period there is a change in the titulary of royal sons in that the name of the father begins to be incorporated, for example 'King's Son of Osorkon'. Unfortunately, this innovation corresponds with the increasing tendency for royal names to become formulaic and repetitive so that they can potentially be confused with one another, and it is often not straightforward to distinguish the specific father of a royal son.[48] The 3rd Intermediate Period also sees a number of individuals bearing the title 'King's Son of Ramesses'. Since no kings of that name ruled during the period this cannot be a direct filiation. There are two possibilities: one is that it is a priestly title, akin to 'King's Son of Amun', 'King's Son of Ptah' and other deities, and implies a role in the mortuary cult of (probably) Ramesses II or III. The other is that the individual had Ramesside blood in his veins, although if this were the case, one might expect a more explicit statement of descent on occasion.

The King's Daughter

Like its male equivalent, the title 'King's Daughter' (*s3t-nsw*) goes back to the earliest times. In contrast with other royal family titles, there are few complications with the use of it, the only extension regularly used being *n ht.f*, 'of his body', although a few ladies were 'Eldest' or 'First' royal daughters.[49] There is little evidence of its widespread bestowal in an honorary fashion, except for occasional use by grandchildren of the king. Although it is difficult to quantify the latter, unequivocal examples are fairly rare, the earliest case being Meresankh III, granddaughter of Khufu. No clear instances are known from the Middle Kingdom, and the most obvious New Kingdom example is Nebetia, daughter of Prince Siatum A.

The God's Wife of Amun, Shepenwepet II – daughter of Piye – offers to Harakhty, Isis and her adoptive mother, Amenirdis I, in the latter's tomb-chapel at Medinet Habu. The chapel was built for Amenirdis by her 'daughter'.

As already noted, a number of King's Daughters acted as King's Great Wife for their fathers, but the details of their role remain unclear. Such 'marriages' were uncommon and attempts to identify a specific regalia denoting a daughter-wife have not been convincing.[50] Few changes in the titles of princesses are to be seen in periods subsequent to the New Kingdom, the main one being the inclusion of a father's nomen in his daughter's title, paralleling male practice at that time.

The King's Sister

As we have already noted, the title of 'King's Brother' is unknown essentially until the end of the Late Period, with an appearance of the wholly anomalous 'King's Brother and Father' appellation given to Tjahapimu, father of Nakhthorheb.[51] However, 'King's Sister' (*snt-nsw*) is found occasionally during the Middle Kingdom, and more frequently during the New Kingdom and later. It is most commonly found in the titularies of kings' sister-wives, but also in that of a married-out princess such as Tia C. However, it does not seem to be universal for such individuals to employ the title, some preferring to stick to 'King's Daughter' alone.[52]

One issue surrounding the sisterly title is whether it necessarily applies to the contemporary king or whether a predecessor can be implied. On the basis of the apparent New Kingdom practice with royal sons, it is likely that the former was the case, but no unequivocal data is available to rule out the second option as a possibility.[53]

During the 25th Dynasty a new sisterly title, 'Sister-wife' (*snt-hmt*, generally '... of the Dual King/Son of Re') appears in the record. Although not found in the Late Period, it reappears in Ptolemaic times, doubtless influenced by the importance of the brother-sister dynamic at that time – although applied on occasion to non-sibling spouses, for example Berenice II and Cleopatra I.

God's Father

In spite of some problems, the titles designating royal spouses and offspring are essentially clear in their implications; 'God's Father' (*it-ntr*), however, is one of the most problematic.[54] On the one hand, it is a well-known priestly title, borne by a series of Old Kingdom High Priests at Heliopolis, and then apparently revived from the end of the 18th Dynasty onwards. These priests marched in front of the god's bark when it was carried in procession, sprinkling purifying water before it; theirs seems to have been in general a middle-ranking title, in between ordinary (*wʿb*) priests and the prophets (*hmw-ntr*), although it was also used as a secondary title by higher-ranking individuals. In any case, its priestly use seems to have carried neither political nor genealogical implications.

In contrast, earlier on, the title is found in at least some instances with a non-sacerdotal, and very definitely political/genealogical, significance. During the Old Kingdom, Khui (father-in-law of Pepy I) had the title, as did Shemay, son-in-law of Neferkauhor. Another bearer, Khety A, has been

The God's Father Yuya and his wife, Tjuiu, parents-in-law of the pharaoh Amenhotep III, as depicted on their mummy-masks; from tomb KV46 in the Valley of the Kings, Western Thebes (CM CG51008–9).

proposed as the ancestor of the 9th Dynasty, while during the Middle Kingdom there are clear examples of its use to designate the non-royal father of the king.[55] The earliest example is Mentuhotep I, ancestor of the 11th Dynasty, with one of the best-documented instances being Haankhef, father of Sobkhotep III and Neferhotep I of the 13th Dynasty. There is also a case of it being used to denote an actual king as the father of the reigning monarch, when Inyotef III is shown with his son, Mentuhotep II (see p. 88).

The title is not found with the implication of 'father of the king' during following periods, with the exception of one statement by Ramesses II with reference to Sety I. However, this may simply be an accident of preservation; for example, we know nothing whatever of the father of Horemheb and have no definite memorials to Sety A, father of Ramesses I, that clearly date to Ramesses' reign.[56] On the other hand, a number of non-priestly God's Fathers exist during the 18th Dynasty. A number are found amongst royal tutors,[57] for example Heqareshu and Heqaerneheh, who served in the middle of the 18th Dynasty, but the most prominent holders of the title are the generals Yuya and Ay. The importance the latter attached to the epithet is shown by the fact that he incorporated it into his nomen after coming to the throne. It is Yuya, however, who may give the clue to the title's 18th Dynasty meaning, in that his daughter was Tiye A, King's Great Wife of Amenhotep III.

On Yuya's example, it has been proposed that holders of the title were likely to be fathers-in-law of a pharaoh, following the Old Kingdom precedent of Khui. There are attractions to this; for example, at least one royal wife was the daughter of a royal nurse, implying that they could spring from this particular court milieu. Also, Ay's wife, Tey, was nurse to Akhenaten's wife, Nefertiti, and it has been suggested that this could reflect Ay as being Nefertiti's father by a wife who had died, giving Tey's title the implication of 'stepmother'. Unfortunately, apart from the case of Yuya, no other God's Father of the period can be shown with certainty to have fathered a queen and thus, although highly attractive, a consistent 18th Dynasty translation of the title as 'King's Father-in-Law' remains unproven.

Even if proven, this meaning of the title had changed again – or perhaps broadened – by the middle of the 19th Dynasty, when it was held by the king-to-be, Merenptah. He could not conceivably have been the father-in-law of the king, who was his own father, Ramesses II. The God's Father title is thus one which has to be evaluated with great care; it may be usable to confirm a

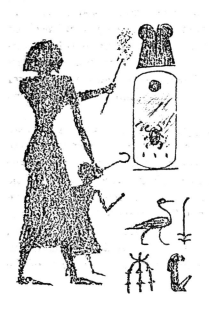

The tutors of the royal children were important figures. They appear to have taken their charges on visits around the country, a fruit of which are the graffiti that they left around the First Cataract area. Left: Thutmose A and his (unnamed) tutor before a damaged cartouche of his father (Sehel); Right: the name of the tutor Heqareshu stands before two small figures of princes Amenhotep D and Akheperure (Konosso).

relationship which is hinted at by other data, but cannot be used on its own to proclaim an individual's relationship – by blood or by marriage – to a king.

The Harem [58]

It is clear that many of the various title-bearers discussed above were amongst the members of the institution (known in Egyptian as *ipt nswt*, and later *ḫnrt*) that we generally refer to by the Turkish word 'harim', in English 'harem'. Unlike the meaning denoted by 'harem' in the Ottoman world, it was not a closed body, but rather the institution concerned with the private affairs of the royal family – a community of women and children that could function as a separate unit from the main royal palace.

Evidence for the formal existence of harems is somewhat equivocal before the New Kingdom, with the added complication that the term often used for them at this period (*ḫnrt*) was identical to a word used during the Old and Middle Kingdoms to refer to a troupe of musicians! Nevertheless, from the beginning of the New Kingdom we begin to find titles clearly belonging to the administrators of the harems, major examples of which were to be found at Memphis and at Gurob, near the entrance to the Fayoum.

Contrary to the modern implications of the word, the females who belonged to the harem were not all offspring or potential sexual partners of the king. The title *ḫkrt nsw* ('Royal Ornament') is sometimes translated as 'Royal Concubine' but, given what we know of many holders, it seems merely to have denoted highly regarded women attached to the royal household, many being the wives of important officials. Indeed, the harem seems to have been an institution with various purposes, tied together in the service of the royal women and outputting goods such as linen cloth, amongst other things.

Further 'output' was the offspring of the king, children who would be educated in the harem; the fact that so many princes of the 18th Dynasty have left monuments around Memphis was due to the presence of the harem there, where they had doubtless been brought up, or even born. It appears that individuals who later bore the title 'Child of the Kap' (*ḥrd n kꜣp*) may have been those who had shared the royal princes' education. Some may have been foster-siblings, their mothers having acted as royal wet-nurses, while others were perhaps the sons of the pharaoh's foreign vassals and sent to Egypt for education, indoctrination – and to act as hostages against their fathers' good behaviour.

Thus rather than the exotic world typified in *1001 Nights*, the Egyptian royal harem was a varied establishment that formed a key part of the royal household. One example has been excavated at Gurob, showing it to have comprised a small city with a temple and an extensive necropolis, some of the tombs of which belonged to royal offspring. The residential areas have revealed many objects of daily life, as well as others with kings' names; amongst other finds was a magnificent wooden head (now in Berlin) of Tiye, wife of Amenhotep III, and certainly a sometime resident of the harem; altogether they reveal a rich community that was at the heart of the pharaonic state.

Granite statue of Senenmut, tutor of Princess Neferure A, whom he holds in his arms; perhaps from Karnak (Field Museum, Chicago 173800).

Genealogical Groupings

The pages that follow are arranged around dynasties or parts of dynasties, grouped into sections by period. Each section is arranged in the same way, alongside one or more genealogical trees:

- **Historical Background**: a brief historical overview of the time in question;

- The basic order of the **Royal Succession** (a more detailed chronology, with royal titularies, is given on pp. 287–94);

- A survey of the evidence for the relationships within the **Royal Family**, and any particular areas of controversy or interest;

- **Brief Lives** of known royal relations, including the pre-accession careers of any kings who have left monuments from before their kingship (otherwise, they are only shown in the Royal Succession section). Generally, lines outside the direct succession are followed, where known, for up to two generations, and occasionally further;

- The **Genealogical Trees** link together all individuals whose relationships are known, or can be surmised with some degree of confidence (an uncertain/hypothetical relationship is indicated by the lines employed).

- A **Bibliography** of the principal sources for the royal relationships of the period is provided at the end of the book;

Nomenclature

Most royal individuals bearing the same name are distinguished by capital letters (e.g. Thutmose C); where it is not altogether certain whether a person is distinct, and may actually be a previously lettered individual at a different stage in their career, a letter from later in the alphabet may be used (e.g. Nefer-hetepes Q, who may be identical with Neferhetepes A). Most private persons are given lower-case roman suffixes (e.g. Hor viii), with capital roman ordinals restricted to kings, major queens, and certain High Priest/esses of royal ancestry, unless necessitated by long usage by Egyptology, where old designations are retained for clarity; some lettering also falls into this category.

It should be noted that several names (e.g. Sobkemsaf, Bebi, Mentuhotep) were used by both males and females; to avoid undue confusion such homonyms are lettered/numbered in a single sequence.

Titulary

High-status Egyptians possessed a myriad titles, and any attempt to list all those possessed by the individuals dealt with in this book would lengthen it to a quite unwarranted degree. Accordingly, only the most important, from the point of view of relationships or political role, are included; for reasons of space, they are given on the following pages in an abbreviated form:

The northern figures from the façade of the Great Temple at Abu Simbel. Ramesses II is shown on a colossal scale, accompanied by the much smaller members of his family. From the left we have: Nefertiry D; Ramesses B; Nefertiry D again (obscured); Tuy A; Meryetamun E; Nefertiry D (obscured).

Abbreviations used in the Brief Lives, Parts 1–5

Abbreviation	Title	Egyptian form	Remarks
Ador	God's Adoratrix	dwȝt nṯr [dwat-netjer]	A senior female priest in the temple of Amun at Karnak. The title is at some periods synonymous with God's Wife, but is later often used to denote the ultimate heir to the reigning God's Wife.
AL	Army Leader (of the whole army)	hȝwty (n mšᶜ r-ḏrw) [hawty (en mesha er djeru)]	Commander-in-Chief of the Army during the 3rd Intermediate Period; a title generally held by the High Priest of Amun.
ChA	Chantress of Amun	hst ḥnw n 'Imn [heset khenu n Amun]	A lady who sang in the temple of Amun; the title was often held by wives and daughters of senior officials.
ChHA	Chief of the Harem of Amun-Re	wrt ḥnr 'Imn-Rᶜ [weret khener Amun-Re]	Other than the God's Wife, the senior female member of the Amun clergy (or one of its sub-sections: 'phyles') during the 3rd Intermediate Period; a title often held by the wife of the High Priest.
ChMa	Chieftain of the Meshwesh/Ma	wr n Mšwš/Mȝ [wer en Meshwesh/Ma]	An individual of Libyan ancestry, who was the head of the Libyan Meshwesh (or Ma) Tribe.
CTL	Consort of the Two Ladies	smȝyt nbty [semayet nebty]	Queenly title used during the 1st Dynasty.
EKD(B)	Eldest King's Daughter (of his Body)	sȝt-nsw smst (n ḥt.f) [sat-nesu semset (en khet-ef)]	Title only found during the Old Kingdom.
EKSon(B)	Eldest King's Son (of his Body)	sȝ nsw smsw (n ḥt.f) [sa-nesu semsu (en khet-ef)]	The designated heir to the throne during the New Kingdom; earlier, it merely implied high status and, if used without the 'n ḥt.f' suffix, may have been bestowed honorifically.
Exec(H2L)	Executive (at the Head of the Two Lands)	iry-pᶜt (ḥry-tp tȝwy) [iry-pat (hery-tep tawy)]	A title borne by the Crown Prince during the latter part of the New Kingdom, perhaps implying a kind of 'Chief Executive' role outside the normal government structure. For the other usages of iry(t)-pᶜt see above, p. 33.
FW	Foremost (of Women)	ḥnty [khenty]	Queenly title used during the 1st Dynasty.
GBW	Great Beloved Wife	ḥmt mrryt ᶜȝt [hemet mereryt aat]	Borne uniquely by Kiya, the junior wife of Akhenaten.
GChMa	Great Chieftain of the Meshwesh/Ma	wr ᶜȝ n Mšwš/Mȝ [wer aa em Meshwesh/Ma]	See 'ChMa'.
GD(B)	God's Daughter (of his Body)	sȝt nṯr (n ḥt.f) [sat-netjer (en khet-ef)]	A senior daughter of the king during the Old Kingdom.
Gen(mo)	General(issimo)	imy-r mšᶜ (wr) [imy-ro mesha (wer)]	Military commander; with the addition of 'wr' ('great') it indicated overall command of the military forces.
GF	God's Father	it-nṯr [yot-netjer]	1. A junior priest; 2. A person closely related to the king, on occasion his father or father-in-law; see above, pp. 35–36.
GH	God's Hand	ḏrt-nṯr [djeret-netjer]	A senior female member of the Amun clergy during the 25th and 26th Dynasties; she might on occasion be synonymous with the God's Wife, but may also be the immediate heir to the reigning God's Wife following the adoption of an heir to the heir.
GKSon	Great King's Son	sȝ nsw wr [sa-nesu wer]	Used once during the Ptolemaic Period by a scion of the old 30th Dynasty.

Abbreviation	Title	Egyptian form	Remarks
GS	Great of Sceptre	*wrt hts* [weret-hetes]	Queenly title used during the Old Kingdom, revived during the 26th Dynasty.
GUE	Governor of Upper Egypt	*imty-r Šmʿw* [imy-ro Shemau]	Chief official for the area around, and south of, Herakleopolis. It is unclear how far south his authority extended.
GW(A)	God's Wife (of Amun)	*hmt nṯr (n ʾImn)* [hemet-netjer (en Amun)]	Female opposite number of the High Priest of Amun at Karnak from the end of the 17th Dynasty onwards; in the 26th Dynasty she became overall head of the Amun clergy.
HPA	High Priest of Amun at Karnak	*hm-nṯr tpy n ʾImn* [hem-netjer tepy en Amun]	Head of the clergy of the god Amun at Karnak.
HPH	High Priest of Re at Heliopolis	*wr mȝȝw* [wer maau]	Head of the clergy of the sun-god.
HPHrk	High Priest of Arsaphes at Herakleopolis	*hm-nṯr tpy n Hryšf* [hem-netjer tepy en Heryshef]	Head of the clergy of Arsaphes.
HPM	High Priest of Ptah at Memphis	*wr hrp hmwt* [wer kherp henut]	Head of the clergy of Ptah.
HPT	High Priest of Amun at Tanis	*hm-nṯr tpy n ʾImn* [hem-netjer tepy en Amun]	Head of the clergy of the god Amun at Tanis.
KB&F	King's Brother and Father of the King	*sn-nsw it-bity* [sen-nesu yot-bity]	A very rare title only found in the 30th Dynasty.
KD(B)	King's Daughter (of his Body)	*sȝt-nsw (n ht.f)* [sat-nesu (en khet-ef)]	Female offspring of the king; in the Old Kingdom only the absence of 'n ht.f' might imply honorific status. The title was occasionally granted to granddaughters.
KGD	King's Great Daughter	*sȝt-nsw wrt* [sat-nesu weret]	Possibly the eldest female offspring of the king; very rare.
KGW	King's Great Wife	*hmt-nsw wrt* [hemet-nesu weret]	Senior wife of the king from the late 12th Dynasty onwards.
KM	King's Mother	*mwt-nsw* [mut-nesu]	Female parent of the king; possibly on occasion bestowed on the mother of the acknowledged heir.
KSon(B)	King's Son (of his Body)	*sȝ-nsw (n ht.f)* [sa-nesu (en khet-ef)]	Male offspring of the king; in the Old/Middle Kingdoms the absence of 'n ht.f' might imply honorific status. The title was occasionally granted to granddaughters.
KSonK	King's Son of Kush [Viceroy of Nubia]	*sȝ-nsw n Kš* [sa-nesu en Kush]	Head of the Egyptian administration south of Aswan; in the early 18th Dynasty the title is abbreviated to simply 'sȝ nsw'.
KSis	King's Sister	*snt-nsw* [senet-nesu]	Female sibling of the king.
KW	King's Wife	*hmt-nsw* [hemet-nesu]	Spouse of the king.
LH	Lady of the House	*nbt-pr* [nebet-per]	The standard designation for a married woman.
L2L	Lady of the Two Lands	*nbt-tȝwy* [nebet-tawy]	Queenly title used from the late 18th Dynasty onwards.
MoH	Master of Horse	*imy-r ssmt* [imy-ro sesemet]	Head of the chariotry arm of the Army.
MULE	Mistress of Upper and Lower Egypt	*hnwt Šmʿw Tȝ-mhw* [henut-Shemau Ta-mehu]	Queenly title used from the end of the 18th Dynasty onwards.

Abbreviation	Title	Egyptian form	Remarks
M2L	Mistress of the Two Lands	ḥnwt-t3wy [henut-tawy]	Queenly title used from the mid-12th Dynasty onwards.
OPULE	Overseer of the Prophets of Upper and Lower Egypt	imy-r ḥmw-nṯr nw Šmᶜw T3-mḥw [imy-ro hemu-netjer nu Shemau Ta-mehu]	Senior official responsible for priesthood of the various gods throughout Egypt.
P[DEITY]	Prophet of [DEITY]	ḥm-nṯr n [DEITY] [hem-netjer en (DEITY)]	Middle-ranking priest.
PH	Prophetess of Hathor	ḥm(t)-nṯr Ḥwt-ḥr [hemet-netjer Hathor]	Female involved in the cult of Hathor, frequently of high social status.
RO	Royal Ornament	ḥkrt-nsw [khekeret-nesu]	High-ranking female at Court, usually the wife of a senior official.
ScH	Sceptre of Horus	ḥts-Ḥr [hetes-Hor]	Queenly title during the 1st Dynasty.
SH	One who Sees Horus	m33t Ḥr [maat-Hor]	Queenly title between the 1st and 3rd Dynasties.
SonL2L	Son of the Lord of the Two Lands	s3-nb-t3wy [sa-neb-tawy]	Variant of 'KSon' used in the late 3rd Intermediate Period.
SPP	Sem-Priest of Ptah at Memphis	sm n Ptḥ [sem en Ptah]	Deputy to the High Priest.
SWSR	Sister-Wife of the Son of Re	snt-ḥmt n s3-Rᶜ [senet-hemet en sa-Re]	Female partner in a sibling marriage; used only during the Ptolemaic Period.
UWC	United with the White Crown	ḥnmt-nfr-ḥḏt [khnemet-nefer-hedjet]	Queenly title used from the 12th to early 18th Dynasties.
Viz	Vizier	(t3yty s3b) t3ty [(taty sab) tjaty]	Head of the Egyptian government; the office was sometimes divided in two, with separate Viziers responsible for Lower and Upper Egypt.
1ChHA	First Chief of the Harem of Amun-Re	wrt ḥnr tpyt nt 'Imn-Rᶜ [weret khener tepyt ent Amun-Re]	The wife of a 3rd Intermediate Period High Priest of Amun at Thebes.
1Genmo	First Generalissimo	imy-r mšᶜ wr tpy [imy-ro mesha wer tepy]	Used by some Ramesside Crown Princes in their role as head of the Army.
1GKW	First Great King's Wife	ḥmt-nsw ᶜ3t tpyt [hemet-nesu aat tepyt]	Queenly title found during the 25th Dynasty.
1KSon	First King's Son	s3-nsw tpy [sa-nesu tepy]	New Kingdom title, denoting the eldest surviving son of a king by a given mother.
2PA	Second Prophet of Amun at Karnak	ḥm-nṯr 2-nw 'Imn [hem-netjer sen-nu en Amun]	Immediate subordinate of the High Priest.
3PA	Third Prophet of Amun at Karnak	ḥm-nṯr 3-nw 'Imn [hem-netjer khemet-nu en Amun]	Immediate subordinate of the High Priest.
4PA	Fourth Prophet of Amun at Karnak	ḥm-nṯr 4-nw 'Imn [hem-netjer fed-nu en Amun]	Immediate subordinate of the High Priest.

Note • Abbreviated titles after names in the Brief Lives sections are only given when monuments exist bearing that title.
• Square brackets – [ ] – in names indicate elements destroyed in the original inscription(s), and either restored (if evidence is available) or with the gap indicated by '...'. Parentheses – ( ) – are used where an element of a name is used inconsistently in the ancient sources.

1

The Early Dynastic Period and Old Kingdom

The Founders

1st, 2nd and 3rd Dynasties

The Royal Succession

1st Dynasty 3150–?
NARMER
HOR-AHA
DJER
DJET
DEN
ADJIB
SEMERKHET
QAA

2nd Dynasty ?–2584
HOTEPSEKHEMWY
NEBRE
NINETJER
WENEG
SENED
PERIBSEN
(period of civil war)
KHASEKHEMWY

3rd Dynasty 2584–2520
DJOSER
SANAKHT
SEKHEMKHET
KHABA
HUNI

(previous page) The Step Pyramid of Djoser at Saqqara – the first major structure built of stone in the world.

(right) Ivory figurine of an Early Dynastic king; Abydos (BM 37996).

Historical Background

The latest prehistoric cultures in Upper Egypt correspond to the cultural phases known as Naqada I (formerly Amratian), Naqada II (Gerzean) and Naqada III. By Naqada II times, it appears that various statelets were coming into existence along the Nile Valley, with certain large and elaborate graves likely to be those of local chieftains. Naqada III ('Dynasty 0') witnessed the consolidation of these statelets into something approaching regional kingdoms, possibly under indirect influence from Mesopotamia, where a complex of city-states came into existence in the second half of the 4th millennium.

It would seem that just before 3000 BC most of southern Egypt was under the control of one man. A slate palette appears to depict the last stage of the inevitable conflicts between the regional kingdoms: the unification of the whole of Egypt under one ruler, the 'Horus Narmer', perhaps the legendary 'Menes'. During the initial part of the 1st Dynasty we have our first records of military expeditions, eastwards into Sinai and perhaps beyond. Later in the dynasty there is evidence for trouble within the royal family, with certain royal names erased on objects from the tomb of a successor.

The 2nd Dynasty is a period of extreme obscurity. The order of the first few kings is reasonably clear, but later in the dynasty hierarchy becomes much more uncertain and there are definite signs of disorder, if not full-scale civil war. Immediately prior to this we find a king who, rather than employing a Horus-name, calls himself 'the Set Peribsen'. In later mythology Set is the enemy of Horus, and some have wondered whether this divine antipathy might have its origins in a conflict between a 'Set-king' and an orthodox 'Horus-king'.

Following the end of this apparent conflict Djoser – the son of the last 2nd Dynasty king – became monarch, starting what posterity regarded as a new dynasty: the 3rd. As with most of the early kings, little is known about the events of his reign apart from the building of his Step Pyramid at Saqqara, the first such monument known, and a shrine at Heliopolis. An expedition to the mines of Sinai is also recorded, Djoser's inscription being the earliest known record of such work, but those of subsequent reigns are plentiful, including depictions of his two immediate successors.

After Djoser, our knowledge of the very royal succession becomes sketchy. The main information

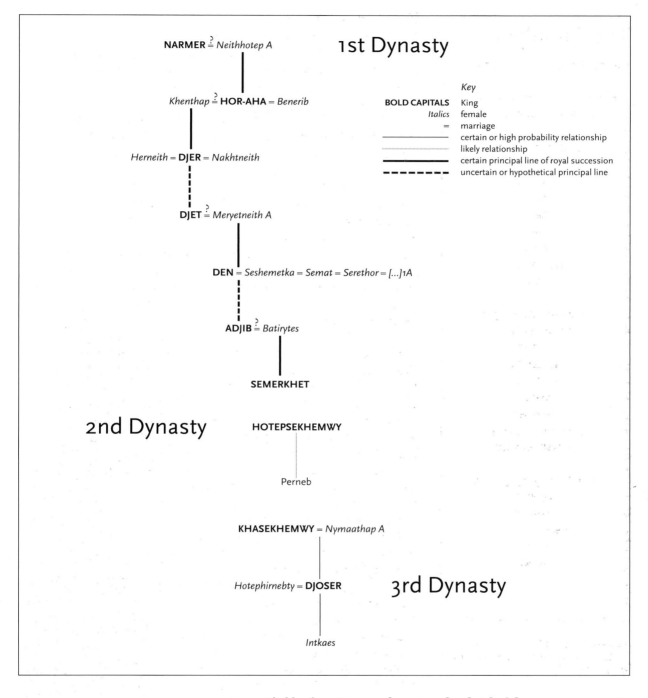

NARMER ⸘ *Neithhotep A*

1st Dynasty

Khenthap ⸘ **HOR-AHA** = *Benerib*

Herneith = **DJER** = *Nakhtneith*

DJET ⸘ *Meryetneith A*

DEN = *Seshemetka* = *Semat* = *Serethor* = *[...]1A*

ADJIB ⸘ *Batirytes*

SEMERKHET

2nd Dynasty

HOTEPSEKHEMWY

Perneb

KHASEKHEMWY = *Nymaathap A*

Hotephirnebty = **DJOSER**

3rd Dynasty

Intkaes

Key

BOLD CAPITALS — King
Italics — female
= — marriage
——— — certain or high probability relationship
·········· — likely relationship
━━━ — certain principal line of royal succession
╶╶╶╶╶ — uncertain or hypothetical principal line

is provided by the existence of a series of unfinished funerary monuments, and it is not until the end of the dynasty that there can be any confidence in the historical reconstruction. According to both king lists and literary sources Huni was the last king of the dynasty, followed by Seneferu, founder of the 4th Dynasty.

One of the pair of funerary stelae of Queen Meryetneith (CM JE34450).

(opposite) King Djoser taking part in the heb-sed (jubilee) festival. Relief in the blue tiled chambers of the South Tomb of the Step Pyramid.

(below) Colossal head of an unknown king of around the end of the 3rd/beginning of the 4th Dynasty (Brooklyn 46. 167).

The Royal Family

Sources for reconstructing the families of the kings of the earliest dynasties are sparse in the extreme. Whilst females, perhaps queens, are shown on ceremonial maceheads of the Predynastic king 'Scorpion' and **Narmer**, the earliest named royal lady seems to be Neithhotep A. Her name is found in the so-called royal tomb at Naqada, along with sealings and labels of Hor-Aha. On the basis of this she is generally believed to be the king's mother, and thus probably Narmer's wife. It should be pointed out, however, that an object bearing her name was also found in the tomb of Djer, and it is not impossible that she could instead have been Hor-Aha's wife. On the other hand, the tombs of Djer and Hor-Aha are close together, making it is possible that the piece could have 'strayed'.

A clear candidate for **Hor-Aha**'s spouse is provided by Benerib, the signs interpreted as her name being written alongside his on a number of pieces, in particular from tomb B14, directly adjacent to the king's sepulchre. The mother of Djer, given on the Cairo Annals Stone, was presumably also a wife of Hor-Aha.

One nameless wife of **Djer** is probably represented by human remains from his tomb, but one Herneith, possibly buried at Saqqara in tomb S3507, may also have been a spouse, given the presence of the king's name on items from the sepulchre. A further lady, Nakhtneith, possessed a subsidiary grave in the funerary complex of the king at Abydos.

No direct evidence exists for the wife of **Djet**, but she may have been Meryetneith A, who was buried in a tomb indistinguishable from that of a king at Abydos, containing material bearing the names of Djer, Djet and Den. She was the mother of Den, apparently serving as regent during his minority, and the terminal signs of her name are visible on the Palermo Stone – a fragment of the annals of the first dynasties, whose entries included the name of a king's mother.[59] This connection suggests that Djet had a relatively short reign.

Four stelae from the subsidiary cemetery that surrounded the tomb of **Den** are likely to have belonged to spouses of that monarch. They are the last-known royal family members from 1st Dynasty contemporary sources. To them may be added Batirytes, however, named as the mother of **Semerkhet** in the Cairo Annals Stone, and presumably a wife of **Adjib**.

The situation is less clear in the 2nd Dynasty, where five princesses are known from their tombs, but in no case does any indication of the name of their fathers survive. Names of a number of princes and a princess can be identified from sealings and vessel-fragments, but apart from Perneb – presumably a son of **Hotepsekhemwy** judging by the appearance of his name in the king's tomb – even their dynasty is uncertain. Only at the end of the dynasty do matters improve, where Nymaathap's naming in both the tomb of **Khasekhemwy** and tomb K1 at Beit Khallaf, dated to Djoser's reign, provides a father-son link between the kings and the two dynasties.

Information on the next generation is supplied by a number of sources, perhaps most importantly a relief-fragment from Heliopolis showing the ladies Hotephirnebty and Intkaes in front of **Djoser**. Both are also named on

Little is known of the royal family of the 3rd Dynasty; even the kings are generally obscure, for example Sekhemkhet (Wadi Maghara, Sinai).

stelae of the king from the Step Pyramid complex at Saqqara. Unfortunately, nothing whatsoever is known about the relationships of the remaining, generally obscure, kings of the dynasty; only a single and unattached princess, Redji, is known from a statuette. It is not until the beginning of the 4th Dynasty that meaningful information about the royal family is available in quantity, bringing the frequently shadowy formative years of Egyptian history to a close.

Brief Lives ●

*Males in **bold**, females in **bold italic**.*

Batirytes
Mother of Semerkhet; named on the Cairo Annals Stone.

Benerib
Name written alongside that of Hor-Aha and presumably his wife; possibly owner of tomb B14 at Umm el-Qaab.

Herneith (CTL; FW)
Probable wife of Djer, and possible owner of Saqqara S3507 which contains vases bearing her name, as well as seals showing the names of Den and Qaa.

Hotephirnebty (SH; KD; GS)
Wife of Djoser. Named on a series of boundary stelae from the Step Pyramid enclosure (now in various museums) and a fragment of relief from a building at Heliopolis, now in Turin.

Intkaes (KD)
Daughter of Djoser. Named on a series of boundary stelae from the Step Pyramid

Fragment of relief showing the lower part of a seated figure of Djoser, with his daughter Intkaes, and wife Hotephirnebty; from Heliopolis (Turin 2671/21).

enclosure (now in various museums) and a fragment of relief from Heliopolis.

Khenthap
Stated to have been the mother of the Horus Djer on the Cairo Annals Stone.

Meryetneith A (FW; KM)
Mother of Den. Owner of Umm el-Qaab tomb Y, the stela from which is in the Cairo Museum. The tomb and stela are like those used for contemporary kings, but on the stela Meryetneith's name is written without the *serekh* used on kingly examples. She is named as Den's mother on a seal from Abydos and probably on the Palermo Stone. One of her officials was buried in Saqqara tomb S3503.

Nakhtneith (ScH)
Known from her stela (number 95), from a grave in the funerary complex of Djer at Umm el-Qaab.

Neithhotep A (CTL; FW)
Known from the Royal Tomb at Naqada, an ivory lid found in the tomb of Djer at Abydos, and on a label from Helwan.

Nymaathap A (GS; KM; KW)
Named on sealings from the funerary complex of Khasekhemwy at Abydos, and from tomb K1 at Beit Khallaf. Her posthumous cult is referred to in the early-

4th Dynasty tomb of Metjen at Saqqara (LS6).

Perneb (KSon)
Seal-impressions bearing his name were found in Hotepsekhemwy at Saqqara.

Semat (SH)
Known from her stela (number 129), found in a grave in the funerary complex of Den at Umm el-Qaab.

Serethor
Known from her stela, excavated in a grave in the funerary complex of Den at Umm el-Qaab and now in the Louvre.

Seshemetka (SH; ScH)
Known from her stela (number 126), discovered in a grave in the funerary complex of Den at Umm el-Qaab.

[...]1A (SH)
Known from her stela (number 128), from a grave in the funerary complex of the Horus Den at Umm el-Qaab.

Unplaced ● ● ● ● ● ● ● ● ● ●

Khnemetptah (KD)
Buried in tomb 175 H8 at Helwan.[60]

Menehpet (KSon)
Known from a seal of unknown origin.

Slab stela of Princess Shepsesipet from Saqqara S3477, perhaps usurped from another.

Neithhotep B (KD)
Known from an inscribed vessel of unknown provenance.

Nysuheqat (KSon)
Owner of tomb 964 H8 at Helwan.

Qaienneith (KD)
Known from a seal of unknown provenance.

Redji (KDB)
Owner of a statuette (now in the Turin

Museum) dated stylistically to the 3rd Dynasty.

Shepsetipet (KD)
2nd Dynasty; known from a stela found near tomb S3477[61] at Saqqara, to which it may have belonged. The body found in the tomb was that of a woman at least 60 years old, suffering from a badly deformed jaw.

Sitba (KD)
2nd Dynasty; buried in Helwan tomb 1241 H9.

Princess Khnemetptah from tomb 175 H8 at Helwan.

Mesenka (KSon)
Name inscribed on a diorite vessel found under the Step Pyramid.

Diorite statue of Princess Redji, 3rd Dynasty.

Princess Sitba, from tomb 1241 H9 at Helwan.

Syhefernerer (KD)
2nd Dynasty; buried in Saqqara tomb S2146E, from which came her stela, now in Cairo.[62]

Wadjetefni (KSon)
Named on a diorite vessel from below the Step Pyramid.

The Great Pyramid Builders

4th Dynasty

The Royal Succession

4th Dynasty 2520–2392
SENEFERU
KHUFU
DJEDEFRE
SET?KA
KHAFRE
MENKAURE
SHEPSESKAF

The Giza pyramids, built by Khufu, Khafre and Menkaure. The three small pyramids are the subsidiary pyramid of Menkaure himself (left), and those of two of his wives.

Historical Background

The 4th Dynasty marks the full flowering of the Old Kingdom upon the foundations laid during the 3rd. Its monuments include some of the most massive structures erected by humans, together with some of the most exquisite works of sculpture. Amongst them are the Bent and Red Pyramids of Seneferu at Dahshur, and the Giza monuments of Khufu (Cheops), Khafre (Chephren) and Menkaure (Mycerinus), also known as the Great, Second and Third Pyramids.

Knowledge of actual events remains sketchy, but it is known that Seneferu's reign included expeditions against Libya and Nubia, and activity in the turquoise mines of the Sinai. Another commodity-bearing activity was the import in a single year of 40 ship-loads of cedar, probably from the port of Byblos in the Lebanon. Some of this was used in the king's pyramids.

Little is also known of the reigns of the remaining kings of the dynasty, apart from their pyramid-building efforts. Khufu, for example, who erected the Great Pyramid at Giza, worked the quarries of the Sinai, but this is the limit of our knowledge. A raised profile for the cult of the sun-god Re has been inferred from the inclusion of his name in the cartouches of most of the dynasty's later kings. Conversely, some kind of religious upheaval at the end of the dynasty has been suggested on the basis that Shepseskaf's name was *not* included, and that he did not build a pyramid – a symbol of the sun. However, no corroborative evidence exists.

Nothing is known of the events that surrounded the transition between the 4th and 5th Dynasties although it is possible that a woman, Khentkaues I, may have exercised royal power for a period (see pp. 62–65).

The Royal Family

Far more genealogical information is available for the 4th Dynasty than any previous period of Egyptian history.[63] However, many problems remain, in particular those caused by the Old Kingdom practice of favoured nobles being given King's Son titles.

The principal sources of data on the 4th Dynasty royal family are the cemeteries at Giza, supplemented by those at Meidum and Dahshur. As to the ancestry of the dynastic founder, **Seneferu**, we know from Papyrus Prisse ('The Instruction for Kagemni') that his predecessor was Huni. A New Kingdom source, as well as the Cairo Annals Stone, implies that his mother may have been one Meresankh (I), but whether Huni was Seneferu's father is unknown.

The wife of Seneferu has been determined by the presence of his names on furniture in the tomb of Hetepheres I, whose King's Mother title is generally assumed to refer to Khufu, during whose reign the tomb was constructed and sealed. She was also a God's Daughter, the implication being that she was an offspring of a predecessor of Seneferu, most likely Huni. Children of Seneferu other than Khufu have been identified through the

(below) Only one three-dimensional image of Khufu survives, this ivory statuette from Abydos (CM JE36143).

(below, right) Upper part of a statue of Seneferu, from the valley temple of the Bent Pyramid complex at Dahshur (CM JE98943).

4th Dynasty

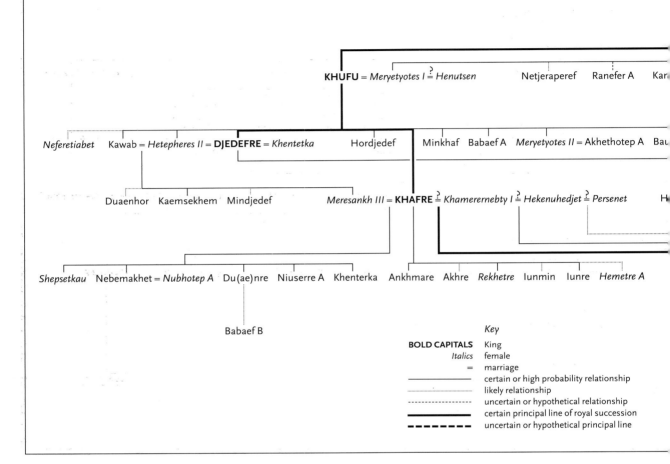

Key

BOLD CAPITALS	King
Italics	female
=	marriage
———————	certain or high probability relationship
··················	likely relationship
- - - - - - - - - -	uncertain or hypothetical relationship
▬▬▬▬▬▬	certain principal line of royal succession
▬ ▬ ▬ ▬ ▬ ▬	uncertain or hypothetical principal line

presence of their tombs in the principal cemeteries of the reign, with the exception of Hetepheres A and Nefertnesu A, who are explicitly stated to be his daughters on monuments of their families. Debate continues on a number of these individuals, partly as regards the controversy over ownership of the Meidum pyramid (which now seems resolved in favour of Seneferu's exclusive proprietorship), and partly as regards whether or not some were actually honorary title-holders.

The identification of one of **Khufu**'s wives is on the basis of the now-lost false-door stela of Meryetyotes I, who is known to have been the mother of Kawab and Hetepheres II. Interestingly, as well as being 'Great of Sceptre' of Khufu, she held the same status vis-à-vis Seneferu. A second spouse, Henutsen, is named on a 26th Dynasty stela found in the temple of Isis that had

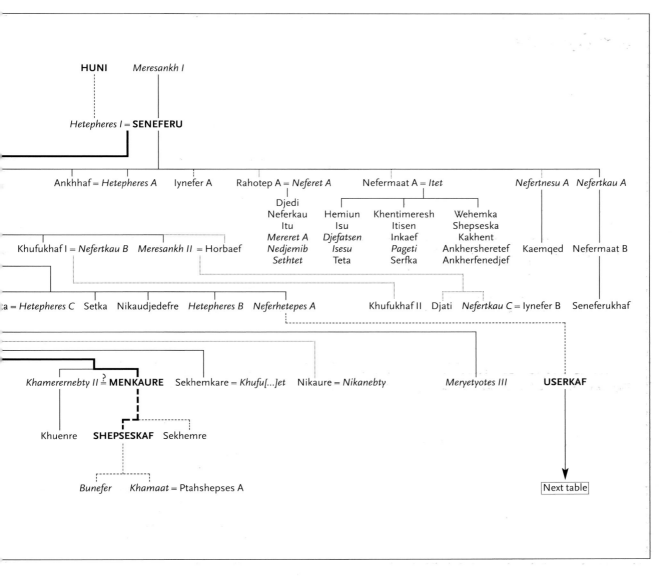

been built against one of the pyramids of Khufu's queens during the 21st Dynasty, but has no certain contemporary attestations.

The principal source for Khufu's children is the East Cemetery at Giza, where many of them were buried. In addition, there is Papyrus Westcar,[64] in which a number of Khufu's sons are presented as telling him stories. Most are known from Giza tombs, but one, Bauefre, appears only in a curious list of cartouches by the road through the Wadi Hammamat (between Koptos and the Red Sea) in the Eastern Desert, alongside Khufu, Djedefre, Khafre and Hordjedef.[65] It has been suggested that Bauefre may be the same person as Horbaef.

The family of **Djedefre** is far less well known, owing to the unfinished and destroyed nature of the king's pyramid-site at Abu Rowash. There is

(above) Slab stela of Princess Neferetiabet, probably a daughter of Khufu; from Giza G1225 (Louvre E15591).

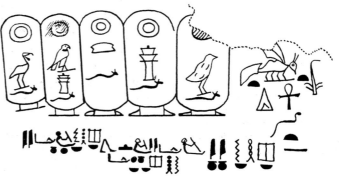

absolutely no basis for the theory that Djedefre murdered Kawab (about whose death nothing is known), nor that his accession saw a split in the royal family. The basis for this view seems to have been that Djedefre was not buried at Giza, and that his pyramid at Abu Rowash was severely damaged and its statuary broken up. However, it is now becoming clear that most of the site's destruction is to be dated to the Roman Period. As for the choice of his tomb-site, Giza had then only been used for one generation, and in Abu Rowash he found the most impressive pyramid site of all, atop a 150-m (500-ft) high ridge, visible for miles around.

The names of one wife and various children of Djedefre are known from items of sculpture from Abu Rowash. The king also appears to have married Hetepheres II, who may also have been a wife of Khafre (the third of her brothers whom she seems to have espoused). It is possible that one of the sons of Djedefre might briefly have been a king, beginning the Unfinished Pyramid at Zawiyet el-Aryan, and may have ruled between Djedefre and Khafre.[66] Unfortunately, the cartouche found at the monument is difficult to read, only the final element '-ka' being unequivocal. Thus although the fact that the names of both Baka and Setka had this ending is highly suggestive, one cannot draw any clear conclusions. Another problematic figure is Neferhetepes A, perhaps the same person as the King's Mother Neferhetepes Q, who had a cult in the 5th Dynasty and was buried in a pyramid that formed part of the funerary complex of Userkaf.

Khafre's wives are generally agreed to have been Khamerernebty I, Persenet, Hekenuhedjet and Meresankh III, but none are explicitly stated as having been married to him. The connection is assumed on the basis of the ladies' indirect dating, or that of their known offspring. For example, a flint knife bearing the name of the King's Mother K[...], found in the mortuary temple of Menkaure, is the best evidence for the affiliations of Khamerernebty I. Similarly, only Iunre is explicitly stated to be a son of Khafre, the remaining royal children being identified through the locations of their tombs and other indirect methods.

Genealogically, the latter part of the 4th Dynasty is problematic. **Menkaure** would seem to have had at least two wives, given the presence of a pair of small pyramids alongside his complex's subsidiary example, one of which contained the skeleton of a young woman. No women are unequivocally known to have been married to him, but Khamerernebty II's son was buried in a cemetery clearly associated with the pyramid of Menkaure, and she is thus likely to have been his spouse. She was perhaps interred in one of the small pyramids, but may have been buried elsewhere at Giza (see p. 59). A woman certainly with her own tomb was Rekhetre, called there both wife and daughter of a king; unfortunately he is left unnamed, but she was possibly married to Menkaure. Clear statements of relationship are generally lacking, but the location of Prince Khuenre's tomb allows us to be confident that Menkaure was his father.

A lady called Bunefer is certainly associated with **Shepseskaf** – assumed to be Menkaure's son – but whether as wife or daughter is unknown. It has

(left) The mysterious MK graffito found in the Wadi Hammamat by Fernand Debono in 1949, which places the names of princes Hordjedef and Bauefre in cartouches after those of Khufu, Djedefre and Khafre.

been suggested that Princess Khamaat may have been Shepseskaf's daughter, but she could just as well have been the offspring of Userkaf. Various ladies with the title of King's Daughter buried at Giza are of even more uncertain affiliation, and may or may not be real royal offspring. Nothing certain is known of any genealogical links between this family and the main line of the 5th Dynasty, although various suggestions have been made (and are expounded in the next section).

Brief Lives

Males in **bold**, *females in* ***bold italic***.

Akhethotep A (Director of the Palace)
Husband of Meryetyotes II, buried in Giza tomb G7650.

Akhre (EKSon)
Probably a son of Khafre, buried in Giza tomb H4. May alternatively be a titular prince of the 5th/6th Dynasty.

Ankherfenedjef
Son of Nefermaat A, shown as a child in Nefermaat's tomb at Meidum.

Ankhersheretef
Son of Nefermaat A, shown as a child in Nefermaat's tomb at Meidum.

Ankhhaf (KSon; Viz)
Son of Seneferu who served as Vizier under Khafre. Buried in Giza tomb G7510, which included a bust of the deceased, now in Boston.

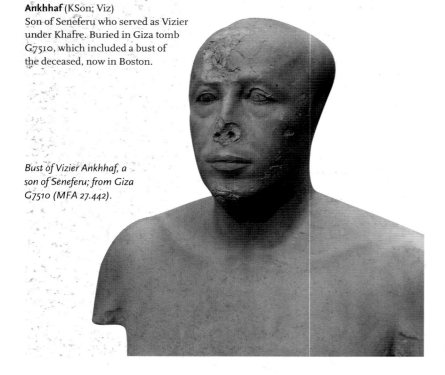

Bust of Vizier Ankhhaf, a son of Seneferu; from Giza G7510 (MFA 27.442).

Ankhmare (EKSon; Viz)
Son of Khafre; served under Menkaure. Buried in a rock-cut tomb in the Central Field at Giza.

Babaef A (KSon)
Son of Khufu, buried in a tomb in the Central Field at Giza.

Babaef B (Viz)
Probably a son of Duaenre and grandson of Khafre. Buried in Giza tomb G5230, which seems never to have been decorated, but equipped with at least 13 statues. He may have started his career as Overseer of Works, with later promotion to Vizier under Shepseskaf.

Baka (EKSon)
Son of Djedefre, known from a statue-base found in his father's mortuary temple.

Bauefre (KSon)
Listed amongst the sons of Khufu in Papyrus Westcar, and also found in the list of cartouches in the Wadi Hammamat. No contemporary monuments, unless he is the same person as Babaef A (as has been suggested).

Bunefer (KW; KD)
Served as Prophetess of Shepseskaf, but unclear whether she was his daughter or his wife. Buried in a rock-cut tomb in the Central Field at Giza.

Djati (KSonB)
Probably a son of Horbaef; served as Overseer of the Expedition at the end of the 4th Dynasty, and buried in Giza tomb G7810.

Djedi
Son of Rahotep A, shown in Rahotep's tomb at Meidum.

Djefatsen
Daughter of Nefermaat A, shown as an adult in his tomb at Meidum.

Duaenhor (KSonB)
Probably a son of Kawab. Buried in Giza tomb G7550, probably under Menkaure.

Dua(en)re (Viz)
Son of Khafre who served as Vizier late in the 4th Dynasty, and buried in Giza tomb G5110. Usually equated with the Duare known to have been a son of Meresankh III.

Hekenuhedjet (KW)
Wife of Khafre, mentioned in the tomb of her son, Sekhemkare.

Hemetre A (KDB)
Parentage not fully certain, but dated to the time of Khafre by the location of her rock-cut tomb, in the Central Field at Giza.

Hemiun (KSB; Viz)
Probably the son of Nefermaat A of the same name depicted in Nefermaat's tomb. Buried in Giza tomb G4000, from which comes his impressive statue, now in Hildesheim, showing him in well-fed middle age. His tomb was completed towards the end of Khufu's reign.

Statue of Prince Hemiun, grandson of Seneferu and Vizier of Khufu; from Giza G4000 (Hildesheim 1962).

(above) Pyramid GIa at Giza, the putative tomb of Hetepheres I; the shaft containing her sarcophagus and furniture lay in front of the pyramid.

Henutsen (KD?)
Name only preserved in a 26th Dynasty stela which calls her a daughter of Khufu. This was found in a temple which had been built against pyramid GIc at Giza in the 21st Dynasty. As the owner of a pyramid, its occupant is more likely to have been a wife of Khufu.

Hetepheres I (GDB; KM)
Wife of Seneferu and mother of Khufu. Sarcophagus and funerary furniture found in shaft G7000X at Giza, in front of pyramid GIa, which may have been built for her.[67]

Hetepheres II (KW; GS; KDB)
Explicitly called daughter of Khufu, and married to Kawab. Known to have subsequently married at least one king. Possessed a joint tomb with her first husband (G7110+7120), but probably ultimately buried in tomb G7350. Owing to her depiction wearing a yellow hair-cover in the tomb of Meresankh III, various erroneous assumptions have been made about her ethnic origins.[68]

(right) Statue of Hetepheres II and her daughter, Meresankh III (MFA 30.1456).

Hetepheres A (KD)
Named in fragments of relief from the tomb of her husband, Ankhhaf. Her tomb is unknown, her husband's G7510 having only a single burial shaft.

Hetepheres B (KDB)
Named on a fragment of statue from the mortuary temple of her father Djedefre at Abu Rowash.

Hetepheres C
Represented on a statue of her husband, Baka, now in Cairo.

Horbaef (KSon)
Probably a son of Khufu and buried in Giza tomb G7420. Horbaef's sarcophagus is in the Cairo Museum, but its provenance is not absolutely certain.

Hordjedef (KSonB)
Son of Khufu. Known from Papyrus Westcar, the Wadi Hammamat cartouche-list and a book of wisdom attributed to him, as well as his tomb at Giza (G7210+7220). The inscriptions in this tomb may have been damaged by an enemy, but a cult was established for him at Saqqara. A later individual calls himself 'Honoured before Hordjedef', as though the prince were deified, and another man is depicted in the pose of adoration with the caption 'Adoring Hordjedef'.[69] He is mentioned in the Book of the Dead as being alive under Menkaure. His unfinished sarcophagus is now in the Cairo Museum.

Hornit (EKSonB)
Son of Djedefre; owner of a statue now in Cairo showing him and his wife.

Inkaef
Son of Nefermaat A, shown as a child in Nefermaat's tomb at Meidum.

Isesu
Daughter of Nefermaat A, shown as an adult in Nefermaat's tomb at Meidum.

Isu
Son of Nefermaat A, shown as an adult in Nefermaat's tomb at Meidum.

Itet
Wife of Nefermaat A, buried in the northern half of the same tomb at Meidum.

Itisen
Son of Nefermaat A, shown as a child in Nefermaat's tomb at Meidum.

Itu
Son of Rahotep A, shown in his father's tomb at Meidum.

Iunmin (EKSonB; Viz)
Assumed to be son of Khafre on the basis of his titles and position of his tomb at Giza (tomb LG92). Served as Vizier around the end of the 4th Dynasty.

Iunre (EKSonB)
Explicitly stated to be the son of Khafre in his tomb in the Central Field at Giza. It has been suggested that he had been Crown Prince, but this is by no means certain, and he may actually have survived his father and been buried early in the 5th Dynasty.

Iynefer A (KSon)
Probably a son of Seneferu; owner of a tomb at Dahshur, parts of which are now in the Cairo Museum.

(below) The chapel from the tomb of Prince Iynefer at Dahshur (CM CG57120–1).

Iynefer B
Husband of Nefertkau C, and grandson-in-law of Khufu. Owner of Giza tomb G7820.

Kaemqed
Son of Nefertnesu A and thus probably grandson of Seneferu; buried at Dahshur in the 5th Dynasty.

Kaemsekhem (KSon)
Son of Kawab and Hetepheres II. Owner of Giza tomb G7660, with his sarcophagus now in the Cairo Museum.

Kakhent
Son of Nefermaat A, shown as a child in Nefermaat's tomb at Meidum.

Kanefer (EKSonB)
Probably a son of Seneferu; the true parentage and dating of Kanefer has been the subject of considerable debate, estimates ranging from the middle of the 4th Dynasty to the end of the Old Kingdom. Buried in tomb 28 at Dahshur, fragments of which are in the British Museum; the tomb's design is consistent with the early 4th Dynasty.

Galarza Tomb at Giza, probably begun for her but completed by Khamerernebty II. She is named in a text in the late-5th Dynasty tomb of Nimaatre at the same site.

Khamerernebty II (GS; KW; KDB)
Probably a wife of Menkaure. Attested by texts and a statue from the Galarza Tomb at Giza, which seems to have been ultimately intended as her burial place, although it is possible that she was actually buried in tomb GIIIa or GIIIb.

Khenterka
Depicted as a child in the tomb of his mother, Meresankh III.

Khentetka (KW)
Known from various fragmentary statues in the mortuary temple of Djedefre at Abu Rowash.

Khentimeresh
Son of Nefermaat A, shown as an adult in Nefermaat's tomb at Meidum.

Statue of Queen Khentetka, kneeling by the leg of her husband, Djedefre; from Abu Rowash (Louvre E12627).

(above) Statue of King Khafre; from Giza (CM CG14).

Kawab (EKSonB)
Appears to have been the intended heir of Khufu, given the prominent position of his tomb (G7110+7120) and his marriage to a senior princess, Hetepheres II. However, he died before the end of his father's reign; his burial chamber seems to have been altered after the prince's death.

Khafre (KSon)
Mentioned in Papyrus Westcar, and later king as **KHAFRE**. It has been suggested that he might have been identical to Khufukhaf I.

Khamaat (EKD)
Based on the dating of her husband, Khamaat could have been a daughter either of Shepseskaf or Userkaf.

Khamerernebty I (KDB; GS; KM; KW)
Probably a wife of Khafre. Known from the

(below) At the foot of the Great Pyramid of Giza lies the Eastern Cemetery, with three queens' pyramids and streets of mastabas built for the king's offspring.

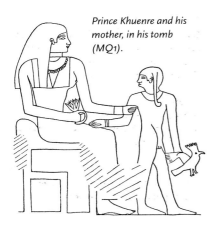

Prince Khuenre and his mother, in his tomb (MQ1).

Khuenre (EKSonB)
Owner of a rock-cut tomb in the Menkaure cemetery at Giza (MQ1), in which he is depicted with his mother, a queen.

Khufu[...]et
Named as wife of Sekhemkare in his tomb.

Khufukhaf I (KSonB; Viz)
Owner of Giza tomb G7130+7140; served as Vizier, probably under Khufu, who seems to have been his father, with his appointment coming after the completion of his tomb. It has been suggested that he might actually have come to the throne as **KHAFRE**, but this is very uncertain.

Khufukhaf II
Perhaps a son of Khufukhaf I on the basis of the proximity of their tombs – Khufukhaf II's tomb G7150 was built directly adjacent to tomb G7140. Lived into the reign of Niuserre.

Mereret A
Daughter of Rahotep A, shown in his tomb at Meidum.

Meresankh I (KW)
Named alongside Seneferu in an 18th Dynasty graffito in the pyramid-temple at Meidum and perhaps on the Cairo Annals Stone; an estate of hers may be named in the tomb of Pehernefer at Saqqara.

Meresankh II (KDB; KW; GS)
Daughter of Khufu and owner of Giza tomb G7410; her sarcophagus is in Boston.

Meresankh III (KDB; GS; KW)
Daughter of Hetepheres II. Bearer of a wide range of titles. Owner of Giza tomb G7530+7540, with an extensively decorated rock-cut chapel, where she was interred 272 days after her death. Her sarcophagus and skeleton are in Cairo, the latter showing her to have been about 1.54 m (5 ft) tall and 50–55 years old at death.

Meryetyotes I (GS; KW)
Great of Sceptre of both Seneferu and Khufu, according to her now-lost stela from Giza, recorded by the 19th-century French archaeologist, Mariette.

Meryetyotes II (KDB)
Daughter of Khufu, who shared Giza tomb G7650 with her husband, Akhethotep A.

Meryetyotes III
Granddaughter of Djedefre; shown on a statue with her father, Hornit (now in Cairo).

Mindjedef (KSonB)
Possible grandson of Khufu; that Kawab was his father is suggested by the location of his tomb, Giza G7760.

Minkhaf (EKSonB; Viz)
Son of Khufu, apparently appointed Vizier fairly early in his career; probably died in the reign of Djedefre or early in that of Khafre. Owner of Giza tomb G7430+ 7440, with his sarcophagus now in the Cairo Museum.

Nebemakhet (KSB; Viz)
Shown in his mother Meresankh III's tomb both in reliefs and statuary. Owner of Giza tomb LG86.

Nedjemib
Daughter of Rahotep A, shown in his tomb at Meidum.

Neferet A (RO)
Wife of Rahotep A, buried in tomb 6B at Meidum. Owner of a famous painted statue in Cairo Museum.

Neferetiabet (KD)
Possibly a daughter of Khufu. Known from her tomb at Giza (G1225), the superb slab stela from which is now in the Louvre; a statuette said to come from her tomb is in Munich.

Statue of Rahotep and Neferet A; from Meidum 16 (CM CG3–4).

Neferhetepes A (KDB; GW)
Known from a broken statue from Abu Rowash. It has been suggested that she might have been the mother of Userkaf or Sahure (see 'Neferhetepes Q' in next section).

Neferkau
Son of Rahotep A, shown in his tomb at Meidum.

Nefermaat A (EKSon; Viz)
Probably a son of Seneferu and owner of Meidum tomb 16, which had a unique system of decoration, allegedly devised by Nefermaat himself, in which blocks of pigment were sunk into a stone surface. The principal pieces are in Cairo.

Nefermaat B (KSonB; Viz)
Stated in his tomb (Giza G7060) and the tomb of Seneferukhaf to have been a son of Nefertkau A.

Nefertkau A (KDB)
Explicitly stated to have been a daughter of Seneferu in the inscriptions of her descendants. Possibly the owner of Giza tomb G7050.

Nefertkau B
Wife of Khufukhaf I.

Nefertkau C
Possible daughter of Meresankh II, buried with her husband in Giza tomb G7820.

Nefertnesu A (KD; GD)
Daughter of Seneferu, known from the false door of her son, Kaemqed.

Netjeraperef (KSon)
Probable son of Seneferu; owner of tomb II/I at Dahshur.

Nikanebty
Wife of Nikaure, named in his tomb.

Nikaudjedefre (KSonB)
Owner of Abu Rowash tomb F15; possibly only a titular prince of later date, rather than a son of Djedefre.

Nikaure (EKSonB; Viz)
Filiation from Khafre is assumed because of the location of Nikaure's tomb (Giza LG87).

Niuserre A (KSonB)
Named in the tomb of his mother, Meresankh III, and owner of an unfinished rock-cut tomb in the Central Field at Giza.

Nubhotep A
Wife of Nebemakhet.

Pageti
Daughter of Nefermaat A, shown as a child in his tomb at Meidum.

Persenet (GS; KW; KDB)
Owner of Giza tomb LG88, dated to Khafre's reign on account of its location.

Ptahshepses A
Probably a son-in-law of Shepseskaf, buried in Saqqara tomb 48, around the reign of Niuserre. May be depicted in the mortuary temple of Sahure at Abusir.

Rahotep A (KSonB; HPH)
Probable son of Seneferu, buried in Meidum tomb 6A; owner of a famous painted statue in the Cairo Museum, which also houses the remains of his tomb's chapel.

Ranefer A (KSon)
Possible son of Seneferu; owner of tomb 9 at Meidum. His name is not absolutely certain.

Rekhetre (KD; KW)
Daughter of Khafre and owner of a stone mastaba with a rock-cut chapel in the Central Field at Giza. Rekhetre's cult was maintained well into the next dynasty, with her priests buried in nearby tombs.

Sekhemkare (EKSonB; Viz)
Owner of the Giza rock-cut tomb LG89. Stated to have been honoured before Khafre, Menkaure, Shepseskaf, Userkaf and Sahure, and to have been the offspring of Hekenuhedjet.

Sekhemre (EKSonB)
Known from a statue in the Galarza Tomb at Giza, and therefore probably related to one or other of the queens Khamerernebty.

Seneferukhaf
Great-grandson of Seneferu. Owner of tomb G7070 at Giza; his sarcophagus is in the Cairo Museum.

Serfka
Son of Nefermaat A, shown as a child in Nefermaat's tomb at Meidum.

Sethtet
Daughter of Rahotep A, shown in his tomb at Meidum.

Setka (EKSonB)
Known from a scribal statue from his father Djedefre's pyramid complex at Abu Rowash. Conceivably identical with **SETH?KA.**

Shepseska
Son of Nefermaat A, shown as a child in Nefermaat's tomb at Meidum.

Shepsetkau (KDB)
Named in her brother Nebemakhet's tomb.

Teta
Son of Nefermaat A, shown as an adult in Nefermaat's tomb at Meidum.

Wehemka
Son of Nefermaat A, shown as a child in Nefermaat's tomb at Meidum.

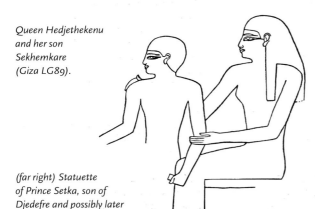

Queen Hedjethekenu and her son Sekhemkare (Giza LG89).

(far right) Statuette of Prince Setka, son of Djedefre and possibly later pharaoh (Louvre E12629).

Children of the Sun-God

5th Dynasty

The Royal Succession

5th Dynasty 2392–2282

USERKAF

SAHURE

NEFERIRKARE I

SHEPSESKARE

NEFEREFRE

NIUSERRE

MENKAUHOR

ISESI

UNAS

Granite doorjamb of Queen Khentkaues I, with her image and the remains of her name. The former seems to show her with a royal beard (Giza LG100).

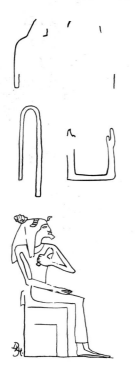

Historical Background

The 5th Dynasty is often regarded as the poor relation of the 4th, with the latter's vast monuments replaced by much more modest pyramids, albeit now adjoining elaborately decorated temple complexes. In addition, the massive centralism illustrated by the clustering of the tombs of the nobility around the foot of Khufu's tomb is replaced by a much wider distribution, both within the Memphite necropolis and elsewhere throughout the country.

The period seems to have been one of prosperity nevertheless, with fairly extensive state-sponsored foreign enterprises, both peaceful and otherwise. During the 4th Dynasty the vizierate had been largely in the hands of the royal princes; under the 5th Dynasty this was no longer the case and, although officials maintained royal links, no longer did kings' sons aspire to major posts in the administration, a situation that was to last until well into the New Kingdom.

A feature of the 5th Dynasty kings is their building of a sun-temple, as well as a pyramid; the former comprised a bulky obelisk, a chapel and a causeway, the surviving examples lying just north of the principal 5th Dynasty royal cemetery, Abusir. Isesi ended this tradition and moved the royal cemetery back up to Saqqara. Isesi's reign also saw alterations in the system of ranking titles bestowed upon the nobility, and a brief return of royal sons to the senior administration was ended. Perhaps the most significant administrative change was a recognition of the status of the provinces by the appointment of more than one Vizier, one of whom was based in the southern part of the country.

The Royal Family

A tale written later (Papyrus Westcar)[70] states that the first three kings of the dynasty were triplets, born to the wife of a priest of Re. While this cannot be squared with contemporary evidence, there is material to suggest that at least one pair of brothers ruled. This is tied up intimately with the genealogical conundrum known as the 'Khentkaues Problem'.

The huge and highly unusual tomb of this lady, Khentkaues (LG100) lies at Giza, and is neither a conventional mastaba nor a pyramid. On part of the granite doorway leading into the mortuary chapel is a set of titles that form the nub of the problem. The titles read in hieroglyphs: , which can be read either as *mwt-nswy-bitwy*, 'Mother of Two Dual Kings' or *nsw-bity mwt-nsw-bity*, 'Dual King and Mother of a Dual King'. The second has led to suggestions that she might have ruled during the minority of her son(s), perhaps in conjunction with Userkaf, particularly since her image had been altered to show her in kingly pose and sporting a false beard. The alternative translation fits in fairly well with the Westcar story, one scholar suggesting that the heroine was actually a pseudonym for Khentkaues I.

Other sources confirm the existence of a King's Mother Khentkaues, including documents from the pyramid-archive of Neferirkare I at Abusir, an offering table from that pyramid, and a mention of the lady's mortuary temple in the Abusir tomb of Mersetjefptah. But Neferirkare is shown with a

The tomb of Queen Khentkaues I is partly carved from the native rock, whose stratigraphy is clearly visible here on the west side.

Colossal head of Userkaf; from his mortuary temple at Saqqara (CM JE52501).

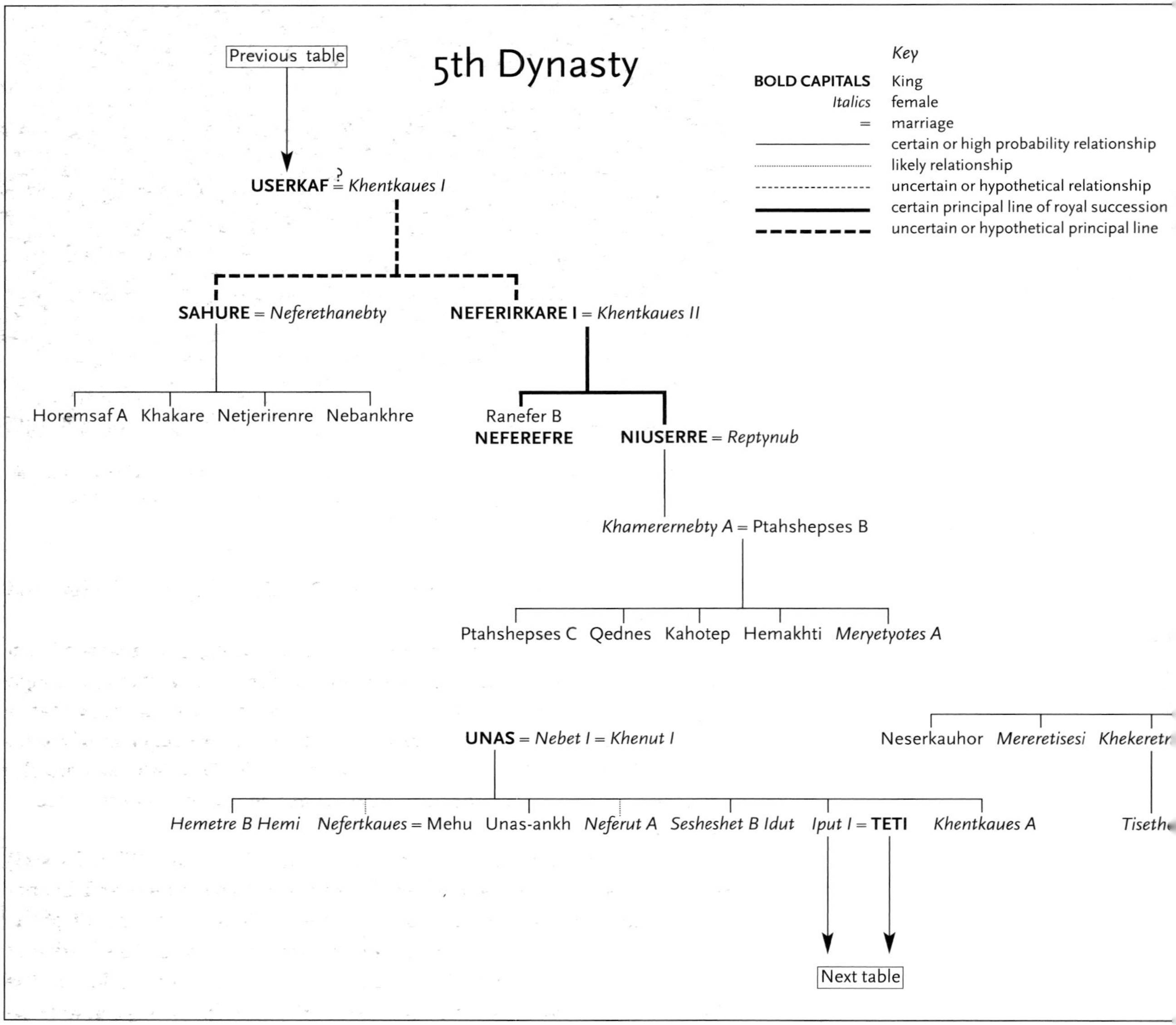

5th Dynasty

Previous table

Key

BOLD CAPITALS	King
Italics	female
=	marriage
————	certain or high probability relationship
··············	likely relationship
- - - - - - -	uncertain or hypothetical relationship
▬▬▬▬	certain principal line of royal succession
▬ ▬ ▬ ▬	uncertain or hypothetical principal line

USERKAF =? *Khentkaues I*

SAHURE = *Neferethanebty*   **NEFERIRKARE I** = *Khentkaues II*

Horemsaf A   Khakare   Netjerirenre   Nebankhre

Ranefer B **NEFEREFRE**   **NIUSERRE** = *Reptynub*

Khamerernebty A = Ptahshepses B

Ptahshepses C   Qednes   Kahotep   Hemakhti   *Meryetyotes A*

UNAS = *Nebet I* = *Khenut I*   Neserkauhor *Mereretisesi* *Khekeretr*

Hemetre B Hemi   *Nefertkaues* = Mehu   Unas-ankh   *Neferut A*   *Sesheshet B Idut*   *Iput I* = **TETI**   *Khentkaues A*   Tiseth

Next table

---

wife named Khentkaues, the mother of his heir, on a relief from Abusir. Also at Abusir next to the king's pyramid is a small pyramid, its construction begun for a King's Wife Khentkaues, but then interrupted and continued with the word 'Mother' added to her title.

An initial stone chapel against the east side of the queen's pyramid was enlarged in brick. The final decoration of the inner part of the chapel was carried out under Niuserre, in which he was shown standing in front of a Khentkaues who bore exactly the same title as the Khentkaues of Giza! A seal-impression of the reign of Isesi repeats the title and, on a pillar from the Abusir chapel, a Khentkaues is shown bearing the kingly cobra, or 'uraeus', on her forehead rather than the queen's vulture-head. How do

Pyramid complex of Khentkaues II at Abusir, with a particularly large mortuary chapel, enlarged in later times. The pyramid itself is very badly damaged, with the internal chambers visible. Beyond is an anonymous queen's pyramid, L.XXV.

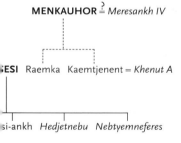

MENKAUHOR [?]= *Meresankh IV*

ESI Raemka Kaemtjenent = *Khenut A*

si-ankh *Hedjetnebu Nebtyemneferes*

these individuals relate to one another? Or might they even be one and the same?

The appearance of the uraeus and beard strongly suggests that the 'Dual King and Mother of a Dual King' translation may be the correct one, although the lack of a cartouche points to the 'Dual King' role being actually that of regent – perhaps paralleling Meryetneith A and her fully fledged kingly tomb but lack of *serekh* back in the 1st Dynasty (see p. 46). Or might *both* translations be possible, given the 'constructive ambiguity' we so often see in Egyptian texts?

A possible solution seems to be that the Khentkaues of Giza (Khentkaues I) was indeed both regent and mother of an early-5th Dynasty king, and that her presence at Abusir in the form of the uraeused figure was a result of the extension of the pyramid complex of her namesake, the wife of Neferirkare I (Khentkaues II), to provide for a cult of the ancestress of the line at the dynasty's royal necropolis. Khentkaues II, on the other hand, was certainly the mother of Neferefre and probably Niuserre, in which case she may have used the title with its *other* meaning during Niuserre's reign. With both ladies thus commemorated in the same monument, posterity's confusion was inevitable.

The identity of Khentkaues I's son (or possibly sons) is problematic. The most likely options are **Userkaf** or Sahure, depending on which of these kings was the son of Neferhetepes Q, who seems to have been buried in a pyramid directly adjacent to that of Userkaf. One would normally have expected the pyramid to have belonged to Userkaf's wife, but Neferhetepes Q lacks the title of King's Wife in a later record of her cult, although this may not be significant. Her mortuary chapel seems to have been later modified, probably by Sahure, a fragment of whose name was found there. This may or may not suggest that Neferhetepes Q was Sahure's mother.

(right) Scene from the pyramid complex of Sahure, showing the king with, behind him, three rows of figures. The top and bottom registers originally showed priests, while the middle rank shows, from the right, princes Netjerirenre, Khakare and Nebankhre. The first figure in the lower register was later altered to one of King Neferirkare I (formerly in Archäologisches Institut, Königsberg [Kaliningrad]).

(below) Neferefre had a short reign, and as a result his Abusir pyramid was never properly completed. However, the complex has revealed many interesting items, including a considerable amount of sculpture like this piece (CM JE98181).

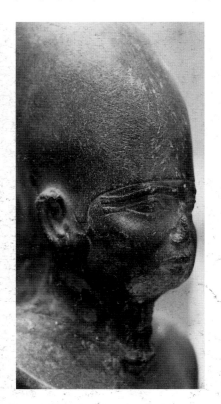

Sahure's mortuary temple contains the names of his wife and children, plus a scene in which a figure has been altered into that of his successor, Neferirkare. It is uncertain whether the figure had previously been his, or whether Neferirkare was related to Sahure: the frequent assumption that he was Sahure's brother is just that – an assumption – albeit influenced by the Westcar tale.

Khentkaues II is **Neferirkare I**'s only known spouse, although one of the small pyramids adjacent to hers might have belonged to another wife. His eldest son (by Khentkaues II) is known to have been Ranefer B, almost certainly the same man as his direct successor, **Neferefre**. Nothing is known of the latter's family, nor whether his evident ephemeral successor, Shepseskare, was a relation. However, it is generally accepted that Niuserre, who ultimately came to the throne, was a brother of Neferefre. Whether any kind of dynastic dispute followed Neferefre's death, as has been suggested, is uncertain.

At least one of the pyramids south of Khentkaues II's probably belonged to a wife of **Niuserre**. The only one known by name is Reptynub; likewise only one child is known, Khamerernebty A, who married the Vizier Ptahshepses B and had a number of children named in his tomb and the adjacent tomb of their son.

There is no known connection between Niuserre and the next king, **Menkauhor**, whose relationships remain completely unknown. Some genealogical break is hinted at by the fact that subsequent kings were buried at Saqqara. On the other hand, a number of definite children of **Isesi** (Menkauhor's successor) were interred at Abusir. Another daughter, Mereretisesi, can be attributed to Isesi on the basis of her name, and a wife and two sons have been linked to that king on the basis of the stylistic dating of their group of tombs at Saqqara.

These sepulchres are, however, much closer to the probable pyramid of Menkauhor than that of Isesi and may instead be members of the former's family, an idea bolstered by Menkauhor's cartouche being found in another tomb in the group (S904), close to the north wall of the Step Pyramid. Nevertheless, judging by this tomb owner's name (Isesi-ankh) and assuming he was not merely a titular prince, he would certainly date to the later reign despite being buried in the cemetery. A large pyramid adjacent to that of Isesi will have belonged to Isesi's principal wife, but unfortunately her name is not preserved there.

Once again, nothing is known of the antecedents of **Unas**, the last king of the dynasty. However, a number of members of his family are known from the tombs surrounding his pyramid at Saqqara. In addition, it is assumed that the King's Daughter Iput I, who married his successor, Teti, was a daughter of Unas and thus provides the genealogical link into the 6th Dynasty.

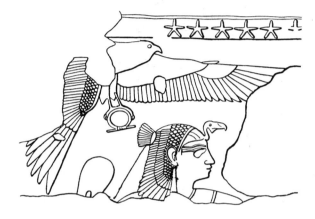

(below) Queen Iput I, from the chapel of her pyramid at Saqqara.

(bottom) The funerary complex of Unas; the double-mastaba of his queens lies on the right of the photograph.

Brief Lives ●

Males in **bold**, *females in **bold italic**.*

Hedjetnebu (KDB)
Daughter of Isesi. She was buried at
Abusir, in a tomb apparently built prior to
the extension of Khekeretnebty's for
Tisethor.

Hemakhti
Named as a son of Ptahshepses B in the
latter's tomb.

Hemetre B Hemi (1KD; GW)
Buried in Saqqara tomb D65, in which she
is explicitly called Unas' daughter. Served
in a cult role in a temple of Teti.

Horemsaf A (KSon)
Depicted in the mortuary temple of his
father, Sahure.

Iput I (KD; KM; GS; KW)
Daughter of Unas; for further details see
p. 76.

Isesi-ankh (KSon)
Son of Isesi. Buried in tomb 85 at Saqqara.
Held the offices of Overseer of Works and
Overseer of the Expedition.

Kaemtjenent (KSon)
Buried in Saqqara tomb 84. Probably the
son of Menkauhor, or perhaps Isesi, on
the basis of the general date and location
of his tomb.

Kahotep
Named as a son of Ptahshepses B in the
latter's tomb and buried in an adjacent
sepulchre at Abusir.

Khakare (KSon)
Son of Sahure. Depicted in the mortuary
temple of the latter.

Khamerernebty A (KD)
Daughter of Niuserre. She was buried
with her husband, Ptahshepses B, in tomb
L.XIX at Abusir.

Khekeretnebty (KDB)
Daughter of Isesi. Buried at Abusir in
a tomb found partially intact . Her skull
seems to suggest that she died in her
30s.

Khentkaues I (King; KM)
Apparently the ancestress of the 5th
Dynasty. Owner of tomb LG100 at Giza.
She appears to have served as regent at
some point in her career and been revered
by later members of the dynasty.

Khentkaues II (KW; KM)
Wife of Neferirkare I. Owner of a pyramid
at Abusir, and once shown on a block with
her husband and Ranefer B.

Khentkaues A (EKDB)
Daughter of Unas. Her tomb lies in his
cemetery at Saqqara, shared with a man
(presumably her husband).

Khenut I (KW)
Wife of Unas. Owner of half of a double-
mastaba tomb adjacent to her husband's
tomb at Saqqara.

Khenut A
Daughter-in-law of either Menkauhor or
Isesi.

Mehu (Viz)
Probable son-in-law of Unas; buried at
Saqqara in the middle of the 6th Dynasty.

Mereretisesi (KDB)
Known from a relief, now in Brooklyn and
probably from Abusir.

Meresankh IV (GS; KW)
Probably a wife of Menkauhor. Owner of
Saqqara tomb 82; her affiliation is based
on the general date and location of this
tomb.

Meryetyotes A (KD)
Named as a daughter of Ptahshepses B in
the latter's tomb.

Nakhtkare (KSon)
Owner of a mastaba at Abusir and,
judging by its location, presumably the
son of Neferefre or Niuserre.

Nebankhre (KSon)
Son of Sahure. Depicted in the latter's
mortuary temple.

Nebet I (GS; KW)
Wife of Unas. Owner of a mastaba adjacent

*The funerary stela of Queen Meresankh IV,
from tomb 82 at Saqqara.*

to her husband's tomb at Saqqara, forming
part of the same building as that of
Khenut I.

Nebtyemneferes (KD)
Daughter of Isesi. Buried at Abusir.

Neferethanebty (KW)
Depicted in the mortuary temple of her
husband, Sahure.

*Queen Nebet, as depicted in her tomb at
Saqqara.*

Neferhetepes Q (KM)
Possibly identical with Neferhetepes A; a reference to her cult is found in the tomb of Persen at Saqqara (D45).

Nefertkaues (KDB)
Wife of Mehu. On the basis of the location of his tomb and its date, she may be a daughter of Unas.

Neferut A (KDB)
Probable daughter of Unas. Known from a single block found near the tomb of Khenut I.

Neserkauhor (EKSonB)
Son of Isesi. Buried at Abusir, in a tomb founded somewhat later than that of Khekeretnebty.

Netjerirenre (KSon)
Depicted in the mortuary temple of his father, Sahure.

Ptahshepses B (Viz)
Owner of a very large mastaba (L.XIX) at Abusir, and married to Khamerernebty A. Served as Vizier under Niuserre.

Ptahshepses C
Named as a son of Ptahshepses B in the latter's tomb.

Qednes
Named as a son of Ptahshepses B in the latter's tomb.

Raemka (EKSonB)
Possibly a son of Menkauhor; usurping owner of Saqqara tomb 80 (now in the Metropolitan Museum of Art, New York). Filiation on the basis of the general date and location of his tomb adjacent to other royal contemporaries.

Ranefer B (EKSon)
Son of Neferirkare I. Shown as a prince alongside his mother and father on a block found in Abusir village, probably from Neferirkare's pyramid. Likely to have become king as **NEFEREFRE**.

Reptynub (GS; KW)
Wife of Niuserre. Known from a fragmentary statuette in her husband's mortuary temple as well as fragments in the tomb of Ptahshepses B.

Sesheshet B Idut (KDB)
Usurped a tomb close to the pyramid of Unas, suggesting that this king may have been her father.

Tisethor (KD)
A granddaughter of Isesi. Buried at Abusir in an extension of the tomb of her mother, Khekeretnebty.

Unas-ankh (KSon)
Son of Unas, buried close to the latter's pyramid; tomb-chapel now in the Field Museum, Chicago.

(left) Block probably from the funerary complex of Neferirkare showing in the top-right corner Crown Prince Ranefer – probably the future King Neferefre.

(above) Throne fragment of a calcite statue of Queen Reptynub, from her husband's pyramid complex at Abusir (Berlin 17438).

Unplaced ● ● ● ● ● ● ● ● ● ●

Neferhetepes B (KDB)
Owner of tomb G4714 at Giza. Identity of her father remains uncertain, but she dates to the first half of the 5th Dynasty.

Nubnebti A (GS; KW)
Buried in tomb 64 at Saqqara; dates to the 5th Dynasty or later.

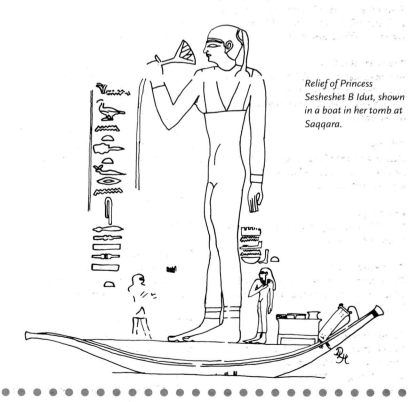

Relief of Princess Sesheshet B Idut, shown in a boat in her tomb at Saqqara.

The House of Teti and Pepy

6th to 8th Dynasty

The Royal Succession

6th Dynasty 2282–2117
TETI
USERKARE
PEPY I
NEMTYEMSAF I
PEPY II
NEMTYEMSAF II

7th to 8th Dynasty 2117–?
NETJERKARE
MENKARE
NEFERKARE II
NEBY
SHEMAY
KHENDU
MERENHOR
NIKARE
TERERU
NEFERKAUHOR
PEPYSONBE
NEFERKAMIN
IBI
NEFERKAURE
KHUIHAPY
NEFERIRKARE II

Historical Background

The latter part of the Old Kingdom is characterized by an increase in the number and quality of the tombs built at provincial centres, in particular by the nome-governors, or nomarchs. This factor becomes most noticeable in the 6th Dynasty, which was traditionally regarded as having begun at the death of Unas, although there is no real evidence for a break in the royal line at this point.

There are some indications of problems during the earlier part of the dynasty. According to later tradition (recorded by Manetho), the founder of the dynasty, Teti, was 'murdered by his eunuchs', while his successor, Userkare, is a distinctly shadowy figure, ignored by some subsequent lists. Furthermore, Pepy I changed his prenomen during his reign – a rare occurrence, later parallels of which suggest some important event in his life. Finally, we know that one of his numerous wives was prosecuted for unknown reasons late in the reign.

A considerable number of trading expeditions are known from the 6th Dynasty, in particular southwards into Africa, led by the governors of Aswan. However, following the long reign of Pepy II there seems to have been a rapid decline in royal authority, with the dynasty ending in a number of short-reigned kings, classified as the 7th and 8th Dynasties. Initially, these kings seem to have been recognized as ruling the whole of Egypt, but it is likely that by the end they were being challenged by a family based at Herakleopolis, known as the 9th Dynasty. Few monuments of theirs survive, most being known only from the Abydos king lists.

The Royal Family

A possible genealogical starting-point for the 6th Dynasty is provided by a rather unlikely source: a remedy against baldness in the Ebers Medical Papyrus! It mentions one Shesh(et) as mother of a king **Teti**, the same name borne by the 6th Dynastic founder.[71]

Estates of a King's Mother Sesheshet are mentioned in the tomb of the Vizier Mehu at Saqqara, dating to the first half of the 6th Dynasty, and thus the two ladies have often been equated. However, final proof is lacking: a pillar fragment from the mortuary temple of Pepy I once named Teti's mother, but only her title survives. The title is simply 'King's Mother', which may suggest that Teti was not the son of a king.

Teti's two principal wives, Iput I and Khuit A, are known from their tombs in his pyramid-cemetery, while a stela shows that the former was the mother of Pepy I. However, there is evidence of another king, **Userkare**, reigning briefly between Teti and Pepy; his mother may be the Khent[kaues III?] named on a block from Pepy I's pyramid-temple. The South-Saqqara Stone, the remains of the annals of the beginning of the dynasty, seem to confirm the existence of his reign (although not his name), and that his mother's name ended in a 't'.

Ink marks on a number of blocks from the pyramid of **Pepy I** name a number of princes, including Teti-ankh, whilst five wives are attested by their

(right) Pepy I with his mother, Iput I, making an offering to Min; from Koptos (CM JE41891).

(below) Uni, who prosecuted an unnamed wife of Pepy I from Abydos (CM CG1435).

possession of pyramids to the south of the king's at South Saqqara. In addition to these ladies, Pepy I had at least one other wife. She is mentioned in the autobiographical inscription of the high official Uni, who records that 'when there was a secret charge in the royal harem against the Great of Sceptre, his person made me go and listen alone. No Chief Judge or Vizier, no official was there, only I alone'. The fact that this trial was recorded suggests that the queen was found guilty and therefore unlikely to have received a proper burial, and is therefore not to be found amongst the royal ladies buried adjacent to the king's pyramid. It is possible that her unused tomb might have been used for the later Queen Ankhenespepy III.

Of the named wives of Pepy I, the most important are the Ankhenespepys – with their names written 'Ankhenesmeryre' on some monuments. They were sisters, named as such on the stela of their brother, Djau, from Abydos, which also gives the siblings' parentage. They also appear in a text from the reign of Pepy II, both documents indicating that they were respectively the mothers of Nemtyemsaf I and Pepy II. A son of Pepy I, Hornetjerkhet, is known from his tomb adjacent to that of the king, with his mother Mehaa named on the remains of a doorway from Hornetjerkhet's sepulchre.

There is no information as to the wife of **Nemtyemsaf I**, but Ankhenespepy III, whose pyramid lies in the complex of Pepy I, is described in a line of invocations along the tops of the walls of her burial chamber as a daughter of Nemtyemsaf I and wife of her uncle Pepy II.

(above) The last great pyramid of the Old Kingdom was that of Pepy II. Although nowhere near as well built as the 4th Dynasty monuments, it is far better preserved than others of the 6th Dynasty; parts of the mortuary temple have been restored, and may be seen in the foreground.

(above, right) Three of Pepy II's wives had pyramids alongside his own. Here, the ruins of the pyramid of Udjebten show the remains of the casing, at the steep angle of 60 degrees.

6th Dynasty

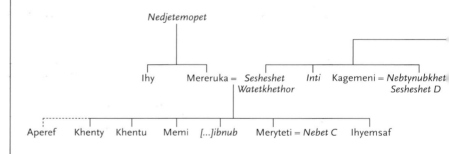

Nedjetemopet

Ihy   Mereruka = *Sesheshet*   *Inti*   Kagemeni = *Nebtynubkhet*
                    Watetkhethor   *Sesheshet D*

Aperef   Khenty   Khentu   Memi   *[...]ibnub*   Meryteti = *Nebet C*   Ihyemsaf

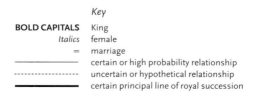

Key

BOLD CAPITALS	King
Italics	female
=	marriage
————	certain or high probability relationship
------------------	uncertain or hypothetical relationship
▬▬▬▬	certain principal line of royal succession

Two of the remaining spouses of **Pepy II** were his sisters, Neith A and Iput II, known – together with another wife, Udjebten – from their pyramids at South Saqqara, around that of their husband. A son of Pepy II, Nemtyemsaf, is known from a stela found near the pyramid of Neith, perhaps his mother. He is usually equated with **Nemtyemsaf II**, given as Pepy II's successor in the Abydos king list. It is likely that a number of Crown Princes may have died during Pepy II's long reign. Nebkauhor-Idu, whose tomb at Saqqara has been dated to approximately this time, may have been one of these men.

A final wife of Pepy II, Ankhenespepy IV, was buried in a store room of the mortuary chapel of Queen Iput II. Texts from her improvised tomb show her to have been a wife of Pepy, and mother of a king named **Neferkare (II)**. No fewer than five kings with this prenomen are known from the Abydos king list to have lived in the period following Nemtyemsaf II's death: Ankhenespepy IV's son will presumably have been one of the earlier of them, apparently Nemtyemsaf II's third and fourth successors.

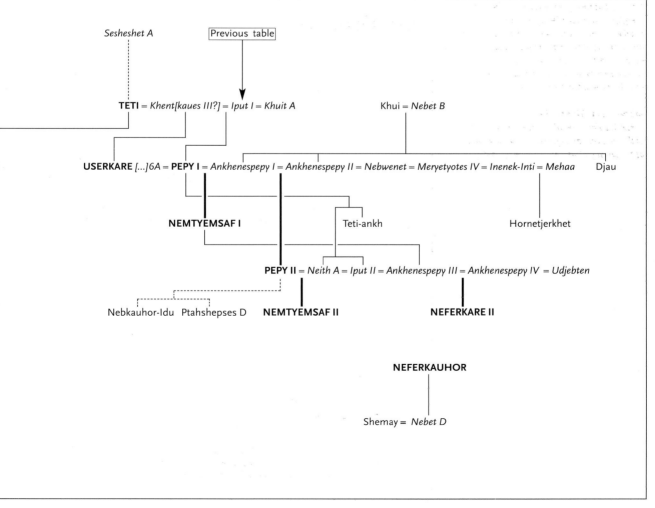

Prince Ptahshepses (D), who received a similar burial to Ankhenespepy IV – in a borrowed sarcophagus in a royal funerary temple (in this case the valley temple of Unas) – is likely to be similarly dated to her, and was probably another son of Pepy II.

Beyond these last scions of the family of Pepy II, our knowledge of not only the royal family but of the very royal succession becomes distinctly sketchy. The successors of Nemtyemsaf II are generally classified as the 7th/8th Dynasties and given an order by the Abydos king list, but their mutual relationships are unknown. One royal offspring, Nebet D, is known from a number of monuments from Koptos, where her husband was nomarch. These include decrees issued by her father, **Neferkauhor**.

Prince Nemtyemsaf A, from the mortuary stela he had carved prior to probably becoming his father's successor; from South Saqqara.

Brief Lives •

Males in **bold***, females in* ***bold italic***.

Ankhenespepy I (KW; KM; GS)
Also referred to as ***Ankhenesmeryre I***.
Wife of Pepy I and mother of Nemtyemsaf I. Along with her sister, Ankhenespepy II, named on a stela of Djau, her brother. Also named on a fragmentary inscription in Berlin; a decree relating to a statue-cult at Abydos; and at her pyramid at Saqqara.

Ankhenespepy II (GD; KM; KW; GS)
Also referred to as ***Ankhenesmeryre II***.
Wife of Pepy I and mother of Pepy II. Named on a stela of Djau; a decree relating to a statue-cult at Abydos; a rock-text in the Sinai; a statue in Brooklyn showing her with her son on her lap; and at her pyramid. A decree regarding her cult and that of Neith A was found at the latter's pyramid.

Ankhenespepy III (KD; KW)
Daughter of Nemtyemsaf I and wife of Pepy II. Buried in a pyramid amongst the pyramids of the wives of Pepy I near that of the king at South Saqqara. Her sarcophagus was carved out of a huge conglomerate flooring block, bearing her names and titles, and containing scattered bones. Fragments of a decree of Pepy II in

(left) Alabaster statuette of Queen Ankhenesmeryre II with her young son, Pepy II, on her lap (Brooklyn 39.119).

(opposite) The Vizier Mereruka was a son-in-law of King Teti, whose eldest daughter he had married. One of the false doors in his tomb at Saqqara is unusual in incorporating a three-dimensional image of the deceased Vizier.

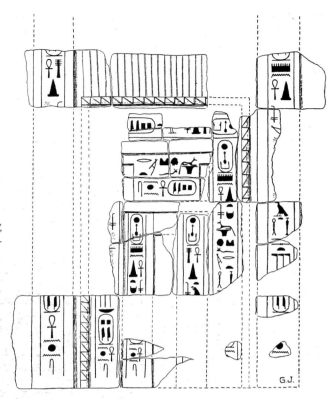

The stela of Ankhenespepy IV, carved on a storeroom wall in the chapel of Iput II.

honour of the queen were found north of the pyramid's enclosure wall.

Ankhenespepy IV (GD; KM; KW; GS)
Wife of Pepy II and mother of King Neferkare (II?). Buried in the mortuary chapel of Iput II at South Saqqara.

Aperef
Possibly a grandson of Teti. Depicted in the tomb of Mereruka at Saqqara.

Djau (Viz)
A brother-in-law of Pepy I. Served as Upper Egyptian Vizier under this king and was buried somewhere at Abydos, although the exact location is lost.

Hornetjerkhet (KSon)
Son of Pepy I, buried near his pyramid at South Saqqara.

Ihy
Brother of Mereruka; depicted in his tomb.

Ihyemsaf
Grandson of Teti. Depicted in the tomb of

Mereruka at Saqqara.

Inenek-Inti (KW)
Wife of Pepy I. Buried in a pyramid adjacent to that of Pepy I at South Saqqara.

Inti (EKDB)
Daughter of Teti. Buried in a tomb at Saqqara.

Iput I (KM; GS; KW; KD)
Daughter of Unas and wife of Teti. Buried in a pyramid near that of her husband at Saqqara. Also depicted with her son, Pepy I, on a decree-stela from Koptos. Bones now in the Cairo Museum (formerly in Qasr el-Aini Medical School).

Iput II (KW; EKD)
Sister and wife of Pepy II, buried at South Saqqara.

Kagemeni (Viz)
Son-in-law of Teti; buried in tomb LS10 adjacent to the king's pyramid.

Khent[kaues III?] (KM)
Mother of Userkare, and perhaps a wife of Teti. She is known from a relief fragment in the mortuary temple of Pepy I. She may have been the owner of a mastaba that lay south of the tombs of Iput I and Khuit, but whose structure was later incorporated into the mastaba of a noble named Khentika.

Khentu
Grandson of Teti. Depicted in the tomb of Mereruka.

Khenty
Grandson of Teti. Depicted in the tomb of Mereruka.

Khui
Father-in-law of Pepy I. Nothing is known of him, other than identity of his children.

Khuit A (GS; KW)
Wife of Teti, near whose pyramid at Saqqara she was buried. Bones now in the Cairo Museum (formerly in Qasr el-Aini Medical School).

Khuit B (KD; KW)
Owner of tomb 70 at Saqqara. Affiliations unknown, other than general date provided by the style of her tomb.

Mehaa (KM)
Wife of Pepy I. Depicted on a doorway from the tomb of her son, Hornetjerkhet.

Memi
Grandson of Teti. Depicted in the tomb of Mereruka.

Mereruka (Viz)
Son-in-law of Teti. Buried in a huge tomb adjacent to the king's pyramid.

Meryetyotes IV (KW)
Wife of Pepy I. Buried in a pyramid adjacent to that of her husband.

Meryteti (EKSonB; Viz)
Grandson of Teti. Buried in the tomb of Mereruka.

Nebet B
Mother-in-law of Pepy I. Named on

monuments of her son Djau.

Nebet C (PH)
Granddaughter-in-law of Teti; depicted in the tomb of Mereruka.

Nebet D (KD)
Daughter of Neferkauhor. Known from her funerary stela from Koptos (Nag Kom el-Kuffar), together with two decrees found in the temple at that site.

Nebkauhor-Idu (EKSonB)
Possibly a son of Pepy II. Buried near the causeway of Unas, in a tomb datable to the latter part of the 6th Dynasty.

Nebtynubkhet Sesheshet D (KDB)
Daughter of Teti; depicted in the Saqqara tomb of her husband, the Vizier Kagemeni.

Nebwenet (KW)
Wife of Pepy I. Buried in a pyramid adjacent to that of her husband.

Nedjeftet (KW)
Known from three limestone blocks found near the pyramid of Inenek-Inti, but nothing is known of her affiliations, although she was clearly related to one of the kings of the 6th Dynasty.

Nedjetemopet
Mother of Mereruka, a son-in-law of Teti.

Neith A (KD; GS; KM; KW)
Sister and wife of Pepy II. Buried adjacent to her husband; the remains of her mummy are in Cairo (formerly in Qasr el-Aini Medical School).

Nemtyemsaf A (EKSonB)
Son of Pepy II. Mentioned in a stela found near Neith A's pyramid complex; probably identical with King **NEMTYEMSAF II**.

(below) Pepy II's 'eldest son of his body', as depicted in this relief at the king's mortuary temple at Saqqara. This may be the Nemtyemsaf (II) who succeeded him on the throne.

Ptahshepses D (KSon)
Possibly a son of Pepy II. Buried in a reused 4th Dynasty sarcophagus in the valley temple of Unas. Mummy in the Cairo Museum (formerly in Qasr el-Aini Medical School).

Sesheshet A (KM)
Probable mother of Teti. Estates belonging to her are mentioned in the tomb of Mehu at Saqqara.

Sesheshet C Watetkhethor (EKDB)
Daughter of Teti; wife of Mereruka, in whose tomb she was buried; bones in the Cairo Museum (formerly in Qasr el-Aini Medical School).

Shemay (Viz; GF)
Son-in-law of Neferkauhor. Held successively the titles of nomarch of Koptos, governor of Upper Egypt and Vizier.

Shesh (KM)
The Ebers Medical Papyrus mentions an anti-baldness remedy that was 'devised by Shesh, mother of the person of the Dual King Teti, true of voice'. Perhaps identical with Sesheshet A.

(below) The golden inlaid belt of Ptahshepses (CM JE87078).

(above) The royal family members of the very end of the Old Kingdom were unable to afford their own tombs. Prince Ptahshepses was buried in the valley building of Unas at Saqqara.

(left) Prince Ptahshepses' sarcophagus had been made at the end of the 4th Dynasty, and must have been usurped from an earlier owner (CM JE87077).

Teti-ankh (KSon)
Son of Pepy I. Named in an ink notation on a block from the pyramid of his father at Saqqara.

Udjebten (KW; GS)
Wife of Pepy II. Buried in pyramid adjacent to that of her husband at South Saqqara.

[...]ibnub
Granddaughter of Teti. Depicted in the tomb of Mereruka.

[...]6A (GS)
Wife of Pepy I. Her prosecution for an unknown crime is recorded in the inscription of Uni; nothing else known.

2

The 1st Intermediate Period, the Middle Kingdom and 2nd Intermediate Period

The House of Akhtoy

9th and 10th Dynasties

*(previous page) The first face of the Middle
Kingdom: Mentuhotep II (CM JE36195).*

The tomb-chapel of Ankhtify at Mo'alla,
which contains the autobiographical text that
is an important source of information on the
conflicts of the 1st Intermediate Period.

Historical Background

The dynasty that seems to have supplanted the 8th Dynasty is extremely obscure. Some royal names survive in the Turin Canon and contemporary objects, but only fragments of the royal succession can be discerned. That the take-over by the rulers of Herakleopolis – just south of the fertile Fayoum basin and 90 kilometres (56 miles) from Memphis – was violent is reflected in Manetho's description of Akhtoy I, the dynastic founder, as 'more terrible than his predecessors', who 'wrought evil things for those in all Egypt'.

Akhtoy may have initially gained power as far as Aswan in the south, but the Herakleopolitans' rule seems after a while to have become restricted to the territory north of the area of Abydos, the southern nomes banding together under the leadership of the hitherto-minor city of Thebes. The accession of Inyotef I as king of Upper Egypt is generally taken as marking the division between the 9th and 10th Dynasties.

Although Akhtoy I and his successors acted as nominal overlords, the actual governance of the Nile Valley was essentially feudal, with the local magnates regularly jockeying for position. Some nomarchs formally acknowledged their loyalty to the royal house, but others went as far as to date events by their own years of office, rather than by their king's regnal years.

Under Akhtoy's second successor, Neferkare III, Ankhtify – the nomarch of Hierakonpolis based at Mo'alla, less than 30 km (18 miles) south of Thebes – led a coalition of his own and the Edfu nomes against the Thebans. This presumably constituted a pre-emptive strike against a polity that was already showing signs of challenging Ankhtify's Herakleopolitan overlords for dominance. This was but the first episode of a conflict that was to last as long as the House of Akhtoy – around a century. Some decades later, the nomarch Tefibi of Asyut tells of how he fought against the Thebans and their allies, presumably the same campaign which is referred to by his king, Akhtoy V, in

The funerary stela of Gemeni (Ny Carlsberg ÆIN 1616), who was a mortuary priest of both the 6th Dynasty King Teti and the 10th Dynasty monarch Merykare. Stelae of his priests constitute the sole evidence for the existence of his pyramid, which presumably lay close to Teti's, but has never been positively identified.

an instruction addressed to his heir. In it he regrets that his troops, having regained the Abydene area from the Thebans, set about plundering the ancient cemetery.

The Herakleopolitan success was apparently short-lived, the Thebans regaining the territory and agreeing some kind of truce by the time the throne had passed to Akhtoy V's son, Merykare. The alliance with Asyut remained strong, the king attending the installation of Tefibi's son, Akhtoy B, in person. Nevertheless, fighting once again broke out around Abydos, with the fall of the Herakleopolitan kingdom occurring not long after the death of Merykare.

The Royal Family

It is possible that the line may have traced itself back to the Overseer of Treasurers and God's Father, Akhtoy (A), the owner of large granite offering table in Cairo Museum. On the basis of his second title, it is conceivable that he could have been the father of **Akhtoy I**. Otherwise, our only information on family relationships is in the text known as the 'Instruction for Merykare',[72] which indicates that **Merykare**'s father was a king, whose name was probably Akhtoy, and that his mother was the daughter of a ruler. It has been suggested that the father was Nubkaure **Akhtoy V**.

81

The Head of the South

11th Dynasty

The Royal Succession

11th Dynasty 2160–1994

MENTUHOTEP I

INYOTEF I

INYOTEF II

INYOTEF III

MENTUHOTEP II

MENTUHOTEP III

MENTUHOTEP IV

Historical Background

The collapse of the nation state during the period after the end of the 6th Dynasty, which had led to the establishment of the Herakleopolitan-led 9th/10th Dynasties in the north, had been paralleled in the south by the eventual emergence of a Theban-ruled polity, now referred to as the 11th Dynasty. Initially simple nomarchs, the line soon adopted Horus-names and nomen-cartouches, although not yet the full five-fold titulary of a pharaoh.

The 11th Dynasty's territory seems to have been consolidated as the land south of the area of Abydos. A Herakleopolitan conquest of Abydos was apparently short-lived, the Thebans subsequently regaining the territory. However, in the 14th regnal year of Mentuhotep II, there was an attempt to re-take the Thinite nome, the fighting ultimately resulting in the conquest of the whole of Egypt by the king's forces. This achievement was well remembered by posterity: in later inscriptions, Mentuhotep II was set alongside Menes as being the second founder of the Egyptian state.

The reuniter of Egypt, Mentuhotep II, is here shown in a relief from his mortuary temple at Deir el-Bahari (BM EA1397).

Having secured the country internally, Mentuhotep II soon began to extend his influence beyond its borders, undertaking police actions in the surrounding deserts and penetrating southwards into Nubia. The king also built extensively, in particular in the area occupied by the original Theban kingdom. Fragments of his works survive at a number of sites, but his most impressive monument is the mortuary temple complex he erected at Deir el-Bahari at Western Thebes.

After a reign of over half a century, he was succeeded by Mentuhotep III, who continued his predecessor's work of renewal, before being in turn followed by a fourth King Mentuhotep, with whom the 11th Dynasty was to come to an end.

The Royal Family

The starting point of this dynasty seems to have been one Inyotef (A), son of a lady named Ikui, who is commemorated as an important figure in the late 11th Dynasty and early in the 12th. He is likely to be identical with the nomarch Inyotef who is known from the mid-1st Intermediate Period, and the *iry-pᶜt ḥȝty-ᶜ* Inyotef who is shown at the head of a series of 11th Dynasty rulers in Thutmose III's king list from the Karnak temple. After him is the figure of the Horus Tepya ('the Ancestor'), **Mentuhotep (I)**, who seems to be identical with the man of the name commemorated by one of a series of three statues dedicated by Inyotef II at Elephantine. On it he is called *it-nṯrw*, 'Gods' Father', in the plural. This would imply that Inyotef II (presumably, as dedicator, one of Mentuhotep's divine sons) had a ruling sibling, who can only be **Inyotef I**. That the mother of at least the younger Inyotef was named Neferu (I) is indicated by **Inyotef II** being called 'born of Neferu' on a number of stelae. The succession of these two Inyotefs is confirmed by a block from

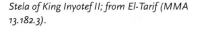

Stela of King Inyotef II; from El-Tarif (MMA 13.182.3).

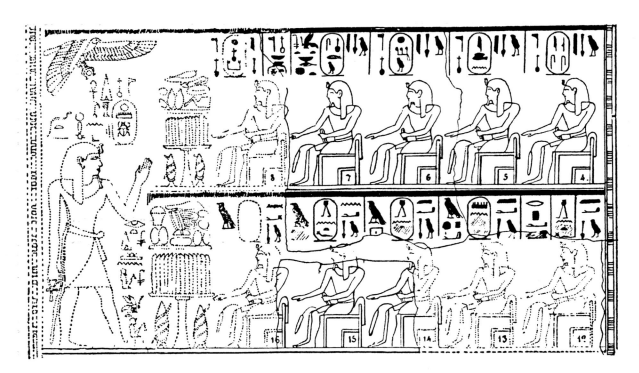

(above) A part of the Karnak king list, compiled by Thutmose III during the 18th Dynasty. In this section, the king offers to a group of ancient monarchs, including, on the lower register from the right, the nomarch Inyotef (A), Mentuhotep I and Inyotefs I and II (Louvre E13481bis).

Reliefs of kings Inyotef I, II and III, from a memorial erected by Mentuhotep II in the temple at Tod (CM JE66331).

11th Dynasty

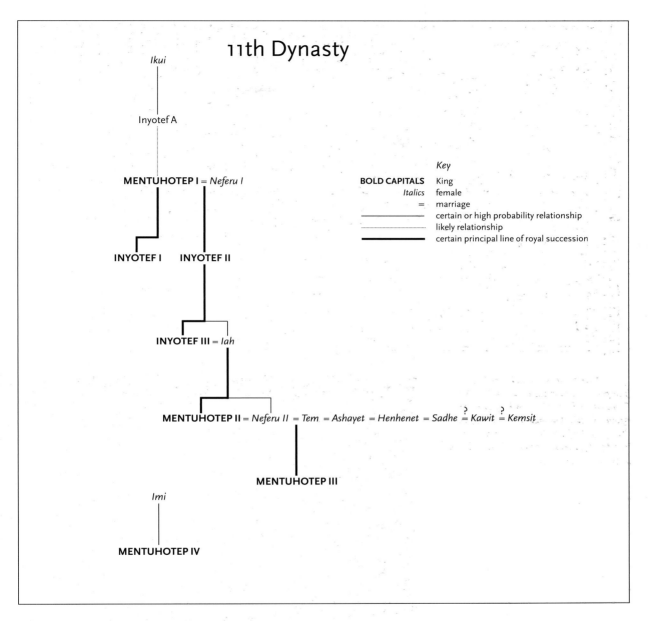

Ikui

Inyotef A

MENTUHOTEP I = *Neferu I*

INYOTEF I   **INYOTEF II**

INYOTEF III = *Iah*

MENTUHOTEP II = *Neferu II* = *Tem* = *Ashayet* = *Henhenet* = *Sadhe* =? *Kawit* =? *Kemsit*

MENTUHOTEP III

Imi

MENTUHOTEP IV

Key

BOLD CAPITALS	King
Italics	female
=	marriage
————	certain or high probability relationship
··········	likely relationship
▬▬▬	certain principal line of royal succession

Tod, which also shows the next king – **Inyotef III**. The latter is stated to have been the son of Inyotef II in the biographical text of one Tjetji in the British Museum.

For evidence as to **Mentuhotep II**'s parentage, one needs to turn to a rock-inscription at Shatt el-Rigal, in which the king is shown flanked by the 'King's Mother ..., Iah', and the 'God's Father, the Son of Re, Inyotef'. The latter is given a cartouche, and is now generally identified with the deceased Inyotef III.[73] This reinforces the stela of Henun in Cairo which, although badly broken, can be reconstructed as stating that Mentuhotep II was indeed Inyotef III's son.

A number of wives of Mentuhotep II are known; one, Neferu II, is shown by her tomb-inscriptions to have been his full sister; another, Tem, is also known from her tomb, alongside that of the king; her title of Mother of the Dual King would indicate that she was also the mother of **Mentuhotep III**. Other spouses are among a group of six females who were buried in the Deir el-Bahari temple early in the reign; this is indicated by the fact that the entrances to their tomb shafts were subsequently covered by the columns and paving of a later phase of the temple. In addition, the name of the king is in all cases given in its second form, which was only current during the middle years of his reign; to reflect the progress of his reunification, Mentuhotep II changed his name or its spelling twice. One burial

View of Deir el-Bahari looking north with the terraced temple of Mentuhotep II in the foreground. Beyond are the 18th Dynasty temples of Thutmose III and Hatshepsut.

belonged to a child, Mayet (whose status remains unknown), while the other five were all Prophetesses of Hathor (as had been the king's mother); three were also definitely King's Wives, with the remaining two of uncertain identity due to the damaged state of their texts.

Curiously, no children of the king are known other than Mentuhotep III – and even he is without any attestation during his father's reign. The younger king's own family remains a mystery,[74] and it is not known whether his successor, **Mentuhotep IV**, was related to him. The latter's mother is given in a quarry inscription in the Wadi Hammamat as being called Imi, but without any further titles to clarify whether she was also Mentuhotep III's wife.

(below, right) Statue of Mentuhotep II, from his cenotaph at Deir el-Bahari. The black flesh is symbolic of resurrection, the image having been made to mark the king's jubilee, part of which involved his physical and spiritual renewal (CM JE36195).

Brief Lives ●

*Males in **bold**, females in **bold italic**.*

Ashayet (PH; KW)

Wife of Mentuhotep II; buried in tomb DBXI.17 within the king's mortuary chapel during the second third of his reign. Her sarcophagus and coffin are in the Cairo Museum, as is her mummy (previously in Qasr el-Aini Medical School).

Henhenet (PH; KW)

Wife of Mentuhotep II; died in childbirth and buried in tomb DBXI.11 within the king's mortuary chapel during the second third of his reign. Her sarcophagus is in

Rock inscription in the Wadi Shatt el-Rigal, showing Mentuhotep II with his mother Iah behind him, and his deceased father Inyotef (III) before him, along with the chancellor Khety (B).

New York, while her mummy is in Cairo (previously in New York and then Qasr el-Aini Medical School).

Iah (KM; KD; PH)

Daughter of Inyotef II, wife of Inyotef III and mother of Mentuhotep II and Neferu II. Depicted with her son and late husband at Shatt el-Rigal, and on a block now in the British Museum; she is also named in the tomb of her daughter.

Ikui

Mother of Inyotef A; her name is coupled with that of her son on two of his posthumous memorials.

Imi (KM)

Mother of Mentuhotep IV; named in an inscription in the Wadi Hammamat recording an expedition to quarry stone there for the king's sarcophagus.

Inyotef A (Nomarch)

Son of Ikui, and probable father of Mentuhotep I; commemorated by the 11th Dynasty stela of Maat (New York) and a scribe-statue dedicated by Senwosret I at Karnak (Cairo), as well as much later in Thutmose III's Karnak king list.

Kawit (PH; KW?)

Possibly a wife of Mentuhotep II; buried in tomb DBXI.9 within the king's mortuary chapel during the second third of his reign. Her sarcophagus is in the Cairo Museum.

Painting of Queen Ashayet enjoying the scent of a lotus, as seen on the interior of her sarcophagus; from Deir el-Bahari DBXI.17 (CM JE47267).

(above) Relief of Kawit, possibly a wife of Mentuhotep II, having her hair arranged; from the exterior of her sarcophagus from DBXI.9 (CM JE47397).

(above, right) Fragment of painted limestone relief of figure of Kemsit; from her tomb chapel in the funerary temple of her husband Mentuhotep II at Deir el-Bahari (BM EA1450).

Kemsit (PH; KW?)
Possibly a wife of Mentuhotep II; buried in tomb TT308 within the king's mortuary chapel during the second third of his reign. The fragments of her sarcophagus are in the British Museum.

Neferu I
Mother of Inyotef II; her son is given the epithet 'born of Neferu' on the stelae of Tjetji (British Museum), Heny (Moscow), and Djari (Cairo and Brussels), as well as one of his own (Metropolitan Museum of Art).

Neferu II (KW; KD)
Daughter of Inyotef III and Iah, and wife of Mentuhotep II; buried in tomb TT319 at Deir el-Bahari.

Sadhe (PH; KW)
Wife of Mentuhotep II; buried in tomb DBXI.7 within the king's mortuary chapel during the second third of his reign.

Tem (KW; GS; KM)
Wife of Mentuhotep II and mother of Mentuhotep III; buried in tomb DBXI.15, within the mortuary temple of her husband.

Unplaced ●●●●●●●●●●●●●

Neferkayet (KW; KD)
Daughter and wife of unknown kings; named on the stela of her steward, Rediukhnum, from Dendara, now in Cairo.

Fragment of a relief of Queen Neferu II; from her tomb chapel, TT319, at Deir el-Bahari (Brooklyn 51.231).

Seizers of the Two Lands

12th Dynasty

The Royal Succession

12th Dynasty 1994–1781

AMENEMHAT I

SENWOSRET I

AMENEMHAT II

SENWOSRET II

SENWOSRET III

AMENEMHAT III

AMENEMHAT IV

SOBKNEFERU

Sphinx of Senwosret III (MMA 17.9.2).

Historical Background

Nothing is known of the means by which Amenemhat I acquired the throne from Mentuhotep IV. It is possible that a series of texts at Deir el-Bersha describing famine and other troubles could be assigned to this point in time and might provide some background. Be that as it may, with the accession of Amenemhat I, the Middle Kingdom, inaugurated by the reunification, moved towards maturity.

A key act of the new king was to transfer the royal seat from Thebes to a new site in the north, the city of *Itj-tawy* ('Seizer of the Two Lands'). This city was established in the area of modern Lisht and was to remain the main residence of the pharaoh for the next 400 years. Amenemhat I died at the hands of assassins, but the conspiracy was unsuccessful, and the years of the 12th Dynasty were to continue as those of great stability and development. The long reign of Senwosret I saw Nubia occupied down as far as Buhen, with a presence extended even further south. Extensive building took place, including the core of the temple of Karnak, and various works at Heliopolis. Senwosret I's co-regent and successor, Amenemhat II, had led a Nubian expedition while still a prince, and more campaigns are recorded on the great annalistic inscription produced during his lengthy occupation of the throne.

The next king, Senwosret II, is less well attested, but seems to have been responsible for the large-scale development of the Fayoum, the 'oasis' region some 70 km (45 miles) south of modern Cairo. He was followed by his son, Senwosret III, who was to become a most distinguished occupant of the Egyptian throne, and worshipped as a god for many centuries after his death. Material dating to his reign is found at a number of locations, particularly in the southern part of Egypt. The king's statues are notable for their extremely naturalistic treatment of the features, in contrast with the idealism of earlier works.

The reign of Senwosret III is the last in which one finds widespread examples of the monuments of the nomarchs. It was long believed that this reflected a conscious 'breaking' of the power of the nomarchs, but it now seems more likely to have been the indirect result of an increasing centralization of the administration, leading to a gradual withering away of the great local 'courts' as their leaders moved to work for the king in the national capital.

There is relatively little evidence for Egyptian military activity in the direction of Palestine during the Middle Kingdom. On the other hand, Senwosret III's expeditions into Nubia were extensive, and marked the full subjugation of Nubian territory by the Egyptian crown. A fortified southern boundary for Egypt was set at Semna, where a whole complex of forts was built or rebuilt to house Egyptian governors and garrisons.

Senwosret III's successor was Amenemhat III; he would appear to have served as co-regent for a considerable period before the elder king's death. Unlike his father, Amenemhat III has left few memorials of military activities but was a major builder, particularly in the Fayoum. The region had received the attention of Senwosret II, but it was only under Amenemhat III that more extensive works were carried out there. The latter king also worked the turquoise mines of the Sinai. Other regions which saw Egyptian expeditions bent on the extraction of raw materials were the Wadi Hammamat and the diorite quarries of the Nubian desert. In his final few years, Amenemhat III seems to have shared the throne with his nominated successor – Amenemhat IV – whose independent reign was short. He was succeeded by Amenemhat III's daughter, Sobkneferu.

Double statues of 'fish offerers', probably representing the co-regents Senwosret III and his son Amenemhat III; from Tanis (CM JE18221=CG392).

(right) Torso of Sobkneferu, showing her wearing a kingly nemes headdress and kilt over her conventional female attire (Louvre E27135).

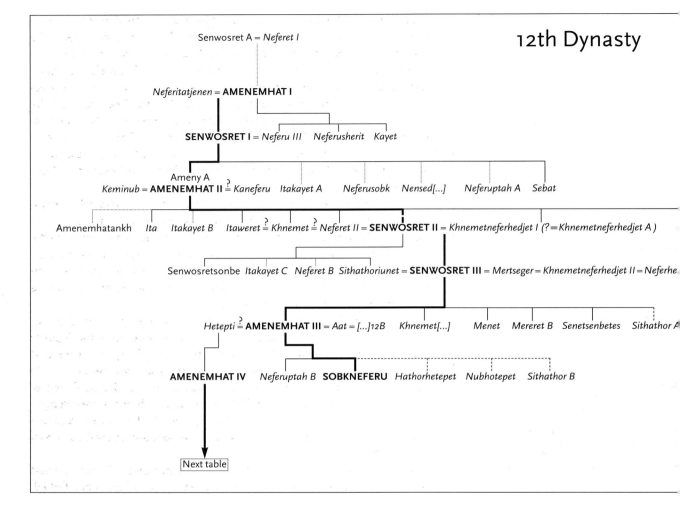

12th Dynasty

The Royal Family

The paternity of **Amenemhat I** is nowhere stated; however, that he was not a member of the 11th Dynasty royal family is implied by the so-called 'Prophecy of Neferti', a propagandistic work written after Amenemhat's accession. Set back in the Old Kingdom, it foretells that after a period of disorder, 'a king will come from the south, Ameny [Amenemhat] his name, son of a woman of the Elephantine nome, a child of Upper Egypt: he will take the White Crown, he will wear the Red Crown ... Rejoice, O people of this time, for this son of man will make his name for ever ....' Amenemhat I is also generally identified with the Vizier Amenemhat (A) who, in the second year of Mentuhotep IV's reign, led a large expedition to the Wadi Hammamat to obtain stone for the king's sarcophagus.

Although definitive proof is lacking, it is likely that Amenemhat I's father was the God's Father Senwosret (A), who is listed after Mentuhotep II and III in a series of recipients of offerings in a chapel of Amenhotep I from Karnak.[75] First, there is the not-infrequent bestowal of his title on non-ruling fathers of kings during the Middle Kingdom; and second, Senwosret was to be the name of Amenemhat's successor, as well as two other kings of the dynasty – a naming pattern that fits well with usual Egyptian practice.[76]

Amenemhat I's mother was probably the King's Mother Neferet I, whose offering table was found near the king's pyramid at Lisht; tellingly, she bears no other titles, confirming the king's non-royal birth. One wife, and the mother of his successor, **Senwosret I**, was Neferitatjenen, whose relationships are given on a statuette of her son. A daughter, Neferu III, is explicitly mentioned in the 'Story of Sinuhe', one of the great works of Egyptian literature, as wife of her brother, Senwosret I;[77] two other daughters, Neferusherit and Kayet, are named on items from the king's pyramid complex.

Apart from this wife, four daughters of Senwosret I – Itakayet A, Neferusobk, Nensed[...] and Neferuptah A – are apparently named on material from his pyramid complex. A further daughter, Sebat, is amongst members of the king's family included in a shrine in Sinai. The eldest son, Ameny, is mentioned in the autobiographical text of Amenemhat, the nomarch of Beni Hasan; 'Ameny' is a shortened form of the name 'Amenemhat', the prince certainly being the later king **Amenemhat II**.

The names of a number of royal family members were found in Amenemhat II's funerary complex, although the dates of a number of the deposits have been questioned, with it being argued that they belong to the latter part of the 12th Dynasty.[78] However, there remain strong archaeological grounds for making the tombs integral parts of Amenemhat II's architectural conception, and it seems most likely that all those interred in his enclosure belonged to his immediate family, although some may not have been interred until a reign or two later.[79] Amongst them was a queen, Keminub, as well as at least four daughters.

Another potential daughter, Itakayet B, is named on a cylinder seal that also bears the cartouche of an Amenemhat; we also have Khnemetneferhed-

nathormeryet   *Sit[...]A*

A

Key

•LD CAPITALS	King
Italics	female
=	marriage
≡	equivalent to
——————	certain or high probability relationship
··············	likely relationship
– – – – – –	uncertain or hypothetical relationship
▬▬▬▬	principal line of royal succession

The pyramid of Senwosret I at Lisht; in the right foreground lie the ruins of two pyramids of members of the royal family – perhaps including one or more wives, since such ladies were generally buried in this position during the Old Kingdom.

jet A, named on a cylinder seal alongside her father, and a lady named Kane-feru, who may have been a wife of the king. Finally, a son, Amenemhatankh seems to be indicated by the presence of fragments of his stela in Amen-emhat II's funerary complex, although he might possibly be the latter's brother.

The relationship between Amenemhat II and Senwosret II is nowhere stated. However, two statues show that Neferet II was one of his wives; her title of King's Daughter indicates that she was also a daughter of Amenemhat II. Another spouse was Khnemetneferhedjet I Weret, known to have been the mother of Senwosret III through her burial in his complex, and her mention in a Kahun papyrus alongside other members of Senwosret II's family.[80] This document lists offerings to the family of the king, and also includes a Prince Senwosretsonbe; also enumerated are two daughters, Itakayet C and Neferet B.[81] Buried in Senwosret II's pyramid complex was the King's Daughter Sithathoriunet; her jewellery included material with the names of Senwosret II and Amenemhat III, suggesting that she was a daughter of the former, buried under the latter. She was also a King's Wife, presumably of Senwosret III.

Senwosret III's parentage seems certain; he had three definite wives – one is known from a stela, another from two statues, and a third from her tomb in his pyramid complex. This last monument also provides names of five of the king's probable daughters,[82] as well as evidence for the existence of others, whose anonymous sarcophagi were found alongside those of their sisters.

Statue of Queen Neferet II; from Tanis (CM CG381).

The northern part of the pyramid complex of Senwosret II at Lahun, showing the rock-cut mastabas of the royal family. The substructures of these sepulchres lay on the opposite side of the pyramid, one of the earliest examples of separating super-structures and substructures for reasons of security. The queen's pyramid lies at the far end of the row.

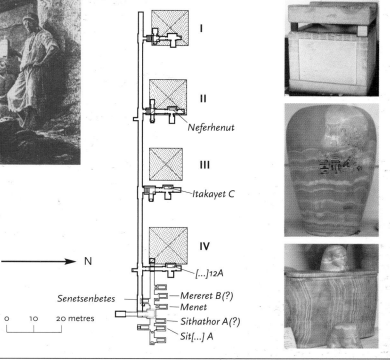

The Gallery of the Princesses in the enclosure of Senwosret III at Dahshur. At an upper level, a long gallery gives access to the substructures of a row of four pyramids (I–IV); at a lower level is a collective catacomb, first excavated in 1894 by De Morgan (above). Along with many items of jewellery were found, amongst others, the canopic chest of Sithathor A and jar of Menet (top right and centre: CM CG4050 and 4005), and a strange canopic jar of Itakayet C (bottom right, CM CG4049).

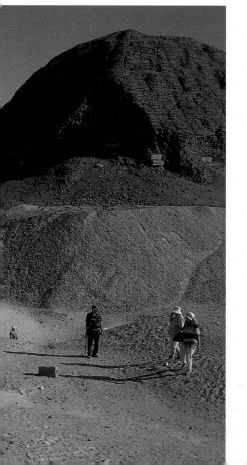

No sons are explicitly attested, but the assumption must be that **Amenemhat III**, who seems to have served as Senwosret III's co-regent for some years prior to assuming the throne in his own right, was an offspring. Two definite wives of Amenemhat III are known, both of whom were buried under his Dahshur pyramid. There remains uncertainty as to whether Hetepti, shown in an inscription at Medinet Maadi to be the mother of his successor, **Amenemhat IV**, was also a spouse. Although Amenemhat IV calls the elder king 'his father', this term can simply mean 'predecessor', while Hetepti does not include King's Wife amongst her otherwise extensive titulary.

Funerary material of three princesses was found in Amenemhat III's Dahshur complex but, as the monument was not used for the king's burial, and was being used as a royal cemetery down to the middle of the 13th Dynasty, it is not certain that they were actually members of his family. One definite daughter was, however, Neferuptah B, who had an improvised sarcophagus in the burial chamber of Amenemhat III's second pyramid at Hawara, and later seems to have had her mummy moved to her own pyramid nearby. Another likely child is **Sobkneferu**, who was to become Amenemhat III's second successor. On her monuments, she consistently associates herself with the third Amenemhat rather than the intervening Amenemhat IV, which supports the assumption that she was the daughter of Amenemhat III, and thus a sister of the cartouche-bearing Neferuptah B.

Brief Lives ●

*Males in **bold**, females in **bold italic**.*

Aat (KW; UWC)
Wife of Amenemhat III; buried under his pyramid at Dahshur – a false door, an offering table, funerary equipment and a sarcophagus being recovered.

Amenemhatankh (KSon)
Probable son of Amenemhat II; known from fragments of false door found reused in the tombs of Khnemet and Siese (Dahshur tomb L.LV), a text on a block statue recording his appointment of the priest Tetiemsaf (from Saqqara, now in Cairo), the block statue of a certain Horemsaf (B) (Saqqara), a statue-base from the temple of Mut at Karnak (now in Cairo), and from a posthumous mention

False door of Prince Amenemhatankh; from Dahshur.

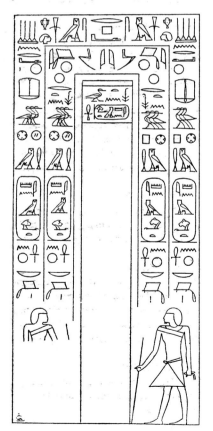

in the autobiographical text of Khnumhotep (Dahshur tomb 2).

Ameny A (EKSonB)
Eldest son of Senwosret I; later king as **AMENEMHAT II**. Amenemhat, nomarch of Beni Hasan, states that the prince sailed with him when he went 'southward … to bring gold for the person of the Dual King, Kheperkare, … with 400 of the choicest of [his] troops, who returned safely, without loss' (text in Beni Hasan tomb BH2).

Hathorhetepet (KD)
Possibly a daughter of Amenemhat III; a fragment of her canopic jar was found in his complex at Dahshur.

Hetepti (KM; M2L; UWC)
Mother of Amenemhat IV, and possibly a wife of Amenemhat III; depicted in a relief at Medinet Maadi.

Ita (KD)
Daughter of Amenemhat II. Owner of a sphinx, found at Qatna in Syria, and now in the Louvre; buried in a double-tomb with Khnemet in their father's funerary enclosure.

Itakayet A (KDB)
Probable daughter of Senwosret I; owner of Pyramid 2 in the latter's pyramid complex, but possibly not buried there. It is not impossible that she may be identical with Itakayet B.

Itakayet B (KD)
Probably a daughter of Amenemhat II; named on a cylinder seal in Berlin that also bears the cartouche of an Amenemhat; conceivably identical with Itakayet C.

Itakayet C (KD)
Probably a daughter of Senwosret II; buried in Pyramid III in the funerary complex of Senwosret III at Dahshur, and probably the lady of the name listed with other members of the royal family on a papyrus from Kahun.

Itaweret (KD; UWC)
Daughter of Amenemhat II, and probably

wife of Senwosret II; buried in a double-tomb with Sithathormeryet in her father's funerary enclosure.

Kaneferu (Mistress of All Women)
Probably a wife of Amenemhat II; named with him on a seal in Tübingen.

Kayet (KDB)
Daughter of Amenemhat I; known from a fragment of relief from Lisht.

Keminub (KW)
Wife of Amenemhat II; buried in a tomb in her husband's funerary enclosure at Dahshur, shared with a certain Amenhotep (i).

Khnemet (KD; UWC)
Daughter of Amenemhat II, and probably a wife of Senwosret II; buried in a double-tomb with Ita in her father's funerary enclosure.

Khnemetneferhedjet I Weret (KM; KW; M2L)
Wife of Senwosret II and mother of Senwosret III. Known from a seal found at Lahun and now in Tonbridge; a mention in a Kahun papyrus in Berlin; a statue in the British Museum; and her cenotaph in the pyramid complex of her son (Pyramid VIII). She was probably buried in the small pyramid in her husband's complex at Lahun.

Khnemetneferhedjet II Weret (GS; KW)
Wife of Senwosret III; known from a statue of her husband in the British Museum and another from Herakleopolis (now in Cairo). Buried in Pyramid IX in her son's complex, where a set of her jewellery was found in 1994.

Khnemetneferhedjet A (KDB)
Daughter of Amenemhat II; named on a cylinder seal in New York, alongside her father. Conceivably identical with Khnemetneferhedjet I Weret.

Khnemet[...] (KDB)
Daughter of Senwosret III; known from a fragment of relief from his pyramid complex at Dahshur.

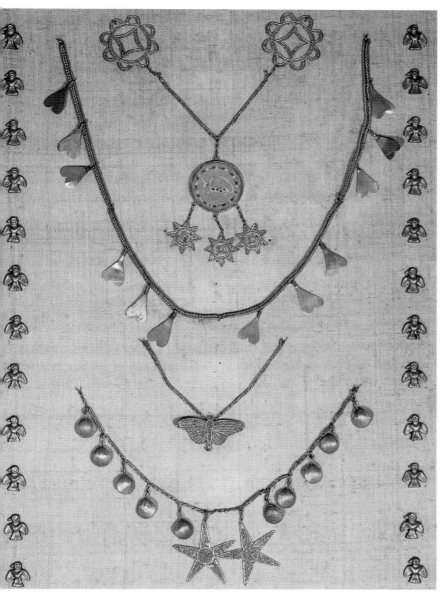

Jewellery from the tomb of Princess Khnemet at Dahshur; much of it seems to be of foreign origin (CM CG52975–9).

Menet (KD)

Daughter of Senwosret III; buried in the lower galleries in his pyramid complex at Dahshur. Two sets of canopic jar fragments are in the Cairo Museum.

Mereret B (KD)

Daughter of Senwosret III; buried in the lower galleries in his pyramid complex at Dahshur. Her jewellery is now in the Cairo Museum, and includes items bearing the name of Amenemhat III.

Mertseger (KW; KGW)

Wife of Senwosret III; depicted on a broken stela in the British Museum and in an inscription at Semna dating to the time of Thutmose III in honour of her husband.

Neferet I (KM)

Probable mother of Amenemhat I; named on an offering table found reused in a later house near the king's pyramid at Lisht.

Neferet II (KDB; GS; M2L)

Daughter of Amenemhat II and wife of Senwosret II; owner of two statues, from Tanis and now in Cairo. Possible owner of the small pyramid in the complex of Senwosret II at Lahun.

Neferet B (KD)

Probably a daughter of Senwosret II; listed with other members of the royal family on a papyrus from Kahun, now in Berlin.

Neferhenut (KW; UWC)

Wife of Senwosret III; buried in tomb II in her husband's funerary complex at Dahshur.

Neferitatjenen (KM)

Wife of Amenemhat I and mother of Senwosret I. Named on a statuette of her son, stolen from the Louvre in 1830.

Neferu III (KD; KW; KM)

Daughter of Amenemhat I and wife of Senwosret I; mentioned in the Story of Sinuhe and known from a fragment of stone found in Amenemhat I's complex at Lisht, Amenemhat II's shrine of Senwosret I at Serabit el-Khadim, and her pyramid in her husband's cemetery. This pyramid may not have been used for her burial, in which case it is possible she was interred at Dahshur near her son, Amenemhat II.

Neferusherit (KD)

Daughter of Amenemhat I; known from a granite object found amongst the shaft-tombs west of her father's pyramid at Lisht.

Neferusobk (KD)

Probable daughter of Senwosret I; a fragment of a granite bowl bearing her name was found near his pyramid. It is conceivable that the bowl may be from a later offering, and that this lady is identical with Sobkneferu.

Neferuptah A (KD)

Probable daughter of Senwosret I; an ivory wand bearing her name was found near his pyramid.

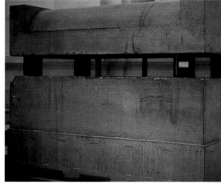

Neferuptah B (GS; KDB)

Daughter of Amenemhat III; towards the end of her life she obtained the use of a cartouche, and it is possible that she may have been regarded as a potential female king before her premature death. She was originally provided with a burial place alongside her father in his burial chamber at Hawara, but seems to have been translated to her own pyramid at Hawara-South; this was found to be intact in 1956, the contents now in Cairo. Besides her funerary equipment, she is also known from a relief in the temple at Medinet Maadi, a statue from Elephantine, a sphinx of her father, and a reference in a Kahun papyrus.

Nensed[...] (KD)

Probable daughter of Senwosret I; a fragment of a dish bearing her name was found near his pyramid.

Nubhotepet (KD)

Possibly a daughter of Amenemhat III; a fragment of her canopic jar was found in his complex at Dahshur.

Sebat (KD)

Daughter of Senwosret I; mentioned in

(above) The scanty remains of the pyramid of Neferuptah B at Hawara-South. In the foreground is the burial chamber, now flooded and filled with reeds.

(right) The huge quartzite sarcophagus of Neferuptah B (CM).

Amenemhat II's shrine of Senwosret I at Serabit el-Khadim.

Senetsenbetes (KD)

Daughter of Senwosret III; buried in the lower galleries in his pyramid complex at Dahshur.

Senwosret A (GF)

Probable father of Amenemhat I; named alongside Mentuhotep II and III on a block from a chapel at Karnak of the time of Amenhotep I.

Senwosretsonbe (KSon)

Son of Senwosret II; included in a papyrus from Kahun, now in Berlin, listing offerings to the family of the king.

Sit[...]A (KD)

Daughter of Senwosret III; buried in the lower galleries of his complex at Dahshur.

Sithathor A (KD)

Probably a daughter of Senwosret III; buried in the lower galleries in his pyramid complex at Dahshur. Her jewellery is in the Cairo Museum, including a pectoral of Senwosret II.

Sithathor B (KD)

Possible daughter of Amenemhat III; buried in a cutting in the entrance staircase of the king's pyramid at Dahshur.

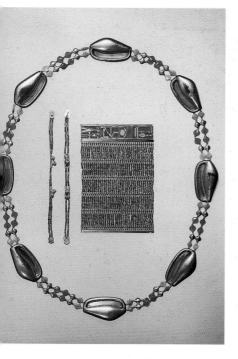

(above) Girdle, bracelet and armlet of Sithathoriunet, from her tomb at Lahun (MMA 16.1.5,8).

(right) Wig ornament and crown of Princess Sithathoriunet (MMA 31.10.8 and replica of CM CG52641).

Sithathoriunet (KD; KW)
Daughter of Senwosret II and probably wife of Senwosret III; buried at Lahun, where her jewellery (now in Cairo and New York) was found in 1914.

Sithathormeryet
Probably a member of the family of Amenemhat II; buried in a double-tomb with Itaweret in the king's funerary enclosure.

Sobkneferu (KD)
Daughter of Amenemhat III; **later female king**, and probably the owner as a princess of statue-base from Gezer, and perhaps a bowl from Lisht.

[...]12A (KD; UWC)
Daughter of Senwosret II and wife of Senwosret III; owner of Pyramid IV in the complex of her husband at Dahshur.

[...]12B
Wife of Amenemhat III; buried under his pyramid at Dahshur.

Unplaced ● ● ● ● ● ● ● ● ● ●

Didit (KSis)
Sister of an unknown king; mother of Neferet Q; named on the latter's stela in Munich.

Neferet Q (KSis)
Sister of an unknown king; named on her funerary stela in Munich alongside her mother, Didit.

Sithathor Q
Mother of Didit, named on the funerary stela of Neferet Q in Munich.

Kings and Commoners

13th Dynasty

The Royal Succession

(NB: the order of some kings is still a matter for debate)

13th Dynasty 1781–1650

SOBKHOTEP I	SOBKHOTEP V
SONBEF	SOBKHOTEP VI
NERIKARE	IAIB
AMENEMHAT V	AYA
QEMAU	INI I
AMENEMHAT VI	SEWADJTU
NEBNUNI	INED
IUFENI	HORI
SIHORNEDJHIRYOTEF	SOBKHOTEP VII
SWADJKARE	INI II
NEDJEMIBRE	NEFERHOTEP II
SOBKHOTEP II	(5 unknown kings)
RENISENEB	MER[...]RE
HOR	MERKHEPERRE
AMENEMHAT VII	MERKARE
WEGAF	?
KHENDJER	MENTUHOTEP V
IMYROMESHA	[...]MESRE?
INYOTEF IV	IBI II
SET(Y)	HOR[...]
SOBKHOTEP III	SE[...]KARE
NEFERHOTEP I	SANKHPTAHI
SIHATHOR	SEKHAENRE
SOBKHOTEP IV	SENEBMIU

Historical Background

The transition between the 12th and 13th Dynasties seems to have been peaceful enough, but the contrast between the two is striking: in place of well-documented reigns of substantial lengths, we have a huge number of kings with brief tenures of the throne, and of such obscurity that the exact order of many of them is unknown. The unfinished remains of a handful of the tombs of the 13th Dynasty kings lie at South Saqqara and Dahshur; while the pyramid remained the ideal tomb, certain kings had to resort to simple shaft-burials, either through poverty or lack of time.

The 13th Dynasty being replete with short-lived kings, it had long been felt that the real power was usually in the hands of a series of closely related Viziers, the actual pharaohs being little more than figureheads. More recent work has cast doubt on this interpretation, and it is unclear how far, if at all, matters diverged from normal Egyptian governmental practice.

Double scene of Sobkhotep III offering to the local goddesses Anukis and Satis; from the island of Sehel, near Aswan (Brooklyn 77.194).

A curious stone shrine from Karnak, containing two figures, both apparently representing Neferhotep I (CM CG42022 =JE37497).

Although much is obscure about the dynasty, one thing that *is* clear is that it did not comprise a single family line, there being a number of monarchs who were undoubtedly born commoners. Some suffered the erasure of their names from certain monuments, while others had apparently been denied burial in their own pyramids. The evidence is certainly suggestive of an irregular succession in a number of such cases.

In contrast to many of these kings, some are fairly well attested; for example, Sobkhotep III is known particularly by his work at Medamud, while a number of places preserve traces of Neferhotep I's activities, from Byblos in the Lebanon to Buhen in Nubia. These foreign attestations suggest that Egyptian influence was still in place in some of its old spheres, while the national capital remained at Itj-tawy for much of the dynasty.

The last 50 years of the 13th Dynasty seem, however, to represent a gradual decline. Although featuring some of the dynasty's longest reigns, a withdrawal from Levantine and Nubian commitments was accompanied by the establishment of a whole new state in Upper Nubia and the consolidation of the control of the north-east Delta under a line of Palestinian rulers, based on the site of Tell el-Daba. Ultimately, however, these rulers were in turn displaced by a new group of Asiatics, who would pursue a far more aggressive policy that would soon engulf the whole of northern Egypt. This group is known to history as the 'Hyksos'.

The Royal Family

The 13th Dynasty presents many problems, not just from the point of view of genealogical reconstruction, but also from that of the very royal succession. The key source is the Turin Canon – a Ramesside compilation of royal names, successions and reign lengths – although analysis is hampered by the badly damaged state of the surviving papyrus copy. Although our knowledge can be augmented by contemporary monuments, there remain many gaps and uncertainties in the various reconstructions that have been put forward, with no real consensus on some of the more opaque parts of the dynasty.

A feature of the nomina of a number of the kings of the 13th Dynasty is their length and formulation, a good example being 'Ameny-Inyotef-Amenemhat'. It is now becoming recognized that such 'names' actually contain the name of the king himself, together with that of his father and, in cases such as this, his grandfather as well. We should thus read here: 'Amenemhat (VI), (son of) Inyotef, ([grand]son of) Ameny (= Amenemhat V)'; this kind of arrangement is known as a 'filiative nomen', and is thus of very considerable help in reconstructing the notoriously opaque genealogy of the dynasty.[83] On the other hand, a further suggestion that any king without such a form of nomen should be judged to be without royal ancestry and thus a 'usurper' is certainly stretching the material too far.[84]

Using the criteria of their nomina, the first two kings of the dynasty, **Sobkhotep I** and **Sonbef** ('Amenemhat-Sobkhotep' and 'Amenemhat-Sonbef' respectively), are probably to be recognized as the sons of Amenemhat IV, penultimate ruler of the 12th Dynasty. In support of the suggestion (cf. above, p.95) that Amenemhat IV was of non-royal birth, there is the fact that the previously untitled mother of the Overseer of the Fields Ankhu A suddenly became a King's Sister late in the 12th Dynasty, suggesting that her royal brother had not previously been a King's Son.

Nothing is known of the relationships – nor the nomen – of **Nerikare**, and similarly the nomina of **Nebnuni** and **Iufeni** give no clues as to their relationships. However, the cartouche 'Ameny-Qemau' suggests that **Qemau** was a son of **Amenemhat V**, while the addition of 'Qemau' to the nomen of **Sihornedjhiryotef** indicates that the latter was an offspring of Qemau – who seems to have ruled four reigns before him. In between them seems to have fallen the reign of **Amenemhat VI**, proclaimed by his aforementioned cartouche, 'Ameny-Inyotef-Amenemhat', to have probably been the grandson of Amenemhat V by an apparently non-reigning Inyotef.

The next king on whom we have genealogical information is **Sobkhotep II**, whose father is named in his entry in the Turin Canon as a commoner named Nen?[...]. His successor **Reniseneb**, however, seems on the basis of his nomen cartouche to have been a son of Amenemhat VI. Since Reniseneb may have been a co-regent of his successor, **Hor**,[85] the two kings may have been father and son; a probable daughter of Hor, Nubhoteptikhered, was buried next to the king's tomb at Dahshur. Her name (right) King Hor: his wooden ka statue from his tomb at Dahshur (CM CG259). This tomb was found almost intact, and gives us the earliest hint of what once lay within a pharaoh's tomb. Adjacent to the king's tomb was that of Princess Nubhoteptikhered, completely intact. It is likely that Nubhoteptikhered was Hor's daughter.

(below) The capstone of the pyramid of King Khendjer; from South Saqqara (CM JE53045).

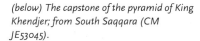

makes it not improbable that her mother was the Nubhotepti (A) who is known from seal impressions, and whose King's Mother title indicates that an offspring also became a king, possibly after some time.

Hor's direct successor was certainly not his son; rather, the nomen of **Amenemhat VII** shows his ancestors to have been a certain Seb and Kay. The former is not known as a king, while the equation of the latter with an unplaced ruler of that name is questionable.

The paternity of **Wegaf** and **Khendjer** remains unknown, although the former may have been a military commander before coming to the throne, on the basis of a scarab. A fragment of canopic jar from the pyramid complex of Khendjer names a King's Wife, Seneb[henas] A, who was thus likely to have been his wife. Probably the wife of either **Imyromesha** or **Inyotef IV** was a Queen Iy who, together with many of her relations, is mentioned in court accounts, probably dating to the period following the reign of Khendjer – on the basis of some of the personnel mentioned – but not as late as Sobkhotep III, whose family does not resemble that described in the accounts. The other intervening king, **Set(y)**, is probably to be ruled out as his monuments suffered attack under Sobkhotep III, while Iy's memorials remained intact.

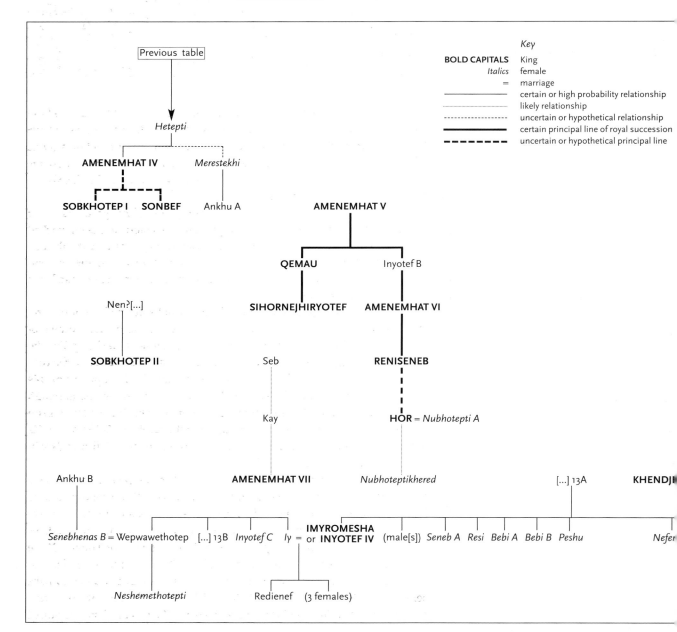

King Sobkhotep III, his parents and siblings. Behind him on the right are his father, Mentuhotep A, and brothers Seneb B and Khakau. On the left, the king is supported by a man whose identity is not recorded, his mother Iuhetibu A and his sister Reniseneb A. From now-lost parts of an altar at Sehel.

13th Dynasty part 1

b[henas A]

emheb A   Neferetiu   Khemmet   Sithathor C

After a further series of kings of unknown antecedents, we come to a king whose family is remarkably well known. **Sobkhotep III**, who seems to have been a senior official prior to his accession, has his family set out on a series of scarabs, along with an altar, a rock-inscription and a stela. Interestingly, his brothers are given the title of King's Son, although it is clear that his father, Mentuhotep A, was a commoner.

The family of Sobkhotep III did not retain power, although the fact that Iuhetibu B used a cartouche might suggest that she could have been marked out as a potential female pharaoh. Instead, **Neferhotep I** came to the throne, his commoner parents known from various sources, including the notation of his father in the Turin Canon. His paternal grandparents are recorded on a stela of their son, Haankhef A.

Texts of Neferhotep from Philae and Sehel also list his wife, children and siblings, the last called King's Sons in the same manner as the brothers of Sobkhotep III. The fact that only the Sehel text names Neferhotep I's wife and children suggests that he may have married after his accession; the consequent youth of his children may be the reason for his appointing his brothers, **Sihathor** and **Sobkhotep** C (**IV**) successively as co-regents, although there may be doubts as to whether Sihathor actually held kingly titles.[86] A son of Sihathor may be named on a scarab, while the family of Sobkhotep IV is given on a stela in the Wadi Hammamat, with others known from a box in Cairo, including a son and his wife.

Sobkhotep V seems to have been unrelated to his predecessor, a seal-impression stating him to have been the son of a God's Father whose name is lost. The name of his mother – Nubhotepti B – is, however, known from two complete scarabs. His spouse is unknown, but might be the queen Nubkhaes A, whose extensive relationships are known from a stela in the Louvre. While listing almost all of her family, it crucially omits the name of the king to whom she was married! However, her uncle, Nebankh, is known to have served under Neferhotep I and Sobkhotep IV, while a relation in the next generation was a descendant of Neferhotep I's wife. The latter link is mentioned

King Sobkhotep V wearing jubilee dress; from Karnak (CM JE37421=CG42027).

in a text in the tomb of Reniseneb B. Thus, if not **Sobkhotep V**, Nubkhaes is almost certain to have been the queen of **Sobkhotep VI** or **Iaib**.

There are no certain links between the Sobkhoteps and the next kings for whom we have evidence for their affiliations – **Aya** and his successor, **Ini I**. On the other hand, the name of Aya was common in the family of the governors of El-Kab, who had been related by marriage to Queen Nubkhaes A, suggesting that he may have been part of that family. The same family also provides key data in the form of the so-called 'Juridical Stela', from Karnak. This indicates that in year 1 of Ini's reign, the Vizier Aya B (previously

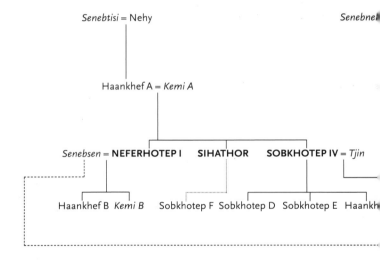

13th Dynasty part 2

Senebtisi = Nehy   Senebne[

Haankhef A = Kemi A

Senebsen = **NEFERHOTEP I**   SIHATHOR   **SOBKHOTEP IV** = Tjin

Haankhef B *Kemi B*   Sobkhotep F Sobkhotep D Sobkhotep E   Haankh[

Key

BOLD CAPITALS	King
Italics	female
=	marriage
————	certain or high probability relationship
··············	likely relationship
- - - - - - -	uncertain or hypothetical relationship
▬▬▬▬	certain principal line of royal succession
▬ ▬ ▬ ▬	uncertain or hypothetical principal line

governor of El-Kab and perhaps a son of Aya A, son-in-law of Nubkhaes) had already been married for some years to a King's Daughter Reditenes, who must have been the offspring of a predecessor – most likely King Aya, whose reign had lasted for two decades. Since Aya B was an appointee of the new king, it would seem likely that Ini was a son of his predecessor, rather than a usurper. The descendants of Aya B are also given in the stela. King Aya's wife may have been a lady called Inni, who is the possessor of more scarabs than any other queen of the dynasty; this would fit in with the length of her putative husband's reign.

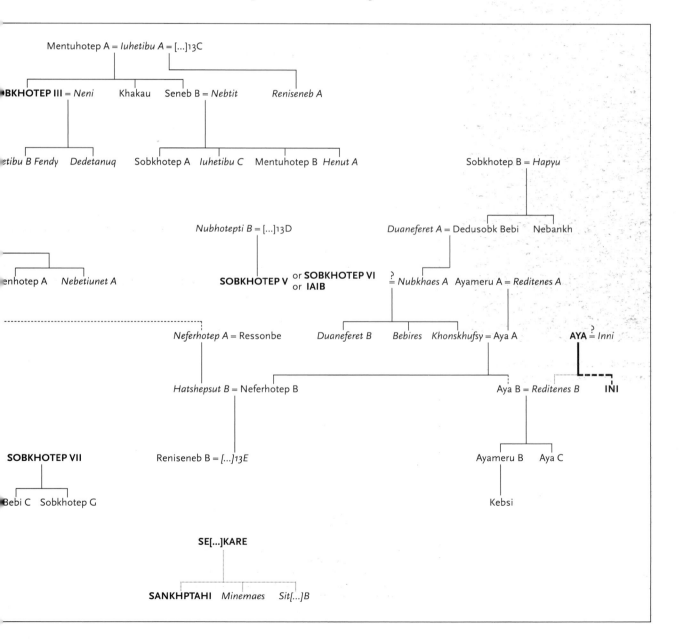

A further gap in our knowledge of the royal families stretches until the time of **Sobkhotep VII**, two of whose sons are named on one of his statues, after which the only surviving data seems to relate to one of the very last kings of the dynasty, **Sankhptahi**. This is in the form of a stela which records a prince, apparently of that name, two of his sisters and other individuals, most of whose names and titles are lost. If the prince and the king were one and the same, this set of siblings may have been the offspring of Sankhptahi's probable predecessor, **Se[...]kare**.

Brief Lives ●

*Males in **bold**, females in **bold italic**.*

Amenhotep A (KSon)
Son of Sobkhotep IV and Tjin; named on a box in Cairo.

Ankhu A (Overseer of the Fields)
Son of Merestekhi, and so possibly nephew of Amenemhat IV; known from a number of sources, in particular a block in Boston.

Ankhu B (Viz)
Father of the wife of the brother of Iy; in office under Khendjer and known from a series of statues and Papyrus Bulaq 18.

Aya A (Governor of El-Kab)
Son-in-law of Nubkhaes A; mentioned in a genealogy in the tomb of Reniseneb B.

Aya B (Viz; Governor of El-Kab)
Husband of Reditenes B; known from the Juridical Stela from Karnak (Cairo).

Aya C (Governor of El-Kab)
Son of Aya B and Reditenes B; known from the Juridical Stela from Karnak (Cairo).

Ayameru A
Father of Aya A; mentioned in a genealogy in the tomb of Reniseneb B.

Ayameru B (Viz; Governor of El-Kab)
Son of Aya B and Reditenes B; known from the Juridical Stela from Karnak (Cairo).

Bebi A (KSis)
Sister-in-law of Iy; named in palace accounts in Cairo (Papyrus Bulaq 18).

Bebi B (KSis)
Sister-in-law of Iy; named in a set of palace accounts in Cairo (Papyrus Bulaq 18).

Bebi C (EKSon)
Son of Sobkhotep VII; depicted on a statue of his father from Karnak, now in Cairo, and the owner of two stelae set up at Abydos by his steward, Ptaha (Cairo and Bologna).

Bebires
Daughter of Nubkhaes A; mentioned in her stela in the Louvre.

Dedetanuq (KD)
Daughter of Sobkhotep III; shown with her sister on a stela from Koptos (Louvre) and with other members of her family on a stela in Wadi el-Hol.

Dedusobk Bebi (Chief Scribe of the Vizier)
Father of Nubkhaes A; mentioned in her stela in the Louvre.

Duaneferet A
Mother of Nubkhaes A; mentioned in her stela in the Louvre.

Duaneferet B
Daughter of Nubkhaes A; mentioned in her stela in the Louvre.

Haankhef A (GF)
Father of Neferhotep I, Sihathor and Sobkhotep IV; owner of a stela (probably from Heliopolis) in Rio de Janeiro, and named on a number of scarabs of his elder sons, together with inscriptions of Neferhotep I.

Haankhef B (KSon)
Son of Neferhotep I; named in his father's Sehel inscription.

Haankhef C Ikherneferet (KSon)
Son of Sobkhotep IV; named on a stela of his father in the Wadi Hammamat.

Hapyu
Grandmother of Nubkhaes A; mentioned in her stela in the Louvre.

Hatshepsut B
Wife of Neferhotep B and descendant of Senebsen; mentioned in a genealogy in the tomb of Reniseneb B.

Henut A
Niece of Sobkhotep III; named on the Vienna stela of her father, Seneb B.

Hetepti (KM; M2L; UWC)
See previous section.

Horemheb A (KSis)
Sister-in-law of Iy; named in palace accounts in Cairo (Papyrus Bulaq 18).

Inni (KGW; UWC)
Possible wife of Aya; known from at least 21 scarabs and one seal-impression, the latter from Kerma in Nubia.

Inyotef B
Probable son of Amenemhat V and father of Amenemhat VI; known only from the filiative nomen of his son.

Inyotef C (RO)
Sister of Iy; known from a stela of her probable brother in Würzburg.

Two daughters of Sobkhotep III, Iuhetibu B and Dedetanuq, stand before Min on a stela from Koptos (Louvre C8).

Iuhetibu A (KM)
Mother of Sobkhotep III, shown with him on an altar from Sehel and a stela in the Wadi el-Hol.

Iuhetibu B Fendy (KD)
Daughter of Sobkhotep III; shown with her sister on a stela from Koptos (Louvre) and with other members of her family on a stela in Wadi el-Hol.

Iuhetibu C
Niece of Sobkhotep III; named on the Vienna stela of her father, Seneb B.

Iy (KW)
Probably wife of either Imyromesha or Inyotef IV; mentioned in palace accounts in Cairo (Papyrus Bulaq 18) and on a stela in Würzburg.

Kay
Father of Amenemhat VII, on the basis of the latter's filiative nomen.

Kebsi (Governor of El-Kab)
Son of Ayameru B; known from the Juridical Stela from Karnak (Cairo), in which he sold the Governorate to one Sobknakhte (B) in the time of Nebiriau I.

Kemi A
Mother of Neferhotep I, Sihathor and Sobkhotep IV; named on a number of scarabs of her sons, inscriptions of Neferhotep I from around the area of the First Cataract of the Nile, near Aswan, and on two statues of Sihathor.

Kemi B (KD)
Daughter of Neferhotep I; named in her father's Sehel inscription and two scarabs.

Khakau (KSon)
Brother of Sobkhotep III; shown with the king and other members of his family on a stela in the Wadi el-Hol and on an altar from Sehel.

Khemmet (KSis)
Sister-in-law of Iy; named in palace accounts in Cairo (Papyrus Bulaq 18).

Khonskhufsy (KD)
Daughter of Nubkhaes A and wife of Aya A; mentioned in a genealogy in the tomb of Reniseneb B and on her mother's stela in the Louvre.

Mentuhotep A (GF)
Father of Sobkhotep III; named on scarabs of his son, as well as being depicted with his sons, his wife and step-daughter on an altar from Sehel and a stela at Wadi el-Hol.

Mentuhotep B (Attendant of Dog-Keepers)
Nephew of Sobkhotep III; named on the Vienna stela of his father, Seneb B.

Merestekhi (KSis)
Mother of Ankhu A and possibly sister of Amenemhat IV; known from the monuments of her son.

Minemaes (KD)
Possibly the daughter of Se[...]kare, depicted on a stela now in Cairo alongside her brother, Sankhptahi.

Nebankh (High Steward)
Uncle of Nubkhaes A; mentioned in her stela in the Louvre, and also in the family lists of Neferhotep I at Philae and Sehel.

Nebetiunet A (KD)
Daughter of Sobkhotep IV and Tjin; named on a now-lost vase and a scarab in Basel.

Nebtit
Sister-in-law of Sobkhotep III; named on the Vienna stela of her husband, Seneb B.

Neferetiu (KSis)
Sister-in-law of Iy; named in palace accounts in Cairo (Papyrus Bulaq 18).

Neferhotep A
Descendant of Senebsen; mentioned in a genealogy in the tomb of Reniseneb B.

Neferhotep B
Grandson of Nubkhaes A; mentioned in a genealogy in the tomb of Reniseneb B.

Neferu A (KSis)
Sister-in-law of Iy; named in palace accounts in Cairo (Papyrus Bulaq 18).

Nehy (Townsman)
Grandfather of Neferhotep I, Sihathor and Sobkhotep IV; named on the Rio de Janeiro stela of Haankhef A.

Nen?[...]
Father of Sobkhotep II, named in the Turin Canon.

Neni (KW)
Wife of Sobkhotep III; named as the mother of Iuhetibu B and Dedetanuq on a stela in the Louvre, and also probably shown on stela in the Wadi el-Hol.

Neshemethotepti
Niece of Iy; known from a stela of her father in Würzburg.

Nubhotepti A (KGW; UWC; KM)
Probable wife of Hor; known from two distinct groups of scarabs, one of which gives her the title of King's Mother.

Nubhotepti B (KM)
Mother of Sobkhotep V; named on two scarabs in London and New York.

Nubhoteptikhered (KD)
Probable daughter of Hor; buried in a shaft-tomb alongside that of Hor on the north side of the pyramid of Amenemhat III at Dahshur. Her tomb was found intact in 1894, its contents now being in the Cairo Museum.

Nubkhaes A (KGW; UWC)
Probable wife of either Sobkhotep V, Sobkhotep VI or Iaib; owner of a stela in the Louvre and mentioned in the tomb of Reniseneb B at El-Kab.

Peshu (KSis)
Sister-in-law of Iy; named in palace accounts in Cairo (Papyrus Bulaq 18).

The Black Pyramid at Dahshur, built for Amenemhat III, but used only for the burial of members of the royal family; shafts on the north side held the burials of King Hor and his probable daughter, Nubhoteptikhered. In the background is the Bent Pyramid.

Redienef (KSon)
Son of Iy; named in palace accounts in Cairo (Papyrus Bulaq 18).

Reditenes A
Wife of Ayameru A; mentioned in a genealogy in the tomb of Reniseneb B.

Reditenes B (KD)
Probable daughter of King Aya and wife of Aya B; known from the Juridical Stela from Karnak (Cairo).

Reniseneb A
Half-sister of Sobkhotep III, shown with him on an altar from Sehel.

Reniseneb B
Husband of a descendant of Senebsen; owner of tomb 9 at El-Kab.

Resi (KSis)
Sister-in-law of Iy; named in palace accounts in Cairo (Papyrus Bulaq 18).

Ressonbe
Husband of Neferhotep A; mentioned in a genealogy in the tomb of Reniseneb B.

Sankhptahi (KSon)
Possibly the son of Se[...]kare, depicted on a stela now in Cairo; probably **later king**.

Seb
Grandfather of Amenemhat VII, on the basis of the latter's filiative nomen.

Seneb A (KSis)
Sister-in-law of Iy; named in palace accounts in Cairo (Papyrus Bulaq 18).

Seneb B (KSon)
Brother of Sobkhotep III; shown with his brother and other members of his family on a stela in the Wadi el-Hol and on an altar from Sehel, while a stela of his own is in Vienna.

Seneb[henas A] (KW)
Probable wife of Khendjer; known from a canopic jar fragment from the king's pyramid complex and a number of scarabs.

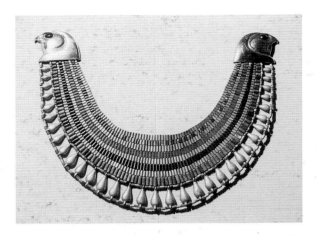

The rich burial of a lady named Senebtisi may be that of the grandmother of Neferhotep I. It includes a fine falcon collar (above) and gold hair ornaments (right); from Lisht (MMA 08.200.30, 07.227.6–7).

Senebhenas B
Sister-in-law of Iy; known from the monuments of her husband.

Senebhenas C (KW; UWC)
Wife of Sobkhotep III; shown with him on an altar from Sehel and a stela in the Wadi el-Hol.

Senebsen (KW)
Wife of Neferhotep I. Recorded in the Sehel inscription of the king. Mentioned in the tomb of Reniseneb B.

Senebtisi
Grandmother of Neferhotep I, Sihathor and Sobkhotep IV; named on the Rio de Janeiro stela of Haankhef A; conceivably the lady of this name who was buried at Lisht, and has her funerary equipment in the Metropolitan Museum of Art.

Sihathor (KSon)
Brother of Neferhotep I and Sobkhotep IV; known from the Philae and Sehel texts of his elder brother and the Wadi Hammamat stela of Sobkhotep IV, as well as two statues of his own from Elephantine and another, dedicated by Sobkhotep IV, in the Qurna temple of Sety I. It is possible he was briefly co-regent with his elder brother, but the last

monument only refers to him as a prince.

Sit[...]B (KD)
Possibly the daughter of Se[...]kare, depicted on a stela now in Cairo alongside her brother, Sankhptahi.

Sithathor C (KSis)
Sister-in-law of Iy; named in palace accounts in Cairo (Papyrus Bulaq 18).

Sobkhotep A (Elder of the Portal)
Nephew of Sobkhotep III; named on the Vienna stela of his father, Seneb B.

Sobkhotep B (High Steward)
Grandfather of Nubkhaes A; mentioned in her stela in the Louvre.

Sobkhotep C (KSon)
Brother of Neferhotep I; known from the Philae and Sehel texts of that king, and perhaps a few scarabs. Later co-regent and king as **SOBKHOTEP IV**.

Sobkhotep D Miu (KSon)
Son of Sobkhotep IV; named on a stela of his father in the Wadi Hammamat, and probably on another from Wadi el-Hudi (Aswan Museum).

Sobkhotep E Djadja (KSon)
Son of Sobkhotep IV; named on a stela of

his father in the Wadi Hammamat.

Sobkhotep F (KSon)
Probable son of Sihathor; named as the offspring of a prince of that name on a scarab.

Sobkhotep G (KSon)
Son of Sobkhotep VII; depicted on a statue of his father from Karnak, now in Cairo.

Tjin (KW)
Wife of Sobkhotep IV; named on a box in Cairo, on a vase of her daughter and on a bead in the British Museum.

Wepwawethotep (Royal Representative)
Brother of Iy; known from a stela of his probable brother in Würzburg.

[...]13A
Non-royal father of either Imyromesha or Inyotef IV, on the basis of the data from the court accounts of his son's reign.

[...]13B
Brother of Iy; known from his stela in Würzburg.

[...]13C
Second husband of Iuhetibu A and step-father of Sobkhotep III; shown with the latter on an altar from Sehel.

[...]13D (GF)
Father of Sobkhotep V; known from a broken seal-impression from Tukh.

[...]13E
Wife of Reniseneb B and the descendant of Senebsen, as well as Aya A.

Unplaced ● ● ● ● ● ● ● ● ● ● ● ●

Ahhotepti (KW; KM)
Wife and mother of unknown kings; known from a scarab, once in a Cairo private collection, the design of which suggests that she lived prior to the reign of Sobkhotep III.

Anuqneferetweben (KD)
Daughter of an unknown king; known from three seals, roughly datable to the time of Sobkhotep IV or Sobkhotep V.

Dedetamun (KD)
Daughter of a king whose prenomen included the syllable 'hotep' (perhaps Sobkhotep V, Sobkhotep VI or Ini I); wife of the God's Seal-Bearer, Nebsenet, son of one Bembu. Known from a stela from Abydos (Vatican).

Dedetsobk (KSis)
Sister of an unknown king, daughter of Iuhetibu Q and Dedusobk A; known from a stela from Abydos (Cairo).

Dedusobk A (GF)
Father of an unknown king, husband of Iuhetibu Q and son of a certain Bebiankh (Q); known from a stela from Abydos (Cairo).

Haankhef Q (KSon)
Son of an unknown king; known from a stela from Abydos (Cairo) that also names Neferhotep Q, Horhotep Q and [...]djeb.

Hatshepsut C (KD)
Daughter of Neferet R and an unknown king; known from a stela of her husband, Nedjesankh-Iu.

Horhotep Q (KSon)
Son of an unknown king; known from a stela from Abydos (Cairo) that also names

Haankhef Q, Neferhotep Q and [...]djeb.

Iuhetibu Q (KM)
Mother of an unknown king, wife of Dedusobk A and daughter of a certain Senwosret (Q); known from a stela from Abydos (Cairo).

Neferet R (KW)
Wife of an unknown king; known from a stela of a man named Nedjesankh-Iu, one of whose wives (Hatshepsut C) was Neferet's daughter.

Neferhotep Q (KD)
Daughter of an unknown king; known from a stela from Abydos (Cairo) that also names Haankhef Q, Horhotep Q and [...]djeb.

Neferu Q (KD)
Daughter of an unknown king and wife of the Chief of Police of the temple of Anubis, Sobkhotep, the son of Dediresu and Ptahqeni. Known from a stela from Abydos (Cairo).

Reniseneb Q (KD)
Daughter of an unknown king; known from a seal, roughly datable to the time of Sobkhotep IV or Sobkhotep V.

Reniseneb R (KD)
Daughter of an unknown king, and perhaps sister of Sobkhotep Q; known from a seal, roughly datable to the latter part of the 13th Dynasty.

Senetmut (KSis)
Sister of an unknown king, daughter of Iuhetibu Q and Dedusobk A; known from a stela from Abydos (Cairo).

Sobkhotep Q (KSon)
Son of an unknown king, and perhaps brother of Reniseneb R; known from a seal, roughly datable to the latter part of the 13th Dynasty.

[...]djeb (KD)
Daughter of an unknown king; known from a stela from Abydos (Cairo) that also names Haankhef Q, Horhotep Q and Neferhotep Q.

Iuhetibu Q and Dedusobk A, parents of a king whose identity is not revealed on their stela, from the temple of Osiris at Abydos (CM).

Rulers of Foreign Countries

14th and 15th Dynasties

The Royal Succession

Until the second half of the 15th Dynasty, there is no general agreement on the succession of the Hyksos kings; the following represents a recent assessment of the 15th Dynasty only:[87]

15th Dynasty 1650–1535

SEMQEN

APER-ANATI

SAKIRHAR

KHYAN

APEPI

KHAMUDY

Key sources for the latter part of Hyksos history are the texts of the 17th Dynasty king Kamose. Carved on a pair of stelae at Karnak, an extract is also preserved on a writing-board, perhaps used by a student for copying practice; from tomb HC9 on the Asasif (CM JE41790).

Historical Background

While the archaeological evidence from Tell el-Daba (Avaris) shows Palestinian and Syrian groups settling in the north-east Delta from 12th Dynasty times,[88] nothing is known as to the political development of the area. Recently, it has been proposed that it became an independent polity early in the 13th Dynasty, being the historical basis for Manetho's 14th Dynasty.[89]

It is possible that the 14th Dynasty's rulers also controlled parts of southern Palestine and beyond. However, after over a century in power, the rulers of Avaris had to cope with famine and plague, trouble that seems to have culminated in their overthrow by a new Palestinian group – the Hyksos (meaning in Egyptian 'Rulers of Foreign Countries', 15th Dynasty).

At Avaris, the arrival of these incomers is shown by changes in the pottery forms and other aspects of material culture, together with an expansion of the city. The Hyksos were expansionist, and appear to have taken over Lower Egypt fairly swiftly, driving the rump of the 13th Dynasty regime into the south, where it may have become the 16th Dynasty. Halfway though their period of rule, the Hyksos leader Khyan appears to have managed to conquer Thebes and beyond, at least as far as Gebelein – control over the latter being maintained into the reign of his successor, Apepi. This expansion seems to have been accompanied by a looting of standing monuments, with various items of sculpture (including the cap stones of two pyramids) finding their way back to the Hyksos heartland.

Control over the south was short-lived, the new Theban 17th Dynasty soon ruling at least as far north as Abydos. Some form of accommodation would then appear to have been reached between the two regimes, as it appears from one of the stelae of Kamose that the Thebans were able to pasture their cattle in Hyksos territory. However, under Taa II hostilities had begun between the two regimes, culminating in the final expulsion of the Hyksos from Egypt during the reign of the 18th Dynasty king Ahmose I.

14th and 15th Dynasties

```
        KHYAN                    [...]15A
          |                         |
          |              _____|_____
          |             |          |          |
       Yanassi ——    APEPI        Tani      Ziwat
                       |
                 _____|......
                |           :
              Harit      Apepi B
```

Key

BOLD CAPITALS	King
Italics	female
··················	certain or high probability relationship
————————	likely relationship

The Royal Family

A number of the seals dated to the 14th Dynasty include the names of members of the royal family, but with very little definite evidence of their relationships, other than the typology of the seals. As nothing certain is known of them other than their names, they will not be listed here.[90]

The 15th Dynasty is also very little known, with information confined to the families of **Khyan** and **Apepi**. The relationship between Khyan and his eldest son, Yanassi, is indicated by their names and titles appearing together on a stela from Avaris. Two sisters of Apepi appear to be named alongside the king on a number of pieces; the fact that neither are also King's Daughters suggests that their father was not a king. A lady who did bear this title is named with Apepi on a vase, and was presumably his offspring. Another child may be Apepi B, whose seal is to be dated to the very end of the 15th Dynasty.

Brief Lives ●

*Males in **bold**, females in **bold italic**.*

Apepi B (KSon)
Probably a son of Apepi; owner of a seal in Berlin.

Harit (KD)
Daughter of Apepi; named on a vase found in the tomb of Ahmes-Nefertiry at Dira Abu'l-Naga (New York).

Tani (KSis)
Sister of Apepi; named on door jambs from a shrine at Avaris, now in Vienna and Cairo and on an offering stand from Medamud (Berlin).

Yanassi (EKS)
Son of Khyan; named with his father on the lower part of a broken stela from Avaris.

Ziwat (KSis)
Sister of Apepi; named on a vessel found in Spain (Almuñécar Town Hall).

[...]15A
The non-royal father of Apepi, inferred from the titles of Apepi's sisters.

● ●

The Southern Kingdom

16th Dynasty;
17th Dynasty part 1

Historical Background [91]

Following the Hyksos takeover of Lower Egypt, the heirs of the 13th Dynasty appear to have decamped to Thebes, forming the 16th Dynasty.[92] Very little is known of this period, except for the names of the kings (whose order of succession is less than certain), although it appears that business continued much as usual in Upper Egypt. However, there was certainly conflict with the Hyksos and suggestions of famine, which may have contributed to the Hyksos occupation of Thebes and the territory southwards, at least as far as Gebelein.

It is unclear how the Thebans regained control over their capital and the area northwards to Abydos, but having done so they appear to have reached some agreement with the Hyksos, since peace seems to have lasted for some decades until the final confrontation during the last part of the 17th Dynasty.

The Royal Family

The earliest known king of the dynasty was **Djehuty**; his wife, Mentuhotep C, is attested by the canopic chest which he presented to her. Her sarcophagus has texts that name her parents – her father, Senebhenaef A, being a well-known figure from his stela from Deir el-Bahari, dedicated by his half-brother, Senebhenaef B. Their father was a contemporary of King Iaib, forming a handy chronological link between the 13th and 16th Dynasties. It is not known how **Neferhotep III** was related to Djehuty, if at all.

A Karnak stela of **Mentuhotepi** names a King's Son, Mentuser, but it is not clear whether he was a true son of the king; furthermore, if he was, it is uncertain whether he is connected with a king of that name whose

(right) King Djehuty, as depicted on a column at the temple of Edfu.

(far right) King Mentuhotepi: a sphinx from Edfu (CM JE48874).

16th Dynasty

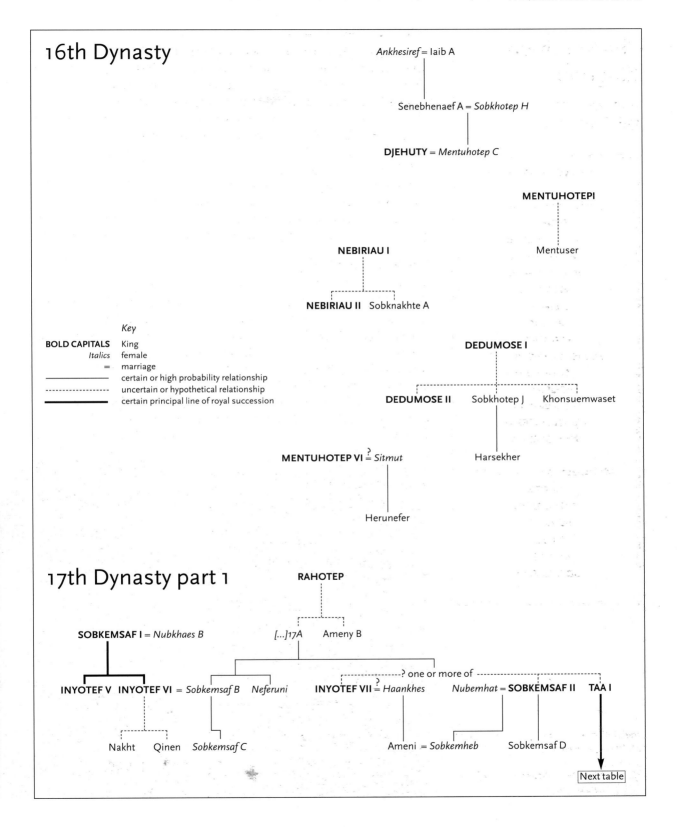

Ankhesiref = Iaib A

Senebhenaef A = *Sobkhotep H*

DJEHUTY = *Mentuhotep C*

MENTUHOTEP I

Mentuser

NEBIRIAU I

NEBIRIAU II Sobknakhte A

Key

BOLD CAPITALS	King
Italics	female
=	marriage
————	certain or high probability relationship
------------	uncertain or hypothetical relationship
▬▬▬▬	certain principal line of royal succession

DEDUMOSE I

DEDUMOSE II Sobkhotep J Khonsuemwaset

Harsekher

MENTUHOTEP VI ⸮= *Sitmut*

Herunefer

17th Dynasty part 1

RAHOTEP

SOBKEMSAF I = *Nubkhaes B*

[...]17A Ameny B

⸮ one or more of

INYOTEF V **INYOTEF VI** = *Sobkemsaf B* *Neferuni* **INYOTEF VII** ⸮= *Haankhes* *Nubemhat* = **SOBKEMSAF II** **TAA I**

Nakht Qinen *Sobkemsaf C* Ameni = *Sobkemheb* Sobkemsaf D

Next table

117

prenomen is unknown (but conceivably Semenre). Similarly, was a man called Sobknakhte (A) of **Nebiriau I**'s reign really his son or merely a titular prince? Given the rarity of his name, it is not improbable that **Nebiriau II** was an offspring of the first king of the name.

The unusual name borne by the two kings **Dedumose** is also suggestive of a father-son relationship. Under one of them lived a man named Harsekher, who held the title of King's Son, but was actually the son of another King's Son, according to his stela. On this basis, Harsekher may have been a grand-son of the king. A stela of Dedumose I's time commemorates a further King's Son, Khonsuemwaset, who might have been his own child.

The wife and son of a King **Mentuhotep** are named on a fragment of the king's coffin, which shows close textual similarities to the coffin of Mentu-hotep C. It is uncertain which King Mentuhotep is in question here but, in view of the probable Theban provenance of the fragment, it is likely that he was the 16th Dynasty king of that name.[93]

Inyotef VI is crowned; from Koptos (Petrie UC14784).

With this possible exception, nothing is known of the families of the later kings of the dynasty, and it is not until the advent of the 17th Dynasty that some relationships of the Theban polity may be reconstructed. A stela of **Rahotep** indicates that a close female relative was probably named Sobkem-saf (A), but her exact relationship is lost. The same king presented a bow to a King's Son, Ameny, who may have been his offspring.

It is unknown whether **Sobkemsaf I** was a son of Rahotep; however a temple-inscription indicates that Sobkemsaf I was the father of a King Inyotef; on the basis of the spelling of his nomen, the latter can be identified as the sixth of the name. The same spelling is used for the brother of **Inyotef V** (whom an inscription on the latter's coffin proclaims as its donor), thus making Inyotefs V and VI the sons of Sobkemsaf I.[94] As far as their mother is concerned, papyri dealing with the robbery of Sobkemsaf's tomb indicate that his wife was one Nubkhaes (B), and thus possibly the mother of his sons.

Inyotef VI's names are found together with those of Sobkemsaf B on her jewellery, confirming that she was his spouse. A stela identifies a number of members of the queen's family; a Princess Sobkemsaf (C) named on another stela may have been her daughter, as it also shows Sobkemsaf B, who is here also given the title of King's Sister. This would imply that a brother later became a king – presumably **Inyotef VII**, **Sobkemsaf II** or **Taa I**. The name of Sobkemsaf B's mother is lost on this second stela, but she is apparently given the title of *(right) Sobkemsaf II, depicted within a gateway now in the Open Air Museum at Karnak.*

(below) Prince Sobkemsaf D, as shown on his father Sobkemsaf II's statue; from Abydos (CM CG386).

King's Daughter; she could therefore have been a daughter of Rahotep. Two bearers of the King's Son title are known under Inyotef VI from inscriptions; they may have either been actual sons or titular princes.

A real royal son was Ameni, known from a stela that also names his wife as a daughter of **Sobkemsaf II** and Queen Nubemhat. Unfortunately, while Ameni's mother is given, the name of his royal father is not. Since he is unlikely from the context also to be Sobkemsaf II, the father may have been Inyotef VII (or conceivably Taa I), who seems to have been of the same generation. Sobkemsaf D, an actual son of Sobkemsaf II is, however, known from an Abydos statue of the king.

Brief Lives ●

*Males in **bold**, females in **bold italic**.*

Ameni (KSon)
Son of Haankhes and perhaps Inyotef VII; owner of a stela from Koptos (split between the Petrie Museum, London, and the Pushkin Museum, Moscow).

Ameny B (KSon)
Possible son of Rahotep, who gave him a bow, now in Moscow.

Ankhesiref
Grandmother-in-law of Djehuty, known from the stela of her son, from Deir el-Bahari and now in New York.

Haankhes (KW)
Mother of Ameni and perhaps a wife of Inyotef VII; named on the stela of her son.

Harsekher (KSon)
Possibly a grandson of Dedumose I (or II); owner of a stela from Edfu, now in Cairo.

Herunefer (EKSon; Gen)
Son of Sitmut and possibly Mentuhotep VI; owner of a fragment of coffin in the British Museum.

Iaib A (Viz)
Grandfather-in-law of Djehuty, known from stelae at Elephantine and others now in London and New York, together with statues from Elephantine and one now in Bologna. Lived under kings Iaib and Aya.

Khonsuemwaset (KSon; Gen)
Possibly a son of Dedumose I, who donated a stela to him at Edfu (Cairo Museum).

Mentuhotep C (KGW; UWC)
Wife of Djehuty; known from a now-lost coffin from Dira Abu'l-Naga, and a canopic chest given to her by her husband (Berlin).

Mentuser (KSon)
Possible son of Mentuhotepi; named on a stela from Karnak.

Prince Nakht, possible son of Inyotef VI, as shown behind the king on a stela from Abydos (Chicago OI 64).

Nakht (KSon; Chief of Archers)
Possibly a son of Inyotef VI; named on his stela, now in Chicago.

Neferuni
Sister of Sobkemsaf B; named on a stela from Edfu, now in Cairo.

Nubemhat (KGW)
Wife of Sobkemsaf II; named on the stela of her son-in-law and probable owner of a fragment of statuette from Kawa (Brussels).

Nubkhaes B (KGW)
Wife of Sobkemsaf I; burial robbed together with that of her husband, as mentioned in papyri relating to tomb robberies in the late 20th Dynasty.

Qinen (KSon; Commander of Koptos)
Possibly a son of Inyotef VI; named on the king's Koptos Decree (Cairo Museum).

Senebhenaef A (Viz)
Father-in-law of Djehuty; known from his stela from Deir el-Bahari (New York) and the sarcophagus of his daughter.

Sitmut (KGW)
Possible wife of Mentuhotep VI; named on the coffin of her son, Herunefer.

Sobkemheb (KD)
Daughter of Sobkemsaf II and Nubemhat; named on the stela of her husband.

[Sobk]emsaf A
Mother, wife or daughter of Rahotep; shown on a stela from Koptos (Petrie Museum).

Sobkemsaf B (KW; KSis; UWC)
Wife of Inyotef VI and sister of an unknown king; named on bracelets (British Museum) and a pendant, as well as on a contemporary stela from Edfu (Cairo) and another from the same site (also in Cairo), dating from the beginning of the 18th Dynasty and commemorating the restoration of her daughter's tomb.

Sobkemsaf C (KD)
Daughter of Sobkemsaf B; the restoration of her tomb at the beginning of the 18th Dynasty is commemorated on a stela from Edfu (Cairo Museum).

Sobkemsaf D (KSon)
Son of Sobkemsaf II; shown on a statue of the king from Abydos and now in Cairo.

Sobkhotep H
Mother-in-law of Djehuty.

Sobkhotep J (KSon)
Father of Harsekher; named on his stela.

Sobknakhte A (KSon)
Possibly a son of Nebiriau I; named on the Juridical Stela from Karnak (Cairo Museum).

[…]17A (KD)
Mother of Sobkemsaf B and possibly a daughter of Rahotep; named on a stela in Cairo, found at Edfu.

Unplaced ● ● ● ● ● ● ● ● ● ●

Iuef (KSis)
Sister of an unknown king, of non-royal birth; married to Ipu A, their daughter Harmose marrying a Lector Priest, Ib.

● ●

3
The New Kingdom

The Taosids

17th Dynasty part 2;
18th Dynasty part 1

The Royal Succession

17th Dynasty part 2 1558–1549
TAA I
TAA II
KAMOSE

18th Dynasty part 1 1549–1491
AHMOSE I
AMENHOTEP I
THUTMOSE I

(previous page) The giant coffin of
Meryetamun B.

*Relief fragment from
Karnak showing
Amenhotep I
(Brooklyn 71.82).*

Historical Background

By the start of the latter part of the 17th Dynasty, Egypt had essentially been divided between the Hyksos (15th Dynasty) and the southern, native Egyptian line (16th/17th Dynasties) for over half a century. In spite of earlier hostilities, the two sides seem to have settled down into a broadly symbiotic relationship. Southern Egyptian cattle were allowed to pasture in the Delta while, presumably, the Hyksos were able to trade with Nubia via the Thebaid (the area around Thebes). The Nubians seem to have been formal Hyksos allies, and at one point actually invaded the Thebaid, as recorded in a newly discovered text at El-Kab.

The memory of the Thebes–Hyksos break was later enshrined in a folktale, and made concrete in the state of the body of the Theban king, Taa II, killed by violence – perhaps in battle with the Hyksos. His successors continued the struggle: Ahmose I ultimately reasserted Egyptian rule over Upper Nubia, expelled the Hyksos, and possibly advanced into the Levant as far as the Euphrates.

The following reign of Amenhotep I appears to have been fairly uneventful, without any further known action in Asia. However, it was clearly a time of major consolidation, and provided the basis for the major expansion of Egyptian power in the following generations.

The Royal Family

We know nothing of what, if any, family relationship linked Sobkemsaf II with the Taosids – the family that occupied the throne during the final phase of the 17th Dynasty, named for their most famous early member. It is possible that **Taa I** might have been the unnamed royal brother of Sobkemsaf B, but this remains pure speculation. Our knowledge of the first king of the Taosid line is decidedly sketchy, and the most concrete thing known about him was that his wife was one Tetisherit, the commoner daughter of Tjenna and his wife, Neferu (B).

Even this 'fact' has been arrived at indirectly, as King Ahmose I, founder of the 18th Dynasty, calls Tetisherit the 'mother of his mother' and 'mother of his father', as well as King's Great Wife, on a great stela from her cenotaph at Abydos. Working backwards two generations (counting Taa II and Kamose as one generation, as explained

(right) Ahmose I makes offerings to his grandmother, Tetisherit; stela from her cenotaph at Abydos (CM CG34002).

(below) 19th-century copy of a now badly damaged scene in TT359 (Inherkhau) at Thebes showing the 'Lords of the West', many of whom belonged to the Taosid royal family. Top row from right: Amenhotep I; Ahmose I; Ahhotep I, Meryetamun B, Sitamun A; Siamun A; unknown; Ahmes-Henuttamehu; Ahmes-Tumerisy; Ahmes-Nebetta, Ahmose-Sipairi; bottom row from right: Ahmes-Nefertiry; Ramesses I; Mentuhotep II; Amenhotep II; Taa II; Ra(?)mose; Ramesses IV; unknown; Thutmose I.

below), we come to the king who seems to have been Tetisherit's husband. On the basis of the combination of a number of later texts, he seems to have been named Senakhtenre Taa (I). Such documents include lists of deified early New Kingdom royalties (known as 'Lords of the West') in Ramesside tombs at Deir el-Medina.

To be dated sometime during the 17th Dynasty is the burial of a royal wife and her child, found at Qurna. Unfortunately, the lady's name is missing,

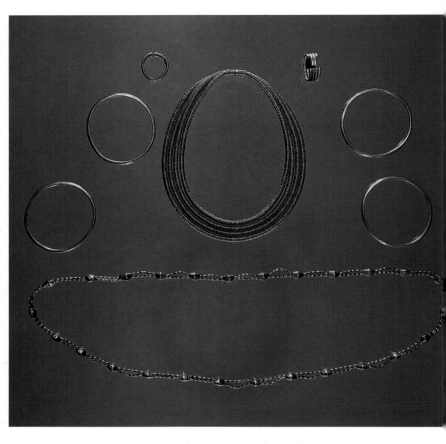

(above; above, right) A queen whose name is missing ([...]17B) was buried in the rubble at Qurna near the beginning of the road to the Valley of the Kings, together with her young child ([...]17C). The burial was found intact by Flinders Petrie in 1909, and featured a fine gilded rishi (feathered) coffin, datable to the middle of the 17th Dynasty. Material from the deposit included pottery suggesting Nubian links for the lady, borne out by the examination of her body. The superb gold jewellery found on the body may also have been derived from the Nubian gold-mines (RMS 1909.527).

and the coffin and other material in the deposit are slightly contradictory in date. While the pottery seems to suggest the end of the dynasty, the coffin points to an earlier time, prior to Sobkemsaf II. The lady's spouse thus remains obscure at present.

Luckily, we are on firmer ground with the next generation. It is centred on Seqenenre **Taa (II)**, known to have been the father of Ahmose I, and who died violently – probably during hostilities against his Hyksos contemporary, Apepi. Taa II's principal wife was his sister, Ahhotep I, although he also married at least two other sisters, Inhapy and Sitdjehuty. Two princesses born to Ahhotep are named on a statue of her prematurely deceased eldest son, Ahmose (A). Both girls bear the name Ahmes, and are almost certainly the women known later under the names Ahmes-Nefertiry and Ahmes-Nebetta. Other daughters of Taa II, of less certain maternity, are known from various sources.

Curiously, Ahmose I did not directly succeed his father, another king – **Kamose** – coming between them. Kamose was once regarded as an elder brother of Ahmose I but, in view of the probable ages-at-death of Taa II and Ahmose I, the general view now is that he was a brother of Taa II, elevated to the throne ahead of his young nephew owing to the critical situation that may have followed Taa II's sudden death. Kamose may have been married to (below) Coffin of Ahmose I; from TT320 at Thebes (CM CG61002).

(below, right) Ahmes-Nefertiry, as wife of Ahmose I, combined all the key titles of an early-18th Dynasty queen, and when dead she was deified alongside her son, Amenhotep I, as patron deity of the Theban necropolis. Here she is depicted c. 150 years after her death in the tomb of Nebamun and Ipuky (TT181), with the black skin of a deity of resurrection (Hanover, Kestner 1962.70).

another Ahhotep (II), whose very existence, however, is based on a single coffin that may in fact have belonged to Ahhotep I.

Like his father, **Ahmose I** took one sister as his Great Wife and a number of the others as lesser spouses. The Great Wife, Ahmes-Nefertiry, lived on to be the dominant figure in the kingdom into the reign of her son, Amenhotep I. Her mother, Ahhotep I, also had a long life, and it is clear that they both played a key role in the affairs of the state.

17th Dynasty part 2

Key

BOLD CAPITALS	King
Bold italics	God's Wife of Amun
Italics	female
=	marriage
————	certain or high probability relationship
··············	likely relationship
━━━━	principal line of royal succession

[Genealogical chart:]

Previous table — ? — **TAA I** = *Tetisherit*

Tjenna = *Neferu B*

TAA II = *Inhapy* = *Sitdjehuty* = ***Ahhotep I***   **KAMOSE** =? *Ahhotep II*

Children: *Ahmes-Henuttamehu*, *Ahmes A*, *Ahmose A*, *Ahmes-Henutemipet*, *Ahmes-Tumerisy*, Binpu, *Ahmose Sipairi* = *Senisonbe A*, *Ahmes-Nebetta*, *Meryetamun A*, ***Ahmes-Nefertiry*** = **AHMO[SE]**

THUTMOSE I = *Mutneferet A*   Ahmose-ankh   **AMENHOTEP I** = ***Meryetamun B***   ***Sitamun A***   Siam[un]

THUTMOSE I → Next table

These two queens were the first holders of the title of God's Wife (of Amun), giving them key roles in Amun's cult; indeed, Ahmes-Nefertiry may have also held the title Second Prophet of Amun, which would be unique for a queen, before becoming God's Wife, perhaps on the death or retirement of her mother. In a scene perhaps marking this transition, Ahmes-Nefertiry is shown with her eldest son, Ahmose-ankh, who presumably died soon afterwards, since Ahmose I was ultimately succeeded by another son, **Amenhotep I**. A sister who did survive was almost certainly Mutneferet A, who was to become a wife of Thutmose I. The remaining children of Ahmose I are little known, although three appear amongst the Lords of the West, and two of their mummies were found together with those of many others of the Taosid family.

These mummies were discovered in 1871 in tomb TT320, near Deir el-Bahari, a tomb apparently originally prepared as the family tomb of the 21st Dynasty High Priest of Amun, Pinudjem II. During the early part of the 22nd Dynasty, many royal mummies had been reburied there, including a large group of Taosid queens, princes and princesses. They all seem to have been buried near one another on Dira Abu'l-Naga, and were moved together to

18th Dynasty part 1

kamose

ose A

their penultimate resting place (prior to the Cairo Museum!) some six centuries later.[95]

Amenhotep I followed the tradition of his immediate ancestors in marrying his sister, in this case Meryetamun B.[96] She may have died fairly young and it is curious that Amenhotep I had no other known wife (nor any children), and on many monuments it is his mother who is shown as his consort: later in the New Kingdom, they were deified together as the patrons of the Theban Necropolis. The king's lack of children and any attested spouse after

(far left) Face of a statue of Amenhotep I from Deir el-Bahari, probably originally placed in his mortuary temple there, and afterwards moved to the monument of Mentuhotep II (BM EA683).

(above, right) Ahmose I, Ahmes-Nefertiry and their son Ahmose-ankh before the god Amun, on a stela found in the Third Pylon at Karnak (Luxor Museum).

(right) Deified after their deaths, Amenhotep I, his mother Ahmes-Nefertiry and grandmother Ahhotep I are shown on this 19th Dynasty stela of the High Priest Roma-Roy (RMO AP59).

Meryetamun could raise questions as to his fertility or sexual orientation. However, there exists no clear evidence one way or the other.

The paternity of Amenhotep I's successor, **Thutmose I**, has long been debated. There is no question that his mother was one Senisonbe, but she was not a King's Wife – bearing simply the title of King's Mother. In 1994, however, it was suggested that the royal father may have been prince Ahmose-Sipairi. It had always seemed curious that such a junior prince should have received so much attention from subsequent generations; if he were Thutmose I's 'missing' father, much would be explained. Nevertheless, no certain evidence exists, and this remains but one possible explanation of Thutmose I's origins. It is equally possible that he could simply have been a trusted subordinate of Amenhotep I whom the childless king nominated as his successor, in the absence of any surviving royal prince.

Brief Lives ●

*Males in **bold**, females in **bold italic**.*

Ahhotep I (KGW; KD; KSis; KM; GW)
Wife of Taa II and mother of Ahmose I; the title of God's Wife only appears on her coffin. A stela of Ahmose I's reign suggests that she might have rallied the troops or the courtiers of Thebes at a crucial moment, perhaps following the death of Taa II or Kamose. Her original tomb is unknown; her outer coffin was ultimately reburied in tomb TT320, but her mummy is unknown – unless she is identical with Ahhotep II.

Ahhotep II (KGW)
Perhaps wife of Kamose, but possibly identical with Ahhotep I; known only from a coffin ultimately reburied at Dira Abu'l-Naga; the mummy was destroyed by the governor of Qena following its discovery in 1859.

Ahmes A (KD; KSis)
Daughter of Taa II and Sitdjehuty; known from the shroud of her mummy, found in her tomb in the Valley of the Queens (QV 47), and now in the Egyptian Museum, Turin.

Ahmes-Henutemipet (KD; KSis)
Probable daughter of Taa II; named on a now-lost coffin and reburied in tomb TT320; her mummy is now in the Cairo Museum.

Ahmes-Henuttamehu (KW; KSis; KD)
Probable daughter of Taa II; reburied in tomb TT320, with her mummy now in the Cairo Museum.

Ahmes-Nebetta (KD; KSis)
Probable daughter of Taa II; named on a statue in the Louvre.

Ahmes-Nefertiry (KGW; KD; KSis; KM; GW; 2PA)
Daughter of Taa II and sister-wife of Ahmose I. One of the most important figures of the period, prominent in both the reign of her husband and her son. As well as her queenly titles, she was also the first God's Wife (of Amun), a title which effectively made her the nominal female opposite number of the High Priest. After her death she became, with Amenhotep I, a patron deity of the Theban Necropolis. Buried at Dira Abu'l-Naga, and later reburied in tomb TT320; her mummy is now in the Cairo Museum.

Ahmes-Tumerisy (KD; KSis)
Probable daughter of Taa II; named on a coffin in the Hermitage, St Petersburg. Body found buried in pit MMA 1019 behind Sheikh Abd el-Qurna.

Ahmose A (EKSon)
Son of Taa II; known from a statue in the Louvre. Although this statue appears to be

The giant wood-and-cartonnage outer coffin of Ahmes-Nefertiry; from TT320 (CM CG61003).

Prince Ahmose A (Louvre E15682).

a funerary one, it has on occasion been suggested that this prince later became Ahmose I.

Ahmose-ankh (1KSon)
Son of Ahmose I and Ahmes-Nefertiry; shown with his parents on a stela from Karnak (Luxor Museum).

Ahmose-Sipairi (KSon)
Probable son of Taa II; appears on a number of early-18th Dynasty, and later, monuments. His prominence has suggested that he may have been the otherwise unknown father of Thutmose I. Buried at Dira Abu'l-Naga.

Binpu (KSon)
Probable son of Taa II; a Lord of the West.

Inhapy (KW; KD)
Wife of Taa II; named in her daughter's Book of the Dead, and in the tomb of Amenemhat (TT53). Had a tomb at Thebes, and was later reburied in tomb TT320; her mummy is now in the Cairo Museum.

Meryetamun A (KD; KSis)
Name also appears as **Ahmes-Meryetamun**; perhaps daughter of Taa II.

Her mummy was found in tomb TT320 and is now in the Cairo Museum.

Meryetamun B (KGW; KD; GW; KSis)
Daughter of Ahmose I and sister-wife of Amenhotep I. Buried in tomb TT358 at Deir el-Bahari, and formerly mistaken for a wife of Amenhotep II; her mummy is now in the Cairo Museum.

Mutneferet A (KM; KW; KSis; KD)
Probable daughter of Ahmose I (see next section).

Neferu B
Mother of Tetisherit; known from the mummy-bandages of her daughter, from tomb TT320.

Ramose A (KSon)
Probable son of Ahmose I; included amongst the Lords of the West, and known from a contemporary statue in Liverpool University.

Senisonbe A (KM)
Mother of Thutmose I; of unknown antecedents.

Face of the inner coffin of Meryetamun B; the original gilding had been stripped off by the 21st Dynasty, when yellow paint was applied to the face, and the now-missing uraeus painted in; from TT358 (CM JE53141).

Siamun A (KSon)
Son of Ahmose I; reburied in tomb TT320, his mummy is now in the Cairo Museum.

Sitamun A (GW; KSis; KD)
Name also appears as **Ahmes-Sitamun**; daughter of Ahmose I, and owner of a colossal statue in front of the Eighth Pylon at Karnak, the upper part of which is in the British Museum; reburied in tomb TT320, with her mummy now in the Cairo Museum.

Sitdjehuty (KW; KD; KSis)
Sister-wife of Taa II; named on the mummy-shroud of her daughter, Ahmes A. The upper part of the lid of her coffin is now in Munich.

Sitkamose (KW; GW; KGW; KD)
On the basis of her name, presumably the daughter of Kamose; her God's Wife title appears to have been posthumous. Reburied in tomb TT320, her mummy is now in the Cairo Museum.

Tetisherit (KGW; KM)
Daughter of an otherwise unknown nobleman named Tjenna and his wife. Lived on into the reign of Ahmose I. Buried at Thebes (exact location unknown), but had a cenotaph built for her at Abydos; probably reburied in tomb TT320, with her possible mummy now in the Cairo Museum.

Tjenna
Father of Tetisherit; known from the mummy-bandages of his daughter, from tomb TT320.

Unplaced ● ● ● ● ● ● ● ● ●

[...]17B (UWC)
Wife of an unknown king. Known from her burial at Qurna, the objects from which are in the Royal Museum in Edinburgh, and are datable to the 17th Dynasty.

[...]17C
Child of an unknown king. Buried alongside *[...]17B*.

The Power and the Glory

18th Dynasty part 2

Historical Background

Thutmose I was a warrior, and undertook extensive campaigns in Nubia and Syria, reaching at least as far as Ahmose I had done; he also carried out many building projects. Relatively little is known, however, of the reign of his son, Thutmose II, which was followed by the minority reign of his heir, Thutmose III. The first part of the latter's reign was under the regency of his aunt, Hatshepsut D, who then became his formal co-regent for a decade and a half. Her reign was punctuated by major building work and a trading expedition to Punt; twenty years after Thutmose III finally achieved untrammelled rule, Hatshepsut's name and image were erased from her monuments.

Although it appears that Thutmose III had undertaken military actions while reigning alongside Hatshepsut, it is only following his re-accession to sole rule that we find extensive accounts of his campaigns – annual expeditions covering two decades that were to cement his reputation as indisputably the greatest of all the warrior-pharaohs. By the end of his reign, Egypt controlled a vast network of client states in Syria–Palestine, together with southern dominion that stretched deep into Upper Nubia. Thutmose III also built extensively, large parts of the temple of Karnak being his work, including the quarrying of the largest obelisk ever completed.

Thutmose III's son, Amenhotep II, imitated his father in martial skill and was also a prolific builder. He was in turn followed on the throne by Thutmose IV, and then Amenhotep III. Both of these kings appear to have consolidated Egyptian power, rather than expanding it, building on a large scale. This was particularly true of Amenhotep III, of whom only one military expedition (into Nubia) is recorded. His reign is generally regarded as the cultural high-point of the New Kingdom, as well as sowing the seeds for perhaps the most remarkable episode in Egyptian history: the Amarna Period.

The Royal Family

The principal wife of **Thutmose I** is well known, from multiple monuments, to have been Ahmes B. Her relationships remain uncertain, depending on whether her title of King's Sister applies to her husband or to a predecessor of his. In favour of the former is the fact that she never carries the title of King's Daughter, which one would have expected if the second option were the case – and as was definitely the case with Thutmose I's other wife, Mutneferet A.

A fragment of a shrine names both Thutmose I and his eldest son, Amenmose; the latter is depicted with a brother, Wadjmose, in the tomb of the royal tutor, Paheri, at El-Kab. That Hatshepsut was a daughter of Thutmose I and Ahmes B is made explicit throughout the female pharaoh's mortuary temple at Deir el-Bahari. A further sibling seems to be Neferubity, who is shown together with Hatshepsut's parents in the sanctuary of the temple; this direct juxtaposition would seem to argue against a suggestion that Neferubity was actually a daughter of Hatshepsut.

It is generally assumed that all these children of Thutmose I were borne by Ahmes B, although her maternity is only explicitly stated (or heavily implied) in the case of the two girls. Thutmose I's successor, **Thutmose II**, is

(above) Relief of Queen Ahmes B, from the Hatshepsut temple at Deir el-Bahari (RMS 1908.378).

(above, right) Senenmut holding his ward, Neferure A, inside his cloak; from Karnak (BM EA174).

confirmed as his direct heir in the tomb-autobiography of the official Ineni (TT81); Thutmose II also dedicated a statue now in Turin to 'his father', Thutmose I. He was, however, the offspring of Mutneferet A, who is represented alongside her son on at least two monuments. From her titles, this lady was the daughter of a king; given the lack of any known offspring of Amenhotep I (see pp. 127–28), it is probable that she may have been a child of Ahmose I.

The marriage between Thutmose II and Hatshepsut is documented by a stela in Berlin that shows them, together with Ahmes B, plus blocks from a monument at Karnak bearing both their images. The latter structure also included the name of Princess Neferure A, conveniently confirming her parentage. No other children of the royal couple are known – Thutmose II's son, **Thutmose III**, being the offspring of a lady called Iset A, as stated on the shroud of Thutmose III's mummy, as well as on a statuette dedicated by him.

It remains unclear whether Thutmose III married his half-sister, Neferure. She is often assumed to have died young and unmarried, but in two

18th Dynasty part 2

Previous table

THUTMOSE I = *Mutneferet A* = *Ahmes B*

Ipu B Amenmose Wadjmose *Iset A* = THUTMOSE II = *HATSHEPSUT D* *Neferubity* *Huy*

Sitiah = THUTMOSE III = *Nebtu* = *Menwi* = *Merti* = *Menhet* ᵉ *Neferure A* ᵉ *Meryetre*

Amenemhat B Siamun B *Beketamun* *Nefertiry B* Menkheperre A AMENHOTEP II = *Tiaa A* *Nebetiunet B* ***Meryetam***

Amenhotep C Ahmose B Akheper[ka?]re Akheperure Amenemopet A Khaemwaset A Nedjem Webensenu *I*

Amenemhat C *Tintamun* Amenemopet B *Pyihia* Siatu*

Nebet

Key

BOLD CAPITALS	King
BOLD ITALIC CAPITALS	Female king
Bold italics	God's Wife of Amun
Italics	female
=	marriage
———	certain or high probability relationship
··········	likely relationship
- - - - - -	uncertain or hypothetical relationship
▬▬▬	principal line of royal succession

inscriptions the names respectively of the mother and a wife (Sitiah) of Thutmose III appear to be written over the cartouche of Neferure; the first text gives her the title of King's Great Wife and Mistress of Upper and Lower Egypt, while the second, although giving her the title of God's Wife, is datable to the early years of Thutmose III's sole reign. The implication would thus seem to be that Thutmose married Neferure, but that her memory later suffered the same opprobrium heaped on her mother.[97]

It has also been suggested that Neferure might have been the mother of Amenemhat B but, given his installation as Overseer of Cattle in year 24, the marriage of his parents would probably then have been at least a decade earlier. If so, one would have expected more mentions of Neferure as a King's Wife, and more than simply her God's Wife title to have been used on a stela dating as late as the period just before her putative son's installation. It would accordingly seem more likely that Thutmose III married Neferure only in the mid-20s of his reign, the lady afterwards disappearing from view.

Amenemhat B's mother thus remains uncertain. Thutmose III's certain wives, Meryetre-Hatshepsut, Sitiah and Nebtu, are shown on a pillar in the king's tomb, a scene which also includes a daughter, Nefertiry B. It is

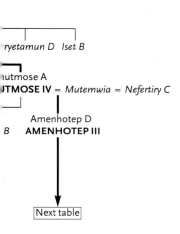

ryetamun D   Iset B

hutmose A
JTMOSE IV = Mutemwia = Nefertiry C

Amenhotep D
B   **AMENHOTEP III**

Next table

(far left) Limestone statue of Hatshepsut as king; from her temple at Deir el-Bahari (MMA 29.3.2).

(above, right) Thutmose III and his eternal family, as depicted on a pillar in his tomb (KV34). On the right he is suckled by his mother, Iset, in the guise of a tree; the king then leads a procession of his wives Meryetre-Hatshepsut, Sitiah and Nebtu, followed by his daughter Nefertiry B.

(right) Statuette of the Royal Nurse Huy, a mother-in-law of Thutmose III and grandmother of Amenhotep II. Here she is shown with Princess Nebetiunet B on her lap. On the sides of her seat are Prince Menkheperre A and his sisters, Iset B and Meryetamun C and D (BM EA1280).

possible that Sitiah, the earlier of these Great Wives, may have been Amenemhat's mother.

Meryetre-Hatshepsut was almost certainly the King's Great Wife and God's Wife borne by the Adoratrix Huy, whose statue is in the British Museum; that Huy's son-in-law was Thutmose III is clear from the names of the royal children named on the statue. Sitiah is known to have had a different mother, while no other contemporary Great Wife is known, with the questionable exception of Hatshepsut's daughter, Neferure. Three lesser wives, apparently of Syrian extraction, named Menwi, Merti and Menhet, are known from their joint tomb, in which the name of Thutmose appears on a number of items.

The images of Prince Menkheperre A and princesses Nebetiunet B, Iset B, Meryetamun C and Meryetamun D on the statue of Huy make it clear that they were all offspring of Meryetre-Hatshepsut and Thutmose III. The fact that Iset was shown smaller than her siblings suggests that she was the youngest. Another child of the couple was the ultimate Crown Prince, Amenhotep B – his mother being mentioned on a number of monuments after his accession. A further son, Siamun (B), is depicted on the statue of an official, which is datable to the reign of Thutmose III, but there is no indication of the identity of his mother. Another daughter, Beketamun, is named on a fragment of a faience votive object from Deir el-Bahari, which also bears the cartouche of Thutmose III.

The family of **Amenhotep II** presents certain problems, some probably stemming from the conflict that seems to have engulfed the royal family at the end of his reign. However, it appears that his principal wife was Tiaa A, albeit on the basis of monuments that all date to the reign of their son, Thutmose IV,[98] and that Tiaa usurped all inscriptions of Meryetre-Hatshepsut dating to Amenhotep II's reign.

The number and identity of the sons of Amenhotep II is also a somewhat complex issue. After his accession, Thutmose IV (Prince Thutmose A) had himself depicted as a miniature king on the lap of his tutor, Heqareshu, in the tomb of the latter's son – and also a royal tutor – Heqaerneheh (tomb TT64); on the same wall were shown a number of other royal sons. Some writers have identified them as Thutmose IV's siblings, but since they are more closely associated in the scene with Heqaerneheh, who has with him the future Amenhotep III (Prince Amenhotep D), they are more likely to be his sons.

However, likely sons of Amenhotep II are to be found in a tomb probably constructed for Heqareshu at the end of his career, under Amenhotep III (TT226).[99] Four children are represented in tomb TT226, two now nameless, the others bearing names of the form Akheper[...]re. They have generally been considered as also appearing among the children shown with Heqaerneheh in tomb TT64, but this does not necessarily follow. The representation in TT226 could be of the royal children who had been in the charge of Heqareshu during a career launched back in the reign of Amenhotep II, remembered in the twilight of his life. Thus, they might be considered as being offspring of one, two or all of Amenhotep II, Thutmose IV and Amenhotep III. Graffiti at Konosso that show princes Akheperure and Amenhotep, and Heqareshu and Heqaerneheh all together need not place the princes in the same generation. What they may represent is a visit of Amenhotep (D), Thutmose IV's eldest son and one of the reigning king's younger brothers,

(below) Fragmentary scene from a pillar in the tomb probably constructed for the royal tutor Heqareshu at the end of his career, under Amenhotep III (TT226). Four children are shown, two now nameless, the others bearing names of the form Akheper[...]re; they seem almost certainly to have been offspring of Amenhotep II.

(below, right) In the tomb of Heqareshu's son, and fellow royal tutor, Heqaerneheh (TT64), we see Thutmose IV depicted as a miniature king on the lap of his tutor, Heqareshu. In front of them is Heqaerneheh, with him the future Amenhotep III (Prince Amenhotep D) and, behind them, other children of Thutmose IV. Unfortunately, only the top two of potentially six figures survive, and only one of these has a name: Amenemhat (C).

who was perhaps a child of Amenhotep II's old age, accompanied by their father-son pair of tutors, Heqareshu being responsible for the late king's offspring, the younger for the child of the reigning king.

The two children whose names are lost may well include Khaemwaset A, Webensenu or Nedjem: the first is named in graffiti alongside the cartouche of Amenhotep II, while Webensenu was buried in Amenhotep II's tomb (KV35); Nedjem is named with Webensenu on the statue of the official Minmose. Another prince, Amenhotep C, is mentioned in a papyrus in the British Museum, to be dated to the reign of Amenhotep II; this gives him the title of Sem-Priest of Ptah, which is useful in identifying his other monuments. Another priestly prince, Ahmose B, can be dated stylistically to the period, most probably to the end of Amenhotep II's reign.

Finally, a Prince Amenemopet A may be attributed to Amenhotep II on the basis of the style and provenance of his one known attestation – a stela from Giza. Only one daughter is known: Iaret, wife of Thutmose IV, was a King's Daughter, and Amenhotep II is the only plausible candidate for her father.

Three wives have been identified for **Thutmose IV**. Iaret and Nefertiry C are both represented alongside the king on a number of monuments, but Mutemwia is only shown on those of her son Amenhotep III. As already noted, as prince Amenhotep D he is shown in the tomb of his tutor, Heqaerneheh, along with a number of other siblings. Unfortunately, only the top two of potentially six figures survive, and only one of these has a name – Amenemhat (C). This boy is also known from his burial in his father's tomb, thus neatly confirming the paternity of the children shown in tomb TT64.

Alongside these seven boys,[100] one daughter – Tentamun (A) – is attested by her interment alongside Amenemhat C in Thutmose IV's tomb. Another, Tiaa (B), is expressly called a daughter of the king on a 21st Dynasty label attached to her mummy on its reburial under Pasebkhanut I, as is a further

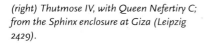

(right) Thutmose IV, with Queen Nefertiry C; from the Sphinx enclosure at Giza (Leipzig 2429).

Between the paws of the Great Sphinx at Giza is the 'Dream Stela' of Thutmose IV. This tells of how, as Prince Thutmose A, the future pharaoh fell asleep in the shadow of the sphinx. The sphinx appeared to him in a dream and promised him the throne of Egypt in exchange for clearing away the sand that enveloped much of the statue. Given the mutilation of the monuments of Thutmose's elder brother, Amenhotep C, this seems likely to have been a tale to justify Thutmose's seizure of power.

lady, Pyihia. Eight other King's Daughters are also known from similar mummy-labels, but their royal ancestor is nowhere mentioned, and as the deposit is a later cache, nothing can be inferred from their presence together as to their date. Tatau, Henutiunu, Meryetptah A, Sithori and Wiay A cannot be placed at all; Pypuy may be the like-named daughter of Rameses II. However, Amenemopet B may well be the same as the girl shown sitting on the knee of the army officer, Horemheb (C), in his tomb (TT78). As Horemheb served under Amenhotep II, Thutmose IV and Amenhotep III, the girl could have been a daughter of any of them, although Thutmose is perhaps most likely.

The last of the ladies represented by a mummy-label from this group is Nebetia. Interestingly, although given the title of King's Daughter, she was actually a granddaughter of a pharaoh. On the label, her father is stated to be Prince Siatum A, and a person of this name is also represented on the knee of his tutor, Meryre, on a slab from the latter's tomb. Stylistically, the relief clearly dates to Amenhotep III's reign, but it is equally clear that such representations do not mean that the royal children shown were actually infants when the scene was carved – merely that the tomb-owner wished to be remembered as having tutored them at some point during his career. Thus, it is not improbable that Siatum was another of the sons of Thutmose IV, particularly as his name corresponds to part of one of that king's Horus names.

Brief Lives ●

*Males in **bold**, females in **bold italic**.*

Ahmes B (KM; KGW; KSis)
Wife of Thutmose I; known from a range of monuments, principally those of her daughter, Hatshepsut, but also from other material, including a statue of her mortuary priest, Nakht, from Karnak.

Ahmose B (KSon; HPH)
Probably a son of Amenhotep II, in office during the reign of Thutmose IV. Known from a stela in Berlin (probably from Heliopolis) and a broken statue in Cairo (probably from Koptos).

Akheper[ka?]re (KSon)
Son of Amenhotep II. Named in tomb TT226.

Akheperure (KSon)
Son of Amenhotep II. Named in graffiti at Konosso and almost certainly in tomb TT226.

Prince Amenhotep B sits on the lap of his tutor – the Mayor of Thinis, Min – in the latter's tomb at Thebes.

Amenemhat B (EKSon; Overseer of Cattle)
Son and heir of Thutmose III. Named on the south side of Festival Hall at Karnak temple in year 24.

Amenemhat C (KSon)
Son of Thutmose IV. Depicted in tomb TT64, died young and buried with his father in KV43, where his canopic jars and probable mummy were found.

Amenemopet A (KSon)
Probably a son of Amenhotep II; owner of stela C from near Amenhotep II's Sphinx Temple. A stela from Saqqara showing a prince of this name with his nurse, Senetruiu, may refer to him.

Amenemopet B (KD)
Possible daughter of Thutmose IV. Her mummy was reburied during the 21st Dynasty; its label was once in Bonn.

Amenhotep B (KSon)
Son of Thutmose III, later king as **AMENHOTEP II**. Depicted in the tomb of Min, Mayor of Thinis (TT109), and perhaps in the anonymous tomb TT143. On a stela from the sphinx at Giza, he states that he came to the throne at the age of 18.

Amenhotep C (KSon; Exec; SPP)
Son, and probably heir, of Amenhotep II. Frequently mentioned in an administrative papyrus in the British

(left) Stela found near the Great Sphinx at Giza, showing a prince and Sem-Priest of Ptah offering to the Sphinx. His name, written in a cartouche, and titles have been erased but he seems almost certainly to be Amenhotep C, heir to Amenhotep II.

Museum, and probably owner of a stela found near the Sphinx at Giza, from which the owner's name, written in a cartouche, had been erased.

Amenhotep D (KSon)
Son of Thutmose IV, later king as **AMENHOTEP III**. Appears in the tomb of his tutor Heqaerneheh (TT64), and on two Konosso graffiti.

Amenmose (EKSon; Genmo)
Son and heir of Thutmose I, whose name was written in a cartouche. Owner of a miniature stone shrine, a fragment of which was bought at Giza, dated to year 4 of his father (Louvre). He accompanies his brother, Wadjmose, in a scene in the tomb of Paheri at El-Kab.

Beket(amun) (KD)
Daughter of Thutmose III; named on a fragment of a faience votive object from Deir el-Bahari (Boston) on a wooden staff (of her servant, Amenmose – now in Brooklyn), and probably on a scarab in the British Museum. She may have been represented in the Hathor Chapel of her father at Deir el-Bahari, where the figure of a princess behind Meryetamun C has lost its name.

Hatshepsut D (GW; KGW; KD; KSis; UWC)
Daughter of Thutmose I, wife of

Thutmose II and **later king**. A range of monuments date to her period as queen, and also as regent for Thutmose III. These include inscriptions from Karnak, Nubia and Sinai, and an (unused) tomb and sarcophagus in the Wadi Siqqat Taqa el-Zeide at Thebes.

Huy (Ador)
Mother of Meryetre-Hatshepsut. Represented on a statue in the British Museum, and played an important role in the cults of Amun, Re and Atum.

Iaret (KGW; KD; KSis)
Daughter of Amenhotep II and wife of Thutmose IV from around year 7 onwards, which is the date of inscriptions at Serabit el-Khadim and Konosso. The transcription of her name is not certain, it being written with a simple cobra, which has a number of possible readings.

Ipu B (Nurse of the God)
Mother of Sitiah. Named on an offering table of her daughter, from Abydos and now in Cairo.

Iset A (GW; KM; KW; KGW)
Mother of Thutmose III; she was given the title of KGW during his reign, as well as GW after her death. Possessor of a statue from Karnak, and mentioned a number of times on her son's funerary monuments and equipment.

Iset B (KD)
Daughter of Thutmose III and Meryetre-Hatshepsut. Represented on the statue of her grandmother, Huy, in the British Museum.

Khaemwaset A (KSon; Overseer of Cattle)
Probable son of Amenhotep II. Named in two Sehel graffiti including the prenomen of Amenhotep II.

Menhet (KW)
Wife of Thutmose III, probably of Syrian extraction. Buried in a tomb in Wadi Gabbanet el-Qurud together with Menwi and Merti; much of the funerary equipment is now in the Metropolitan Museum of Art.

Menkheperre A (KSon)
Son of Thutmose III and Meryetre-Hatshepsut. He is depicted upon a British Museum statuette of his grandmother, Huy. Canopic jar fragments from the Valley of the Queens, in Strasbourg and Cairo, are probably his.

Menwi (KW)
Wife of Thutmose III, probably of Syrian extraction. Buried with Menhet and Merti.

Iset A, mother of Thutmose III; from Karnak (CM JE37417 = CG42072).

Merti (KW)
Wife of Thutmose III, probably of Syrian extraction. Buried with Menhet and Menwi.

Meryetamun C (KD; KSis; GW)
Daughter of Thutmose III and Meryetre-Hatshepsut. Represented on the statuette of her grandmother, Huy, and on the wall of the Hathor shrine of Thutmose III at Deir el-Bahari. She (or Meryetamun D) was also shown on the lap of the Overseer of Works, Benermerut, from Karnak.

Meryetamun D (KD)
Daughter of Thutmose III and Meryetre-Hatshepsut. Represented on the statue of her grandmother, Huy.

Meryetre(-Hatshepsut) (KGW; GW; KM)
Wife of Thutmose III; daughter of the Adoratrix Huy and mother of Amenhotep II. Known from a number of monuments, including the Edifice of Amenhotep II at Karnak. Many of her representations were usurped by Tiaa A during the reign of

(below) Block granite statue of Benermerut with a Princess Meryetamun; from the temple of Amun at Karnak (CM CG42171).

Thutmose IV, into which she seems to have survived. Her disgrace under her grandson is also suggested by her apparent non-use of tomb KV42 in the Valley of the Kings, which had previously been taken over for her burial.

Mutemwia (KGW; KM)
Wife of Thutmose IV and mother of Amenhotep III; shown in the 'divine birth' scenes of her son in Luxor temple. A statue of her probably came from his mortuary temple, with a figure of her in a boat found adjacent to the granite sanctuary of the Karnak temple (British Museum); she is also represented with her son on the Colossi of Memnon and in the tomb of Heqareshu (TT226, now in the Luxor Museum).

Mutneferet A (KM; KW; KSis; KD)
Wife of Thutmose I, mother of Thutmose II and probable daughter of Ahmose I. Represented by the leg of her son on a colossus in front of the south face of the Eighth Pylon, in the temple of Thutmose III at Deir el-Bahari and on a stela found near the Ramesseum. She was also the owner of a statue found in the chapel of Wadjmose.

(below) Queen Mutneferet A, found in the chapel of Wadjmose at Western Thebes (CM CG572).

(below) The bark of Mutemwia, upon which sits the queen, protected by the vulture-goddess, Mut. The whole sculpture is a rebus on Mutemwia's name, which means simply 'Mut in the boat'! From Karnak (BM EA43).

Nebetia (KD)
Daughter of Prince Siatum A, and probably a granddaughter of Thutmose IV. Her mummy was reburied during the 21st Dynasty on Sheikh Abd el-Qurna with a number of other princesses of the period, but was robbed prior to 1857; its label is in Edinburgh.[101]

Nebetiunet B (KD)
Daughter of Thutmose III and Meryetre. Represented on the lap of her grandmother, Huy, on the latter's statuette.

Nebtu (KW)
Wife of Thutmose III. Represented in her husband's tomb, and had an estate whose steward, Nebamun, was buried in tomb TT24.

Nedjem (KSon)
Son of Amenhotep II. Named, with Webensenu, on the statue of Overseer of Works, Minmose, from Karnak.

Nefertiry B (KD)
Daughter of Thutmose III; depicted on a pillar in the king's tomb (KV34).

Nefertiry C (KGW)
Wife of Thutmose IV. Shown on eight stelae from Giza of her and her husband before deities, a stela from Luxor temple, and named on a scarab from Gurob.

Neferubity (KD)
Daughter of Thutmose I and Ahmes B. Depicted on the walls of the sanctuary of Hatshepsut's temple at Deir el-Bahari.

Neferure A (KD; GW; KGW)
Daughter of Hatshepsut, and possibly wife of Thutmose III. Depicted on a number of statues of her tutor, Senenmut, on the walls of the Deir el-Bahari temple, and on stelae from Sinai and Karnak. A tomb that may be hers is in the Wadi Qubbet el-Qurud at Thebes.

Pyihia (KD)
Daughter of Thutmose IV. One of the group of princesses reburied during the 21st Dynasty on Sheikh Abd el-Qurna.

Seneb (KSon)
Son of Thutmose II; known from the tomb of his funerary priest at Qurnet Murai.

Siamun B (KSon)
Son of Thutmose III. Named upon the statuette of the Chancellor, Sennefer, in the Cairo Museum.

Siatum A (KSon)
Probable son of Thutmose IV. Known from two sources: a relief of his tutor, Meryre, from Saqqara, and a label which names him as the father of a lady (Nebetia) reburied during the 21st Dynasty.

Sitiah (GW; KW; KGW)
Wife of Thutmose III, and perhaps the mother of Amenemhat B; daughter of the nurse Ipu B. A number of items were dedicated to her by her husband after her death.

Thutmose A (KSon)
Son of Amenhotep II, later king as **THUTMOSE IV**, and conceivably identical with Thutmose Q. Owner of a statue from the Mut temple at Karnak, which also bears the name of his tutor, Heqareshu.

(below) The name of only one wife of Amenhotep II is known: Tiaa A, mother of Thutmose IV. She is shown with her son on this statue from Karnak (CM CG42080).

Tiaa A (KGW; KM; GW)
Wife of Amenhotep II and mother of Thutmose IV. A number of monuments were created for her by the latter at Giza, Thebes and the Fayoum, including a number of usurpations of material belonging to Meryetre-Hatshepsut. She was buried in tomb KV32, where many fragments of her funerary equipment have been found; some material was washed by floodwater into the adjacent tomb KV47, where it was for a long time thought to belong to a like-named mother of Siptah.

Tiaa B (KD)
Daughter of Thutmose IV. She is probably the owner of three canopic jars from the Valley of the Queens, and also the princess of the name depicted in the tomb of Sobkhotep at Thebes (TT63). Probably one of the group of princesses reburied during the 21st Dynasty on Sheikh Abd el-Qurna.

Tintamun (KD)
Daughter of Thutmose IV; a fragment of one of her canopic jars was found in tomb KV43 and is now in the Cairo Museum.

Wadjmose (KSon)
Son of Thutmose I, perhaps born only a few years before the king's accession to the throne. His major contemporary attestation is in the tomb of Paheri. Perhaps under his brother, Thutmose II,

(above) Wadjmose, shown on the lap of his tutor, Paheri, in the latter's tomb at El-Kab (EK3). Paheri was also tutor to the prince's eldest brother, Amenmose.

a chapel was dedicated to him, in between the sites of the later Ramesseum and the mortuary temple of Thutmose IV.

Webensenu (KSon)
Son of Amenhotep II. Died as a child and buried with his father in tomb KV35, where his probable body still lies. Named on the block statue of Minmose, from Karnak.

Unplaced ● ● ● ● ● ● ● ● ● ● ●

(See also Addenda p. 304)

Amenemhat Q (KSon)
Unplaced, probably in the earlier part of the dynasty. Owner of a rewrapped mummy found in the cliffs north of tomb TT280 and, probably, of the adjacent tomb MMA 1021.

Henut Q (KW)
Wife of a king of the mid-18th Dynasty. Her name is enclosed in a cartouche on canopic fragments from the Valley of the Queens.

Henutiunu (KD)
Her mummy was reburied during the 21st Dynasty on Sheikh Abd el-Qurna, but robbed prior to 1857; its labels are in Edinburgh.

Merybennu (KSon)
Probably a son of Thutmose III or Amenhotep II. Known from a *shabti* figure in the Oriental Museum, Durham.

Meryetptah A (KD)
One of the group of princesses reburied during the 21st Dynasty on Sheikh Abd el-Qurna.

Nebetnehat A (KGW)
Wife of a king of the mid-18th Dynasty. Her name is enclosed in a cartouche on canopic fragments from the Valley of the Queens.

Sithori (KD)
One of the group of princesses reburied during the 21st Dynasty on Sheikh Abd el-Qurna.

Tatau (KD)
One of the group of princesses reburied during the 21st Dynasty on Sheikh Abd el-Qurna.

Thutmose Q (KSon; Captain of the Troops)
Owner of a whip found in the tomb of Tutankhamun; possibly identical with Thutmose A or B, although the latter's titles are otherwise all sacerdotal.

Ti (KD)
Daughter of a king of the mid-18th Dynasty. Owner of canopic fragments from the Valley of the Queens.

Wiay A (KD)
One of the group of princesses reburied during the 21st Dynasty on Sheikh Abd el-Qurna.

[...]pentepkau (KSon)
Unplaced, probably mid-18th Dynasty. Known only from a fragment of sphinx-stela from near the Second Pyramid of Giza.

The Amarna Interlude

18th Dynasty part 3

Stela of Akhenaten and Nefertiti, together with their three eldest daughters; from Amarna (CM JE44865).

Historical Background

Amenhotep III is generally regarded to have been barely into his teens when he ascended the throne of his ancestors. Building work began early on, as recorded by quarry inscriptions of the first two years of the reign, while year 5 saw the king putting down a rebellion in Nubia, possibly the only military operation recorded from his reign.

In year 30 Amenhotep III celebrated his first jubilee. Huge quantities of potsherds from Malqata record items supplied for the celebration, which was repeated in years 34 and 37. Some of the manifestations of the jubilee seem to have been without precedent, apparently associated with his transformation into an apotheosis of the sun-god Re: the king was being elevated to full godhead. Depictions are even known of the king worshipping himself (see p. 13).

There has been much debate over whether Amenhotep III shared the throne with his son (Amenhotep IV) from around year 30 onwards, or whether the latter succeeded only on the former's death. In favour of there having been a co-regency is the possibility that Amenhotep III's divine transformation was directly linked with the new sun-religion to be championed by Amenhotep IV – that of the 'Aten'. Indeed, it may be that Amenhotep III *was* the Aten, and that the jubilee of the god celebrated by the younger Amenhotep in his fourth year was in essence identical with one of those of the older king.

The Aten had long been a designation of the physical body of the sun, but during the 18th Dynasty it had begun to attain a separate divine status and, under Amenhotep IV, the Aten was to be something far more: at first the paramount, and finally the sole, god. Marking the god's progress was a remarkable new art style which at first sight contradicted everything for which Egyptian art stood. The king, family and entourage were all shown with slack jaws, scrawny features, extravagant paunches and swelling hips and breasts. On top of all this, the representation of the Aten as a hawk-headed man was replaced by the sun's disc, from which spread down solar rays, each ending in a human hand; the latter held the sign of 'life' to the nostrils of the king and queen.

Having built a temple at Karnak to coincide with his celebration of a jubilee (apparently that of the Aten), Amenhotep IV moved in year 5 to a desolate plain in Middle Egypt, where he founded a new capital dedicated to the Aten: Akhet-Aten (Amarna). He also changed his name to Akhenaten, overseeing in the next few years the growth of the city, with the construction of palaces, temples, government offices and residential quarters.

Links between Egypt and her neighbours in the ancient world are thrown into sharp relief by the unique survival at Akhet-Aten of letters, which were written in cuneiform script on clay tablets to the pharaoh from his vassals and the kings of the other contemporary great powers. On one reading of the letters from his vassals, one may see a decline in Egyptian power, exacerbated by a gross failure on the part of the pharaoh to act on behalf of his interests in the area. Another view, however, sees merely the usual ebb and flow of the influence of great powers in an area constantly under dispute.

During the last years of his reign, Akhenaten acquired a co-regent, the mystery of whose identity has generated a whole range of mutually exclusive theories. Perhaps the most likely view, however, makes the new joint-pharaoh Akhenaten's elder son, Smenkhkare, later replaced by his (half-?) sister and wife, Meryetaten, under the name of Neferneferuaten. It may have been only after their premature deaths that Akhenaten launched an attack on the god Amun, erasing his names and images wherever they appeared.

Not long afterwards Akhenaten seems to have died and, under his successor Tutankhaten, a steady return to orthodoxy took place. Tutankhaten seems to have spent the first few years of the reign at Amarna, but fairly early on his name was changed to Tutankhamun, with the royal residence shifting back to Memphis.

The military are prominent at court, with a Syrian campaign apparently led by the general who was later to become king: Horemheb. After Tutankhamun's early death, his widow, Ankhesenamun, seems to have attempted to cling to power by offering herself in marriage to a Hittite prince called Zannanza. However, the latter was killed and another military man, Ay, obtained the throne. After his short reign, Horemheb finally became pharaoh.

Tutankhamun and Ankhesenamun, as shown on a small golden shrine from his tomb (CM JE60686).

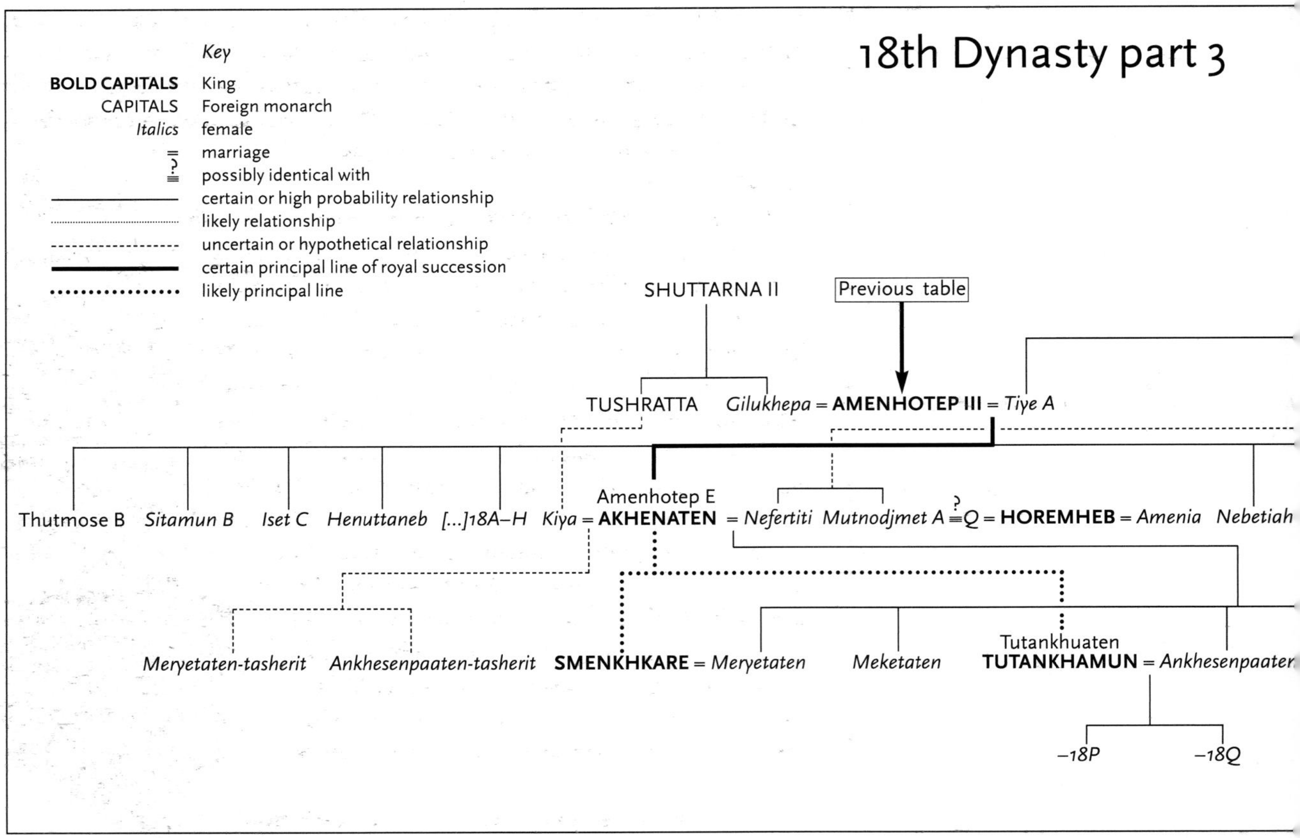

18th Dynasty part 3

Key

BOLD CAPITALS	King
CAPITALS	Foreign monarch
Italics	female
=	marriage
=?	possibly identical with
———	certain or high probability relationship
··········	likely relationship
- - - - - -	uncertain or hypothetical relationship
——	certain principal line of royal succession
••••••••	likely principal line

SHUTTARNA II

Previous table

TUSHRATTA   *Gilukhepa* = **AMENHOTEP III** = *Tiye A*

Thutmose B   *Sitamun B*   *Iset C*   *Henuttaneb*   [...]18A–H   *Kiya* = **AKHENATEN** = *Nefertiti*   *Mutnodjmet A* =? *Q* = **HOREMHEB** = *Amenia*   *Nebetiah*

Amenhotep E

Meryetaten-tasherit   *Ankhesenpaaten-tasherit*   **SMENKHKARE** = *Meryetaten*   *Meketaten*   Tutankhuaten **TUTANKHAMUN** = *Ankhesenpaaten*

–18P   –18Q

Some Akhenaten material had begun to be dismantled back in the time of Tutankhamun. Major attacks on Akhenaten's memory, however, probably began immediately after Tutankhamun's death, and it was with Horemheb that the first attempts seem to have been made to write the Amarna Period out of history. Demolition work began at Amarna, while the Aten temples at Karnak were taken down and immediately employed in the foundations and filling of Horemheb's own monuments to Amun-Re. As one might expect from a former general, some military operations were undertaken during Horemheb's reign, perhaps following on from those which he had carried out under his predecessors, but they seem to have been of strictly limited extent.

The Royal Family

The monuments of the late 18th Dynasty show a massive rise in the public importance of the royal family. During earlier reigns of the dynasty the identity of even the principal wife of the king is often obscure; in contrast, the spouses of the Amarna Period kings are frequently shown alongside their husbands, while daughters (though not sons) are now regularly depicted. In this way, the monuments of the period clearly provide a prototype for the massive display of family seen in the early 19th Dynasty. This change from

Yuya = *Tjuiu*

AY = *Tey*   *Mutemnub* = Nakhtmin A   Anen

ketaten   Nakhtmin B   Ay B   [...]18J   [...]18K–N

rneferuaten-tasherit   Neferneferure   Setpenre A

earlier times clearly had an ideological basis with, in particular, the Great Wife forming a divine duumvirate with her husband. While this had always been the case up to a point, the queen's status was now made much more explicit, equating her with certain female deities, and even temples were built in which the earthly focus was not simply the king, but his Great Wife as well.

In spite of this heightened family focus, some of the relationships of the late-18th Dynasty kings continue to present major problems of interpretation – problems that tie in with many of the historical difficulties as well. The basic relationships are clear, however: **Amenhotep III**'s Great Wife, Tiye A, is known from multiple monuments, which unequivocally describe her as the king's wife. Her parents' names, Yuya and Tjuiu, are also clearly stated on the 'marriage scarabs' issued by Amenhotep III. On the sarcophagus and a coffin of her mother, Tjuiu, there are inscriptions that name a son of hers, Anen, who was thus Tiye's brother. Five of Anen's children are shown in his tomb, but their names are all lost. It has also been suggested – on the basis of the similarity in their names and titles – that Ay, later king, was another son of Yuya; however, while attractive, this idea is without any direct evidence.

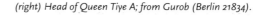

(right) Head of Queen Tiye A; from Gurob (Berlin 21834).

(below) Face of the gilded wood middle coffin of Tjuiu, mother of Tiye A (CM CG51006).

(right) The mummy of Yuya, father of Tiye A (CM CG51190).

Amenhotep III also contracted diplomatic marriages with two daughters of kings of Mitanni (northern Syria). One, Gilukhipa, is commemorated on a series of scarabs, while the other, Tadukhipa, is mentioned in a diplomatic letter and may later have become a wife of Akhenaten. If so, Tadukhipa may have been the same person as Kiya, who bears at Amarna a unique wifely title, perhaps reflecting an exotic origin.[102]

The sons of Amenhotep III are a fairly straightforward issue. One was Amenhotep E, the future **Amenhotep IV/Akhenaten**, who is named on a jar-sealing from the royal palace. The other was the prematurely deceased elder son, Thutmose B, whose paternity is indicated by a group of material found at the Serapeum. Two other individuals, Smenkhkare and Tutankhaten, have been put forward as being amongst Amenhotep III's offspring but, as we will see, they were almost certainly the sons of Akhenaten. Akhenaten was definitely Tiye's son, both shown on more than one occasion in contexts which show that he was the king of her King's Mother title. While Thutmose's maternity is nowhere stated, as the heir, he is very likely to have been Tiye's child as well.

Eight daughters of Amenhotep III are shown in the tomb of Kheruef (TT192), labelled collectively and anonymously as 'royal children', while four were once depicted and named on a mutilated colossus at Medinet Habu. Five daughters' names seem to be known, of whom three (Iset C, Henut-taneb A and Nebetiah) are explicitly linked with their father (and one also with her mother) on monuments. Beketaten is shown alongside Tiye on more than one occasion, and once in close proximity to Amenhotep III as well, making her status apparently clear (although see below, and notes 105 and 106). The fifth princess, Sitamun B, is generally regarded as the eldest daughter, but curiously there seems to be no unequivocal document naming her simply as Amenhotep III's daughter. Where she is named alongside the king, it is also as King's Great Wife, so one could quite easily argue that she was actually a daughter of Thutmose IV and married to her brother. On the other hand, two items bearing the name and titles of a Princess Sitamun were found in the tomb of Yuya and Tjuiu: the most natural assumption would be that they were burial gifts from a granddaughter. In addition, Iset C – an unequivocal daughter of Amenhotep III – also received wifely titles from her father, making a similar status for Sitamun not unlikely. These two ladies are perhaps the first to have certainly held wifely titles under their father and, although the situation is once again found under Ramesses II, it is not common. Neither woman has known offspring (although there have been numerous ingenious speculations), and thus it remains unknown whether one or both or neither had a sexual relationship with their father.

Moving to the next generation, from early in the first stage of his reign as Amenhotep IV, Akhenaten's principal wife on countless monuments is shown to be Nefertiti. Nevertheless, nowhere is Nefertiti's parentage stated, although the fact that she is never called King's Daughter or King's Sister makes it certain that she was not of royal birth.[103] She had a sister, named Mutnodjmet A (read by some as 'Mutbeneret'),[104] who is described as such in a number of tombs, but who is also without any clear indication of parentage. A clue may lie in the fact that a lady named Tey is called Nefertiti's 'nurse' on a number of Tey's monuments. Tey's husband was Ay, whose title of God's Father is one that can sometimes indicate its bearer being the father of a queen (see pp. 35–37). Certainly Ay was proud of this title, incorporating it into his nomen-cartouche when he eventually became king. The suggestion has thus been made that Nefertiti may have been a daughter of Ay, perhaps by a wife who died in childbirth, and that Tey was another wife who actually brought up the queen. While once again very attractive, and capable of explaining a number of historical issues, this can only remain a theory in the absence of direct evidence.

Nefertiti was the mother of at least six daughters who appear frequently on monuments, with label-texts that explicitly name her as their mother, without naming the father. Such labels are otherwise unknown, and have been the basis for a theory that Akhenaten was infertile and Amenhotep III was really their father. However, in only one scene does Amenhotep III appear anywhere near his putative offspring.[105] Needless to say, no real evidence exists for this extraordinary suggestion, which is ultimately grounded on arguments that Akhenaten's odd appearance was caused by a glandular disorder that would have left him unable to father children. Similarly lacking in corroboration is an interpretation that would make the 'common father' Akhenaten, having impregnated his mother and making concrete the notion that the king was the 'bull of his mother'. This concept encapsulated the idea that kingship was a self-engendered cycle.[106] Accordingly, one is willing to embrace neither such extraordinary explanations of the unusual designation

(below) Stela showing Akhenaten and Nefertiti with their three eldest daughters, from the left, Meryetaten, Meketaten and Ankhesenpaaten (Berlin 14145).

(below right) Upper part of a sandstone colossus of Akhenaten, from East Karnak. This shows him wearing the insignia of the god Shu, who played an important role in the early Amarna theology (CM JE99065).

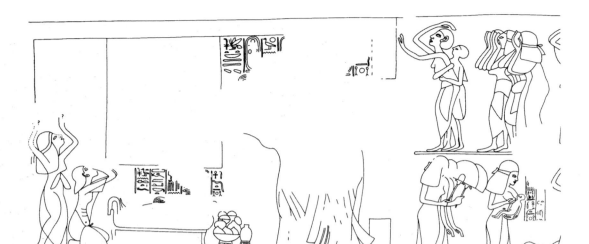

Detail from the left-hand wall of room 'gamma' in the royal tomb at Amarna. Meketaten, of whom only a few traces survive, lies on her death-bed, mourned by her father and mother. On the lower register is to be seen a baby in its nurse's arms. This has been interpreted both as Meketaten's newborn child and as a young child of Nefertiti, conceivably the future king, Tutankh(u)aten.

Relief of Kiya, from Hermopolis; her image has been altered to resemble Meryetaten (Ny Carlsberg 1776).

of Nefertiti's daughters. Rather, these labels most probably simply reinforce the princesses' relationship with the female aspect of the Amarna divine couple.

Certain inscriptions from Amarna seem to show that there were two further princesses: Meryetaten-tasherit ('Meryetaten Junior') and Ankhesenpaaten-tasherit. Because of the presence of a baby in the death-bed scene of Meketaten in Akhenaten's tomb, it has generally been assumed that she died in childbirth; following on from this, it has been argued that he sired children by all three of his eldest daughters. However, the texts accompanying the baby can also be interpreted as making it a further child of Nefertiti.[107] Furthermore, Meketaten may well not have reached puberty at her death,[108] neither Meryetaten nor Ankhesenpaaten bear wifely titles with regard to their father, and the parentage – even the existence – of princesses Meryetaten-tasherit and Ankhesenpaaten-tasherit is problematic. Both only appear in re-worked texts that once involved Kiya, and it is possible that they were daughters of the latter, rather than of Meryetaten and Ankhesenpaaten; indeed the very names may be fictitious, replacing others.[109]

Fragment of a column, apparently showing the same daughter of Akhenaten twice. Traces on the right appear to be from the dress of Nefertiti, suggesting that this figure is her eldest daughter, Meryetaten; from the chapel of the Great Palace at Amarna (Brooklyn 35.2000).

A final issue as regards the children of Akhenaten is whether he had any sons. The preponderance of girls on the monuments may simply be an issue of decorum – male children are a rarity on any pre-Ramesside royal monuments – and is thus not an argument for or against Akhenaten having sons. Indeed, on a block formerly from Amarna is the name and title of a 'King's Son Tutankhuaten', and since it appears that during the 18th Dynasty his title was only current during the life of the king to which it referred, there is a strong presumption in favour of Akhenaten being the father of this prince (presumably the future King Tutankhaten/amun). Indeed, traces in the label-text of the aforementioned baby in Meketaten's death scene have been interpreted as being the end of a male name. If correctly interpreted, this

Brown quartzite head of an Amarna princess, showing the exaggerated skull so typical of art of the period. There is no evidence for the kind of pathology or artificial deformation that would create such a shape in nature. Such distortions are probably part of Akhenaten's desire to stress the 'otherness' of the royal family, who were the sole interlocutors between humanity and the Aten; from Amarna (CM JE44869).

would mean that Nefertiti had at least one son, with the further possibility that the child shown here (and also in another death scene in the Amarna royal tomb, in chamber 'alpha') is indeed Tutankh(u)aten.[110] However, proponents of a long co-regency between Amenhotep III and Amenhotep IV (Akhenaten) continue to suggest that the former might be the prince's father.

Even more controversial is a probable elder son, whose very existence as a male is a matter for debate. Towards the end of his reign, Akhenaten was associated with one or more co-rulers, the confusion deriving from the fact that the principal names involved can be interpreted as belonging either to a single individual who changed their name at least once, or to two separate people. Furthermore, the gender of those involved is also unclear, options ranging from a single male, a single female, or one of each (the females put forward include the former Nefertiti, Meryetaten and Kiya). The latest evidence seems to point to a male, **Smenkhkare**, succeeded by a woman, **Neferneferuaten**, probably the former Princess Meryetaten.[111] Smenkhkare was most probably a son of Akhenaten, since it is otherwise difficult to explain how he could have stood ahead of Tutankh(u)aten in the succession.[112] No positive evidence exists for the maternity of either of these male children, whether a mother was Nefertiti or some other wife such as Kiya, unless Meketaten's death scene does indeed show Tutankh(u)aten; Smenkhkare is ruled out by age.[113]

Smenkhkare is shown alongside Meryetaten at least twice, the latter also bearing the title of King's Great Wife, apparently guaranteeing their

(above) The young Tutankhaten shown on the lap of his nurse, Maya, in her tomb-chapel at Saqqara. The face of the young king has miraculously survived the destruction of the wall directly to the right of it.

On the rear wall of Tutankhamun's burial chamber in KV62, the far right scene shows Ay carrying out the Opening of the Mouth ceremony on Tutankhamun's mummy. By doing so, he was staking a claim to be the king's legal son and heir.

Outer coffins of the still-born children of Tutankhamun; from KV62 (CM JE60692/ 60695).

marriage. On this basis, might Meryetaten-tasherit be their daughter? The union between Ankhesenpaaten and **Tutankhaten/amun** is demonstrated by numerous texts and depictions, while a pair of embalmed foetuses found in the tomb of Tutankhamun would seem to show that Ankhesenpaaten (later Ankhesenamun) had at least two abortive pregnancies.[114] With these two tiny corpses, the line of the 18th Dynasty seems to have come to an end.

The origins of General **Ay**, who ultimately obtained the throne, remain uncertain – we have already noted the various speculations as to his affiliations. That he had a son in the form of Nakhtmin is suggested by a statue of the latter giving him the title of King's Son. The statue is broken after the signs for 'King's Son of', and there has been considerable debate as to whether it continued to say 'Kush', making Nakhtmin a Viceroy of Nubia, or 'of his body', making him an actual royal son. Since there is no other evidence for Nakhtmin as a Viceroy – with another man attested in office at this period as well – the latter suggestion seems the more likely. As Nakhtmin donated items to the burial of Tutankhamun without such a title, it follows that he only became a King's Son subsequently, presumably under Ay. This theory is supported by the evidence of intentional damage to Nakhtmin's statue, since Ay was amongst the Amarna pharaohs whose memories were execrated under later rulers.

Nakhtmin's mother will presumably have been Tey, although the putative earlier wife of Ay would also be a possibility. Tey is shown with Ay on numerous monuments, both private and royal. She is presumably the queen whose

(above and right) The principal fragments of the statue of Prince Nakhtmin B and his wife (CM CG779A and B).

estate is mentioned on the statue of Ay B, and also the King's Wife whose sister was this man's mother, given that the statue also bears the cartouche of King Ay.[115] It appears that Ay may also have married Tutankhamun's widow, Ankhesenamun (since a ring bears both their cartouches), but no other monuments show her as royal consort, a role taken exclusively by Tey.

Nakhtmin seems to have predeceased his father, since Ay's successor was one **Horemheb**, of obscure ancestry. His coronation inscription cites 'Horus of Hnes', suggesting that he may have come from Hnes, modern Kom el-Ahmar Sawaris, south of the Fayoum.[116] A restoration inscription in the Upper Colonnade of the temple of Hatshepsut at Deir el-Bahari that calls Thutmose III the 'father of his fathers' might imply collateral royal descent, although it may simply reflect the fiction of the unbroken descent of the institution of kingship itself.

Material from Horemheb's original tomb at Saqqara shows that his first wife, apparently dead before his accession, was called Amenia. His second wife and queen was Mutnodjmet Q, shown with him on his Coronation Statue in Turin. She is without any direct indication of ancestry, although is often equated with Mutnodjmet A, sister of Nefertiti. This cannot be proven, however, and if the latter two ladies were indeed daughters of Ay, Mutnodjmet Q's lack of the title of King's Daughter would seem curious. On the other hand, there seems to have been at best little posthumous regard for Ay, and this might have led to his putative daughter's failure to use a title linking her to him.

No living children of Horemheb are known; but the possible skeleton of Mutnodjmet was that of a woman who had given birth on a number of occasions, and was buried with a still-born (if not unborn) baby. It thus seems that no fewer than three lines came to an end during the last phase of the 18th Dynasty; Horemheb's heir was thus yet another General, Paramessu, the founder of the 19th Dynasty.

(right) Mutnodjmet Q, perhaps the younger sister of Nefertiti, sits alongside her husband, Horemheb, on his 'Coronation Statue' from Karnak (Turin Cat. 1379). She is also shown on the side of her throne as a winged sphinx, recalling some of the images of Tiye A under Amenhotep III (eg. p. 157).
The inscription on the rear tells the story, unfortunately in very flowery language, of how Horemheb rose to the highest levels of the Egyptian administration, and then beyond to the very kingship itself. There are various allusions to events we would dearly love to know more about, especially regarding the time when 'the Palace fell into rage, and [Horemheb] opened his mouth and answered the king (Tutankhamun? Or even Akhenaten?) and appeased him with the utterance of his mouth.'

Brief Lives ●

*Males in **bold**, females in **bold italic**.*

Amenhotep E (KSon)
Son of Amenhotep III; his estate is mentioned on a wine-jar seal from Malqata, and he later became king as **AMENHOTEP IV/AKHENATEN**.

Jar-sealing from Malqata naming an estate of Amenhotep E – the future Akhenaten.

Amenia (ChA)
Wife of Horemheb; named on a column in his Saqqara tomb, and possibly buried in the upper suite in shaft IV, perhaps dated to the reign of Ay.

Anen (2PA)
Brother of Tiye A; left office some time during the final decade of Amenhotep III's reign when he was replaced by Simut, previously Fourth Prophet. Owner of tomb TT120 on Sheikh Abd el-Qurna, where his figure has been mutilated, a *shabti* in The Hague and a statue in Turin.

Ankhesenpaaten (KDB; KGW; L2L)
Third daughter of Akhenaten and Nefertiti

Face of a statue of the goddess Mut, with features probably belonging to Queen Ankhesenamun; from Luxor temple, statue cache (Luxor Museum).

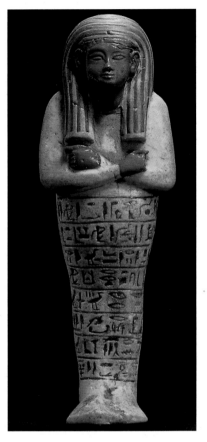

Shabti figure of Ay A, of unknown provenance (private collection).

and wife of Tutankhamun, later known as **Ankhesenamun**. Known as a princess from numerous depictions from Amarna and others at Karnak; as queen, she is depicted or mentioned on various items from her husband's tomb, in his 'resthouse' at Giza, scenes in the colonnade of the temple of Luxor, on a lintel in Berlin and a number of faience items. Amongst these last items is a ring in Berlin that joins her cartouche with that of King Ay, perhaps indicating a brief marriage.

Ankhesenpaaten-tasherit
Perhaps a daughter of Akhenaten and Kiya, or Smenkhkare and Meryetaten; named on blocks from Hermopolis, originally deriving from Amarna.

Ay A (GF; MoH; Viz?)
Possibly father of Nefertiti and perhaps son of Yuya; owner of tomb TA25 at Amarna and **later king**. He may have become Vizier under Tutankhamun, if a fragment of gold leaf from KV58 refers to him.

Ay B (2PA; 1PMut; Steward of Queen Tiye A/Tey)
Probably a nephew of Ay; depicted by a block statue in the Brooklyn Museum, probably from Dahamsha.

Beketaten (KDB)
Youngest daughter of Amenhotep III and Tiye A; depicted with her mother (and once near her father) in the tomb of Huya at Amarna (TA1). A statue of the princess is shown being painted in another scene in the tomb.

Gilukhipa
Wife of Amenhotep III and daughter of Shuttarna II of Mitanni. A series of scarabs record that she arrived in Egypt with a retinue of 317 women in year 10 of her husband's reign.

Henuttaneb A (KD)
Daughter of Amenhotep III and Tiye A; shown with her parents and sister, Iset C, in the temple at Soleb, on a carnelian plaque (Metropolitan Museum of Art) and on a colossus from Medinet Habu (Cairo). Mentioned on a stela from Malqata and owner of faience fragments, two once in private collections and one from Gurob.

Horemheb B (Exec; Gen)
Army officer who may have been designated heir to Ay, and **later king**. Possibly began his career as Paatenemheb (Amarna tomb TA24), but certainly originally from the Herakleopolitan area. Acted as Deputy under Tutankhamun, when he also led military expeditions and built a tomb at Saqqara.

Iset C (KD; KW)
Daughter of Amenhotep III and Tiye A;

Statue of Horemheb B in the pose of a scribe (MMA 23.10.1).

shown as her father's wife on a statue in the G. Ortiz Collection, and as a simple princess at Soleb and on a carnelian plaque (Metropolitan Museum of Art). Also probably hers are a box from Gurob and a pair of kohl-tubes, all now in Cairo.

Kiya (GBW)
Wife of Akhenaten, and conceivably the former Tadukhipa – the daughter of Tushratta, king of Mitanni. Kiya is named and depicted on various blocks originating at Amarna, on vases in London and New York, four fragmentary kohl-tubes in Berlin and London, and a wine-jar docket. She may also be depicted by three uninscribed sculptor's studies. Her coffin and canopic jars were taken over for the burial of a king (probably Smenkhkare), which was ultimately discovered in tomb KV55 in the Valley of the Kings. Almost all of Kiya's monuments were usurped for daughters of Akhenaten, making it fairly certain that she was disgraced some time after year 11, although one researcher has suggested that she actually became king as Smenkhkare.

Meketaten (KDB)
Second daughter of Akhenaten and Nefertiti; known from a large number of

reliefs from or at Amarna and Karnak, and a writing palette in New York. Her death (interpreted by some as in childbirth) and mourning are shown in chamber 'gamma' of the Royal Tomb at Amarna.

Meryetaten (KDB; KGW)
Eldest daughter of Akhenaten and Nefertiti; wife of Smenkhkare. Known as a princess from a large number of reliefs from or at Amarna and Karnak, together with others usurped from Kiya, and a writing pallet found in Tutankhamun's tomb (KV62). As a queen, she is shown with her husband in tomb TA2 at Amarna (belonging to a nobleman called Meryre ii), and named alongside Smenkhkare on a block from Memphis (lost) and a box from tomb KV62. She may have become female king **NEFERNEFERUATEN** towards the end of her father's reign.

Meryetaten-tasherit
Perhaps a daughter of Akhenaten and Kiya, or Smenkhkare and Meryetaten; named on blocks from Hermopolis, originally from Amarna.

Mutemnub
Mother of Ay B, and probably sister of Tey; named on the statue of her son.

Mutnodjmet[117] A (Sister of KGW)
Sister of Nefertiti; depicted adjacent to Nefertiti's daughters, and attended by two dwarfs in the tombs of Ay, Panehsy, Parennefer, Tutu, and May at Amarna

Relief of a royal couple, generally identified as Smenkhkare and Meryetaten; said to have been found in a house at Amarna (Berlin 15000).

(tombs TA25, 6, 7, 8 and 14); perhaps identical with Mutnodjmet Q.

Mutnodjmet Q (KGW; MULE; L2L)
Wife of Horemheb, and possibly identical with Mutnodjmet A. She appears with her husband on the Coronation Statue in Turin, in the tomb of Roy (TT255), and was the usurper of a number of inscriptions of Ankhesenamun at Luxor temple. A statue and other items of hers were found in the substructure of the tomb of Horemheb at Saqqara, suggesting that she may have been buried there. Human remains found near the lower burial chamber of shaft IV may thus be hers, accompanied by the bones of a foetus or newborn child. If so, Mutnodjmet may have been in her mid-40s at death, having lost all her teeth early in life; this burial may be dated soon after year 13 by a wine-jar docket found in the burial chamber. A canopic jar of the queen is in the British Museum.

Nakhtmin A
Father of Ay B; named on the statue of his son.

Nakhtmin B (Genmo; KSon; Exec)
Probable son of Ay; represented on one, and possibly another, statue in Cairo. He donated five *shabti*s to the burial of Tutankhamun.

Nebetiah (KD)
Daughter of Amenhotep III, shown on a colossal statue from Medinet Habu (Cairo).

Neferneferuaten-tasherit (KDB)
Fourth daughter of Akhenaten and Nefertiti; known from reliefs from or at Amarna. It is possible that she may be the now-anonymous person buried in chamber 'alpha' in the royal tomb.

Neferneferure (KDB)
Fifth daughter of Akhenaten and Nefertiti; known from a large number of reliefs from or at Amarna, a seal-impression from the Royal Wadi there, and a box-lid from the tomb of Tutankhamun. It is possible that she may

(above) Painting of princesses Neferneferuaten-tasherit and Neferneferure; from a palace at Amarna (Ashmolean 1893.1).

be the now-anonymous person buried in chamber 'alpha' in the royal tomb.

Nefertiti (KGW; L2L)
Wife of Akhenaten; known from year 5 onwards as **Neferneferuaten-Nefertiti**. Represented in many reliefs from Amarna and Karnak alongside her husband and daughters, and by large numbers of statues and statuettes, including the famous bust in Berlin. She appears to have married her husband soon after he came to the throne and is constantly at his side until around year 13, when she disappears from view. It has been suggested that she then became king as first Neferneferuaten, and later as Smenkhkare, but it seems more likely that she had died. There is no evidence to substantiate the assertion that her disappearance was the result of disgrace – the alleged data in fact refers to Kiya (see p. 148). *Shabti*-fragments of Nefertiti are in the Louvre and Brooklyn. Attempts to

(right) Unfinished quartzite head intended to form part of a composite statue of Nefertiti; from Amarna (CM JE59286).

identify Nefertiti's mummy as one of two bodies in KV35 (Amenhotep II's tomb) are not based on any compelling evidence.

Setpenre A (KDB)
Sixth daughter of Akhenaten and Nefertiti; known from a number of reliefs from or at Amarna. It is possible that she may be the now-anonymous person buried in chamber 'alpha' in the royal tomb.

Shuttarna II (King of Mitanni)
Father-in-law of Amenhotep III.

Sitamun B (KGD; KW; KGW)
Wife and probable daughter of
Amenhotep III; shown as a princess on
the stela of her nurse, Nebetkabeny, from
Abydos and on a chair from the tomb of
Yuya and Tjuiu (all now in Cairo). The
pedestal of a statue of the senior nobleman
Amenhotep-son-of- Hapu, from Karnak
(Cairo), names her as a King's Wife,
showing that she attained the rank before
the former died between years 30 and 34.
She is named as Great Wife on a kohl-tube
and a disc now in Oxford.

Tadukhipa
Wife of Amenhotep III and later of
Akhenaten; daughter of Tushratta, king
of Mitanni, whose arrival is mentioned
in Amarna Letter 17. It is possible that
she was the same person as **Kiya**.

Tey (Nurse of KGW; KGW)
Wife of Ay A and 'nurse' (= stepmother?)
of Nefertiti; shown with her husband in
his tomb at Amarna and later became his
queen. As such, she is depicted with Ay in
his royal tomb in the Valley of the Kings
(WV23) and in the rock-chapel of Min at
Akhmim. If she were the mother of
Nakhtmin B, she will also have held the
title of Adorer of Min.

Thutmose B (EKSon; HPM; SPP; OPULE)
Eldest son of Amenhotep III, and
conceivably identical with Thutmose Q
(p. 141); known in particular from material
from the burial of Apis I at the Serapeum
at Saqqara, carried out while he was only
Sem-Priest at Memphis. A small figure of
the prince as a miller is in the Louvre,
while a recumbent mummiform figure is
in Berlin; the coffin of a cat, dedicated by
him, is in Cairo. The prince seems to have
died some time during the third decade of
his father's reign.

Tiye A (KGW; MULE; M2L; L2L; KM)
Wife of Amenhotep III, her union with
whom was commemorated by the series
of marriage scarabs; mother of Akhenaten.
Known from a wide variety of sources,
including temple reliefs at Soleb and
Sedeinga. Sculptures of her together

(above, top) Relief of Tiye A; from the tomb
of Userhat (TT47; Brussels E2157).

(above) Bracelet plaque of Queen Tiye as a
winged sphinx holding Amenhotep III's
cartouche (MMA 26.7.1342).

with her husband include a colossus
from Medinet Habu, and the Colossi
of Memnon. Individual heads from
particularly fine statuettes of Tiye are in
Cairo (from Sinai) and Berlin (Gurob),
with small objects in various collections.
Tiye is also depicted in the tombs of
Userhat (TT47), Kheruef (TT192) and
Huya (TA1), the last suggesting that she
may have resided at Amarna later in her
son's reign. *Shabtis* of hers were found
in Amenhotep III's tomb, but a broken
sarcophagus made for her was found in
the Royal Tomb at Amarna, and a gilded
funerary shrine (showing her with
Akhenaten) ultimately found its way to
tomb KV55 in the Valley of the Kings.
A lock of Tiye's hair was found in a nest
of miniature coffins in the tomb of
Tutankhamun; it seems very unlikely that
her mummy could be the so-called 'Elder
Lady' in the tomb of Amenhotep II.[118]

Tjuiu (KM of KGW)
Mother of Tiye A; buried with her

(right) Block
from
Hermopolis
giving the
name and
titles of Prince
Tutankhuaten.

husband in Valley of the Kings tomb
KV46, with her mummy and funerary
equipment now in the Cairo Museum.

Tushratta (King of Mitanni)
Possible father-in-law of Akhenaten.

Tutankhuaten (KSonB)
Probable son of Akhenaten, later king
as **TUTANKHATEN/AMUN**. Named on
a block from Hermopolis, and possibly
shown as a baby in his nurse's arms in
chambers 'alpha' and 'gamma' in the royal
tomb at Amarna.

Yuya (GF; MoH)
Father of Tiye A; buried with his wife in
tomb KV46, with his mummy and funerary
equipment now in the Cairo Museum.

[...]18A–H
Daughters of Amenhotep III, shown in
the tomb of Kheruef (TT192; see p. 30);
some may be identical with named
daughters.

[...]18J
Son of Anen; depicted with his siblings
in tomb TT120.

[...]18K–N
Daughters of Anen; depicted with their
siblings in tomb TT120.

–18P
Unnamed, still-born daughter of
Tutankhamun and Ankhesenamun,
found in her father's tomb and now in
Cairo.

–18Q
Unnamed, still-born daughter of
Tutankhamun and Ankhesenamun, found
in her father's tomb and now in Cairo.

The House of Ramesses

19th Dynasty part 1

The founder of the 19th Dynasty, Ramesses I, in the guise of Paramessu, Vizier of Horemheb; from Karnak (CM JE44861).

Historical Background

The dynastic founder, General Paramessu, had been Horemheb's military colleague, Deputy and Executive, and may have served for a short period as Horemheb's co-regent. As Ramesses I, he served but briefly as sole king – his son, Sety I, leading an expedition to Palestine during the last months of his father's reign. Already an old man, Ramesses' death occurred less than two years after his appearance on the throne of the Two Lands.

The first year of the reign of Sety I saw a major campaign into Palestine. The territory up to the area of Tyre seems then to have been pacified, before the king returned to the fortress of Sile in the north-east Delta. Further campaigns in the immediately succeeding seasons pushed up deeper into Palestine and southern Syria, while in year 8 military intervention became necessary in Nubia. A considerable building programme was initiated by Sety I, adorned with some of the most outstanding examples of Egyptian art. However, many buildings were left unfinished on the king's death after a reign of only a dozen years.

His successor, Ramesses II, continued the building work, expanding it on a massive scale during his 67 years on the throne. This included buildings throughout Egypt and Nubia, and a new northern capital, Piramesse ('The House of Ramesses'), on part of the site of the old Hyksos stronghold of Avaris.

The fourth regnal year marked the beginning of Ramesses' independent campaigning into the Levant, the next year seeing the famous Battle of Qadesh against the Hittites. This proved a tactical defeat for the Egytians, although strategically the status quo remained unaffected. Further military action followed in subsequent years, but in the face of resurgent Assyria, a formal peace treaty was agreed between the two powers in year 21. This agreement was marked by correspondence between Ramesses II and the Hittite king, Hattusilis III – and also between their wives, Pudukhepa and Nefertiry – together with the exchange of presents that formed the underpinning of much ancient diplomacy. In year 34, the alliance was firmly cemented by Ramesses' marriage to a daughter of the Hittite king.

A series of sons held the title of Crown Prince, the last – Merenptah – effectively acting as regent for his father in the latter's declining years. A motif of Ramesses II's

(above) Detail of Sety I offering Osiris a small statue of himself. Part of the West Wall of a chapel built by Sety I for his father Ramesses I at Abydos (MMA 11.155.3).

(right) Colossal statue of Ramesses II, the so-called 'Young Memnon', from his mortuary temple. The hole in the shoulder was drilled during an abortive French attempt to remove the piece. It was ultimately removed by Giovanni Belzoni, working for the British Consul General, Henry Salt, in 1816 (BM EA19).

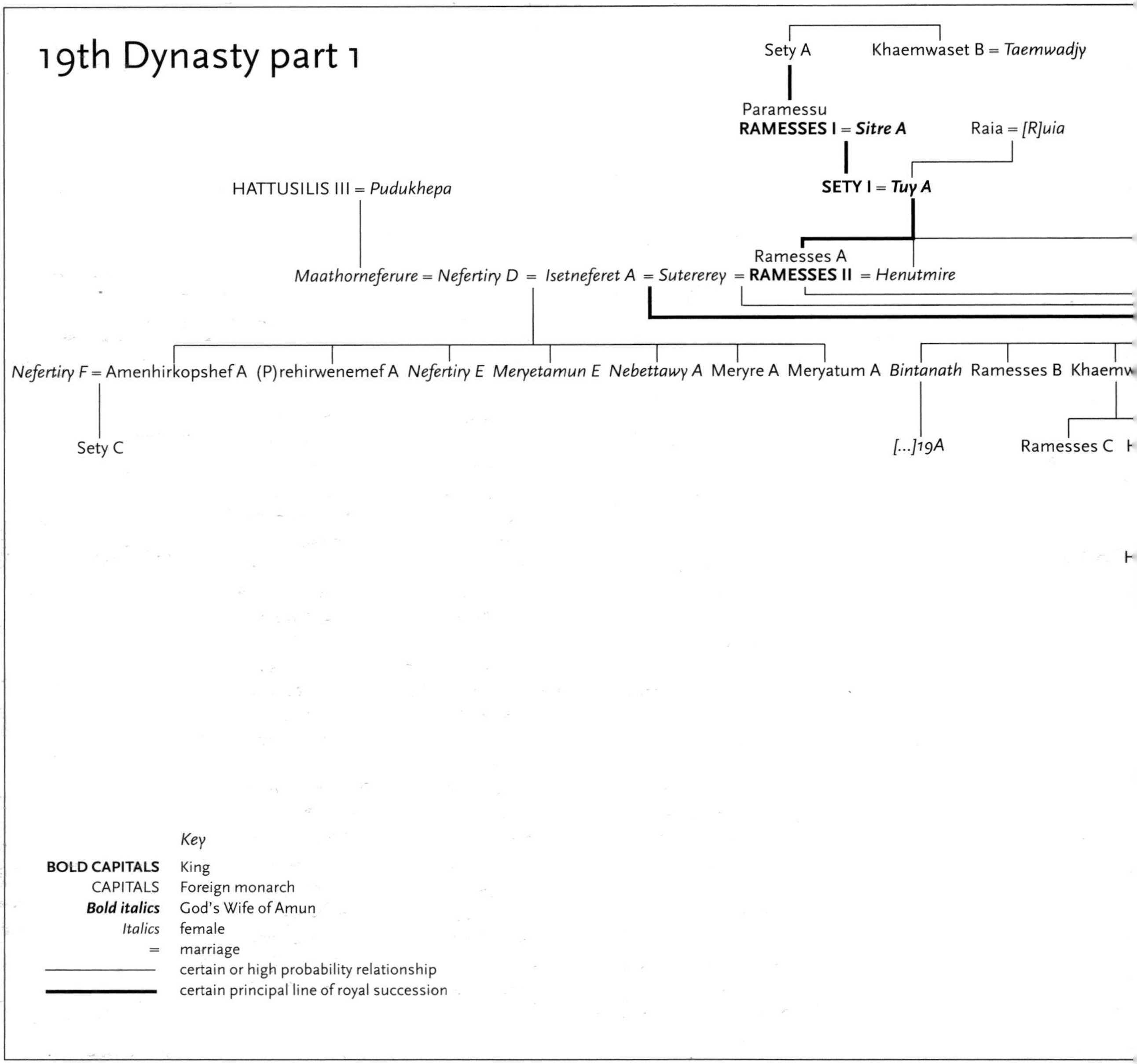

19th Dynasty part 1

Sety A   Khaemwaset B = *Taemwadjy*

Paramessu
RAMESSES I = *Sitre A*   Raia = *[R]uia*

HATTUSILIS III = *Pudukhepa*   **SETY I** = *Tuy A*

Ramesses A

Maathorneferure = *Nefertiry D* = *Isetneferet A* = *Sutererey* = **RAMESSES II** = *Henutmire*

Nefertiry F = Amenhirkopshef A   (P)rehirwenemef A   *Nefertiry E*   *Meryetamun E*   *Nebettawy A*   Meryre A   Meryatum A   *Bintanath*   Ramesses B   Khaemw

Sety C   *[...]19A*   Ramesses C   H

H

Key

BOLD CAPITALS	King
CAPITALS	Foreign monarch
Bold italics	God's Wife of Amun
Italics	female
=	marriage
————	certain or high probability relationship
——	certain principal line of royal succession

reign is a further increase in the profile of the royal family, the High Priesthoods at both Memphis and Heliopolis being held by princes, and
processions of the king's children featuring in temples.

The Royal Family

The origins of the 19th Dynasty seem to have been wholly non-royal.
Ramesses I is usually equated with the Vizier Paramessu, whose titles make
it quite clear that he was the designated successor of Horemheb. Paramessu
may have begun his career as a stable-master, advancing later to the positions

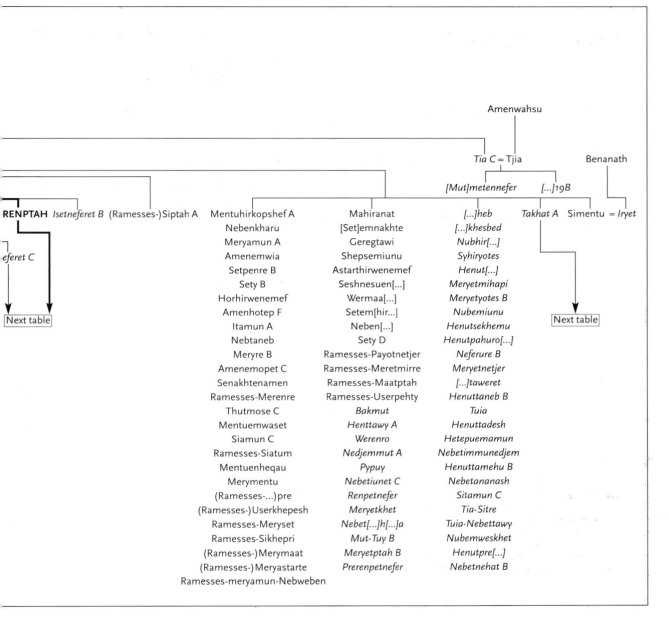

of Master of Horse, Troop Commander, King's Envoy, Generalissimo and finally Vizier. It has been suggested that he may be an unnamed army officer depicted in the tomb of Horemheb at Saqqara.

Paramessu's father, Sety A, is mentioned on statues of the Vizier; relatives of Paramessu are named on a stela and a statue belonging to him. There remains some debate as to the wife of Ramesses I.[119] Sitre A is generally assumed to be his wife (and the mother of Sety I) on the basis of her being shown with Sety I and Ramesses in Sety I's temple of Abydos, bearing the title King's Great Wife; on the other hand she bears the same title in Sety I's

(above) The so-called Year 400 Stela, from Tanis. The scene at the top shows Set being worshipped by Ramesses II and a man who is described as one Sety, son of Paramessu and Tia (Q); he is exceptionally shown with the royal/divine bull's tail. The most generally accepted interpretation of the stela is that it refers to the commemoration of a 400th anniversary relating to the god Set, which had been carried out by Ramesses II's father, Sety I, while he was still a commoner, under Horemheb. Such was the significance of this act that when the stela was carved, some four decades after Sety's death, he was depicted as he had been perhaps 60 years before, with only the bull's tail to show his later royal status (CM).

(opposite) Sety I and his son Ramesses A, as shown on the stela of Miya; from Abydos (Brussels E5300).

(right) [R]uia and Raia, the parents of Queen Tuy, as depicted on a block at Medinet Habu.

tomb, rather than the expected King's Mother – a title borne, however, by the King's Mother Sitre who owned tomb QV38 in the Valley of the Queens.

In addition, the 'Year 400 Stela' from Tanis seems to indicate that Sety's mother was actually named Tia (Q). This stela was carved under Ramesses II, apparently to commemorate a celebration of the god Set by the Vizier Sety, son of the Vizier Paramessu, who seem to be none other than Sety I and Ramesses I, seen back in the reign of Horemheb. On the other hand, tomb QV38 seems to be datable stylistically to no later than the early 19th Dynasty, leaving perhaps the best suggestion one that makes Sitre an additional name taken by Tia Q when she became queen. In this connection, it may be significant that a daughter of Ramesses II had the compound name, Tia-Sitre.

Nevertheless, **Sety I** is clearly stated to be Ramesses I's son on a number of monuments. Likewise well attested is Sety's wife, Tuy; her parents are known from a block at Medinet Habu, dating to Ramesses II's reign. Here, one Raia is called the father of the king's mother, and his wife ([R]uia) the king's

grandmother. The family of Sety I are little known; apart from his heir, Ramesses A (Ramesses II), a daughter, Tia C, is only attested on monuments of her brother's reign (two daughters of hers are shown in her tomb). An elder son of Sety I, identified by early Egyptologists on the basis of an erased figure in Sety I's reliefs at Karnak, has turned out to be a phantom, actually being a simple army officer. A further possible daughter is Henutmire; she is shown on a statue of Tuy in the Vatican, and the assumption has generally been that she must have been Tuy's daughter. However, on the basis of the fact that she is not called King's Sister, it has been argued that she was actually one of the younger daughters of Ramesses II,[120] in spite of the fact that this would make it difficult to see why she would have been so closely linked with Tuy, a lady possibly dead before she was born. Thus it remains more probable that Henutmire was a sister, rather than daughter, of Ramesses II.

The key documents for the study of the children of **Ramesses II** are the series of processions of royal offspring that are to be found in a number of the king's temples. Such depictions reversed the earlier practice of keeping royal children – particularly boys – in the background, except where they held substantive state offices (e.g. the various Sem-Priests of Ptah during the latter part of the 18th Dynasty). The motivation behind this probably lies in the plebeian origins of the new Ramesside royal house. The royal line of the 18th Dynasty, which probably traced its origins back into the late Middle Kingdom, had come to an abrupt end with Tutankhamun, and had been

Daughters of Ramesses II, as depicted in the Great Temple at Abu Simbel; from the right, Bintanath; Bakmut; Nefertiry E; Meryetamun E; Nebettawy; Isetneferet B; Henttawy A; and Werenro.

followed by a series of generals who quite clearly had little or no royal blood in their veins. It was probably against this background that a desire to build up a full-scale 'royal family' to back up the parvenu pharaohs of the new dynasty came about. In addition, the increased status of the royal family under Akhenaten[121] may also have played a part – ironically, in that the Ramesside Period saw the definitive demolition of so many of the heretic king's monuments.

Processions of princes and princesses, in no particular historical context, are to be found in the Ramesseum, and in the temples of Abu Simbel, Derr, Luxor, Wadi el-Sebua and Abydos (Sety I temple). Blocks now incorporated into a 29th Dynasty extension to the 18th Dynasty temple at Medinet Habu show parts of another procession, originally in the Ramesseum, and showing princes not otherwise known; yet more are listed on an *ostrakon* (stone fragment) of unknown provenance in Cairo. Other more specific groupings of royal children include one on the outer wall of the great Hypostyle Hall at Karnak of the triumph following the Battle of Qadesh, and the war scenes in the temple of Beit el-Wali and at the Ramesseum (siege of Dapur). At least one name – Meryre – appears twice in the processions; this is clearly the result of the elder prince of the name dying and being 'replaced' by the next-born son (such an instance is also seen later, under Ramesses III). All the processions are more or less damaged, and often a sequence can only be reconstructed by combining a number of separate processions – not all of

One of the many lists of sons of the king is to be found in the Ramesseum; here we see, from the right, Amenhirkopshef A, Ramesses B, Prehirwenemef A and Khaemwaset C.

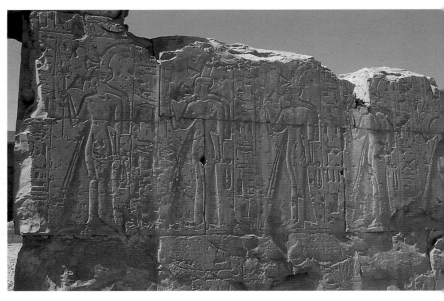

(above) Detail of one of the Abydos processions, showing a princess shaking a systrum.

(above, right) Daughters of Ramesses II, as shown in a procession in the Sety I temple at Abydos; from the left: Meryetmihapi; Meryetyotes B; Nubemiunu; Henutsekhemu; Henutpahuro[...].

which are wholly consistent with one another, and some of which are much shorter than others. Amongst the princes missing from the processions, either through damage or as a result of their having been born after the latest surviving list was carved (at Wadi el-Sebua, dating to the late 30s/40s of the reign) are Ramesses-Maatptah, known from a private letter, and Ramesses-meryamun-Nebweben, attested by his burial at Gurob.

Similar problems exist with the daughter-processions, which tend to follow the figures of their brothers and, like their younger brethren, suffer from the damage found at the farthest end of the processions. Some of these apparently missing ladies seem, however, to be listed on an *ostrakon*, which originally gave fifteen names (two of which are now lost). Taken together, the evidence seems to indicate that Ramesses II had around 100 children – 48 to 50 sons and 40 to 53 daughters – rather than the 170 claimed by some early Egyptologists due to the double-counting of some of the evidence, especially aspects of the Wadi el-Sebua processions.

(right) Plan of KV5 in the Valley of the Kings, the tomb of a number of the sons of Ramesses II. In spite of the large number of chambers, only five names of occupants had been recovered by 2004.

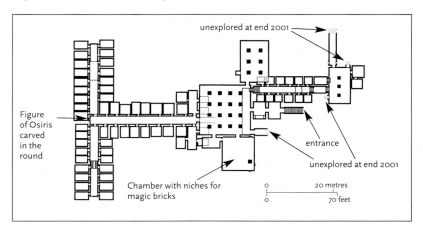

unexplored at end 2001

Figure of Osiris carved in the round

entrance

unexplored at end 2001

Chamber with niches for magic bricks

0   20 metres
0   70 feet

It is clear that such a large brood of children, of whom at least half seem to have been born during the first three decades of the reign of Ramesses II, must have been born of more than one mother. During the first part of his tenure of the throne, two contemporary King's Great Wives are known. By far the best attested is Nefertiry (D) Meryetmut, made famous by her wonderful tomb in the Valley of the Queens. Nothing is known for sure about her background, except for an oblique hint from amongst her funerary equipment: a faience knob, bearing the cartouche of King Ay. Given his lack of posthumous regard, the presence of such an item is suggestive. Also suggestive is the unusual pink complexion given to Nefertiry in her tomb, perhaps best paralleled by the Berlin bust of Nefertiti, who has also been mooted as a relation of Ay (see above, p. 146). However, definitive evidence is wholly lacking.

It is possible to identify a number of Nefertiry's offspring, particularly from the façade of the small temple at Abu Simbel, dedicated to both Hathor and the queen. Here are to be found statues of Ramesses II and Nefertiry, along with a number of royal children who are clearly their joint offspring: Amenhirkopshef (A), (P)rehirwenemef (A), Meryetamun (E), Nebettawy,

The façade of the Great Temple at Abu Simbel.

In contrast to Nefertiry D, Isetneferet A is seen little on the monuments. However, in the rock-temple at Gebel el-Silsila are a number of stelae, carved by her sons and including a depiction of her and her offspring. This one shows Ramesses II worshipping Ptah, with Isetneferet and Bintanath behind him, and Ramesses B and Merenptah A below; the small figure in front of the king is almost certainly Khaemwaset, completing this family group, and probably the one responsible for the stela.

Meryre (A) and Meryatum (A). Additionally, it is likely that Nefertiry E will have been named for the lady who was her mother. An old suggestion that Sety B was also Nefertiry D's son was based on the misreading of an *ostrakon*, actually naming Sety C, son of Amen/Sethirkopshef A.

The second Great Wife of Ramesses II, Isetneferet A, is also lacking any data on her ancestry; as to her children, we have two basic sources of information. First, there is the rock-temple at Gebel el-Silsila, where a stela shows Ramesses II and Isetneferet with four of their children: Ramesses, Khaemwaset, Merenptah and Bintanath. Second, a similar list of offspring is

Detail of a battle scene in the temple of Beit el-Wali, showing the young Prince Khaemwaset (C) in his chariot (plaster cast in BM).

Hori A, High Priest of Ptah, and apparently a son of Prince Khaemwaset C, as shown on three faces of a pillar from his tomb at Saqqara. Interestingly, his father's titles, as preserved, do not include King's Son; however, by this time, Ramesses II was long dead, and Khaemwaset was doubtless now remembered as High Priest par excellence. It may also reflect a practice whereby, once a king was dead, filiation from him no longer counted (CM JE4327).

given in a rock-stela on the Aswan–Shellal road, this stela making it clear that Bintanath was older than Khaemwaset. Ramesses B is also shown as Khaemwaset's elder, something already implied by the prince-processions. No other definite maternity information is known, although one would suspect that Isetneferet B was the offspring of Isetneferet A.

Around the end of their mothers' lives, Meryetamun E and Bintanath also became Great Wives, as is indicated by numerous monuments; later still, Nebettawy also took the title. Whether this involved a sexual relationship with their father, or merely represented their assumption of Nefertiry and Isetneferet's ritual roles, remains uncertain. However, Bintanath may have borne an unnamed daughter at some point during her career, since an adult King's Daughter of his Body is depicted with Bintanath in her tomb. On the other hand, royal grandchildren are sometimes given this title, so the matter remains unresolved. Clearly, Ramesses II will have had many other wives and sexual partners as mothers of further offspring, but only Sutererey is known from a relief of her son, Ramesses-Siptah (A).[122]

As usual, little information is available on grandchildren of the king outside the direct line of succession. However, a number of Khaemwaset C's children are known:[123] Ramesses C is shown on the back pillar of a statue of his father; another son has been identified as Hori A, son of a High Priest Khaemwaset, although the latter is not called King's Son on the monuments in question. If this equation is correct, Hori followed his father into the Ptah priesthood. A daughter named Isetneferet (C), after her grandmother, is known from a figure of Khaemwaset C from Medinet Maadi. Khaemwaset's brother, **Merenptah**, had a wife named Isetneferet (as is shown by a stela in the Gebel el-Silsila rock-temple) who is not, however, called a King's Daughter. This title would be expected if, as early writers believed, she were Merenptah's sister, Isetneferet B. While no definitive evidence exists, an alliance between Merenptah and his niece, daughter of his powerful elder brother, seems not improbable.

Brief Lives ●

Males in **bold**, *females in* ***bold italic**.*

Amenemopet C (KSonB)
Son of Ramesses II and number 19 in the
processions of sons.

Amenemwia/Setemwia (KSonB)
Son of Ramesses II and number 8 in the
processions of sons; changed his name –
perhaps at the same time as
Amen/Sethirkopshef A. Present at the
siege of the Syrian city of Dapur in year 10.

Amenhirwenemef/Amenhirkopshef A
 (1KSonB; EKSonB; Genmo)
Eldest Son of Ramesses II and Nefertiry D,
and number 1 in the processions of sons;
changed his name early in the reign. First
heir to the throne, he took part in his
father's early campaigns, appearing on the
wall of the temple of Beit el-Wali along
with Khaemwaset C, and in the triumph
that followed the Battle of Qadesh.
Depicted with his father lassoing a bull in
the Sety I temple at Abydos, and
frequently on Ramesses II's statues, but
seems to have changed his name once
again around year 20 to **Sethirkopshef (A)**.
Involved in the exchange of
correspondence following the Hittite

*Crown Prince Amenhirkopshef A helps
Ramesses II in the ritual capture of a bull;
temple of Sety I at Abydos.*

peace treaty in year 21, but died around
year 25. Buried in tomb KV5 in the Valley
of the Kings, his interment being
apparently inspected in year 53 of his
father's reign.

Amenhotep F (KSonB)
Son of Ramesses II and number 14 in the
processions of sons.

Amenwahsu
Father of Tjia; shown with him, Ramesses
II, and Sety B on a block in Chicago.

Astarthirwenemef (KSonB)
Son of Ramesses II; depicted on a block
from the Ramesseum, reused at Medinet
Habu.

Bakmut (KDB)
Daughter of Ramesses II; number 2 in the
processions of daughters.

Benanath
Syrian ship's captain and father-in-law of
Simentu.

Bintanath (KDB; KGW; L2L; MULE)
Eldest daughter of Ramesses II and
Isetneferet A. Served as one of her
father's Great Wives following her
mother's death and was represented on
a number of monuments throughout
Ramesses II's reign. Survived into the
reign of her brother, Merenptah, when

she was depicted on a statue usurped by
him, and buried in tomb QV71 in the
Valley of the Queens.

Geregtawi (KSonB)
Son of Ramesses II; depicted on a block from
the Ramesseum, reused at Medinet Habu.

Hattusilis III (King of Hittites)
Father-in-law of Ramesses II.

Henttawy A (KDB)
Daughter of Ramesses II; number 7 in the
processions of daughters.

Henut[...] (KDB)
Daughter of Ramesses II; number 20 in
the Abydos procession of daughters.

Henutmire (KD; KGW)
Wife of Ramesses II and probably
daughter of Sety I. Depicted on a statue
of Tuy A in the Vatican and statues of
Ramesses II from Abukir and
Hermopolis. Buried in tomb QV75 in the
Valley of the Queens; the trough of her
coffin was later usurped by Harsiese A
for his interment at Medinet Habu.

Henutpahuro[...] (KDB)
Daughter of Ramesses II; number 26 in
the Abydos procession of daughters.

Henutpre[...] (KDB)
Daughter of Ramesses II; number 58 in the
Wadi el-Sebua procession of daughters.

Henutsekhemu (KDB)
Daughter of Ramesses II; number 25 in
the Abydos procession of daughters.

Henuttadesh (KDB)
Daughter of Ramesses II; number 6 on
the Louvre *ostrakon* list.

Henuttamehu B (KDB)
Daughter of Ramesses II; number 9 on
the Louvre *ostrakon* list.

Henuttaneb B (KDB)
Daughter of Ramesses II; number 4 on
the Louvre *ostrakon* list.

Hetepuemamun (KDB)
Daughter of Ramesses II; number 7 on the Louvre *ostrakon* list.

Horhirwenemef (KSonB)
Son of Ramesses II; number 12 in the processions of sons.

Hori A (HPM)
Probably a grandson of Ramesses II and son of Khaemwaset C. Depicted on a pillar from his tomb at Saqqara (Cairo Museum), and a stela from Memphis. His probable sarcophagus and canopic jars are in Berlin and the British Museum/Liège respectively.

Hori B (Viz)
Son of Hori A, shown with him on a stela from Memphis. First northern, and then southern, Vizier.

Iryet
Wife of Simentu and daughter of Benanath, a Syrian ship's captain. Possibly died in year 42 of Ramesses II's reign.

Isetneferet A (KGW; L2L)
Wife of Ramesses II and mother of Merenptah. Seen on a number of mounuments, and appears to have died around year 34. Her tomb has not been identified, but work on it (and that of Meryatum A) is recorded on an *ostrakon* that may imply her burial in the area of the Valley of the Queens. Otherwise, she is commemorated alongside her son, Khaemwaset C, on a number of his monuments, as well as others at Saqqara.

Isetneferet B (KDB)
Daughter of Ramesses II; number 6 in the processions of daughters. A letter from two palace singers to the princess enquiring after her health survives. It is possible that she may have been the wife of Merenptah, rather than Isetneferet C.

Isetneferet C (KGW)
Granddaughter of Ramesses II, daughter of Khaemwaset C and possibly wife of Merenptah (see next section).

Itamun A (KSonB)
Son of Ramesses II and number 15 in the processions of sons.

Khaemwaset B (Fanbearer)
Uncle of Ramesses I, mentioned on a stela of his brother, Sety A. He seems to have been the owner of a statue from Kawa, now in Khartoum.

Khaemwaset C (KSonB; SPP; HPM; ExecH2L)
Son of Ramesses II and Isetneferet A, and number 4 in the processions of sons. By far the best-known son of the king, remembered for centuries after his death, and the hero of a cycle of stories written in Late/Ptolemaic times. Crown Prince during the early 50s of his father's reign, but died soon after year 55 and probably buried at Saqqara, perhaps below his hilltop sanctuary between Abusir and Saqqara.[124]

Maathorneferure (KGW)
Daughter of Hattusilis III of Hatti and wife of Ramesses II from year 34. The marriage is commemorated in a contemporary stela at Abu Simbel, but also remembered in the so-called Bentresh stela of Ptolemaic times. She is represented on a colossus of Ramesses II,

but seems to have retired to Gurob later in the reign.

Mahiranat (KSonB)
Son of Ramesses II; depicted on a block from the Ramesseum, reused at Medinet Habu.

Mentuemwaset (KSonB)
Son of Ramesses II and number 24 in the processions of sons.

Mentuenheqau (KSonB)
Son of Ramesses II and number 28 in the processions of sons.

Mentuhirkopshef A (KSonB; MoH)
Son of Ramesses II and number 5 in the processions of sons. Owner of a statue from Bubastis, and depicted on a stela in Copenhagen. Present at the siege of the Syrian city of Dapur in year 10.

Merenptah A (KSonB; EKSonB; ExecH2L; Genmo)
Son of Ramesses II and Isetneferet A, and number 13 in the processions of sons; heir to the throne and effective regent during the last ten years of Rameses II's reign. Early in the reign he was explicitly called the 'younger brother' of Khaemwaset C, Bintanath and Ramesses B on a rock-

(below) Queen Maathorneferure, daughter of Hattusilis III of Hatti, depicted with her father on a stela at Abu Simbel.

(below) Prince Mentuhirkopshef A offers flowers to the Mnevis bull, an incarnation of Re of Heliopolis (Ny Carlsberg 589).

carving at Aswan, and also appeared with them and their parents on a stela in the rock-temple at Gebel el-Silsila. During the fifth decade of his father's reign he obtained the title of Generalissimo, and finally an heir's titles after year 55. As such, he is known from monuments at Karnak, the Serapeum, Memphis, Tanis (ex-Piramesse) and Athribis. Other monuments, attributed to Merenptah B, may also be his. He later became **king**.

Meryamun A (KSonB)
Also known as **Ramesses-Meryamun**. Son of Ramesses II and number 7 in the processions of sons. Present at the triumph that followed the Battle of Qadesh and at the siege of the Syrian city of Dapur in year 10, and buried in tomb KV5 in the Valley of the Kings, where remains of his canopic jars were found.

Meryatum A (KSonB; HPH)
Son of Ramesses II and Nefertiry D, and number 16 in the processions of sons. Appears to have visited Sinai during the second decade of his father's reign, and been appointed Heliopolitan High Priest in the late 20s; two statues of him are in Berlin, plus a stela in Hildesheim. He served for around twenty years, work on his tomb (and that of Isetneferet A) being recorded on an *ostrakon* that may imply his burial in the area of the Valley of the Queens. On the other hand, a fragment of canopic jar found in tomb KV5 may be his.

Meryetamun E (KDB; KGW; L2L; MULE)
Daughter of Ramesses II and Nefertiry D; number 4 in the processions of daughters. Served as one of her father's Great Wives following her mother's death and appears on a number of monuments; buried in tomb QV68 in the Valley of the Queens.

Meryetkhet (KDB)
Daughter of Ramesses II; number 13 in the Luxor procession of daughters.

Meryetmihapi (KDB)
Daughter of Ramesses II; number 22 in the Abydos procession of daughters.

Meryetamun E from Western Thebes (CM JE31413=CG600).

Meryetnetjer (KDB)
Daughter of Ramesses II; number 32 in the Abydos procession of daughters.

Meryetptah B (KDB)
Daughter of Ramesses II; number 16 in the Luxor procession of daughters.

Meryetyotes B (KDB)
Daughter of Ramesses II; number 23 in the Abydos procession of daughters.

Merymentu (KSon)
Son of Ramesses II; depicted at Wadi el-Sebua and Abydos.

Meryre A (KSonB)
Son of Ramesses II and Nefertiry D; number 11 in the processions of sons.

Meryre B (KSonB)
Son of Ramesses II; number 18 in the processions of sons.

[Mut]metennefer
Daughter of Tjia and Tia C; depicted in their tomb at Saqqara.

Mut-Tuy B (KDB)
Daughter of Ramesses II; number 15 in

the Luxor procession of daughters.

Nebenkharu (KSonB)
Son of Ramesses II; number 6 in the processions of sons.

Neben[...] (KSon)
Son of Ramesses II; named on an *ostrakon* in the Cairo Museum.

Nebet[...]h[...]a (KDB)
Daughter of Ramesses II; number 14 in the Luxor procession of daughters.

Nebetananash (KDB)
Daughter of Ramesses II; number 10 on the Louvre *ostrakon* list.

Nebetimmunedjem (KDB)
Daughter of Ramesses II; number 8 on the Louvre *ostrakon* list.

Nebetiunet C (KDB)
Daughter of Ramesses II; number 11 in the Luxor procession of daughters.

Nebetnehat B (KDB)
Daughter of Ramesses II; number 59 in the Wadi el-Sebua procession of daughters.

Nebettawy A (KDB; KGW; L2L; MULE)
Daughter of Ramesses II and Nefertiry D; number 5 in the processions of daughters. Served as one of her father's Great Wives and buried in tomb QV60 in the Valley of the Queens.

Nebtaneb (KSonB)
Son of Ramesses II and number 17 in the processions of sons.

Nedjemmut A (KDB)
Daughter of Ramesses II; number 9 in the processions of daughters.

Nefertiry D Meryetmut (KGW; L2L; MULE)
Wife of Ramesses II; perhaps a descendant of Ay. Numerous monuments known, including the small temple at Abu Simbel, and others from sites throughout Egypt. Corresponded with her Hittite counterpart, Pudukhepa, in year 21, and attended the inauguration of the

Close-up of painting of Nefertiry D wearing the vulture headdress; from QV66.

Abu Simbel temples in year 24. Appears to have died soon afterwards and buried in tomb QV66 in the Valley of the Queens; her sarcophagus lid and various remains of her funerary equipment are in Turin, along with the knees from her mummy.

Nefertiry E (KDB)
Daughter of Ramesses II; number 3 in the processions of daughters.

Nefertiry F
Wife of Amenhirkopshef (Sethirkopshef A) and mother of Sety C; mentioned on an *ostrakon* in the Louvre; conceivably identical with Nefertiry E.

Neferure B (KDB)
Daughter of Ramesses II; number 31 in the Abydos procession of daughters.

Nubemiunu (KDB)
Daughter of Ramesses II; number 24 in the Abydos procession of daughters.

Nubemweskhet (KDB)
Daughter of Ramesses II; number 15 on the Louvre *ostrakon* list.

Nubhir[...] (KDB)
Daughter of Ramesses II; number 18 in the Abydos procession of daughters.

Pudukhepa
Wife of Hattusilis III; corresponded with Nefertiry D.

Paramessu (Viz; Exec)
Son of Sety A and later king as **RAMESSES I**. Known from two statues from Karnak and his unused stone coffins from Medinet Habu and Gurob.

(P)rehirwenemef A (KSonB; MoH)
Son of Ramesses II and Nefertiry D, and number 3 in the processions of sons. Also depicted at Abu Simbel and in the triumph that followed the Battle of Qadesh.

Prerenpetnefer (KDB)
Daughter of Ramesses II; number 12 in the Luxor procession of daughters.

Pypuy (KDB)
Daughter of Ramesses II; number 10 in the processions of daughters. Perhaps the princess of the name, the daughter of a lady named Iwy, whose mummy was reburied with others during the 21st Dynasty on Sheikh Abd el-Qurna (see pp. 135–37).

Raia (Adjutant of the Chariotry)
Father-in-law of Sety I. Known from a block at Medinet Habu.

Ramesses A (EKSon; Exec)
Eldest son of Sety I, and later king as **RAMESSES II**. Depicted with his father in the latter's Abydos temple.

Ramesses B (KSonB; EKSonB; 1Genmo)
Son of Ramesses II and Isetneferet A, and number 2 in the processions of sons. Heir to the throne from around year 25 to year 50. Attested in various inscriptions and sculptures, including the triumph that followed the Battle of Qadesh. Buried in tomb KV5 in the Valley of the Kings.

Ramesses C (KSon; SPP)
Grandson of Ramesses II. Dedicator at

Prince Ramesses A, later Ramesses II, in a relief in the temple of his father at Abydos.

Memphis of a statue of his father, Khaemwaset C, now in Vienna.

(Ramesses-...)pre (KSonB)
Son of Ramesses II and number 20 in the Abydos procession of sons.

Ramesses-Maatptah (KSon)
Known only from a letter in which the palace servant Meryotef rebukes him for failing to respond to his communications.

Ramesses-Merenre (KSonB)
Son of Ramesses II and number 21 in the processions of sons.

Ramesses-Meretmirre (KSonB)
Son of Ramesses II and number 48 in the Wadi el-Sebua procession of sons.

Ramesses-meryamun-Nebweben[125] (KSon)
Son of Ramesses II; does not appear in the surviving processions of sons, and therefore likely to have been one of the king's younger children. Known only from the addition of his name to two stone coffins of his grandfather, Ramesses I, made while the latter was still only

(above) The granite outer coffin of Ramesses I, made before his accession, used for the burial of Ramesses-meryamun-Nebweben at Gurob (CM JE30707+46764).

Vizier. The outer one was used for the prince's interment in tomb W5 at Gurob: bones found alongside it were those of a man with a badly deformed spine. The inner coffin was found in a pit at Medinet Habu.

(Ramesses-)Meryastarte (KSonB)
Son of Ramesses II and number 26 in the Abydos procession of sons.

(Ramesses-)Merymaat (KSonB)
Son of Ramesses II and number 25 in the Abydos procession of sons.

Ramesses-Meryset (KSon)
Son of Ramesses II; depicted on a block from the Ramesseum, reused at Medinet Habu; at Abydos (number 23 in the procession); on a door lintel from Qantir (Hildesheim); on a doorjamb in Cairo; and on a stela in Berlin.

Ramesses-Payotnetjer (KSon)
Son of Ramesses II; named on an *ostrakon* in the Cairo Museum.

Ramesses-Siatum (KSonB)
Son of Ramesses II and number 19 in the Abydos procession of sons.

Ramesses-Sikhepri (KSonB)
Son of Ramesses II and number 24 in the Abydos procession of sons.

(Ramesses-)Siptah A (KSonB)
Son of Ramesses II and probably Sutererey, and number 26 in the processions of sons. A Book of the Dead probably belonging to him is in the Florence Museum, while a relief of the prince and his mother is in the Louvre.

(Ramesses-)Userkhepesh (KSonB)
Son of Ramesses II and number 22 in the Abydos procession of sons.

Ramesses-Userpehty (KSonB)
Probably a son of Ramesses II, named on a plaque formerly in the Fraser Collection and on a column-base at Memphis.

Renpetnefer (KDB)
Daughter of Ramesses II; number 12 in the Luxor procession of daughters.

[R]uia
Mother-in-law of Sety I. Known from a block at Medinet Habu.

Senakhtenamen (KSonB)
Son of Ramesses II and number 20 in the processions of sons. A faience votive plaque showing Ptah and Sekhmet, dedicated by one Amenmose who was employed in the prince's household, suggests that the latter may have been resident at Memphis.

Seshnesuen[...] (KSon)
Son of Ramesses II; named on an *ostrakon* in the Cairo Museum.

Setem[hir...] (KSon)
Son of Ramesses II; named on an *ostrakon* in the Cairo Museum.

[Set]emnakhte (KSonB)
Son of Ramesses II; depicted on a block from the Ramesseum, reused at Medinet Habu, and on a doorway from Qantir (Cairo).

Setpenre B (KSonB)
Son of Ramesses II; and number 10 in the processions of sons. Present at the siege of the Syrian city of Dapur in year 10.

Sety A (Troop Commander)
Father of Ramesses I. Named on the latter's statues as Vizier, a stela of Sety is in the Oriental Institute, Chicago. He may have been a royal envoy in Palestine during the Amarna Period.

Sety B (KSonB)
Name spelled **Sutiy** in his funerary equipment. Son of Ramesses II; number 9 in the processions of sons. Present at the triumph that followed the Battle of Qadesh, and the siege of the Syrian city of Dapur in year 10. Buried in tomb KV5 in the Valley of the Kings, where two of his canopic jars were found; his interment was apparently inspected in year 53 of his father's reign.

Sety C (KSon)
Son of Amenhirkopshef (Sethirkopshef) A and Nefertiry F; mentioned on an *ostrakon* in the Louvre.

Sety D (KSon)
Son of Ramesses II; named on an *ostrakon* in the Cairo Museum and conceivably identical with Sety B.

Shepsemiunu (KSonB)
Son of Ramesses II; depicted on a block from the Ramesseum, reused at Medinet Habu.

Siamun C (KSonB)
Son of Ramesses II and number 25 in the processions of sons.

Simentu (KSonB)
Son of Ramesses II and number 23 in the processions of sons; husband of Iryet.

Sitamun C (KDB)
Daughter of Ramesses II; number 11 on the Louvre *ostrakon* list.

Sitre A (GW; KGW; L2L; GM; KM; MULE)
Wife of Ramesses I and mother of Sety I. Her statue is depicted in the Abydos temple of her son, while her tomb is number QV38 in the Valley of the Queens. She may previously have borne the name Tia (Q).

Sutererey (KW)
Mother of a Prince Ramesses-Siptah and probably a wife of Ramesses II. Shown with her son on a relief in the Louvre.

Syhiryotes (KDB)
Daughter of Ramesses II; number 19 in the Abydos procession of daughters.

Taemwadjy
Aunt of Ramesses I. Shown on a statue with her husband, Khaemwaset B.

Takhat A (KDB; KGW; KM)
Daughter of Ramesses II; number 14 on the Louvre *ostrakon* list. Probable wife of Sety II (see next section).

Thutmose C (KSonB)
Son of Ramesses II; number 22 in the processions of sons.

Tia C (KSis)
Sister of Ramesses II. Buried with her husband, Tjia, in a tomb at Saqqara, and shown alongside him and her mother on a block in Toronto.

Tia Q (Songstress of Pre)
Stated to be the mother of Vizier Sety on the Year 400 stela from Tanis; if Vizier Sety is to be equated with King Sety I, Tia may be identical with Sitre.

Tia-Sitre (KDB)
Daughter of Ramesses II; number 12 on the Louvre *ostrakon* list.

Tjia (Overseer of Treasurers)
Brother-in-law of Ramesses II. Shown along with his mother-in-law and wife on a block in Toronto. Buried with his wife in a tomb at Saqqara.

Tuia (KDB)
Daughter of Ramesses II; number 5 on the Louvre *ostrakon* list.

Tuia-Nebettawy (KDB)
Daughter of Ramesses II; number 13 on the Louvre *ostrakon* list.

Tuy A (KW; KM; GW)
Name also found with the longer form **Mut-Tuy**. Wife of Sety I and mother of Ramesses II; named on many of her son's monuments and represented amongst the colossi at Abu Simbel, and on a broken statue at Tanis. A number of blocks involving her, including a divine birth scene, were reused at Medinet

(below) Ramesses II with his mother Tuy A (Vienna ÄS5091).

(below, right) Statue of the mother of Ramesses II, Tuy A (CM JE37484).

Habu in Ptolemaic times. Buried in tomb QV80 in the Valley of the Queens.

Werenro (KDB)
Daughter of Ramesses II; number 8 in the processions of daughters.

Wermaa[...] (KSon)
Son of Ramesses II; named on an *ostrakon* in the Cairo Museum.

[Anuketem?]heb (KDB)
Daughter of Ramesses II; number 13 on Luxor list of princesses, perhaps the Anuketemheb, whose sarcophagus lid was reused in KV10.

[...]khesbed (KDB)
Daughter of Ramesses II; number 16 in the second Abydos procession of daughters.

[...]taweret (KDB)
Daughter of Ramesses II; number 3 on the Louvre *ostrakon* list.

[...]19A (KDB)
Daughter of Bintanath; depicted with her mother in tomb QV71.

[...]19B
Daughter of Tjia and Tia C; depicted in her parents' tomb at Saqqara.

The Feud of the Ramessides

19th Dynasty part 2

The Royal Succession

19th Dynasty part 2 1201–1187
MERENPTAH

SETY II

AMENMESSE
(*in southern Egypt during years 2 to 5 of Sety II*)

SIPTAH

TAWOSRET

Historical Background

The decade occupied by the reign of Ramesses II's successor, Merenptah, was an eventful one. In particular, an invasion of the 'Sea Peoples' – who were a coalition of Libyan and Mediterranean peoples – had to be repulsed in the fifth year of his reign; more peaceably, grain was shipped to the Hittites to relieve a famine, presumably a manifestation of continued alliance between the Egyptians and Anatolians.

The last years of the 19th Dynasty, however, marked a sad decline from the glory days of Sety I and Ramesses II. Central to this was the usurpation of the throne by a certain Amenmesse. It has often been argued that he seized the throne on Merenptah's death, besting the heir, Sety-Merenptah A. However, it seems more likely that the latter actually succeeded, as Sety II, but was replaced by Amenmesse in the area south of the Fayoum during Sety's second regnal year. The usurper then ruled for some four years, after which Sety II returned, subsequently mutilating and/or usurping the monuments of Amenmesse. A number of officials associated with Amenmesse also seem to have lost their jobs, most notably the Theban High Priest of Amun, Roma-Roy. However, by the time Sety II had regained power, he only had a year or two to live, dying during his sixth regnal year.

The key figure in the days immediately following the death of Sety II was the Chancellor Bay, a man of apparently Syrian origin. Crown Prince Sety-Merenptah B was either dead or unable to assert his rights, for the new king, Siptah, seems to have been a son of the defeated Amenmesse. Only in his early teens, Siptah ruled under the regency of the newly widowed King's Great Wife, Tawosret. Bay's position vis-à-vis Tawosret is well illustrated by the fact that a relief of the queen on one side of a doorway at Amada is balanced on the other side by one of Bay, on exactly the same scale. As the relative size of images in Egyptian art reflects the relative standing of the individuals, this is highly significant; likewise is the frequent presence of Bay's name in the foundation deposits of Siptah's mortuary temple.

A modest number of monuments of Siptah are known from Memphis, Thebes, southern Upper Egypt and Nubia, some of which show that the formulation of his royal names were changed about a year into his reign. For the first years of the reign, Tawosret's role was that of a conventional regent, her rule being wholly in the name of the youthful Siptah. In perhaps the fifth year, however, a radical change took place as Tawosret imitated that other queen-regent, Hatshepsut, in assuming full pharaonic titles. This may have coincided with the downfall, and perhaps execution, of Bay, recorded on an *ostrakon* which refers to the 'king maker' as 'the great enemy'.[126] A later source is generally regarded as referring to him as 'the Syrian upstart'.[127]

A year or less later, Siptah was dead, with Tawosret continuing to rule as sole pharaoh; she was probably responsible for erasing his names in his tomb, and also replacing Siptah's names in her own tomb with those of Sety II. However, there was clearly opposition to her regime that may have grown into a full-scale civil war, in which a certain Setnakhte was ultimately victorious as founder of the 20th Dynasty. Both Tawosret and Siptah were written out of history, with Sety II regarded as the effective predecessor of Setnakhte, much as the Amarna kings had been ignored by Ramesside chroniclers.

The Royal Family

Merenptah's wife is known from a number of monuments to have been called Isetneferet. Since she is never called a King's Daughter, she has been equated with Khaemwaset C's offspring of this name, although it is not impossible that she still could be Merenptah's sister, Isetneferet B.

Of their offspring, Merenptah's ultimate heir – Sety-Merenptah A – is well known from a number of his father's statues, while a daughter – Isetneferet D – may be named in a papyrus. The possibility that Merenptah had a second son is raised by five monuments that clearly belong together and name a Prince Merenptah, whose titulary differs but slightly from those titles borne by Merenptah himself before coming to the throne. Crucially, two of them are Middle Kingdom statues usurped (apparently for the first time) by Merenptah as king. The only difficulty with the apparent implication that the prince is a new bearer of the name is the fact that he bears in all cases a *uraeus*, a feature normally indicating accession to the throne. Since the actual heir, Sety-Merenptah, used his double name both as prince and as pharaoh **Sety II**, and also had a slightly different string of titles as prince, it is unlikely that these representations are actually him. It is possible that

Crown Prince Sety-Merenptah B is depicted with his father Sety II in the small temple of the Sety II monument at Karnak. It has been suggested that the prince's figure has been inserted to replace one of the Chancellor Bay.

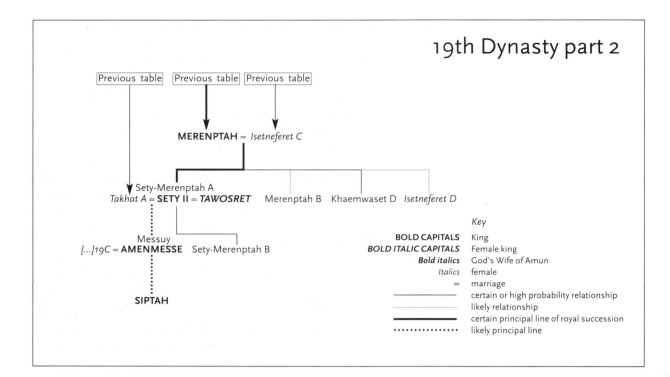

19th Dynasty part 2

| Previous table | Previous table | Previous table |

MERENPTAH = *Isetneferet C*

Sety-Merenptah A
Takhat A = **SETY II** = ***TAWOSRET*** Merenptah B Khaemwaset D *Isetneferet D*

Messuy
[...]19C = **AMENMESSE** Sety-Merenptah B

SIPTAH

Key
BOLD CAPITALS King
BOLD ITALIC CAPITALS Female king
Bold italics God's Wife of Amun
Italics female
= marriage
——— certain or high probability relationship
············· likely relationship
——— certain principal line of royal succession
·············· likely principal line

The chapel of Sety II in the first courtyard of the Karnak temple. It was intended as a temporary resting-place for the barks of Amun, Mut and Khonsu during festivals. Its decoration includes the scene of the king and Prince Sety-Merenptah B seen on the previous page.

the addition of the *uraeus* may reflect some facet of the civil war between Sety and Amenmesse, but this can only be a suggestion. A further son of Merenptah, Khaemwaset D, is shown in the king's Palestinian war reliefs at Karnak.[128]

There has long been debate as to the identity of **Amenmesse**. Certain threads of evidence point to his having served as Viceroy of Nubia under Merenptah, under the abbreviated name Messuy. In particular, two representations of him on the temple at Amada seem to have had royal *uraei* added to their brows, in a manner consistent with others who had later become kings (e.g. Horemheb, Merenptah A and some of the sons of Ramesses III). As to Messuy's origins, a reference to himself as 'the king's son himself' at Amada might point to his having been a prince of the blood; on the other hand, it could simply be a reference to the Viceroy's title, 'King's Son of Kush'.

Be that as it may, key evidence as to the parentage of Amenmesse is provided by a pair of statues that (as they exist today) are inscribed with the names of Sety II. They both bear reliefs labelled as belonging to the (Great) Wife Takhat, but on one, still at Karnak, the word 'wife' has been carved in the place of, and over, 'mother'. This statue belongs to a group all of which had originally been made together for Amenmesse, but had been reinscribed after his defeat by Sety II. Thus, on the basis of the relief's original title, one is led to the conclusion that Amenmesse's mother was named Takhat.

On the left-hand side of the back pillar of a statue of Amenmesse at Karnak, usurped by Sety II, is a figure of Takhat A; she was originally entitled King's Daughter and King's Mother. After her son's defeat, the latter title was replaced by that of King's Wife, when the statue was taken over by her husband.

However, the fact that the only change made to Takhat's figure when the statue was reinscribed by Sety II was the replacement of 'mother' by 'wife' strongly suggests that the mother of Amenmesse either became Sety's consort, or had always been. In favour of the latter interpretation is the figure of Takhat on the second statue, now in Cairo. Here, the inscription accompanying the queen's figure seems to be original, unlike that which names the king. The most likely solution is that the Cairo statue had been made for Sety II, with his wife, Takhat, carved on the side of its back pillar. It had then been usurped by their son, Amenmesse, who did not make any attempt to change his mother's titles, and was then finally reclaimed by Sety II.

The parentage of Takhat is nowhere stated, but it is not improbable that she was the daughter of Ramesses II of the same name, and thus an aunt of her husband; however, as certainly one of the younger daughters of Ramesses II she may have been of the same age, or even younger than Sety.

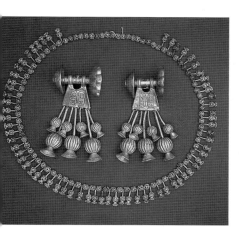

Earrings bearing the names of Sety II, together with a necklace, all found in a pit tomb in the Valley of the Kings (KV56) which contained various items of jewellery. It has been suggested that the burial may have belonged to a young child of the king (CM CG52397–8; 82679).

On the other hand, nothing is known of the ancestry of a second wife of Sety II, **Tawosret**, whose existence is indicated by the appearance of both their names (singly and jointly) on jewellery found in tomb KV56 in the Valley of the Kings.[129]

The recognition that Amenmesse was the son of Sety II and his Great Wife provides important background to the accession of **Siptah**, known from an *ostrakon* to be Sety II's direct successor. The Chancellor Bay states in texts at Aswan and Gebel el-Silsila that he had 'established the king in the seat of his father', as well as making other less explicit, but still suggestive, comments. A statue in Munich once depicted Siptah on the lap of another king, by context clearly his father, but the image of the latter has been entirely cut away. The only ruler of the period who could have provoked such destruction was Amenmesse, and likewise he is the only king whose offspring is likely to have required such explicit promotion. The demolition of his figure is likely to have closely followed the fall of Bay or the death of Siptah himself, when any short-lived rehabilitation of Amenmesse will have ended.

Siptah's mother is thus likely to be the wife of Amenmesse who is represented on one of his Karnak statues, but whose cartouche has been completely erased.[130] Material naming a 'King's Mother Tiaa' found in Siptah's tomb seems actually to be 'strays' belonging to the mother of Thutmose IV from the adjacent KV32 (see p. 140). Siptah, who was probably not even 20 years old at his death, has no known wife.[131]

Mutilated statue of Siptah, apparently seated on the lap of his father, Amenmesse, whose image has been entirely cut away (Munich Gl.122).

Brief Lives ●

Males in **bold**, *females in* **bold italic**.

Isetneferet C (KGW)
Wife of Merenptah. Depicted on a statue
usurped for her husband from
Amenhotep III in his chapel at Gebel el-
Silsila, on the stelae of the Vizier Panehsy
at the same site, and on a statuette
dedicated by Panehsy.

Isetneferet D (KD)
Probably a daughter of Merenptah, named
in a ship's log in Leiden.

Khaemwaset D (KSon)
Son of Merenptah. Depicted in his father's
war reliefs in the Cour de Cachette in the
Karnak temple.

Merenptah B (KSon; ExecH2L; Genmo)
Probable son of Merenptah. Known from
reliefs on two statues of Senwosret I
(usurped by Merenptah and found at

Alexandria and Tanis) and on three statue
fragments from Bubastis. Assumed a
uraeus at some point in his career.

Messuy (KSonK)
Probably identical with King
AMENMESSE, and thus probably a son of
Sety II and Takhat A. Served as Viceroy
during much of Merenptah's reign, but
was succeeded by Khaemtjitry (who was
promoted to Vizier under Amenmesse)
prior to Merenptah's death.
Commemorated by a number of kneeling
figures and inscriptions in the Nubian
temples at Amada, Aksha and Beit el-Wali,
plus *shabti* figures from Wadi el-Sebua
and Aniba, as well as a doorjamb inscribed
by one of his subordinates at Aniba. In
Egypt proper, an Aswan/Philae road
inscription shows Messuy greeting the
chariot-borne Merenptah, while Messuy's
name appears on the island of Bigeh, near
Aswan. It was doubtless the power-base
provided by his viceregal background and
his close relationship with the current
Viceroy, Khaemtjitry, which allowed
Messuy/Amenmesse's bid for power to be
backed by the resources of Nubia, and
explain how he managed to maintain his
position for nearly four years.

*Prince Merenptah B offering to Amun on a
block at Bubastis.*

Sety-Merenptah A (KSonB; ExecH2L;
Genmo)
Son of Merenptah; depicted on the side
of the rear pillar of six of his father's
statues, and on two stelae of the Vizier
Panehsy at Gebel el-Silsila. Also shown

*Viceroy Messuy greets his sovereign, and
probably grandfather, King Merenptah, in a
rock inscription on the road running south
from Aswan.*

in battle scenes where, given Merenptah's advanced age, he may have been in actual charge. Later king as **SETY II**.

Sety-Merenptah B (EKSon; Exec)
Son of Sety II; depicted behind his father in the small temple of the latter at Karnak, possibly replacing a figure of the Chancellor Bay. It has recently been suggested that he was actually a baby, born in the last year of his father's reign, who died in year 4 of Siptah; this, however, remains doubtful.

Takhat A (KGW; KD)
Wife of Sety II, mother of Amenmesse, and probable daughter of Ramesses II. Depicted on a number of statues of her husband and her son. Perhaps buried in the former tomb of Amenmesse (KV10), with a sarcophagus lid that once belonged to Anuketemheb, probably a daughter of Ramesses II (see p. 175). The lid may, however, be from the burial of Takhat B, who subsequently usurped the tomb with Baketwernel A (pp. 191, 192, 194).

Tawosret (KGW; L2L; MULE; GW)
Wife of Sety II, regent for Siptah and later king. Jointly provided jewellery with Sety II to a burial in tomb KV56 in the Valley of the Kings; depicted during the regency with the Chancellor Bay in the temple of Amada, and also on various small items. Assumed full pharaonic titles around the time of Siptah's death and ruled for two years – continuing Siptah's regnal numbering sequence – until apparently overthrown by Setnakhte. Owner of tomb KV14 in the Valley of the Kings, apparently begun in the second regnal year of Sety II, enlarged during the regency, and then once again extended during Tawosret's reign; the tomb was later usurped for Setnakhte. Nothing is known about the fate of the queen's body,[132] although her original sarcophagus was later reused for the burial of Amenhirkopshef D in tomb KV13 under Ramesses VI.

[...]19C (KGW)
Wife of Amenmesse; represented on a statue of the king at Karnak.

(right) On silver bracelets from tomb KV56, Tawosret pours a drink for her husband, Sety II (CM JE52577–8).

(below) Queen Tawosret as depicted on the right doorjamb of the inner part of the temple of Amada, with the titles of God's Wife and King's Great Wife. An image of the Chancellor Bay is on the opposite jamb.

The Decline of the Ramessides

20th Dynasty

Historical Background

Setnakhte was probably past middle-age when he took power from the regime of Tawosret; his reign was certainly extremely short, followed by that of his son, Ramesses III. The earliest years of the new reign were probably taken up with repairing the damage of the late-19th Dynasty conflicts, but by Ramesses III's fifth year, external threats had emerged that would test the mettle of the man who would prove to be the last truly great pharaoh. The first threat came from the west, where Libyan tribes advanced on the western Delta. In the battle that followed, Ramesses' forces were wholly successful: thousands of the enemy were killed, and many more captured. Nevertheless, the Libyan population of the western Delta continued to increase by peaceful infiltration, and would form the basis for a line that would ultimately take the throne of Egypt. The second, far more serious, threat came three years later when the Sea Peoples attacked. A confederacy from the Aegean area, they had previously liquidated the principal states of Syria and Asia, and – in order to face them – Ramesses III established a defensive line in southern Palestine. Fighting on land and water, the king was able to defeat them, as recorded in his mortuary temple at Medinet Habu.

The late 20s of the reign saw economic problems, against which background was hatched a plot against the king's life, known today as the 'Harem Conspiracy'. In addition, a popular rebellion was to be stirred up, with a magical element that involved the use of waxen images. Only one of these plans apparently succeeded however: the murder of the king. In the aftermath, the main conspirators were tried and condemned.[133]

The new king was the legitimate heir, Ramesses IV. There is slender evidence for some sea-borne conflict, perhaps the outcome of a final thrust on the part of the Sea Peoples. Although he began various pieces of building work, and on a stela from Abydos prayed that he might be allowed the span of Ramesses II, Ramesses IV's sixth regnal year was his last. Similarly short was the reign of Ramesses V Amenhirkopshef I, cut off by what appears to have been smallpox. Since Ramesses V died without a surviving heir, the throne accordingly reverted to Ramesses IV's younger brother, Prince Amenhirkopshef C, known today as Ramesses VI Amenhirkopshef II. The new king is the last known king to have worked the turquoise mines of the Sinai and, although a Karnak relief and a number of martial statues are known, there is no certain evidence of his foreign policy. Dynastic misfortune struck again only a few years after Ramesses VI's death, when his son and successor Itamun (Ramesses VII) had to be followed, for a brief period, by yet another son of Ramesses III: Sethirkopshef B (Ramesses VIII).

Ramesses IX Khaemwaset I reigned for 19 years, a time marked by various problems, both economic and political, which continued during the reigns of Ramesses X and XI. The resulting lawlessness was manifested in large-scale looting in the Theban necropolis; amongst the most interesting documents to survive from ancient times are the transcripts of the trials of a number of persons accused of plundering both royal and private tombs. A

Prince Khaemwaset E, shown holding a fan in his tomb, QV44 in the Valley of the Queens. Behind him stands the god Ptah-Sokar-Osiris, to whom the prince's father, Ramesses III, makes an offering.

fair few monuments survive from Ramesses IX's reign, both in the Nile Valley and out at Dakhla Oasis.

There is some evidence to suggest that the reigns of Ramesses X and XI might have overlapped with that of Ramesses IX. In any case, their monuments are few and far between, with clear proof of some fairly dramatic events during the final decade of the reign of Ramesses XI. The High Priest of Amun, Amenhotep G, was 'suppressed' for a nine-month period as part of some kind of major civil upheaval, which included an attack on the fortified temple complex of Medinet Habu. These troubles were ultimately brought to a conclusion by the Viceroy of Nubia, Panehsy, marching north to Thebes to restore order. For possibly a period of years he held sway over both southern Egypt and Nubia, until perhaps he overreached himself and had to be removed by the General Piankh. Panehsy was driven into Nubia; he seems to have survived there, and it was perhaps his heirs (or those of his associates) who were to be responsible for establishing a new Nubian monarchy, whose descendants we shall be meeting later as conquerors of Egypt.

For his part in the war, Piankh additionally received the office of High Priest of Amun from the king. He thus effectively became the military dictator of much of Upper Egypt, the new regime instituting its own dating era

20th Dynasty

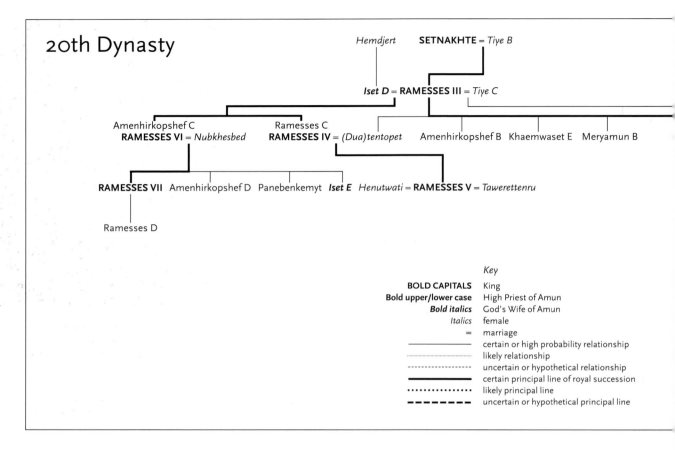

Key

BOLD CAPITALS	King
Bold upper/lower case	High Priest of Amun
Bold italics	God's Wife of Amun
Italics	female
=	marriage
————————	certain or high probability relationship
··················	likely relationship
- - - - - - - -	uncertain or hypothetical relationship
▬▬▬▬▬▬	certain principal line of royal succession
••••••••••••	likely principal line
▬ ▬ ▬ ▬ ▬	uncertain or hypothetical principal line

(the 'Repeating of Births'), which lasted until Ramesses XI's demise – an event that marked the end of the New Kingdom. The period also embraced the rule in Thebes of another General and High Priest called Hrihor. It remains uncertain whether he preceded or followed Piankh in office; the debate continues.[134]

The Royal Family

The origins of **Setnakhte** are obscure. His name's compounding with that of the god Set would suggest familial links with the 19th Dynasty royal family, whose devotion to the god is shown by the currency of the otherwise unusual name, Sety. Most probably, he was a grandson of Ramesses II by one of the latter's numerous offspring. That Ramesses III was Setnakhte's son is explicitly stated in the introduction to the Great Harris Papyrus in the British Museum. Setnakhte's wife and Ramesses' mother, Tiye B Merneiset, is shown with the former on a stela from Abydos.

It is very clear that **Ramesses III** was a great devotee of Ramesses II: not only was his prenomen based on that of Ramesses II, but his sons were named after those of the earlier king and often received the same offices as their namesakes. A particular example of this is Khaemwaset E, who became Sem-Priest of Ptah at Memphis just like the famous prince of earlier times,

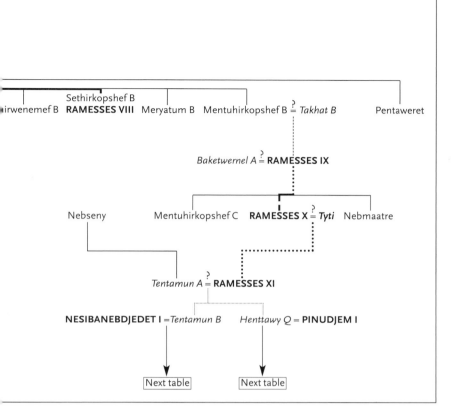

irwenemef B **Sethirkopshef B**
RAMESSES VIII Meryatum B Mentuhirkopshef B = *Takhat B*   Pentaweret

Baketwernel A = **RAMESSES IX**

Nebseny Mentuhirkopshef C **RAMESSES X** = *Tyti* Nebmaatre

Tentamun A = **RAMESSES XI**

NESIBANEBDJEDET I = *Tentamun B*   *Henttawy Q* = **PINUDJEM I**

| Next table | | Next table |

(above) The so-called 'Migdol' at Medinet Habu has a number of unusual scenes of Ramesses III in intimate poses with unnamed women.

(below) View of Ramesses III's buildings at Medinet Habu. The Syrian-style Migdol is in the foreground.

187

although he never rose to the dignity of High Priest. The 'system' so established even went so far as to demand that if a child died, the next to be born would take his name.

The key evidence for the study of these sons is a double procession of figures, carved into either side of the doorway that leads from the Second Court of Ramesses III's mortuary temple into its rear rooms (see pp. 32–33). The figures represent princes and princesses worshipping deep-cut cartouches of Ramesses III, the whole motif being borrowed from Ramesses II's own mortuary temple, the Ramesseum (see pp. 164–65). By Ramesses III's death, although the figures were complete, the accompanying titles and names had not yet been added. Ultimately however, such details were added to most of the figures. Prince 1 received the simple nomen cartouche 'Ramesses' – the nomen most commonly used by Ramesses IV. The initial labelling of princes 2 and 3 gave respectively the prenomen and nomen cartouches of King Ramesses VI, but prince 4 was simply tagged for Prince Sethirkopshef B (his cartouches as Ramesses VIII were added only later). Behind him come further prince figures with the names and titles of non-ruling princes. It is thus clear that, with the possible exception of prince 1, all must have had their basic labels added after the accession of Ramesses VI, but before that of Ramesses VIII.

Prince 1's label could at first sight have been added at the same time, or during the preceding reign of Ramesses IV, with the later figures left blank. The decision between these options very much depends on how one interprets the simple cartouche 'Ramesses'. It is this interpretation that has caused much scholarly dispute. Sir Flinders Petrie took the view that all individuals named in the processions were sons of Ramesses III, so that prince 1 became Ramesses IV. However, he misread Ramesses VI's nomen as 'Itamun' (Ramesses VII), and further identified the figures labelled Khaemwaset, Amenhirkopshef and Meryamun as Ramesses IX, X and XI respectively. He thus produced a theory that the last eight kings of the 20th Dynasty were *all* the sons of Ramesses III!

This was rejected by Eric Peet, who decided that figure 1's lack of a prenomen and his simple cartouche precluded his being Ramesses IV, in spite of the latter being identified as a son of Ramesses III in the Great Harris Papyrus. He therefore invented a non-reigning father of Ramesses VI, who was nevertheless believed by the latter to have had a right to the throne actually held by Ramesses IV and V. Further embroidery led certain writers to speculate that this 'Prince Ramesses' might be none other than the Harem Conspiracy protagonist, Pentaweret. Peet then declared the princes following Ramesses VI's figures to be the sons of that king, and thus only great-grandsons of Ramesses III. This interpretation became very popular, and is still followed by a number of Egyptologists.

However, a far simpler option was set out by Kenneth Kitchen in 1972. He pointed out that the simple cartouche 'Ramesses' was actually that most frequently affected by Ramesses IV, that the titles given for him were attested as those of Ramesses IV as a prince and that, while individuals with all the

names given could be demonstrated to have lived under Ramesses III, this was not true of the reign of Ramesses VI. Also, if the princes listed were Ramesses VI's sons, where was Itamun (Ramesses VII), demonstrably Ramesses VI's son?

The most likely interpretation of the Medinet Habu procession is as follows: Ramesses IV inscribed his kingly cartouche below his princely titles soon after his accession, but left the remaining figures unlabelled; his brother, Ramesses VI, added his own royal cartouches and former titles, along with the name and titles of his still-living sibling, Sethirkopshef, during his reign; junior and long-dead brothers were commemorated by labels affixed to some of the remaining figures. The final addition to the procession occurred after Sethirkopshef's accession as Ramesses VIII, when his cartouches were placed alongside his image.

The daughters shown following their brothers at Medinet Habu were unfortunately never named. Amongst them is likely to have been the Adoratrix Tentopet, shown with a king who is probably Ramesses III in the temple of Khonsu at Karnak. She is likely to be identical with the later Queen Duatentopet (see p. 190).

Ramesses III's principal wife was Iset D Ta-Hemdjert, depicted on a statue of the king in the temple of Mut at Karnak. Hemdjert (with the alternate spelling, 'Hebnerdjent') will have been the mother of the queen, the syllable 'Ta' meaning 'She of'. Iset's tomb in the Valley of the Queens was built for her by Ramesses VI, and since the only title he gives her is King's Mother, the implication is that she was his mother. This is confirmed by her appearance as the King's Mother 'Hemdjert' (clearly an abbreviation for the queen, *not* her mother) in an inscription commemorating the installation of her granddaughter, Iset E, as God's Wife of Amun.

That there was also a second wife is suggested by the titles of some of

(above) Queen Iset D Ta-Hemdjert, on a statue made for Ramesses IV but usurped by Ramesses VI (Luxor Museum, ex-CG42153).

(below) A King's Great Wife is shown behind Ramesses III in this relief in his temple at Medinet Habu. Curiously, her cartouche is blank, perhaps reflecting problematic familial relationships leading up to the Harem Conspiracy; the temple's processions of sons were also left unlabelled at the king's death.

Ramesses III's sons – two of whom (Prehirwenemef B and Khaemwaset E) were First King's Sons, implying first-birth and thus two separate mothers. However, no monuments give this wife's name: could she have been Tiye C, the spouse who is known to have been a member of Ramesses III's harem and who instigated the plot that ended his life? Her name is given in the record of the trial of the conspirators, as is that of Pentaweret – her son who was to be the beneficiary of the plot.[135]

Ramesses IV's wife is nowhere stated, but the titles borne by Duatentopet, owner of tomb QV74 in the Valley of the Queens, would fit with her being his sister, consort and the mother of his successor – particularly given the possibility that she is identical with the Ramesses III/IV-dated Adoratrix Tentopet. **Ramesses V** had two known wives – Henutwati and Tawerettenru – both mentioned in Papyrus Wilbour, a land-holding inventory of the time. No children are known.

A hitherto-unknown prince, Amenhirkopshef (D), was revealed by the 1993 excavation of tomb KV13 in the Valley of the Kings. This tomb had been built for the late-19th Dynasty Chancellor Bay, but a rough extension terminated in the burial chamber of an Amenhirkopshef. That the appropriation of the tomb (and the prince) dates to the reign of **Ramesses VI** is suggested by a fragmentary inscription naming that king's wife, Queen Nubkhesbed. The latter's relationship with the king is indicated by a stela from Koptos commemorating their daughter, Iset (E); this explicitly calls Ramesses VI her father, and Nubkhesbed her mother. Two other children are known: Ramesses VII Itamun's paternity is explicitly stated on a doorjamb found at Deir el-Medina, while a probable final male offspring, Panebenkemyt, is to be found depicted on the side of a statue of Ramesses VI (now in the Luxor Museum). The statue had been usurped from Ramesses V but, like the figure of Iset D also inscribed on it, it is likely that the prince's figure had been added by its final owner.

Iset E, as depicted on a stela from Koptos; her mother, Nubkhesbed, is also mentioned on the stela (Manchester 1781).

A son of **Ramesses VII** seems to be mentioned on an *ostrakon* in the Louvre, which records the foundation of a tomb for a Prince Ramesses (D). However, no children of **Ramesses VIII** are known, with the ancestry of his successor, **Ramesses IX**, obscure. Yet on the basis of the naming of one of the latter's sons, it has been suggested that his father might have been Mentuhirkopshef B, making Ramesses IX the nephew of Ramesses VIII. As far as Ramesses IX's mother is concerned, she may be Takhat B, who certainly dates to the 20th Dynasty, and bears only the title of King's Mother on the walls of her burial place. This lady usurped part of tomb KV10 in the Valley of the Kings, as did Baketwernel A, suggesting that the two were contemporaries. Since Ramesses IX is without any certain wife, ascribing Baketwernel to him fits rather neatly.

Two of Ramesses IX's sons are known: at Heliopolis, a gateway was reinscribed with texts including the king's names and also those of the prince and High Priest Nebmaatre, who was fairly clearly his son. Mentuhirkopshef (C), perhaps the first heir, took over the former tomb of Sethirkopshef B (tomb KV19), in which one of his depictions bears the prenomen cartouche to Ramesses IX on its belt.

No evidence is known to indicate the relationship between the final three kings Ramesses: IX, X and XI. If they were a father-son succession, Tyti, who bears the titles of King's Daughter, King's Wife and King's Mother, would seem a good candidate for the wife of **Ramesses X**, but little else can be discerned. Some Ramesside royal blood may have passed into the 21st Dynasty, suggested by the son and grandson of Pinudjem I bearing the names Ramesses-Pasebkhanut (King Pasebkhanut I) and Ramesses-Ankhefenmut respectively. The link can only be Pasebkhanut's mother, Henttawy Q, who bears a range of titles, including that of King's Daughter. These two strands of evidence thus make it likely that Henttawy was a daughter of one of the last

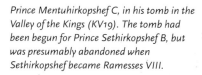

Prince Mentuhirkopshef C, in his tomb in the Valley of the Kings (KV19). The tomb had been begun for Prince Sethirkopshef B, but was presumably abandoned when Sethirkopshef became Ramesses VIII.

Ramessides, most probably **Ramesses XI**. As to the mother of this lady, Hent-tawy's funerary papyrus names her as Tentamun (written in a cartouche), in turn the daughter of one Nebseny. Tentamun A thus becomes the 'missing' wife of Ramesses XI, completing the basic 20th Dynasty picture. It is possible that this Tentamun was also the mother of another lady of the same name who was the consort of Nesibanebdjedet (Smendes) I, founder of the 21st Dynasty (see next section).

Brief Lives ●

Males in **bold**, *females in* **bold italic**.

Amenhirkopshef B (EKSon; ExecH2L)
Name also found as **Ramesses-Amenhirkopshef**. Son of Ramesses III. Depicted in the Medinet Habu procession and owner of tomb QV55 in the Valley of the Queens; died young as heir presumptive.[136]

Amenhirkopshef C (KSon; MoH)
Son of Ramesses III and Iset D. Depicted in the Medinet Habu procession and to be seen in two sets of temple reliefs dating to his father's reign: in the forecourt of the

Ramesses III temple in the first court of the Amun temple at Karnak, and in a scene of games under the Window of Appearances at Medinet Habu. Later king as **RAMESSES VI**.

Amenhirkopshef D (KSon)
Son of Ramesses VI. Buried in an extension of tomb KV13 in the Valley of the Kings.

Baketwernel A (KGW)
Possible wife of Ramesses IX. Buried in the former tomb of Amenmesse (KV10), where one chamber was plastered and redecorated for her.

Ramesses III introduces Prince Amenhirkopshef B to the goddess Isis (QV55).

(Dua)tentopet (Ador; KD; KW; KM)
Wife of Ramesses IV, buried in Valley of the Queens tomb QV74. Appears as Adoratrix, probably under Ramesses III, in the temple of Khonsu at Karnak. Her steward, Amunhotep, was the owner of tomb TT346.

Hemdjert
Mother of Iset D. Given the variant spellings of her name (e.g. 'Hebnerdjent'), she may have been of foreign extraction.

Henttawy Q (KD; KW; KM)
Probable daughter of Ramesses XI (see next section).

Henutwati (KGW)
Wife of Ramesses V; mentioned in Papyrus Wilbour.

Iset D Ta-Hemdjert (KGW; KM; GW)
Wife of Ramesses III. Depicted on a statue of the king in the temple of Mut at Karnak, and participated under Ramesses VI in the installation of her granddaughter, Iset E, as God's Wife of Amun. Owner of tomb QV51 in the Valley of the Queens.

Iset E (KD; Ador; GWA)
Daughter of Ramesses VI; name written with the Adoratrix title within the cartouche. Depicted on a stela from Koptos, now in the Manchester Museum, while her installation as God's Wife of Amun is recorded on a block from Deir el-Bakhit, on Dira Abu'l-Naga.

Khaemwaset E (1KSonB; SPP)
Name also found as **Ramesses-Khaemwaset**. Depicted in the Medinet Habu procession and buried in Valley of

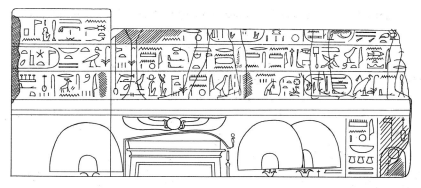

The remains of the inscription commemorating the installation of Princess Iset E as God's Wife, from Deir el-Bakhit (Western Thebes), but now lost.

the Queens tomb QV44; a canopic jar is in the Cairo Museum, while his sarcophagus lid and possible mummy are in Turin.

Mentuhirkopshef B (KSonB)
Son of Ramesses III. Depicted in the Medinet Habu procession and possibly the father of Ramesses IX. Probably the prince of the name buried in the Valley of the Kings tomb KV13.

Mentuhirkopshef C (1KSonB; EKSonB; 1Genmo; ExecH2L)
Name also found as **Ramesses-Mentuhirkopshef**. Son of Ramesses IX; took over tomb KV19 for his burial.

Meryamun B (KSonB)
Name given in full as **Ramesses-Meryamun**. Son of Ramesses III; nothing of his life or death known, other than his representation in the Medinet Habu list.

Meryatum B (KSonB; HPH)
Name also found as **Ramesses-Meryatum**. Son of Ramesses III; depicted in the Medinet Habu procession. Outlived his father, and occupied the High Priesthood of the Sun at Heliopolis on into the reigns of Ramesses IV and V, when he is mentioned in Papyrus Wilbour.

Nebmaatre (KSonB; HPH)
Son of Ramesses IX. Named together with his father on two gateways which they reinscribed in a temple at Arab el-Hisn, Heliopolis.

Nebseny
Father of Tentamun A. Possibly buried in tomb TT320 at Thebes.

Nesibanebdjedet
Governor of Tanis and possible son-in-law of Ramesses XI. **Later king**.

Nubkhesbed (KGW)
Wife of Ramesses VI. Mentioned on a stela of Iset E from Koptos, and also in tomb KV13 in the Valley of the Kings.

Panebenkemyt (KSon)
Son of Ramesses VI. Shown on a statues of the king, now in the Luxor Museum.

Pentaweret
Son of Ramesses III and Tiye C. In the Turin Judicial Papyrus, recording the trial of those involved in the plot against the king, the following is stated: 'Pentaweret, to whom had been given that other name (*perhaps referring to his putative name as pharaoh?*): He was brought in because of his collusion with Tiye, his mother, when she had plotted the matters with the women of the harem, concerning rebellion against his lord. He was placed before the (*court commissioners*) in order to examine him; they found him guilty; they left him in his place; he took his own life.'

Pinudjem I (HPA)
Probable son-in-law of Ramesses XI (see next section).

Ramesses III accompanied by Prince Khaemwaset E, in the latter's tomb QV44.

Prehirwenemef B (1KSon)
Son of Ramesses III. Depicted in the
Medinet Habu procession; predeceased
his father and was buried in the Valley of
the Queens (QV42).

Ramesses C (KSon; Genmo)
Son of Ramesses III and Iset D. Depicted
in the Medinet Habu procession and heir
to the throne for much of his father's
reign. He is to be seen in two sets of
temple reliefs dating to his father's reign:
in the forecourt of the Ramesses III temple
in the first court of the Amun temple at
Karnak, and in a scene of games under the
Window of Appearances at Medinet Habu.
As Crown Prince, he seems to have taken
an increasingly important role in the rule
of Egypt during the closing years of his
father's reign. For example, as early as year
27 he is depicted as being responsible for
the appointment of one Amenemopet as
High Priest of Mut at Karnak in the latter's
tomb (TT148) on Dira Abu'l-Naga at
Western Thebes. A tomb was constructed
for the prince in the Valley of the Queens
(QV53), but remained unused when he
ascended the throne as **RAMESSES IV**.

Ramesses D (1KSon; Genmo)
Son of Ramesses VII. The foundation of
his tomb, presumably in the Valley of the
Queens, is mentioned on an *ostrakon* in
the Louvre.

Sethirkopshef B (KSon; MH).
Son of Ramesses III, and depicted in the
Medinet Habu procession. Except for his
tomb in the Valley of the Queens (QV43),
little is known of this prince during his
father's lifetime, but he survived into the
reigns of his elder brothers and began a
new tomb in the Valley of the Kings
(KV19). However, he ultimately became
king as **RAMESSES VIII**.

Takhat B (KM)
Probable wife of Mentuhirkopshef B and
mother of Ramesses IX. Probably buried
in the former tomb of Amenmesse A
(KV10), where one chamber was plastered
and redecorated for her. The usurpation of
the sarcophagus of Anuketemheb (see pp.

*The future Ramesses IV and VI shown at
Medinet Habu.*

175, 183) may have been part of this
installation. Parts of her probable mummy
were found in the tomb from 1996.

Tawerettenru (KW)
Wife of Ramesses V; mentioned in
Papyrus Wilbour.

Tentamun A
Mother of Henttawy Q and probably wife
of Ramesses XI; mentioned in the
funerary papyrus of her daughter.

Tentamun B
Probable daughter of Ramesses XI and
wife of Nesibanebdjedet I (see next section).

Tiye B Mereniset (KGW; KM)
Wife of Setnakhte, with whom she is
adored by a priest named Meresyotef on a
stela from Abydos, now in Cairo. Shown

with her son, Ramesses III, on another
block from the site.

Tiye C
Wife of Ramesses III; conspired with
others to place her son, Pentaweret, on
the throne. Final fate unknown, but
presumably tried and condemned.

Tyti (KD; KSis; KW; KM; GW)
Possible wife of Ramesses X. Owner of
tomb QV52 in the Valley of the Queens.

Unplaced ● ● ● ● ● ● ● ● ● ● ●
in 19th and 20th Dynasties

Anuketemheb (KD; KW; KGW)
Original owner of a sarcophagus and canopic
jars later usurped for Takhat B in KV10.

Taiay (KW)
Name and title appears written in ink on
an *ostrakon* found in the Valley of the
Kings, between the tombs of Amenmesse
and Ramesses III.

4
The 3rd Intermediate Period

Of Kings and Priests

21st Dynasty

(*previous page*) *For many centuries, the Kushites had simply been a subject-people of the Egyptian pharaohs. Roles were abruptly reversed during the 8th century* BC *when the Kushite king Piye and his successors took control of Egypt from the squabbling native dynasts. Perhaps the most significant king of Piye's 25th Dynasty was Taharqa (see p. 234 ff.), seen here in a colossal stone head from Thebes (Aswan, Nubian Museum ex-CG560).*

Historical Background

Following the end of Ramesses XI's reign, the kingship of Egypt fell to Nesibanebdjedet I, the former governor of Tanis. It may have been at this point that the High Priest of Amun, Hrihor, briefly adopted royal titles at Thebes,[137] the pontificate falling either then or soon afterwards to Pinudjem I. The new political settlement seems to have abandoned the 'Repeating of Births' system in favour of Nesibanebdjedet's regnal years. However, the effective independence of the soldier-priests was clearly established: revealingly, Theban date-lines never actually name the Tanite king whose regnal year they quote.

For the whole of the 21st Dynasty, Egypt was effectively split in two – Lower Egypt being under the direct authority of the king in Tanis, but with the southern portion controlled by the High Priests of Amun at Thebes. The writ of these priests seems to have run from north of El-Hiba to the southern frontier, which (following the expulsion of Panehsy) was probably a short distance into Nubia. As far as one can tell, the division of Egypt seems to have worked fairly well – certainly there are no surviving indications of conflict. However, around year 16 of Nesibanebdjedet's rule, it appears that Pinudjem began taking steps towards full pharaonic titles, although at all times deferring to Nesibanebdjedet as senior king in his datelines. Nevertheless, the reality of Pinudjem's kingship is emphasized by the fact that his High Priesthood was passed on to his sons while he still lived.

Some troubles seem to have occurred after the death of the first of Pinudjem's High Priestly sons, Masaharta B, but the ultimate successor of Nesibanebdjedet at Tanis also seems to have been a son of Pinudjem: Pasebkhanut I (Psusennes). For around fifty years, the brothers Pasebkhanut I and Menkheperre B respectively ruled at Tanis and Thebes, one as king, one as High Priest, during a period which seems to have been of some prosperity.

Interestingly, Pasebkhanut I's second successor, Osorkon the Elder, was of Libyan background and was the uncle of the founder of the next dynasty – Shoshenq I. The significance of this Libyan appearance on the Tanite throne is unclear; Libyans had been amongst the foes of Merenptah and Ramesses III, but there is no evidence of any kind of violent take-over. Rather, the family in question seem to have been resident in Egypt for generations, distinguished mainly by their ancestral names and titles. Indeed, it is possible that the main line of the 21st Dynasty contained Libyan blood since the name of Masaharta is Libyan, as were those of some of the sons of the late-20th Dynasty High Priest, Hrihor.

It is not wholly certain what happened at the end of the 21st Dynasty. High Priest Pasebkhanut II is known to have assumed full royal names and titles, but it is unclear whether he did so as successor to Siamun, who followed Osorkon the Elder as Tanite king, or merely as a junior co-regent like Pinudjem I. The latter seems the more likely,[138] in which case Siamun was followed on the throne by the former Chief of the Ma, Shoshenq B: the nephew of the late king Osorkon the Elder, and now the founder of the 22nd Dynasty. Indeed, it is possible that Shoshenq had acquired quasi-pharaonic

(above) The God's Wife Maatkare A offers to Amun-Re on the façade of the Khonsu temple at Karnak.

(below) The Khonsu temple is a major source of data on the beginning of the 21st Dynasty.

power while Siamun was still alive, since a text from Karnak names him as only a chieftain, but also gives him a second regnal year.

The Royal Family

The roots of the family, or families, that provided the kings and High Priests of the 21st Dynasty lie in the troubles of the late 20th Dynasty.[139] The key figure is the High Priest Piankh, a man of uncertain antecedents; however, given the appearance of Libyan names amongst his descendants – and also amongst the children of his military-priestly contemporary, Hrihor – it is likely that Libyan mercenaries were amongst his ancestors. Piankh has four sons known, the eldest being Pinudjem I. A graffito in the temple of Luxor has a posthumous depiction of Piankh, followed by his sons, honouring the lady Nodjmet, with the request that Amun grant her a long lifespan. Another graffito in the same temple states that Pinudjem I was son of Piankh and a woman whose name may begin with either 'H...' or 'Nodj...'. This lady seems either to be Hrere, known to be the mother of Nodjmet from the latter's funerary papyrus; a hypothetical homonym; or Nodjmet herself.

Nodjmet also appears as wife of Hrihor (as High Priest) on a stela, on her funerary papyrus and in the temple of Khonsu at Karnak (both with him as

(above) Within the Khonsu temple, Hrihor is shown with royal attributes.

(right) Also within the Khonsu temple, although very badly damaged, there is a procession of Hrihor's sons and daughters, modelled on the examples of Ramesses II and III. The top register is headed by Queen Nodjmet, followed by the eldest son, Ankhef(enmut A). The bottom register is headed by princesses [...]amenweret and Nesta[...].

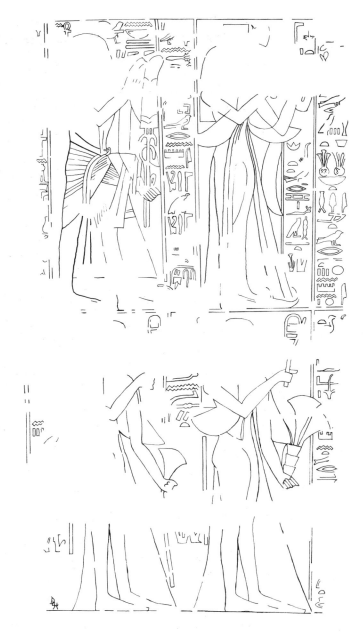

(opposite) Details of Hrihor and his wife Nodjmet, from the latter's Book of the Dead, found with her mummy in TT320 (BM EA10541).

king). The temple has a long list of children of Hrihor, comprising 19 named sons (none of whom are otherwise known for certain) and 5 daughters (with another 15 women's figures unlabelled), but with no statement as to their maternity. In addition, both Nodjmet and her mother, Hrere, have the titles of King's Mother, but the king in question is never mentioned. The data is thus confusing and not easy to interpret.

However, if it is assumed that Nodjmet was married twice – first to Piankh and then, after being widowed, to Hrihor as a later wife – a credible picture seems to emerge. On the basis of known contemporaneities, Hrere would be

21st Dynasty

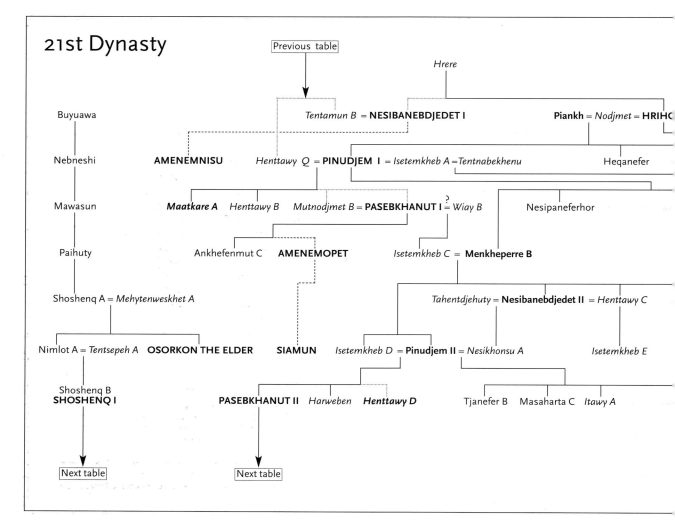

the mother of both Nodjmet and **Nesibanebdjedet I**; no father can be positively identified but, as Hrere was Chief of the Harem of Amun, it is possible that her husband could have been a High Priest – conceivably the 'suppressed' Amenhotep G (p. 185). As noted in the previous section, the wife of Nesibanebdjedet, Tentamun B, may well have been a daughter of Ramesses XI, perhaps a younger daughter of the latter marrying Nodjmet's eldest son, Pinudjem I. It must be emphasized, however, that many of these links are not based on unequivocal evidence, and that a number of other reconstructions have been proposed. One of these includes *two* Nodjmets, on the basis of the existence of two Books of the Dead bearing the name.[140]

Nothing is known of the origins of **Amenemnisu**, the short-lived successor of Nesibanebdjedet, but a number of suggestions have been made, including that he could be a son of Hrihor. Against this argument is the fact that he does not appear amongst his sons in the Khonsu temple, unless as one of the two destroyed male names, or an unnamed baby shown in a scene

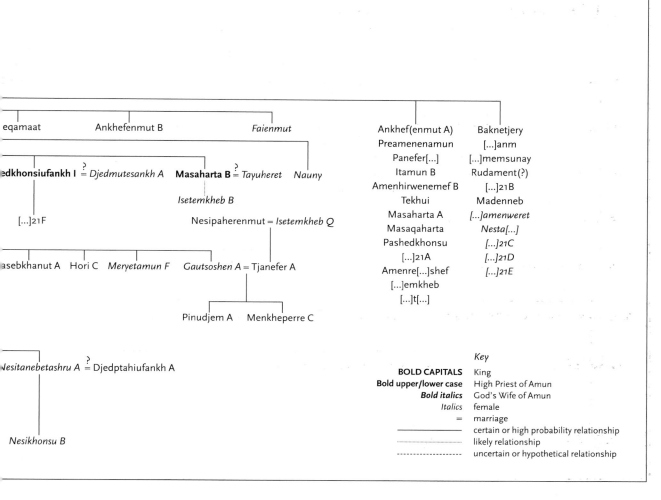

eqamaat — Ankhefenmut B — *Faienmut*

...dkhonsiufankh I ?= *Djedmutesankh A*   **Masaharta B** ?= *Tayuheret*   *Nauny*

Isetemkheb B

Nesipaherenmut = *Isetemkheb Q*

[...]21F

...asebkhanut A   Hori C   *Meryetamun F*   *Gautsoshen A* = Tjanefer A

Pinudjem A   Menkheperre C

...Nesitanebetashru A ?= Djedptahiufankh A

Nesikhonsu B

Ankhef(enmut A)
Preamenenamun
Panefer[...]
Itamun B
Amenhirwenemef B
Tekhui
Masaharta A
Masaqaharta
Pashedkhonsu
[...]21A
Amenre[...]shef
[...]emkheb
[...]t[...]

Baknetjery
[...]anm
[...]memsunay
Rudament(?)
[...]21B
Madenneb
[...]amenweret
Nesta[...]
[...]21C
[...]21D
[...]21E

Key

BOLD CAPITALS	King
Bold upper/lower case	High Priest of Amun
Bold italics	God's Wife of Amun
Italics	female
=	marriage
————————	certain or high probability relationship
····················	likely relationship
- - - - - - - - - - - -	uncertain or hypothetical relationship

in the same temple. Perhaps the most likely view is that he was simply the son of his predecessor, Nesibanebdjedet, but this is without direct evidence.

In contrast, much is known about the family of **Pinudjem I**. Of his siblings, in addition to the three brothers already mentioned, a sister, Faienmut, is named on a bandage used to rewrap one of the ancient royal mummies that were reburied from the late 20th Dynasty onwards. Pinudjem's marriage to Henttawy Q is indicated by their priestly names and titles being found together on an inscribed goblet and on the Khonsu temple's façade; and in a dedication inscription Henttawy, as queen, mentions Pinudjem as king, the two of them also being shown together on a stela from Koptos.

The children of the couple included (according to Henttawy's titles) a king, a High Priest and a God's Wife of Amun. The God's Wife was certainly Maatkare A and, in view of her depiction alongside two sisters – Henttawy B and Mutnodjmet[141] B – at Karnak, these two are also likely to have been born to Henttawy Q. As far as the High Priest is concerned, he could be one, some

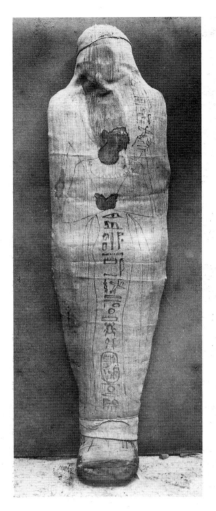

Wrapped mummy of Pinudjem I with an image of Osiris on its shroud. The body was found in TT320, Western Thebes, in 1881 and taken to the Cairo Museum, where it was unwrapped soon afterwards. However, it seems not to have been examined subsequently, and its precise location is currently unknown.

or all of the three sons of Pinudjem I to hold that office: Masaharta B, Djedkhonsiufankh I and Menkheperre B, all of whom are explicitly called his son on their monuments. Regarding the identity of the king, a jar from the tomb of Pasebkhanut I at Tanis bears both his own names and titles and those of Henttawy, who is given the title of 'King's Mother', confirming another link. **Pasebkhanut I**'s wife is also indicated by a dish from his tomb, in this case pairing the king's names with that of Mutnodjmet as his wife, while other sources also indicate that she was his sister – without doubt the Mutnodjmet B who is known from Karnak.

Pinudjem I had at least two other wives, neither of them of known ancestry, Isetemkheb A being identified from stamped bricks bearing her name and that of her husband. Tentnabekhenu is attested solely by the coffins of her daughter, Nauny, which call the latter the offspring of a king; as Nauny's tomb was at Thebes, the Theban king Pinudjem I is most likely to have been the father. One other child of Pinudjem I seems to be known: a son, Nesipaneferhor, who had his own and his father's name written over that of the 18th son of Hrihor in the Khonsu temple.

A daughter of Pasebkhanut I – Isetemkheb C – is known from another bowl in the king's tomb. Her mother is shown to be called Wiay (B) by the funerary papyrus of Pinudjem II, which states that Pinudjem was not only the son of an 'Isetemkheb, daughter of Wiay', but also a descendant of Pasebkhanut. Only one son is certainly attested – Ankhefenmut C, who had a burial chamber within his father's tomb – but it is probable that his successor **Amenemopet** was also a son, although this pure supposition at present. Neither is any wife or child of Amenemopet known.

Of the families of Pasebkhanut's brothers, Masaharta's wife is not known with certainty but may be Tayuheret, whose title is appropriate and whose coffins seem to be contemporary. Djedkhonsiufankh I is only known from the now-lost coffin of a nameless son; it is conceivable that his wife was Djedmutesankh A, who is definitely the wife of an otherwise unknown High Priest.

Menkheperre's kin are rather better known, with both he and his wife, Isetemkheb C, mentioned in the funerary papyrus of a son, Pinudjem II. Three daughters, Isetemkheb D, Gautsoshen A and Meryetamun F are explicitly called 'daughter of Menkheperre' on their funerary equipment; details of Gautsoshen's husband and children are also provided by their funerary equipment. A further daughter may be Henttawy C, on the basis of a property decree at Karnak. Nesibanebdjedet II (possibly the eldest son) is called 'son of Menkheperre' on a pair of bracelets, as is Pasebkhanut A on his funerary stela, and a final son, Hori C, on his coffins.

The property decree of Henttawy C shows that she was the mother of Isetemkheb E and suggests that she may have been the sister-wife of Nesibanebdjedet II – her titles on her coffins indicate that she was married to a High Priest. The same document also seems to indicate that Nesibanebdjedet II had a daughter named Nesikhonsu, who is generally regarded as the same as Nesikhonsu A who married Pinudjem II, and whose mother is given

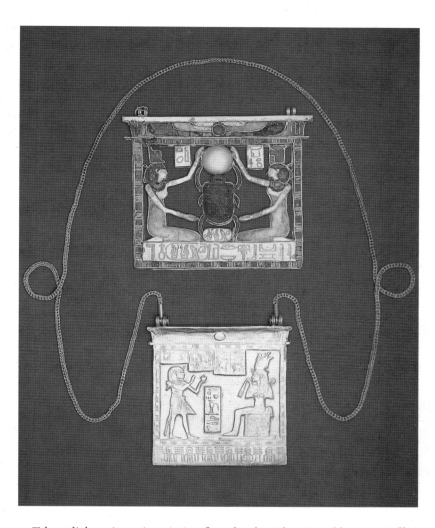

(right) Pectorals of King Amenemopet; from his burial at Tanis (CM JE86037–8).

as Tahentdjehuty in an inscription from her burial; on Nesikhonsu's coffin, her father is simply referred to as a High Priest of Amun, without a name. Nesikhonsu's inscription also gives the names of her children. Of them, Nesitanebetashru A is known to have had a daughter, Nesikhonsu B, on the basis of the latter's funerary papyrus, but there is no direct evidence for her father. Speculation that he may have been Djedptahiufankh (A), Third Prophet of Amun, is based purely upon his burial alongside Nesitanebetashru in tomb TT320.

Pinudjem II's other wife was his sister, Isetemkheb D; this marriage is nowhere stated explicitly, but her titles make it clear that she married a High Priest, the choice being limited to Nesibanebdjedet II or Pinudjem II. The fact that Isetemkheb was buried alongside Pinudjem makes him by far the more likely. Her daughter was Harweben, on the basis of inscriptions on the latter's coffins and papyrus.

Another child of Pinudjem II, Pasebkhanut II, is named in ink inscriptions on the bandages of a number of mummies. There is no indication of his

Pinudjem II offers to Osiris on his funerary papyrus; from TT320, Western Thebes (BM EA10793).

mother although, as Nesikhonsu A's children are apparently listed comprehensively in the aforementioned text from her burial, it is more likely to be Isetemkheb D (assuming that there was no third wife). A final child of this couple might be a God's Wife, Henttawy D, who dates to this period and may be the offspring of a 'Mother of the God's Wife, Isetemkheb', who may in turn be identical with Isetemkheb D.

Returning to the Tanite kings, Amenemopet was followed on the throne by a scion of a long-established Libyan family. Our knowledge of the family is based upon the stela of a remote descendant, Pasenhor B (see p. 221), who included his distinguished genealogy in a stela dedicated at the funeral of the sacred bull known as Apis XXXIII in the Serapeum at Saqqara in year 37 of Shoshenq V's reign. However, King **Osorkon the Elder**'s place in the family derives from another much later text (once on the roof of the Khonsu temple) which gives his mother as a Mehytenweskhet. This ties in with Mehytenweskhet A's title of 'King's Mother' on Pasenhor's stela. This stela also shows that Mehytenweskhet's nephew was none other than Shoshenq I, ultimately founder of the 22nd Dynasty.

Nothing is known of any relationship between Amenemopet and Osorkon the Elder; neither is there any known connection between Osorkon the Elder and his successor, **Siamun**. Indeed, Siamun's Egyptian name contrasts with the uniformly Libyan names adopted by the males of Osorkon the Elder's family, both in earlier generations and later, when his kin had become the 22nd Dynasty, thus suggesting that he was not directly related. It may be therefore that he was a son or grandson of Amenemopet,[142] but this is without any evidence.

Brief Lives ●

Males in **bold**, *females in* **bold italic**.

Amenhirwenemef B (KSonB)
Son of Hrihor; depicted in a procession of his siblings in the peristyle court of the temple of Khonsu at Karnak.

Amenre[...]shef (KSonB)
Son of Hrihor; depicted with his siblings in the Khonsu temple.

Ankhef(enmut A) (KSonB)
Son of Hrihor; depicted with his siblings in the Khonsu temple.

Ankhefenmut B (PMut)
Son of Piankh; depicted in a graffito in the first courtyard of the temple of Luxor.

Ankhefenmut C (KSonB; 1Genmo)
Son of Pasebkhanut I, also known as **Ramesses-Ankhefenmut**. Had a burial chamber within the king's tomb at Tanis (NRTIII), but seems to have suffered disgrace and had his inscriptions mutilated.

Baknetjery (KSonB)
Son of Hrihor; depicted with his siblings in the Khonsu temple.

Buyuawa
Ancestor of Osorkon the Elder and Shoshenq I, entitled simply *thnw* – 'the Libyan'; he probably lived during the 20th Dynasty. Named on the stela of his remote descendant, Pasenhor B, from the Serapeum and now in the Louvre.

Djedkhonsiufankh I (HPA)
Son of Pinudjem I; known only from the filiation on the now-lost coffin of his son.

Djedmutesankh A (1ChHA)
Possibly wife of Djedkhonsiufankh I; her burial (datable to the latter part of the dynasty) was found in Deir el-Bahari tomb MMA60 and is now in New York.

Faienmut (ChA)
Daughter of Piankh, mentioned on a bandage used to rewrap the mummy of Ramesses III around years 13 and 15 of Nesibanebdjedet I.

Gautsoshen A (ChH Mentu)
Daughter of Menkheperre B; wife of Tjanefer A, known from her coffin and funerary papyrus, found in the tomb known as the Bab el-Gasus at Deir el-Bahari and now in Cairo.

Harweben (ChHA–4th phyle)
Daughter of Isetemkheb D; buried in the Bab el-Gasus; her funerary equipment is in the Cairo Museum.

Henttawy B (KD; ChA; Flautist of Mut)
Daughter of Pinudjem I; shown with her sisters and father in a Luxor graffito, and buried at Deir el-Bahari in tomb MMA60. Her coffins are in the Cairo Museum.

Henttawy C (ChHA)
Probable mother of Isetemkheb E and sister-wife of Nesibanebdjedet II. Known from a property decree on the Tenth Pylon at Karnak, and from her burial in Deir el-Bahari tomb MMA60, the coffins from which are in Boston and New York.

Henttawy D (GWA; Ador)
Possible daughter of Isetemkheb D and Pinudjem II; name written with the Adoratrix title within the cartouche. Known only from a number of *shabtis* of unknown provenance.

Henttawy Q (KD; KW; KM; L2L; M2L; Daughter of KGW; 1ChHA; Mother of: KGW, HPA & Genmo)
Wife of Pinudjem I, mother of

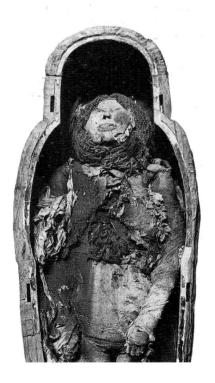

Henttawy Q was reburied in TT320, from which tomb came this shabti (above, Berlin 8530) and her mummy (below, CM CG61090).

Pasebkhanut I, Maatkare A, and one or more of Masaharta B, Djedkhonsiufankh I or Menkheperre B, and probably daughter of Ramesses XI; name written in full is **Duahathor-Henttawy**. A goblet from tomb NRTIII at Tanis, a scene on the pylon of the Khonsu temple at Karnak and a lintel refer to her in the period before her husband's assumption of royal titles. Nevertheless, these sources give Henttawy a number of queenly titles, as well as that of King's Daughter and the cartouche to which she was entitled by virtue of that status. To the subsequent phase of her career date a stela from Koptos, a dedication inscription in the temple of Mut at Karnak, a scene on the façade of the Khonsu temple at Karnak, and a number of inscribed items from the tomb of her son at Tanis. Her funerary papyrus, mummy and coffins were found in tomb TT320 and are now in the Cairo Museum.

Heqamaat (Sem-Priest at Medinet Habu)
Son of Piankh; depicted in a graffito in the first courtyard of the temple of Luxor with brother Heqanefer.

Heqanefer (2PA)
Son of Piankh; depicted in a graffito at Luxor with Heqamaat.

Hori C (PA; PSeth)
Son of Menkheperre B; his mummy and coffins were found in the Bab el-Gasus and are now in the Cairo Museum.

Hrere (ChHA; KM)
Mother of Nodjmet and probably Nesibanebdjedet I; presumably the wife of a High Priest of Amun. Named on a funerary papyrus of her daughter, and the sender of two letters to Thebes concerning the rations of the Theban necropolis workmen. From other correspondence of the late 20th Dynasty, she is seen as active both in Elephantine and Thebes.

Isetemkheb A (ChHA)
Wife of Pinudjem I; named alongside her husband on stamped bricks from El-Hiba.

Isetemkheb B (ChH Min)
Perhaps daughter of Masaharta B. Owner of a leather catafalque (tent for the coffin), bearing the names of Pinudjem I and Masaharta B, and calling her the 'daughter of the High Priest'; it is possible, however, that she could be identical with ***Isetemkheb D***.

Isetemkheb C (1ChHA)
Wife of Menkheperre B and daughter of Pasebkhanut I and Wiay B; mentioned in her son's funerary papyrus, and on a daughter's coffin, with her name alongside that of her husband on stamped bricks at El-Hiba. She may also be mentioned in a decree inscribed on Pylon X at Karnak.

Isetemkheb D (ChHA)
Daughter of Menkheperre B and sister-wife of Pinudjem II. Her mummy, coffins, canopics and other funerary equipment were buried in tomb TT320; they are now in Cairo. A much earlier set of her coffins was reused for the interment of Nesikhonsu A.

Isetemkheb E
Daughter of Henttawy C, and mentioned in her mother's Karnak property decree.

Isetemkheb Q
Mother of Tjanefer A, mentioned on his coffins.

Itamun B (KSonB)
Son of Hrihor; depicted with his siblings in the Khonsu temple.

Itawy A
Daughter of Pinudjem II and Nesikhonsu A; named on her mother's decree text.

Maatkare A (KDB; Ador; GWA: prenomen **Mutemhat**)
Daughter of Pinudjem I and Henttawy Q. Depicted early in life in a graffito in Luxor temple, as God's Wife of Amun on the façade of the Khonsu temple at Karnak and by a statue in Marseilles. Her mummy, coffins, papyrus and *shabtis* were found in tomb TT320; Maatkare's body was accompanied in its coffin by the mummy of her pet baboon.

Madenneb (KSonB)
Son of Hrihor; depicted with his siblings in the Khonsu temple.

Masaharta A (KSonB)
Son of Hrihor; depicted with his siblings in the Khonsu temple.

Masaharta B (KSon; HPA; Genmo)
Son of Pinudjem I. He was responsible for the restoration of the mummy of Amenhotep I in year 16 of Nesibanebdjedet I; inscriptions are known in the temple of Amenhotep II at Karnak, on ram-headed sphinxes at the same site and on a colossal falcon in Brussels. Shown by his mummy to have been a man of considerable girth, Masaharta may have fallen ill and died at El-Hiba around year 24, if a fragment of a letter has been correctly interpreted. His burial was found in tomb TT320 and is now in the Museum of Mummification at Luxor.

Masaharta C
Son of Pinudjem II and Nesikhonsu A; named on his mother's decree text.

Masaqaharta (KSonB)
Son of Hrihor; depicted with his siblings in the Khonsu temple.

Mawasun (ChMa)
Ancestor of Osorkon the Elder and Shoshenq I. Named on the stela of Pasenhor B, from the Serapeum.

Mehytenweskhet A (KM)
Mother of Osorkon the Elder and grandmother of Shoshenq I. Named on the stela of Pasenhor B, from the Serapeum, and also mentioned as Osorkon the Elder's mother in a text formerly on the roof of the Khonsu temple at Karnak.

Menkheperre B (KSon; HPA; Genmo)
Son of Pinudjem I. Assumed the priesthood in year 25 of Nesibanebdjedet I and immediately proceeded southward to Thebes to 'pacify the land and suppress his enemy', as recorded on a stela in the Louvre. As also recorded on the stela, a number of those people implicated in the

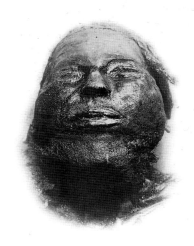

Head of the mummy of Masaharta B (Luxor Museum of Mummification, ex-CG 61092).

troubles were exiled to the western oases, to be recalled a few years later. Menkheperre undertook building work at the fortress of El-Hiba, as well as building other forts further south. On occasion he used a cartouche, and is shown wearing a kingly kilt on a statuette in Rio de Janeiro, but he seems not to have made any substantive claim to kingship. Menkheperre's pontificate lasted for some 50 years, running in parallel with the reign of his brother, Pasebkhanut I. Nothing is known of his burial.

Menkheperre C (3PA)
Grandson of Menkheperre A; his mummy and coffins were found in the Bab el-Gasus and are now in the Cairo Museum.

Meryetamun F (ChA)
Daughter of Menkheperre A; buried in the Bab el-Gasus during the pontificate of Pasebkhanut II. Her coffins are in Cairo.

Mutnodjmet B (KDB; KSis; KGW; L2L; 2PA Tanis)
Probably a daughter of Pinudjem I, and wife of Pasebkhanut I. Depicted as a princess alongside her sisters in a graffito in the peristyle courts of the Luxor temple, and as queen in her burial chamber in her husband's tomb at Tanis (NRTIII).

Various items bearing her name were found in the tomb (Cairo Museum), but her burial chamber was appropriated for the burial of Amenemopet, and her mummy apparently removed.

Nauny (KDB)
Daughter of Tentnabekhenu and (probably) Pinudjem I. Her burial was found in the tomb of Meryetamun B at Deir el-Bahari (TT358), and proved to be that of a woman in her seventies; the material from the interment is in New York.

Nebneshi (ChMa)
Ancestor of Osorkon the Elder and Shoshenq I. Named on the stela of Pasenhor B, from the Serapeum.

Nesibanebdjedet II (High Steward of Amun; HPA)
Son of Menkheperre B, and served as High Steward under his father before assuming the pontificate. His monuments are scarce, limited to an inscription at Karnak, a note on the bandages of a mummy and bracelets bearing his name on the mummy of Pasebkhanut I. A scribal palette in New York may be his, although it may belong to Nesibanebdjedet III.

Nesikhonsu A (1ChHA; KSonK)
Wife of Pinudjem II; known from her burial in tomb TT320, which took place in year 5 of Siamun according to an inscription at the tomb entrance, and which employed coffins originally made for Isetemkheb D. Nesikhonsu's burial included a religious decree, written on a wooden board, that was to ensure her well-being in the next world – and to prevent her doing harm to her husband and children from there. This suggests that family problems may have existed around the time of her death. Nesikhonsu is also named on the funerary papyrus of her daughter, Nesitanebetashru A.

Nesikhonsu B (ChHA–1st phyle)
Granddaughter of Pinudjem II; known from her funerary papyrus in the Guimet Museum, Paris.

Nesipaherenmut (4PA)
Father of Tjanefer A; known from a mention of his son in the Karnak Priestly Annals.

Nesipaneferhor (GFAmun)
Son of Pinudjem I; his name was written in place of that of [...]21B in the procession of sons of Hrihor in the Khonsu temple at Karnak.

Nesitanebetashru A
Daughter of Pinudjem II and Nesikhonsu A; named on her mother's decree text. Her mummy, coffins and *shabti*s were buried in tomb TT320 and are now in Cairo. Possibly married to Djedptahiufankh A.

Nesta[...] (KDB)
Daughter of Hrihor; depicted with her siblings in the Khonsu temple.

Nimlot A (ChMa; GF)
Father of Shoshenq I and brother of Osorkon the Elder. Named on the stela of Pasenhor B, and also commemorated by his son (prior to his accession) on a stela from Abydos, now in the Cairo Museum.

This stela records various endowments made by the then-reigning king (perhaps Siamun) to support a statue-cult of Nimlot at Abydos.

Nodjmet (ChHA; KGW; KM; L2L)
Wife of Hrihor and probably previously Piankh; likely to have been mother of Pinudjem I. Shown behind an erased figure of Hrihor (as High Priest) on a stela in Leiden, and in the company of Piankh and his sons in a graffito in the temple of Luxor, as well as queen of Hrihor in a scene in the temple of Khonsu. She is also the recipient of a letter from Piankh in which she is asked to carry out the interrogation and extra-judicial execution of two policemen charged with sedition. Nodjmet's coffins, mummy, canopic chest (all now in Cairo) and two Books of the Dead (split between the British Museum, Louvre and Munich Museum) were found in tomb TT320's cache.

Panefer[...] (KSonB)
Son of Hrihor; depicted with his siblings in the Khonsu temple.

Paihuty (ChMa)
Ancestor of Osorkon the Elder and Shoshenq I. Named on the stela of Pasenhor B.

Pasebkhanut II (HPA; AL)
Son of Pinudjem II; known from the wrappings of a number of mummies from the Bab el-Gasus, and from a graffito in the temple of Sety I at Abydos which gives him a composite priestly/kingly set of titles. He appears to have assumed full **kingship** as co-regent of Shoshenq I. Buried in NRTIII.

Pasebkhanut A (AL)
Son of Menkheperre B who held various military and priestly offices. He was buried in tomb D22 at Abydos; his funerary stela is in the British Museum.

Pashedkhonsu (KSonB)
Son of Hrihor; depicted with his siblings in the Khonsu temple.

Piankh (Gen; AL; HPA; KSonK)
Father of Pinudjem I. Much of his pontificate was spent campaigning

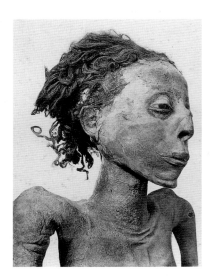

The mummy of Nesitanebetashru A (below, CM CG61096) was buried alongside that of her father in TT320, accompanied by the usual shabti figures (left, in a private collection).

(below) The mummy of Nodjmet, showing the facial packing introduced at the beginning of the 21st Dynasty; from TT320 (CM CG61087).

against the renegade Viceroy of Nubia, Pahehsy, from which period survive a number of letters written by Piankh, his family and associates, known as the Late Ramesside Letters. An oracle in Piankh's favour is recorded in a text at Karnak, while a stela is known from Abydos (Cairo), plus inscriptions in the Khonsu temple at Karnak and a restoration text on the mummy of Ramesses III.

Pinudjem I (Viz; HPA; Genmo)
Son of Piankh. As High Priest he added inscriptions to the Karnak Khonsu temple and the small temple at Medinet Habu. However, a statuette (Cairo, from Karnak) shows him with High Priestly titles but wearing royal garb, and in one case a representation was altered back to showing him in priestly garb, as if to hint at some hesitation on Pinudjem's part. From at least year 16 of Nesibanebdjedet I he took full **pharaonic** titles as well.

Pinudjem II (HPA; Genmo)
Son of Menkheperre B and Isetemkheb C. Assumed the High Priesthood following the short pontificate of Nesibanebdjedet II, and served until year 10 of Siamun. Buried in tomb TT320 near Deir el-Bahari, shared with members of his family, which was used under Shoshenq I to cache a number of earlier royal mummies.

Pinudjem A (4PA)
Grandson of Menkheperre A; his mummy and coffins were found in the Bab el-Gasus, but their location is presently unknown.

Preamenenamun (KSonB)
Son of Hrihor; depicted with his siblings in the Khonsu temple.

Rudament(?) (KSonB)
Son of Hrihor; depicted with his siblings in the Khonsu temple.

Shoshenq A (ChMa)
Father of Osorkon the Elder and grandfather of Shoshenq I. Named on the stela of Pasenhor B.

Shoshenq B (ChMa)
Nephew of Osorkon the Elder, and later king as **SHOSHENQ I**. Dedicated a statue to his father, Nimlot A, at Abydos, in which he indicates a close relationship with the then-king, unnamed but probably Siamun. He seems to have ruled Upper Egypt for at least two years before becoming acknowledged king – to judge from an entry in the Karnak Priestly Annals, which is dated to his second year but only gives his title as Chieftain.

Tahentdjehuty
Mother of Nesikhonsu A; named on Nesikhonsu's 'amuletic decree' from TT320.

Tayuheret (ChHA)
Possibly wife of Masaharta B; known from her mummy, coffins and canopics, found in tomb TT320.

Tekhui (KSonB)
Son of Hrihor; depicted with his siblings in the Khonsu temple.

Tentamun B
Probably daughter of Ramesses XI and wife of Nesibanebdjedet I. Named alongside Nesibanebdjedet in the Report of Wenamun Papyrus as resident at Tanis.

Tentnabekhenu
Mother of Nauny, and probably a wife of Pinudjem I; named on her daughter's funerary papyrus.

Tentsepeh A
Mother of Shoshenq I. Named on the stela of Pasenhor B.

Tjanefer A (3PA)
Husband of Gautsoshen A. Active as Fourth Prophet of Amun in year 40 of Pasebkhanut I, as recorded in the Karnak Priestly Annals; later promoted, as shown by his funerary equipment found in the Bab el-Gasus, now in the Cairo Museum.

Tjanefer B
Son of Pinudjem II and Nesikhonsu A; named on his mother's decree text.

Wiay B
Grandmother of Pinudjem II, and probably wife of Pasebkhanut I; mentioned in her grandson's funerary papyrus.

[...]amenweret (KDB)
Daughter of Hrihor; depicted with her siblings in the Khonsu temple.

[...]anm (KSonB)
Son of Hrihor; depicted with his siblings in the Khonsu temple.

[...]emkheb (KSonB)
Son of Hrihor; depicted with his siblings in the Khonsu temple.

[...]memsunay (KSonB)
Son of Hrihor; depicted with his siblings in the Khonsu temple.

[...]t[...] (KSonB)
Son of Hrihor; depicted with his siblings in the Khonsu temple.

[...]21A (KSonB)
Son of Hrihor; depicted with his siblings in the Khonsu temple.

[...]21B (KSonB)
Son of Hrihor; depicted with his siblings in the Khonsu temple. His name was overwritten by that of Nesipaneferhor.

[...]21C (KDB)
Daughter of Hrihor; depicted with her siblings in the Khonsu temple.

[...]21D (KDB)
Daughter of Hrihor; depicted with her siblings in the Khonsu temple.

[...]21E (KDB)
Daughter of Hrihor; depicted with her siblings in the Khonsu temple.

[...]21F
Son of Djedkhonsiufankh I; known only from a now-lost coffin from Thebes, although a number of uninscribed objects from his tomb are in the British Museum.

The Rise and Fall of the House of Shoshenq

22nd Dynasty

The Royal Succession

22nd Dynasty 948–927
SHOSHENQ I
OSORKON I
HARSIESE
TAKELOT I
OSORKON II
SHOSHENQ III
SHOSHENQ IV
PIMAY
SHOSHENQ V
PEDUBAST II
OSORKON IV

Historical Background

The principal motif of the earlier part of the 22nd Dynasty was the re-estab-lishment of a unitary state; that of the later part was its disintegration. A key part of the first was the ending of the hereditary High Priesthood at Thebes, in favour of a system whereby the pontificate was held by a son of the reigning king, beginning with Iuput A, son of Shoshenq I. The king's commitment to Thebes was further indicated by major building work at Karnak, a whole new forecourt being constructed (albeit left largely undeco-rated at his death). In addition, military intervention in the Levant was once more brought to the fore, with probably at least two campaigns by Shoshenq I – one of them noted in the Old Testament,[143] and another in a relief at Karnak.[144] At home, security of the displaced royal mummies of earlier times was finally achieved by their ultimate reburial in the tomb of Pinudjem II (TT320) some time after Shoshenq's 11th regnal year.

On Shoshenq I's death, the throne passed to Osorkon I. Soon after his accession, the new king's brother Iuput died and was succeeded as High Priest of Amun by Osorkon I's eldest son, Shoshenq Q. Towards the end of Osorkon I's long reign, Shoshenq apparently briefly became his father's co-regent and was replaced as pontiff by a brother, Iuwlot.

The Bubastite Portal, in the south-east corner of the first court of the Great Temple at Karnak, is the major family monument of the Libyan kings.

When Osorkon I himself died soon afterwards, he was followed by Takelot I. Thebes continued to be ruled by the High Priest Iuwlot, and then by his brother, Nesibanebdjedet III; but hardly anything else is known of the events of Takelot I's occupation of the throne, other than the fact that he was succeeded by his son, Osorkon II.

During Osorkon II's reign, the beginnings of a new disintegration of the state was signalled by the High Priest of Amun, Harsiese, doing as Pinudjem I had done: obtaining full pharaonic titles while passing the pontificate itself to a son. On the other hand, elsewhere in Egypt the practice of installing royal sons in positions of power was continued from previous reigns, and extended at Memphis, where the old-established line of High Priests was supplanted by the Crown Prince Shoshenq D, borne to Osorkon II by Queen Karomama B. The approach was also re-adopted at Thebes after the (perhaps forced) end of the pontificate of Harsiese's son, when Prince Nimlot C became High Priest of Amun. On his death, the hereditary principle reasserted itself, with Takelot F taking office, and apparently later taking royal titles at Thebes as Takelot II, first proper king of the parallel 23rd Dynasty. That this split was rapidly recognized abroad is suggested by the mention of 'kings of Egypt' in a Biblical passage that refers to this very period.

(right) Upper part of a statue of Osorkon I, from Jebail, Lebanon. Its torso is covered with a Phoenician inscription of Elibaal, King of Byblos (Louvre, AO9502).

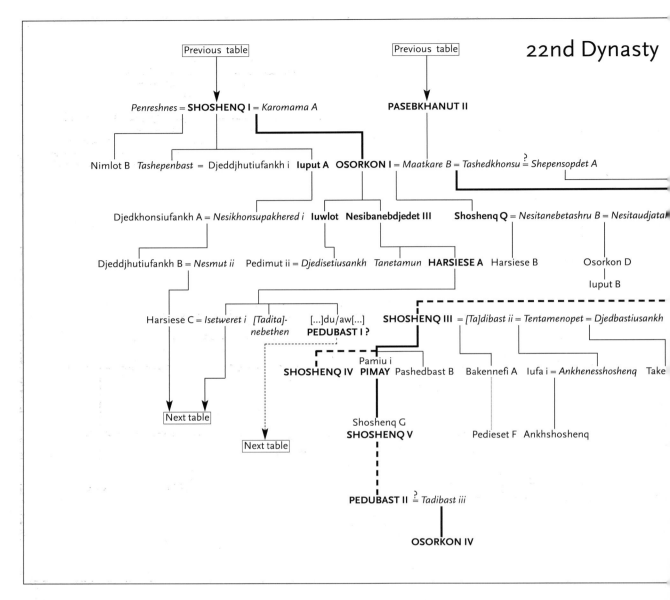

22nd Dynasty

Osorkon II did little to imitate his great-grandfather, Shoshenq I, in the area of foreign relations, although he may have contributed around 1,000 troops to the coalition of Syro-Palestinian polities that opposed the Assyrians at the Battle of Qarqar in 853 BC.

At Tanis, Osorkon II was succeeded by Shoshenq III; however, while Shoshenq's authority was acknowledged by the great array of 'princedoms' and 'chiefdoms' which sprang up throughout the Delta during the middle of the 22nd Dynasty, Thebes was now a separate polity – albeit one in whose affairs the Tanite king is known to have meddled (see next section).

Shoshenq III was a considerable builder at his capital, following usual practice by employing recycled earlier monuments as raw material.

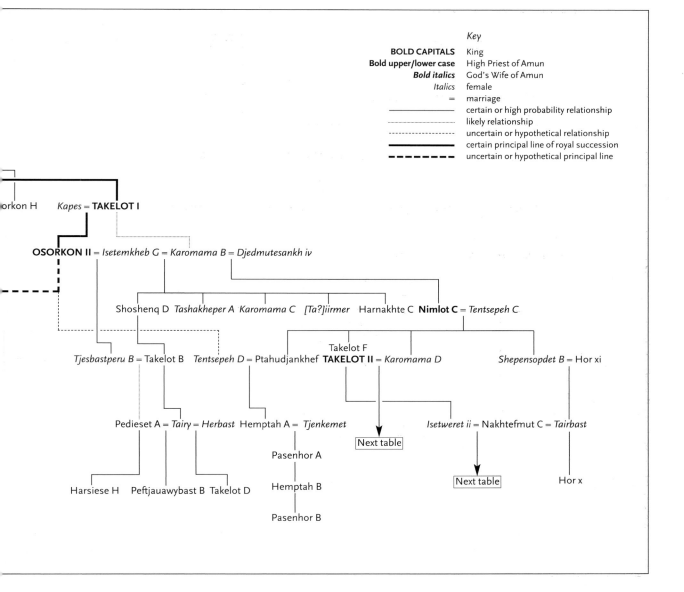

Key

BOLD CAPITALS	King
Bold upper/lower case	High Priest of Amun
Bold italics	God's Wife of Amun
Italics	female
=	marriage
———————	certain or high probability relationship
··················	likely relationship
- - - - - - - -	uncertain or hypothetical relationship
——————	certain principal line of royal succession
- - - - - -	uncertain or hypothetical principal line

After four decades on the throne, he was succeeded by Shoshenq IV, whose reign was so unremarkable that his very existence was only first noticed in the late 1980s. The line was then maintained by Shoshenq III's son Pimay, and then a fifth Shoshenq, before concluding with Pedubast II and Osorkon IV. By this time, the old family's power over the north was little more than nominal – a 'first amongst equals' within the framework of Delta principalities.

The Royal Family

As noted in the previous section, **Shoshenq I** was descended from a series of Libyan chieftains, and was also the nephew of the 21st Dynasty king,

Shoshenq I established his son, Iuput (A), as High Priest at Karnak, thus ending the long-standing independent line of High Priests. The High Priesthood would remain under the firm control of the Tanite king until the appointment of Harsiese A led to the collapse of Shoshenq I's settlement. Here, the king is being suckled by Hathor, while Iuput makes an offering; from the Bubastite Portal at Karnak.

Osorkon the Elder. That Shoshenq was married to Karomama A is stated on the stela of Pasenhor B, but not confirmed by any contemporary monuments. From the same source, we know that Karomama was the mother of the future Osorkon I; however, a second son – Nimlot B – was borne by Penreshnes, the daughter of an unnamed chieftain. The maternity of Shoshenq I's other two known children is uncertain. Of them, Iuput A is well known and is explicitly called Shoshenq I's son on all his monuments. He had a daughter, Nesikhonsupakhered i, who is included in the biographical texts of a number of her descendants, along with her husband. The other child of the king, Tashepenbast, is named (together with her husband) on a statue of their grandson Neseramun ii.

Osorkon I is known to have married Maatkare B, daughter of Pasebkhanut II; this fact, and Maatkare's parentage, is provided by a statue of the personification of the Inundation dedicated by their son, Shoshenq Q. A wife and son of the latter are given on a statuette of the god Bes, which records Nesitanebetashru B and the Prophet of Amun, Harsiese B. The latter is almost certainly the same man who rose to be High Priest under Osorkon II and Shoshenq III. Two papyri in St Petersburg (Papyrus Denon) call Osorkon D 'the son of the High Priest of Amun, Shoshenq, son of King Osorkon', the second of them naming his mother as Nesitaudjatakhet.[145] As the only certain High Priest of Amun who was the son of an Osorkon, Osorkon D's father would seem to have been **Shoshenq Q**.

Three children of **Harsiese A**[146] are known: Isetweret i is named as his daughter on the statue of a descendant; [Tadita]nebethen is recorded on a coffin-fragment; while a son is expressly called the offspring of King Harsiese on a monument from Koptos. Unfortunately, his name has been damaged, only signs reading 'du' or 'aw' surviving. One possible reading is 'Pedubast', and it has been suggested that he could in this case be the future 23rd Dynasty king, Pedubast I; certainly, he belongs to the right generation.

Besides Shoshenq Q, two other sons of Osorkon I are known from contemporary monuments, both Iuwlot and Nesibanebdjedet III being called his sons on a Nile-level inscription at Karnak. Descendants of Iuwlot are listed on a statue of one of them. A further offspring of Osorkon – his successor **Takelot I** – is so designated in the Pasenhor B stela, which also provides the name of his wife, Kapes. A final son may be Osorkon H; he is known from his tomb at Herakleopolis, which also contained *shabtis* of a King's Wife, Shepensopdet (Q), otherwise unknown. If, as seems likely, he was the husband of Tanetamun (daughter of Nesibanebdjedet III and buried in the adjacent tomb), his father can only have been Osorkon I, given that Takelot I already had a son named Osorkon: the future Osorkon II.

Pasenhor also indicates that **Osorkon II** was this royal couple's son, for whose numerous children we have a number of sources. Nimlot C left many descendants (including Pasenhor B) who clearly name him as a son of Osorkon II on their statues and coffins. Pasenhor indicates that Nimlot's mother was Djedmutesankh (iv) and that his wife was Tentsepeh (C); Pasenhor's line then continues through their son, Ptahudjankhef, and onwards.

Relief of Osorkon II and his wife Karomama B, from the entrance to the King's Jubilee Hall in the temple at Bubastis (BM EA1077).

The latter's wife, Tentsepeh D, is stated to have been a king's daughter; the most likely candidate for her father seems to be Osorkon II.

Nimlot and Tentsepeh C's daughter, Shepensopdet B, her husband and son are recorded together on a statue dedicated by their grandson. Nimlot C's two remaining children were Takelot F, as stated on a Karnak inscription of the latter; and Karomama D, as indicated by the Chronicle text of her son, Osorkon B – the same source showing that she was married to Takelot II. That this king was none other than her brother, Takelot F, is suggested by the circumstantial evidence of his period of office as High Priest directly preceding the appearance of Takelot II on the Theban throne.

Osorkon II had at least two other wives. Karomama B appears with her husband on the latter's Jubilee Hall at Bubastis and, judging by her title of King's Daughter, was probably also his sister. Their eldest son was Shoshenq D, as stated on one of his statues. Shoshenq D's descendants are given on a *(right) Queen Karomama B leads her daughters Tashakheper A, Karomama C and [Ta?]iirmer, at the entrance to the Jubilee Hall at Bubastis.*

(below) The lid of the sarcophagus adapted for the burial of Prince Harnakhte C in his father Osorkon II's tomb at Tanis (NRTI), where it is now on display.

stela of his grandson and great-grandsons from the Serapeum, with Tjesbastperu B known to be a daughter of Osorkon II and a certain Isetemkheb G from her canopic jars. An unusual feature of this line of the family is that Shoshenq D's grandchildren, Pedieset A and Tairy, although brother and sister, married one another; such a union is otherwise unknown outside those in direct line to the throne, or a semi-regal High Priesthood.

Three daughters of Osorkon II are shown in his Jubilee Hall at Bubastis. One of them, Karomama C, may be identical with the God's Wife Karomama G, who is known to have served under Osorkon II and his successors; the main obstacle to this identification is Karomama G's lack of the King's Daughter title. On the other hand, since almost all other God's Wives were royal daughters and occasionally omitted the title, this may not be significant. The final known offspring is Harnakhte C, known only from his burial in the tomb of his father at Tanis.

Nothing is known of the relationship between Osorkon II and his successor, since the Pasenhor stela, so useful earlier on, continues its genealogy through Nimlot C's line and not through the main royal succession. In addition, research is now strongly suggesting that – rather than being followed on the throne by Takelot II as had always been assumed – Takelot II was actually the definitive founder of a new independent 23rd Dynasty at Thebes.[147] Thus, unless a hitherto-unrecognized pharaoh is to be interposed,[148] Osorkon II will have been directly succeeded by Shoshenq III, whose ancestry is completely unknown. It is most likely that he was a son of Osorkon II, but this has not been proved.

Another problem from this point onwards is that with the effective independence of Thebes, the useful genealogical material provided by private monuments is now orientated towards the local 23rd Dynasty. Far less is henceforth known about the 22nd Dynasty's links, except where occasionally revealed by Serapeum stelae.

However, the evidence for **Shoshenq III**'s own family is initially fairly good. His eldest son is stated to have been Bakennefi A, son of [Ta]dibast ii, on a Heliopolitan stela that also gives the name of the prince's grandmother. Another spouse, Djedbastiusankh, is named on a stela of her son, Takelot C; and yet a further wife, Tentamenopet, is named together with her descendants on a block that formed part of a monument belonging to one of them. Two more sons are mentioned on monuments of theirs. One of the latter was Pamiu i – probably the same man as King **Pimay**, Shoshenq III's ultimate successor. However, between the two kings ruled **Shoshenq IV**, who was buried in Shoshenq III's tomb and was presumably another son.[149]

Pimay's successor, **Shoshenq V**, is explicitly called Pimay's son on a stela from the Serapeum at Saqqara; he thus may be the same man as Shoshenq G, called 'son of Pamiu' on a scarab. Beyond this, no family information exists for Shoshenq V – even indirect data of the name of his successor. It is generally accepted that the last king of the dynasty was Osorkon IV, who submitted to the 25th Dynasty conqueror, Piye, following his invasion (see below, p. 232). Osorkon's mother seems to have been named Tadibast (iii), on the basis of the names on a miniature headpiece: although no prenomen is given, all other Osorkons had mothers of other names. It is possible that his predecessor was **Pedubast II**, but no family links are known. On the basis of general chronology, they could be either sons of Shoshenq V, or son and grandson.

Brief Lives ●

Males in **bold,** *females in* **bold italic.**

Ankhenesshoshenq (KD)
Daughter of Shoshenq III; named in the biography of a descendant (Cairo).

Ankhshoshenq (GF)
Grandson of Shoshenq III; named in the biography of a descendant, now in Cairo.

Bakennefi A (ELSon; AL)
Eldest son of Shoshenq III, by [Ta]dibast ii; known from a stela from near Heliopolis.

Djedbastiusankh
Wife of Shoshenq III; named on the stela of her son, Takelot C.

Djeddjhutiufankh B (4PA)
Great-grandson of Shoshenq I; named on statues of his descendants.

Djeddjhutiufankh i (3PA)
Husband of Tashepenbast; named on a statue of their grandson Neseramun ii from Karnak.

Djedisetiusankh
Granddaughter of Osorkon I; commemorated on the statue of her husband.

Djedkhonsiufankh A (4PA)
Grandson-in-law of Shoshenq I; known from the biographies of a number of his descendants.

Djedmutesankh iv
Mother of Nimlot C; named on the stela of Pasenhor B.

Harnakhte C (KSon; HPT)
Son of Osorkon II; died aged no more than ten; interred in the burial chamber of his father in Tanis tomb NRTI.

Harsiese B (HPA)
Probably the son of Shoshenq Q who is recorded as a simple Prophet of Amun on a statue of Bes, now in Durham. This man is probably to be identified with a man who became High Priest late in the reign of Osorkon II and continued in office under Shoshenq III and his Theban contemporaries.

Harsiese C
See next section.

Harsiese H (SPP; HPM)
Great-great-grandson of Osorkon II. Served as Sem-Priest alongside his father during the latter's second High Priesthood, and took part in the burial of Apis XXX in year 2 of Pimay. Later became High Priest, and buried as such at Memphis near the tombs of his ancestors.

Hemptah A (GUE; Gen)

(Great-)grandson of Osorkon II; based at Herakleopolis. Known from the stela of Pasenhor B.

Hemptah B (GUE)

(Great-)great-great-grandson of Osorkon II. Known from the stela of his son, Pasenhor B.

Herbast

Wife of Pedieset A; mentioned as mother of Takelot D on her husband's first Serapeum stela.

Hor x (Viz)

Great-great-grandson of Osorkon II; dedicated a statue to his father, Nakhtefmut C; served as Vizier under Osorkon III.

Hor xi (Letter Writer of Pharaoh)

Husband of Shepensopdet B. Known from a statue of their son-in-law.

Isetemkheb G

Wife of Osorkon II; named on the canopic jars of their daughter.

Isetweret i (KD)

Daughter of Harsiese A; named on the statue of her son, Djedkhonsiufankh C, from Karnak and now in Cairo.

Isetweret ii (KD)

See next section.

Iufa i (GF)

Husband of Ankhenesshoshenq; named in the biography of a descendant (Cairo).

Iuput A (KSon; HPA; Genmo)

Son of Shoshenq I; High Priest for much of his reign and into that of his brother, Osorkon I. His first mention is in year 10, on bandages on the mummy of Djedptahiufankh A (3PA, from TT320) and he was involved in the Silsila quarrying in year 21, as shown by the great stela there. He is also shown in the reliefs of the Bubastite Portal at Karnak, mentioned on a stela from there, and in his granite-lined tomb at Abydos.

Iuput B (PA)

Son of Osorkon D; known from fragments of his cartonnage in a private collection.

Iuwlot (KSon; HPA)

Son of Osorkon I; born some time after Shoshenq Q, as he is called a 'youth' in his father's year 10. Probably became High Priest after Shoshenq Q left office late in Osorkon I's reign, but in any case before year 5 of Takelot I, when he recorded the height of the Nile at Karnak. Named on a statue of his son-in-law, Pedimut ii, found at Karnak and now in Cairo.

Kapes

Wife of Takelot I and mother of Osorkon II. Named on the stela of Pasenhor, and apparently also included amongst the mourners for her son in the latter's tomb at Tanis (NRTI). It seems unlikely she outlived him, however, given the probable long length of his reign.

Karomama A

Wife of Shoshenq I and mother of Osorkon I; known only from the stela of Pasenhor B.

Karomama B (KW; KD; MULE)

Wife of Osorkon II and probable daughter of Takelot I. Shown in the Jubilee Hall of the temple of Bubastis, and mentioned on a stela held by a statue of her husband at Tanis and on two scarabs.

Karomama C (KDB)

Daughter of Osorkon II; depicted in the king's Jubilee Hall. She may be identical with **Karomama G**.

Karomama D

See next section.

Karomama G Meryetmut (GWA; L2L; Ador; prenomen: **Sitamen Mutemhat**)

Perhaps identical with **Karomama C**. Her Treasurer was one Ahentefnakhte, who dedicated a superb bronze statue (now in the Louvre) to her, as well as a fragment of a votive figure of the goddess Maat from

Front of a naos held by an 18th Dynasty statue usurped by a 22nd Dynasty priest. A figure of the original owner has been replaced by an image of Karomama G (Berlin 2278).

THE RISE AND FALL OF THE HOUSE OF SHOSHENQ

(opposite) Bronze standing statuette of the God's Wife Karomama G (Louvre N500).

Karnak. In the same complex, she appears in the chapel of Osiris-Nebankh there, while also hers are a stela, canopic jars and *shabtis* (Berlin).

Maatkare B (KD; PH)
Daughter of Pasebkhanut II, wife of Osorkon I and mother of Shoshenq II. Named on two statues made by her son, but curiously not given the title of King's Wife, nor a cartouche. As a princess, she featured in a property settlement carved on the north face of the Seventh Pylon at Karnak.

Nakhtefmut C (Viz)
See next section.

Nesibanebdjedet III (KSon; HPA)
Son of Osorkon I. Served as High Priest during the middle of the reign of his brother, Takelot I, recording the height of the Nile at Karnak in years 8 and 14. His may be a scribal palette in New York, although it may rather belong to Nesibanebdjedet II.

Nesikhonsupakhered i
Granddaughter of Shoshenq I and wife of Djedkhonsiufankh A; named on statues of their descendants.

Nesitanebetashru B (Chantress)
Wife of Shoshenq II and mother of Harsiese A; mentioned on a statue of Bes in Durham.

Nesitaudjatakhet
Wife of Shoshenq II and named with her son, Osorkon D, in Papyrus Denon in St Petersburg.

Nesmut ii
Wife of Djeddjhutiufankh B; named on statues of their descendants.

Nimlot B (KSon; Gen; AL)
Son of Shoshenq I and Penreshnes. Based at Herakleopolis, whence comes an altar and a stela in Cairo, which records the

king's praise for his son in reinstating the daily offering of a bull to the local god, Arsaphes. The lower part of a statue of his was found at Tell Moqdam (Cairo) and another statue, probably from Heliopolis, is now in Vienna.

Nimlot C (KSon; GUE; HPA; HPHrk; Gen; AL)
Son of Osorkon II. Began his career as Commander-in-Chief at Herakleopolis, where he remained until at least year 16, as a donation stela there is dated to that time. Later became High Priest at Thebes until a little before the end of his father's reign. His accession may have followed some troubles there, given the apparent erasure of the name of his predecessor [...]du/aw[...] on the latter's one surviving monument. Nimlot is mentioned in the texts of his son, Takelot F; grandson, Osorkon B; daughter, Shepensopdet B; and grandson-in-law, Nakhtefmut C – from Karnak.

Osorkon D (PA)
Son of Shoshenq Q and Nesitaudjatakhet; named on Papyrus Denon in St Petersburg and cartonnage of Iuput B.

Osorkon H (KSon; Gen; HPHrk)
Son of Shepensopdet A and possibly Osorkon I. Known from his tomb (number 2) at Herakleopolis.

Pamiu i (GChMa; SonL2L)
Son of Shoshenq III, known from a stela from Sais (Cairo). Possibly later king as **PIMAY**, although the spelling of his name differs.

Pasenhor A (GUE; Gen)
(Great-)great grandson of Osorkon II; based at Herakleopolis. Known from the stela of Pasenhor B.

Pasenhor B (PNeith)
(Great-)great-great-great-grandson of Osorkon II; dedicated a stela to the Apis in year 37 of Shoshenq V, in which he recounts his ancestry.

Pashedbast B (KSon; Genmo)
Son of Shoshenq III. Active in the Thebaid

during the period of the 23rd Dynasty civil war, as shown by an inscription formerly on the doorway of the Tenth Pylon at Karnak.

Pedieset A (ChMA; HPM)
Great-grandson of Osorkon II and served as High Priest after his father's death. Apparently passed the office to his own son, Peftjauawybast B, before year 28 of Shoshenq III; he is shown with Peftjauawybast and his second son, Takelot D, on the burial stela of Apis XXIX of that year. Pedieset later resumed the High Priesthood, appearing as such at the burial of Apis XXX in year 2 of Pimay, with his third son – Harsiese H – as Sem-Priest. Buried at Memphis near his father and grandfather, his silver coffin is in Cairo.

Pedieset F
Probably a son of Bakennefi A, mentioned on a stela of his father.

Pedimut ii (3PA)
Son-in-law of Iuwlot, also known as **Patjenfy**; commemorated by a statue dedicated by his son, one Djedkhonsiufankh.

Peftjauawybast B (HPM)
Great-great-grandson of Osorkon II. Took over the post of High Priest from his father prior to year 28 of Shoshenq III – at which time he is shown involved in the burial of Apis XXIX – but had died or retired prior to the next burial in year 2 of Pimay.

Penreshnes
Mother of Nimlot B; mentioned on the Vienna statue of her son.

Ptahudjankhef (GUE; Gen)
Grandson of Osorkon II; based at Herakleopolis. Known from the stela of Pasenhor B.

Shepensopdet A (KW)
Perhaps a wife of Osorkon I and mother of Osorkon H. Known from *shabtis* in the antechamber of the latter's tomb (number 2) at Herakleopolis.

Shepensopdet B
Granddaughter of Osorkon II. Known from a statue of herself in Cairo, a bowl from the Ramesseum, and a statue of her son-in-law, Nakhtefmut C.

Shoshenq Q (KSon; HPA; Genmo)
Son of Osorkon I and Maatkare B; served as High Priest at Karnak for much of his father's reign, during which time he produced two statues – one of himself (Cairo), one of the Inundation (British Museum) – and reinscribed a very fine late-18th Dynasty human figure (Cairo). On the second of these he uses a cartouche, and has often been equated with a king Heqakheperre Shoshenq (IIa), buried in NRT III at Tanis. However, there are various monuments of descendants of Shoshenq Q, and none of them refers to him as a king – unthinkable if he ever held pharaonic titles, no matter how briefly. In any case, he was ultimately succeeded as High Priest by his brother, Iuwlot.

Shoshenq D (KSon; HPM; Great Exec.)
Eldest son and heir of Osorkon II. Probably served as High Priest at Memphis from early in his father's reign, displacing a long-established line of High Priests. Oversaw the burial of Apis XXVII in year 23 of his father, including the dedication of a block-statue (Budapest), and is the probable owner of another block-statue from Saqqara (Brooklyn); a faience relief-chalice of his is in Berlin, with a scarab in the Petrie Museum. He predeceased his father and was buried in a tomb at Memphis, found intact in 1942.

Shoshenq G (HPT)
Named on a scarab in Cairo as the son of Pamiu i (= King Pimay[?]); possibly later king as **SHOSHENQ V.**

[Ta]dibast ii
Wife of Shoshenq III; named in the stela of her son.

Tadibast iii (GM; KW)
Mother of Osorkon IV, named on an electrum headpiece in the Louvre.

[Tadita]nebethen (KD)
Daughter of Harsiese A; named on a coffin(?)-fragment from Abydos, now in Philadelphia.

Tairbast
Great-granddaughter of Osorkon II; named on a statue dedicated by her son.

[Ta?]iirmer (KDB)
Daughter of Osorkon II; depicted in the king's Jubilee Hall.

Tairy
Daughter of Takelot B, and wife of her (half?-)brother, Pedieset A. Named on her husband's first Serapeum stela.

Takelot B (ChMa; HPM)
Grandson of Osorkon II. Succeeded his father, Shoshenq D, as High Priest, and served into the reign of Shoshenq III, with whom he is shown offering to Ptah and Sekhmet on two blocks from Memphis. Married his aunt, Tjesbastperu B, and was buried near his father within the temple precinct at Memphis.

Prince Shoshenq Q, depicted upon a statue of the personification of the Inundation (BM EA8).

Shoshenq D, eldest son of Osorkon II and High Priest of Ptah, offers to Horus, on the façade of his burial chamber; from Memphis (CM JE88131).

Takelot C (SonL2L)
Son of Shoshenq III; active at Busiris in year 18 of his father, when he dedicated a stela from there (now in Paris).

Takelot D (SPP)
Great-great-grandson of Osorkon II; serving as Sem-Priest at the time of the burial of Apis XXIX in year 28 of Shoshenq III, alongside Peftjauawybast B as High Priest.

Takelot F (HPA)
Son of Nimlot C, whom he seems to have followed as High Priest in the last years of

Osorkon II. Known from reliefs in the temple of Osiris-Wepished at Karnak. Probably then became Theban king as **TAKELOT II**.

Tanetamun (ChH Arsaphes)
Daughter of Nesibanebjedet III and probably wife of Osorkon H. Buried in tomb 4 at Herakleopolis.

Tashakheper A (KDB; GW)
Daughter of Osorkon II; depicted in the Jubilee Hall of her father and probably the God's Wife of the name mentioned in a graffito in the temple of Khonsu under Takelot III.

Tashedkhonsu
Wife of Osorkon I and mother of

Takelot I; known from the stela of Pasenhor B.

Tashepenbast (KD)
Daughter of Shoshenq I, named on a statue of her grandson Neseramun ii from Karnak.

Tentamenopet (KW)
Wife of Shoshenq III. Named on the biographical text of a descendant (Cairo) and on the diorite statue-base of her steward, Amenemhat (Petrie Museum).

Tentsepeh C
Wife of Nimlot C; named on the stela of Pasenhor B.

Tentsepeh D (KD; MH)
Probable daughter of Osorkon II and wife of Ptahudjankhef. Known from the stela of Pasenhor B.

Tjenkemet (Chief Sistrum-Bearer of Arsaphes)
Wife of Hemptah A. Known from the stela of Pasenhor B.

Tjesbastperu B (KD)
Daughter of Osorkon II and Isetemkheb G. Married her nephew, Takelot B, and is named on the Serapeum stelae of her son; her canopic jars are in Vienna.

[...]du/aw[...] (KSon; HPA)
Son of Harsiese A; known only from a rectangular basin from Koptos, and presumably took office as High Priest on his father's elevation to the kingship. If his name could be restored as 'Pedubast' he could have later become king as **PEDUBAST I**.

Unplaced ● ● ● ● ● ● ● ● ● ●
in second half of 3rd Intermediate Period

Kama (KW)
Buried at Tell Moqdam (Leontopolis); she may be the wife of the King Iuput II who was ruling there at the time of Piye's invasion, although it has been suggested that she is identical with Karomama B.

The Independence of Thebes

23rd Dynasty

The Royal Succession

23rd Dynasty 867–724
HARSIESE
TAKELOT II
PEDUBAST I
IUPUT I (*co-regent*)
SHOSHENQ VI[151]
OSORKON III
TAKELOT III
RUDAMUN
INY
PEFTJAUAWYBAST

(opposite) The Bubastite Portal at Karnak contains the Chronicle of Prince Osorkon (B), relating his misfortunes and final victory over his enemies.

Historical Background

As we have seen, the High Priest of Amun, Harsiese A, had obtained royal dignity under Osorkon II; now – a few years later – the same seems to have occurred, with the High Priest Takelot F becoming Takelot II. It appears that his rule stretched southwards from Herakleopolis to the Nubian border, centred on Thebes.[150] However, the formal establishment of a Theban monarchy seems to have led to the unleashing of forces that had remained suppressed since the 'troubles' of the mid-21st Dynasty (see pp. 196, 207).

In Takelot II's 11th regnal year his son and High Priest, Osorkon B, was forced to face a potential threat that was initially overcome. However, within a few years, a King Pedubast I had appeared as a direct rival to Takelot II, apparently supported by the Tanite Shoshenq III. Hostilities seem to have lasted for nearly a decade, with Pedubast ultimately recognized as Takelot II's successor, rather than Osorkon B. Later, Iuput I became Pedubast's co-regent, with a certain Shoshenq VI apparently following Pedubast as sole ruler.

Hostilities resumed a year or two later, and it was not until a decade-and-a-half after his father's death that Osorkon B was able to ascend the Theban throne, as Osorkon III, perhaps after overthrowing Shoshenq VI. Power was consolidated by appointing the king's children to the posts of High Priest and God's Wife of Amun – the latter office now being considerably enhanced in its standing.

The latter part of the dynasty under Takelot III and Rudamun saw, however, the dynasty's power eroded by that of Kush, whose ruler Piye effectively took control of Thebes, installing his sister as the heir to the God's Wife. To all intents and purposes deprived of his Theban heartland, Peftjauawybast, last king of the dynasty, initially retained Middle Egypt while ruling from Herakleopolis as a client of the Kushites. Within a few years, however, this would also have ended, the last scions of the line being swallowed up into the other great Theban families.

The Royal Family

Takelot II is likely to have been identical with the High Priest Takelot F, who is stated in Karnak inscriptions to have been a son of Nimlot C, and whose likely period of office falls neatly just before Takelot II's appearance. Of his own family, his principal wife, Karomama D, was a daughter of Nimlot C and thus his sister, if Takelot's equation with the High Priest of the same name is correct. Her relationships are clear from the inscriptions of her eldest son, Osorkon B. A further wife, Tashep, was the mother of Nimlot F, who is called a son of a King Takelot on his stela, which is probably to be attributed to the second Takelot on the basis of its style.

Five other children are known: Bakenptah is described as Osorkon B's brother in the latter's Chronicle text at Karnak; Isetweret ii's father is given as a King Takelot on the coffins of her descendants, whose dating shows that the king must be the second of the name; Shepensopdet ii is also dated by the affiliations of her descendants; Karomama E is explicitly dated by her installation stela; and [...]iufankh is dated by an inscribed slab.

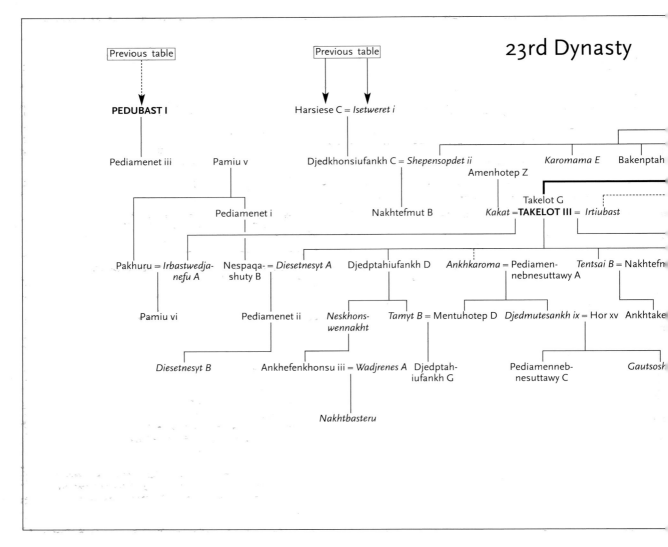

23rd Dynasty

That Osorkon B is the same person as King **Osorkon III** is indicated by the fact that the former's last appearance as High Priest of Amun seems to directly precede Osorkon III's assumption of the throne, reinforcing a stela from Tehna which mentions the latter with the additional title of High Priest – an unusual occurrence.[152] Absolutely nothing is known of the origins of **Pedubast I** and other members of the 'rival' line of the dynasty. It is likely that they were also descendants of the old 22nd Dynasty line, but there is no direct evidence for this. One unproven suggestion is that Pedubast could have been the son of Harsiese A whose name is partially lost.

Osorkon III's eldest son and heir, Takelot G (III), is shown on a stela from Gurob, and stated to be the offspring of Tentsai A on a relief. Another child of Tentsai was a daughter named Shepenwepet (A), who seems to have died young according to her funerary stela. A second daughter of the name was Shepenwepet I, in this case borne by another wife, Karoatjet, as shown by the

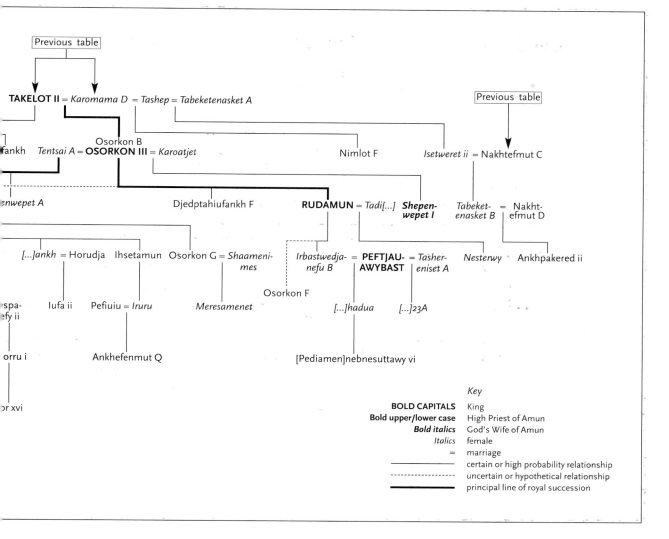

Previous table

TAKELOT II = Karomama D = Tashep = Tabeketenasket A

Previous table

...]ankh   Tentsai A = **OSORKON III** = Karoatjet   Nimlot F   Isetweret ii = Nakhtefmut C
                    Osorkon B

enwepet A   Djedptahiufankh F   **RUDAMUN** = Tadi[...] **Shepen-   Tabeket-   = Nakht-
                                                                                       wepet I**   enasket B | efmut D

[...]Jankh = Horudja Ihsetamun Osorkon G = Shaameni-   Irbastwedja- **PEFTJAU-** = Tasher-   Nesterwy   Ankhpakered ii
                                           mes   nefu B   **AWYBAST** | eniset A
                                                   Osorkon F

spa-   Iufa ii   Pefiuiu = Iruru   Meresamenet   [...]hadua   [...]23A
efy ii

orru i   Ankhefenmut Q   [Pediamen]nebnesuttawy vi

or xvi

Key

BOLD CAPITALS	King
Bold upper/lower case	High Priest of Amun
Bold italics	God's Wife of Amun
Italics	female
=	marriage
——————————	certain or high probability relationship
- - - - - - - - - - - -	uncertain or hypothetical relationship
▬▬▬▬▬▬	principal line of royal succession

texts in the temple of Osiris-Heqadjet at Karnak. Two other sons are attested: Osorkon III's second successor, Rudamun, called his son on a block from Medinet Habu; and Djedptahiufankh F, known from coffin-inscriptions.

Takelot III had one wife named Irtiubast, who is named and described as a King's Daughter on the coffin of their son, Osorkon G.[153] Her father is not stated; he is likely to have been Osorkon III, but was perhaps a 22nd Dynasty monarch. It is possible that Osorkon G was identical to the High Priest of Amun Osorkon F, if the coffin of Osorkon G had been made for him early in his career before promotion to the High Priesthood. Otherwise, Osorkon F may have been a son of Rudamun.

Seven other offspring are attributable to Takelot III. Another son was Djedptahiufankh D, stated to be the son of a Takelot on a statue of his son-in-law, Mentuhotep D, which also gives many of the family's other ramifications; yet more are given on the coffins of various descendants. A key

Bronze statuette of King Peftjauawybast (MFA 1977.16).

chronological link is Mentuhotep's father, who can be dated to the late 23rd Dynasty, allowing Mentuhotep's mother, Ankhkaroma, to be identified as a probable daughter of Takelot III. Her husband, Pediamennebnesuttawy A, is known to have had at least one daughter, Djedmutesankh ix, on the basis of a number of her descendants' coffin-inscriptions. Prince Ihsetamun is known from the stela of his grandson, dated to the 26th Dynasty; his father, 'King Takelot', can thus only be Takelot III.

Of Takelot III's other daughters, two married into a well-known family of Viziers. Of them, Irbastwedjanefu A is expressly called the daughter of a King Takelot, whose identity is narrowed down to Takelot III by a spelling in her coffin-inscriptions; her mother and maternal grandfather are named on her coffins. Similar orthographic data confirm the identity of the father of Diesetnesyt (A), her affiliations being given on her son's coffin. Tentsai B, yet another offspring of a King Takelot, can be dated by the style of the statue of her son Ankhtakelot, as well as the fact that she bears the same name as her putative grandmother. Finally, a lady whose name is destroyed (apart from the final 'ankh') is named as daughter of a King Takelot on a stela which seems to have belonged to her son, probably dating to the time of Taharqa.

The family of **Rudamun** can be reconstructed from two documents: the aforementioned Medinet Habu block, and a coffin-fragment belonging to the king's great-grandson. The latter also shows that the last king of the dynasty, **Peftjauawybast**, was Rudamun's son-in-law; a second wife of Peftjauawybast is known from stelae in Cairo, and his own parentage is unknown, as is that of another king of the end of the dynasty – **Iny**.

Brief Lives ●

Males in **bold**, *females in* **bold italic**.

Amenhotep Z (Beloved of the God)
Father of Kakat; named on the coffins of his descendants.

Ankhefenkhonsu iii (PMentu)
Great-grandson of Takelot III; his ancestry is given on the coffins of his daughter.

Ankhefenmut Q (GF of Amun)
Great-grandson of Takelot III; owner of a stela, now in Croydon and perhaps from Koptos.

Ankhkaroma (KD)
Wife of Pediamennebnesuttawy A, and probably a daughter of Takelot III; named on a statue of Mentuhotep D in Tübingen.

Ankhtakelot (PMentu)
Grandson of Takelot III; owner of a block-statue in Vienna.

Ankhpakered ii (4PMut)
Great-grandson of Takelot II; buried in tomb B29 at the Ramesseum. His coffins and canopic jars are in Berlin.

Bakenptah (Gen; AL)
Son of Takelot II and brother of Osorkon B (III); appointed a Commander-in-Chief at Herakleopolis prior to year 39 of Shoshenq III and in company with his brother at the latter's triumph in that year. Known from both the Chronicle of Prince Osorkon and a stela-fragment from Herakleopolis.

Diesetnesyt A (KD)
Daughter of Takelot III, wife of Nespaqashuty B. Known from her *shabti* boxes and the coffins of her son, Pediamenet ii.

Diesetnesyt B (KD)
Great-granddaughter of Takelot III;
known from a stela found at Deir el-
Bahari, now in Chicago.

Djedkhonsiufankh C (4PA)
Husband of Shepensopdet ii and a
descendant of King Harsiese.

Djedmutesankh ix
Daughter of Pediamennebnesuttawy A
and wife of Hor xv.

Djedptahiufankh D (2PA)
Son of Takelot III; buried in tomb 17 at
Medinet Habu.

Djedptahiufankh F (KSon)
Son of Osorkon III; known from a coffin
in Boston.

Djedptahiufankh G
Great-grandson of Takelot III and son of
Mentuhotep D.

Gautsoshen iii
Daughter of Djedmutesankh ix and Hor
xv; buried at Deir el-Bahari, with her
coffins now in Cairo.

Harsiese C (2PA)
Father of Djedkhonsiufankh C and son-in-
law of Harsiese A; had previously served
as Fourth Prophet of Amun. Known from
an inscribed doorjamb and a statue
dedicated by him and the children of his
sister Tasherenmut in the temple of
Mentu at Karnak.

Hor xv (PMentu)
Husband of Djedmutesankh ix.

Hor xvi (PMentu)
Son of Gautsoshen iii. Buried at Deir el-
Bahari, with his coffins now in Cairo.

Horudja (Overseer of the Singers of
Amun)
Husband of [...]ankh; buried in the
usurped tomb TT367, his stela now in
Cairo.

Ihsetamun (KSon)
Son of Takelot III; known from the stela of

his grandson, Ankhefenmut Q.

Irbastwedjanefu A (KD; LH)
Daughter of Takelot III and Kakat, wife of
Pakhuru and mother of Pamiu vi. Buried
in the temple of Hatshepsut at Deir el-
Bahari; sarcophagus and coffin now in
Paris.

Irbastwedjanefu B (KD)
Daughter of Rudamun and wife of
Peftjauawybast; known from a coffin-
fragment belonging to her grandson.

Irthorru i (PMentu)
Husband of Gautsoshen iii. A descendant
of Besenmut I – Third Prophet of Amun
under Osorkon III; buried at
Deir el-Bahari, with his coffins now in
Cairo.

Irtiubast (KW; KD)
Wife of Takelot III, possibly a daughter
of Osorkon III, and mother of Osorkon G;
named on her son's coffin.

Iruru
Granddaughter of Takelot III, wife of
Pefiuiu, and mother of Ankhefenmut Q,
on whose stela she is mentioned.

Isetweret i
Daughter of Harsiese A. See previous
section.

Isetweret ii (KD)
Daughter of Takelot II and wife of
Nakhtefmut C; named on the coffins of
their daughter and grandson.

Iufa ii (PAmun)
Son of Horudja; buried in the usurped
tomb TT367, his stela now in Cairo.

Kakat (Singer of the Great House)
Wife of Takelot III; named on the coffin
of her daughter.

Karoatjet
Wife of Osorkon III; named in the temple
of Osiris-Heqadjet.

Karomama D (KGW; MULE)
Wife of Takelot II and daughter of Nimlot

C. Known from the Chronicle of
Osorkon B and Nile-level texts of the
reign of Osorkon III.

Karomama E (ChA)
Daughter of Takelot II; a stela from year
25 of her father records a grant of land to
her.

Mentuhotep D (First Royal Scribe)
Grandson-in-law, and probably grandson,
of Takelot III. Owner of a headless block-
statue in Tübingen.

Meresamenet (Singer of the Harem of
Amun)
Granddaughter of Takelot III; buried in
the temple of Hatshepsut at
Deir el-Bahari; coffin now in Cairo.

Nakhtbasteru
Great-great-granddaughter of Takelot III;
buried at Deir el-Bahari, with her coffins
now in Cairo.

Nakhtefmut B (Fanbearer)
Son of Shepensopdet ii and
Djedkhonsiufankh C, to whom he
dedicated a statue.

Nakhtefmut C (Viz)
Husband of Isetweret ii; named on
numerous monuments of his relations
and served under Osorkon III.

Nakhtefmut D
Husband of Tabeketenasket B/Tamyt;
named on the coffins of their son.

Nakhtefmut Q (Lesonis of Khonsu)
Husband of Tentsai B.

Neskhonswennakht
Granddaughter of Takelot III, named
on the coffins of her own
granddaughter.

Nespaqashuty B (Viz)
Husband of Diesetnesyt A; son of
Pediamenet i.

Nespasefy ii (PMentu)
Father-in-law of Gautsoshen iii, on whose
husband's coffin he is named.

Nesterwy (KD)
Daughter of Rudamun; named on a block at Medinet Habu.

Nimlot F (KSon)
Son of Takelot II and Tashep. Known from a stela in the Vatican.

Osorkon B (HPA; Genmo; KSon)
Eldest son of Takelot II; probably appointed High Priest at the time of his father's assumption of the kingship. From year 11 he was involved in a lengthy civil war against Pedubast I and his successors, as recorded in his Chronicle

After his many trials and tribulations, Osorkon B finally obtained his throne as Osorkon III. This statue from Karnak shows him launching a sacred boat (CM CG42197).

text in the Bubastite Portal at Karnak. Although initially successful, in Takelot's year 15 Osorkon and his father seem to have lost control of Thebes until year 24. Then, some kind of agreement allowed the prince to resume his place as High Priest. However, hostilities were renewed only a year or two after Takelot II's death, with Osorkon B's expulsion from Thebes once again, this time lasting nearly a decade. It was not until around the 40th anniversary of his first appointment that Osorkon finally regained office, with the help of his brother Bakenptah; this seems to have been marked soon after by his assumption of the throne as **OSORKON III**.

Osorkon F (KSon; HPA)
Probable son of Rudamun; a statue of him is in Cairo.

Osorkon G (KSon; PA)
Son of Takelot III and father of Meresamenet; buried in tomb B27 at the Ramesseum; his coffin-fragments were destroyed in Berlin in 1944–45. Conceivably identical with Osorkon F.

Pakhuru (Viz)
Husband of Irbastwedjanefu A; son of the Vizier Pamiu v.

Pamiu v (Viz)
Father of Pediamenet i and Pakhuru.

Pamiu vi
Son of Pakhuru and Irbastwedjanefu A. Buried in the temple of Hatshepsut at Deir el-Bahari; his coffin is now in Cairo.

Pediamenet i (Viz)
Son of Pamiu v, and father-in-law of Diesetnesyt A.

Pediamenet ii (PMentu)
Son of Nespaqashuty B and Diesetnesyt A.

Pediamenet iii (KSon; GF)
Son of Pedubast I, inducted in his father's 7th regnal year.

Pediamennebnesuttawy A (3PA)
Husband of Ankhkaroma; named on a statue of Mentuhotep D in Tübingen, and also on other genealogies.

Pediamennebnesuttawy C (3PA)
Possibly great-grandson of Takelot III; served until soon after year 9 of Psametik I.

[Pediamen]nebnesuttawy vi
Grandson of Peftjauawybast and great-grandson of Rudamun; a fragment of his coffin was found in tomb TT83, and is now in Berlin.

Pefiuiu (GF of Amun)
Husband of Iruru; mentioned on the stela of their son, Ankhefenmut Q.

Shaamenimes
Wife of Osorkon G and mother of Meresamenet; if she were also the daughter of a Chief of the Ma, Takelot, her coffin is in Cairo.

Shepensopdet ii (KD)
Daughter of Takelot II and wife of
Djedkhonsiufankh C; named on a statue
dedicated by their son.

Shepenwepet I (KD; Ador; GWA:
   prenomen **Khnemetibamun**)
Daughter of Osorkon III and Karoatjet;
served as GWA from the beginning of
her father's reign. Represented in the
temple of Osiris-Heqadjet at Karnak, and
named on two statues of Osiris (one in
St Petersburg), as well as in a graffito in
the Wadi Gasus, alongside her adoptive
daughter, Amenirdis I.

Shepenwepet A (LH)
Daughter of Osorkon B and Tentsai A;
she died young before her father's
accession, and her funerary stela is in
Turin.

Tabeketenasket A (KW)
Wife of Takelot II and mother of Isetweret
ii; named on the coffins of her
descendants.

Tabeketenasket B/Tamyt (Sistrum-player
   of Amun-Re)
Granddaughter of Takelot II. Buried in
tomb B28 at the Ramesseum; a coffin and
her canopic jars are in Berlin.

Tadi[...] (KW)
Wife of Rudamun and mother of
Nesterwy; named on a block at Medinet
Habu.

Takelot G (KSon; HPA; Great Exec)
Son of Osorkon III. Known from a relief
of the gods Amun and Arsaphes, a stela
from Gurob and a wax impression bearing
his name, titles and pedigree. Later king
as **TAKELOT III**.

Tamyt B
Daughter of Djedptahiufankh D; wife of
Mentuhotep D.

Tashep (KW)
Wife of Takelot II and mother of Nimlot F;
known from her son's stela in the Vatican.

Tashereniset A (KW)
Wife of Peftjauawybast; mentioned on
two donation stelae of her husband's 10th
regnal year.

Tentsai A (KW; KM)
Wife of Osorkon III and mother of
Takelot III. Named on a Nile-level text at
Karnak dating to her son's reign, and on
a relief produced while he was still
serving as High Priest of Amun.
Her damaged name is also to be seen
on the funerary stela of Shepenwepet A.

Tentsai B (KD)
Daughter of Takelot III and wife of
Nakhtefmut Q; named in the statue of
her son.

Wadjrenes A
Wife of Ankhefenkhonsu iii; named
with him on the coffins of their
daughter.

[...]ankh (KD)
Daughter of Takelot III; mentioned on
the stela of her son Iufa ii.

[...]hadua (KD)
Daughter of Peftjauawybast;
mentioned on a fragment of the coffin
of her son.

[...]iufankh (KSon)
Son of Takelot II; mentioned on a slab
in Stockholm.

[...]23A (KD; ChA)
Daughter of Peftjauawybast and
Tashereniset A; installed as a Chantress
of Amun in her father's 10th year.

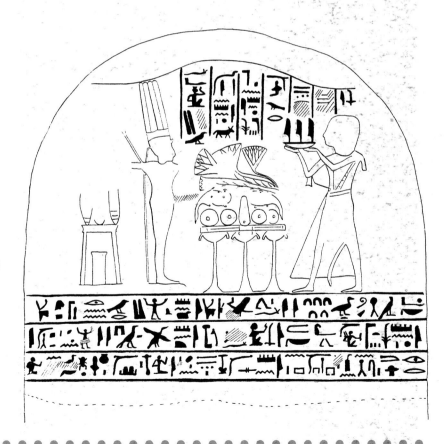

*Stela from Gurob showing Takelot G – soon
to be Takelot III – offering to Amun.*

The Princes of the West

24th Dynasty

The Royal Succession

24th Dynasty 735–721
TEFNAKHTE
BAKENRENEF

Historical Background [154]

One of the polities that came to prominence during the gradual disintegration of the 22nd Dynasty's control over northern Egypt was the Princedom of the West, based on Sais (Sa el-Hagar) in the Delta. By years 36/38 of the reign of Shoshenq V, control was in the hands of a man called Tefnakhte. A few years later his power had expanded into the Nile Valley, as far south as Itjtawy (Lisht); he formed an alliance with the local king, Nimlot D of Hermopolis, while threatening King Peftjauawybast at Herakleopolis. Tefnakhte was later forced to retreat in the face of an invasion by the Kushite king, Piye, during which he lost one son and another son was captured by his southern opponent.

Tefnakhte had in the meantime gained access to Memphis under the cover of darkness, installed a garrison of 8,000 men, and departed on horseback. However, the city then fell to the Kushites, after which the majority of the various regional rulers in Egypt submitted to Piye in person at Memphis or Athribis. The notable absentee was Tefnakhte, who initially continued resistance, but eventually submitted – albeit by messenger, with his oath of allegiance to Piye administered by officials who had to go all the way to Sais.

However, as soon as Piye had returned to the south Tefnakhte proclaimed himself king, controlling at least the western Delta and thus founding the 24th Dynasty. Little is known of his reign, although the dynastic area of control seems to have included Memphis. On Tefnakhte's death eight years

The 'pharaohs' of Egypt submit to Piye: at the bottom kneel Osorkon IV, Iuput II and Peftjauawybast, while above stands Nimlot, leading a horse; from Gebel Barkal (CM JE48862).

Today almost nothing remains of the once-great city of Sais, destroyed by those searching for antiquities and fertilizer.

later he was succeeded by Bakenrenef, who remained in power until deposed (and allegedly burnt alive) by Shabaka in his 6th regnal year.

The Royal Family

The 24th Dynasty line may go back to Pimay who, while a prince, dedicated a statue at Sais. Somewhat later Osorkon C, known from an amulet and *shabtis*, bore similar titles to Tefnakhte and might have been an ancestor.[155] Two unnamed sons of **Tefnakhte** are known from the Victory Stela of Piye: one having been killed and another captured. Another son was, according to the Classical writer Diodorus, his successor **Bakenrenef**.

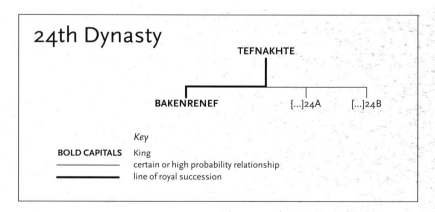

24th Dynasty

TEFNAKHTE

BAKENRENEF   [...]24A   [...]24B

Key
BOLD CAPITALS   King
certain or high probability relationship
line of royal succession

Brief Lives

*Males in **bold**, females in **bold italic**.*

Tefnakhte (ChMa; AL; Chief Libu; PNeith; PEdjo; Ruler of Provinces of the West)
Known from donation-stelae from Buto, dated to years 36 and 38 of Shoshenq V;

mentioned frequently in the Victory Stela of Piye in Cairo; subsequently **king**.

[...]24A
Son of Tefnakhte; according to Victory Stela of Piye, killed during Piye's assault on Tihna.

[...]24B
Son of Tefnakhte; according to Victory Stela of Piye, captured following the surrender of Pisekhemkheperre, near the entrance to the Fayoum.

Lords of the Holy Mountain

25th Dynasty

The Royal Succession

25th Dynasty 721–656

Ancestors of actual 25th Dynasty:
ALARA
KASHTA

PIYE
SHABAKA
SHABATAKA
TAHARQA
TANUTAMUN

Kush only:
ATLANERSA
SENKAMENISKEN
ANLAMANI
ASPELTA

Head of a colossal statue of Taharqa (Aswan, Nubian Museum, ex-CG560).

Historical Background

Control of Nubia, stretching from Aswan far into modern Sudan, and comprising ancient Kush, had been a key Egyptian foreign policy objective since Early Dynastic times. At the end of the 20th Dynasty, difficulties concerning the Viceroy had resulted in warfare for a number of years. While members of the Theban High Priestly family claimed the viceregal title during the 21st Dynasty, it is unclear how far south their power actually extended, with the likelihood that part of Lower (northern) and all of Upper (southern) Nubia was under the rule of elements related to the former viceregal regime.

It would appear that some of these rulers assumed the title of (local) pharaoh, with titularies and relief styles recalling those of kings of the recently ended Ramesside Period. They seem to have flourished around the time of the 21st and early 22nd Dynasty in Egypt and may have initiated a line of rulers who began a series of high-status tumuli and mastabas at El-Kurru. This lies deep in the south of Nubia and is close to Napata (Gebel Barkal), the capital of Kush since the New Kingdom, and dominated by a great flat-topped mountain, sacred to Amun and a key symbol of the Kushite kingdom.

There is then a gap in our knowledge until the appearance of a ruler called Alara, about whom nothing is known, but whose successor assumed full pharaonic titles and rapidly expanded his power into Lower Nubia. Piye then extended Kushite influence down the Nile to Thebes itself, where he had his sister adopted as heir to the God's Wife of Amun, and may have become the city's formal ruler after the death of Rudamun.

In reaction to the southward expansion of the princes of Sais, Piye was later to launch a northern campaign which resulted in the submission of the various rulers of Egypt, and his formal recognition as pharaoh. He seems to have been happy to leave the running of Egypt to his new vassals, shown by his return to Nubia. However, his successor Shabaka seems to have severely curtailed the power of the 'royal' lines that Piye had left in place; he took up residence in Memphis as the fully fledged ruler of the united kingdom of Egypt and Kush, symbolized by his adoption of the twin *uraeus* on his crown.

The next king, Shabataka, became involved in the politics of Syria–Palestine, which were becoming increasingly overshadowed by Assyria to the east. An Egypto-Nubian army marched into Palestine, where the pharaoh's armies – together with those of its local allies – were beaten by the first-rate Assyrian forces. His successor Taharqa seems to have preferred to concentrate on home affairs, organizing major building works in both north and south of Egypt and Nubia. However, the nemesis of the Kushite kings was approaching in the shape of the Assyrian king, Esarhaddon. An initial attack was successfully repulsed, but a further strike reached Memphis, the representatives of the various dynasties who had been humbled by Piye and Shabaka being appointed as Assyrian vassals in the Delta. A counter-attack by Taharqa was aided by the premature death of the Assyrian king, but his successor Assurbanipal was not prepared to forget about Egypt, and launched a fresh campaign which drove Taharqa back to Napata.

The Kushites were later able to reclaim the rule of Thebes, but an attempt by Taharqa's successor, Tanutamun, to reimpose Kushite rule over the whole of Egypt was short-lived. Assurbanipal was not slow in sending an army to subdue Egypt once more, succeeding in driving Tanutamun back down to Thebes, and then into Nubia, sacking Amun's city Napata in passing. Kushite rule in Egypt was now over, but the line continued to rule Upper Nubia for three-quarters of a millennium. Until its extinction in the 4th century AD, there continued to flourish a culture that displayed its Egyptian heritage, made most concrete in the line of pyramids that grew until their number exceeded by some considerable margin those of Egypt itself.

The Royal Family

The relationships of the Kushite kings present many problems. It seems fairly clear that a simple father-to-son succession was not always involved, nor do attempts to substitute a system of fraternal succession fully explain the evidence, which may conceal a set of interrelated families.[156] In addition, there seems to have been some significance attached to a king's maternal ancestry – a stela of Atlanersa for instance lists his seven female ancestors, all of whose names have, unfortunately, been erased.[157]

The ancestor of the Kushite pharaohs was **Alara**. His only known wife was Kasaqa, as shown by the stela of their daughter, Tabiry. Another relationship is shown by an inscription of Taharqa at Kawa indicating that his mother, Abar, was the daughter of Alara's (unnamed) sister. Abar married the next-but-one king, Piye, as did Tabiry, a fact stated in her stela.

The ancestry of the intervening monarch, **Kashta**, is obscure, but three children are known. Peksater names him as her father and Pebatjma as her mother on the doorjambs of her tomb, as does Amenirdis I on one of her statues; Shabaka is called Amenirdis' brother in her own texts. Another child may, on the basis of her name, have been Neferukakashta. It is uncertain whether Pebatjma might be the Paabtamer who was buried at Abydos, since the latter has the additional title of King's Daughter, which fits uncomfortably with the apparent fact that Kashta was the first Kushite monarch of the period to have full royal titles (Alara being merely a chieftain). In this case, Paabtamer would be the wife of a later Kushite king, either Piye or Taharqa, on the basis that she was the mother of an Adoratrix. On the other hand, Paabtamer was also shown on stelae from her tomb to be the mother of Pegattereru, who was not a King's Son, further complicating the issue.

Piye's parentage is also uncertain although, as we have seen, he was certainly the son-in-law of Alara. It has been assumed that Khensa was one of his wives, in which case her titles of King's Sister and King's Daughter might

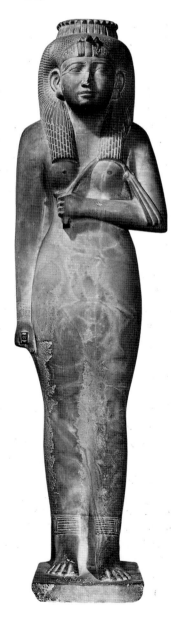

The God's Wife of Amun, Amenirdis I, daughter of Kashta; from Karnak (CM CG565).

Haremakhet, son of Shabaka, and the penultimate male High Priest of Amun at Karnak (Aswan, Nubian Museum, ex-JE38580).

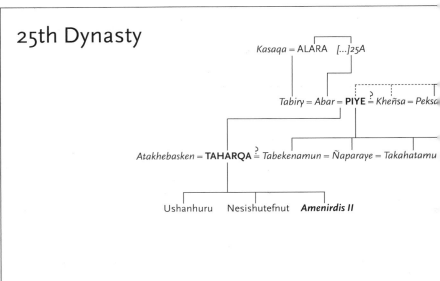

25th Dynasty

Kasaqa = ALARA [...]*25A*

Tabiry = *Abar* = **PIYE** = *Kheñsa* = *Peksa*

Atakhebasken = **TAHARQA** = *Tabekenamun* = *Ñaparaye* = *Takahatamu*

Ushanhuru   Nesishutefnut   ***Amenirdis II***

Key
BOLD CAPITALS	King
CAPITALS	Foreign monarch
Bold upper/lower case	High Priest of Amun
Bold italics	God's Wife of Amun
Italics	female
=	marriage
———————	certain or high probability relationship
····················	likely relationship
- - - - - - - - - -	uncertain or hypothetical relationship

suggest that both she and Piye were children of Kashta. Of Piye's children, Shepenwepet II is so identified on various monuments of her own. Taharqa is stated to be her brother on the stela recording the Nitokris I adoption (see pp. 243, 247), with two other sons of Piye also known: Khaliut, whose paternity is known from a later stela in his honour, and Har, mentioned thus on an inscription of his daughter, Wadjrenes B.[158] Five further daughters are attested: Qalhata, on the basis of a statement in Assyrian records that she (as mother of Tanutamun) was Taharqa's sister; Arty, known from texts on a statue of hers; and Tabekenamun, Ñaparaye and Takahatamun – all stated on their monuments to be sister-wives of Taharqa.

Isetemkheb H is said to have been the daughter of **Shabaka** on her coffin fragments and, on the basis of her title of King's Sister, one of the king's sons must have ruled. This backs up Assyrian records stating that Tanutamun was an offspring of Shabaka, although it is not impossible that Shabataka could have been the brother-husband in question, supporting a statement by Manetho that Shabataka was Shabaka's son. On the other hand, a text of Taharqa could be taken as implying that Shabataka was a brother of Taharqa, and thus a son of Piye. As already noted, the Assyrians

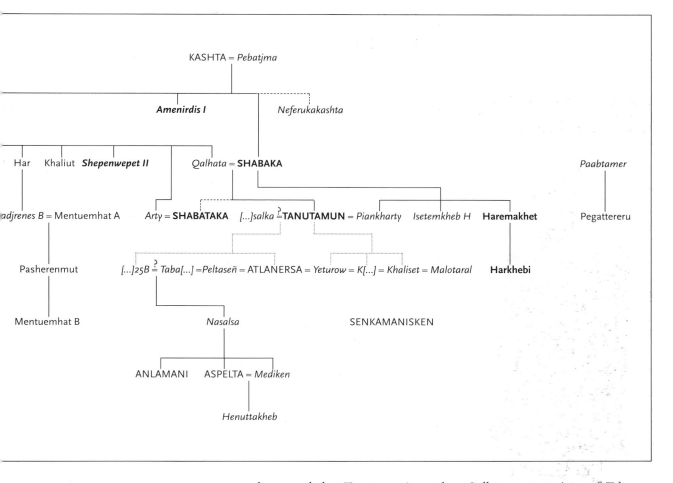

also record that Tanutamun's mother, Qalhata, was a sister of Taharqa. Piankharty was sister-wife of Tanutamun, depicted so on her husband's Dream Stela. Another son of Shabaka was Haremakhet, as stated on one of his statues, and the descent of his own son, Harkhebi, is indicated in a papyrus of Harkhebi's pontificate.

Shabataka has one known wife, Arty, mentioned on the base of a statue of Haremakhet, although (as noted just above) Isetemkheb H might conceivably have been his spouse. No children seem to be attested. As we have seen, Shabataka's successor Taharqa and three of the latter's wives were children of Piye; two more wives are known from inscriptions.

Turning to **Taharqa's** children, his eldest daughter, Amenirdis II, is called such in the Nitokris Adoption Stela. Two other sons are known – Nesishutefnut having been named as Taharqa's son on his statue, although the name of his mother has been erased; Ushanhuru, allegedly the eldest son, is recorded as captured by the Assyrians during their second invasion of Egypt.

That Yeturow, K[...] and Khaliset were also Tanutamun's daughters is implied by their appearance on a temple-element built by their husband,

Atlanersa, who would seem from the context to have been their brother as well. It is possible that **Tanutamun** had a number of other children.[159] This is based on the descent of the later King Aspelta, whose grandmother (her name is destroyed) was an Adoratrix. She might have been an intended successor for Amenirdis II who lost her role when the Kushites evacuated Egypt, and thus is likely to have been a daughter of the ruling Kushite king at the time, Tanutamun. As she was also a King's Sister, it would follow that her brother was probably Atlanersa. While womenfolk of Atlanersa were shown on the pylon of temple B700 at Gebel Barkal, the evidence for the relationships of the later (now entirely Kushite) rulers is distinctly sketchy and often based on no more than the proximity of their pyramids. However, some evidence is available from stelae of the kings of the next two generations, who are accordingly included in the table for completeness.

(left) Members of the family of Atlanersa on the inner face of the west tower of the now-destroyed pylon of temple B700 at Gebel Barkal. In the top register are, from the right: Yeturow, K[...] and Peltaseñ; below: [...]salka and Taba[...].

Brief Lives ●●

Males in **bold***, females in* ***bold italic****.*

Abar (KM; KSis)
Niece of Alara, wife of Piye and mother of Taharqa; a Kawa stela relates that she was dedicated by her father as a sistrum-player at the temple there. She is also recorded in Barkal temple 300 and on a stela from Tanis.

Amenirdis I (KD; Ador; GH; GWA: prenomen Khaneferumut)
Daughter of Kashta; presumably installed by her father as heir to the God's Wife, Shepenwepet I, and then served through the reigns of Shabaka and Shabataka. Depicted in the temple of Osiris-Heqadjet at Karnak, named in the Wadi Gasus (as Adoratrix alongside Shepenwepet I) and known from two offering tables, five statues, a stela and a number of scarabs and other small items. Buried in a funerary chapel at Medinet Habu.

Amenirdis II (KD; Ador; GH)
Daughter of Taharqa; as indicated by the

The tomb of Amenirdis I and the joint sepulchre of Shepenwepet II, Nitokris I and Mehytenweskhet C lie in front of Ramesses III's temple at Medinet Habu.

Nitokris Adoption Stela, adopted as heir by Shepenwepet II, and then she herself adopted Nitokris I as her own heir in year 9 of Psametik I. It appears that on Shepenwepet II's death, Nitokris took the office of God's Wife, Amenirdis retaining the deputy position until her own death, around the end of the reign of Psametik I.

Arty (KW)
Daughter of Piye and wife of Shabataka; mentioned on the base of a statue of Haremakhet, from Karnak and now in Cairo; buried in tomb Ku6 at El-Kurru.

Atakhebasken (KW)
Wife of Taharqa; buried in Nuri tomb Nu36, with her canopics in Boston and an altar in Merowe Museum.

Har (KSon)
Son of Piye and father-in-law of Mentuemhat A; named on an offering table of his daughter from tomb TT34.

Haremakhet (KSon; HPA)
Son of Shabaka; owner of one complete and one broken statue from Karnak, now respectively in Aswan and Cairo.

Harkhebi (HPA)
Grandson of Shabaka; served as High Priest until at least year 14 of Psametik I, having been named in an oracle papyrus of this year, and in the Nitokris Adoption Stela of year 9.

Henuttakheb (KSis; KD; KM)
Daughter of Aspelta and mother of an unknown Kushite king, perhaps Amtalqa or Maleñaqeñ; shown on her father's Adoption Stela and buried in Nuri tomb Nu28.

Isetemkheb H (KGW; KSis; KD)
Daughter of Shabaka, and probably wife of Tanutamun; owner of tomb D3 at Abydos, coffin fragments, canopic jars and *shabtis* from which are now in Cairo.

Kasaqa
Wife of Alara; known from an inscription in temple T at Kawa, and the stela of Tabiry in Khartoum.

Khaliset (KGD)
Possible daughter of Tanutamun and perhaps wife of Atlanersa; depicted on the destroyed east tower of the pylon of Barkal temple B700.

Khaliut (KSon)
Son of Piye; known from a stela from Barkal temple B500 recording donations to his mortuary cult during the reign of Aspelta, which records that he had been governor of the province of Kanad.

Kheñsa (KD; KSis; KGW; M2L)
Probable wife of Piye and daughter of Kashta; named on a statue of Bastet in the Louvre, and buried in El-Kurru tomb Ku4, from which were recovered various items of funerary equipment, now in Boston and Khartoum.

K[...] (KD; KW)
Wife of Atlanersa and possibly daughter of Tanutamun; depicted on the west tower of the destroyed pylon of Barkal temple B700.

Malotaral (KW; KM)
Wife of Atlanersa; known from *shabtis* and a heart scarab from her tomb Nu41 at Nuri.

Mediken (KSis; KW)
Sister-wife of Aspelta; shown on his Adoption Stela from Gebel Barkal and now in the Louvre.

Mentuemhat A (4PA)
Son-in-law of Har; Mayor of Thebes and Governor of Upper Egypt from the reign of Taharqa until soon after year 14 of Psamtik I. Owner of tomb TT34 and a large number of monuments from Thebes.

(below) Upper part of statue of Mentuemhat A, the Mayor of Thebes during the crucial transition from Kushite to Saite rule; from Karnak (CM CG42238).

(below, right) Pasherenmut, a great-grandson of Piye and the son of Mentuemhat A (CM CG42243).

Mentuemhat B
Great-great grandson of Piye; depicted on a leg of the statue of his father, Pasherenmut.

Ñaparaye (KSis; KW; M2L)
Daughter of Piye and wife of Taharqa; buried in El-Kurru tomb Ku3, an offering stone from which is in Khartoum.

Nasalsa (KSis; KM)
Daughter of Atlanersa and mother of Anlamani and Aspelta; named on Anlamani's Enthronement Stela and Aspelta's Election and Adoption stelae, both from Gebel Barkal, and respectively in Cairo and the Louvre.

Neferukakashta
Perhaps a daughter of Kashta; buried in El-Kurru tomb Ku52.

Nesishutefnut (KSon; 2PA)
Son of Taharqa; known from the lower portion of a squatting statue from Karnak (Cairo).

Pasherenmut (Announcing Priest)
Great-grandson of Piye; owner of a statue from Karnak (Cairo), and also named on the base of a statue of his father, Mentuemhat A.

Pebatjma (KW; KSis)
Wife of Kashta; named on a fragment of a statue of her daughter, Amenirdis I, and in the tomb of her other daughter, Peksater, at Abydos.

Peksater (KD; KGW)
Daughter of Kashta and wife of Piye; shown in a relief in room B502 of the Amun temple at Gebel Barkal, on a scribal statue in Berlin and on the stela of Irihor in Bologna. Buried in a tomb in cemetery D at Abydos (parts of the door now in Cairo).

Peltaseñ (KSis; KW)
Wife of Atlanersa; depicted on the west tower of the destroyed pylon of Barkal temple B700.

Piankharty (KSis; KW)
Daughter of Shabaka and sister-wife of Tanutamun; shown with the latter on his Dream Stela.

Qalhata (KSis; KM)
Daughter of Piye, wife of Shabaka and mother of Tanutamun; mentioned in the latter's Dream Stela and buried in El-Kurru tomb Ku5, which has a decorated burial chamber.

Shepenwepet II (Ador; GWA: prenomen **Henutneferumut-iryetre**)
Daughter of Piye; served as God's Wife from the reign of Taharqa until after year 9 of Psametik I. Involved in the building of various structures at Karnak and depicted with Nitokris I in the Wadi Gasus; owner of three statues and a sphinx, together with numerous smaller items. Buried in a funerary chapel at Medinet Habu.

Taba[...] (KW)
Wife of Atlanersa; depicted on the west tower of the destroyed pylon of Barkal temple B700.

Tabekenamun (KD; KSis; KW)
Daughter of Piye and perhaps wife of Taharqa; mentioned on the base of a statue of Haremakhet from Karnak.

Tabiry (KD; 1GKW)
Daughter of Alara and Kasaqa, and wife of Piye; known from her funerary stela from tomb Ku53 at El-Kurru, and now in Khartoum.

Takahatamun (KSis; 1KGW; L2L; MULE)
Daughter of Piye and wife of Taharqa; mentioned in a temple at Barkal and on a statue of Nesishutefnut.

Ushanhuru
Son of Taharqa; the Assyrian king Esarhaddon records that he was captured by the Assyrians during their second invasion of Egypt. The Egyptian form of his name may have been Nesinhuret.

Wadjrenes B (PHathor; ChA)
Granddaughter of Piye and wife of Mentuemhat A; appears in her husband's tomb (TT34), she is with him on the Nitokris Adoption Stela and is also mentioned on the statue of her son, Pasherenmut.

Yeturow (KW; KD; KSis)
Wife of Atlanersa; shown in the latter's burial chamber and depicted on the destroyed pylon of Barkal temple B700. Buried in the decorated tomb Nu53 at Nuri; her heart scarab was found elsewhere at Nuri.

[...]salka (KM)
Mother of Atlanersa; shown on the now-destroyed inscription on the pylon of Barkal temple B700.

[...]25A
Sister of Alara and grandmother of Taharqa; mentioned in the latter's stela IV from Kawa.

[...]25B (KSis; Ador)
Possible daughter of Tanutamun, sister of Atlanersa and grandmother of Aspelta; name erased in the genealogy on Aspelta's Accession Stela.

Unplaced ● ● ● ● ● ● ● ●

Meryetamun G (KD)
Owner of a stela in Cairo, possibly from Abydos, that is dated stylistically to the 25th Dynasty.

Paabtamer (ChA; KSis; KD; Mother of Adoratrix)
Mother of Pekatror; perhaps wife of Piye or Taharqa, and mother of either Shepenwepet II or Amenirdis II. Known from two stelae: her own (Oxford) and that of Pegattereru. Buried at Abydos in tomb D9. Conceivably identical with Pebatjma.

Pegattereru (Gen)
Son of Paabtamer; his stela (Chicago/Moscow), probably originally placed in his mother's tomb, states that he came from Nubia at the age of 20 to carry out his mother's interment.

Sphinx of Shepenwepet II offering a ram-headed jar to Amun; from the Sacred Lake at Karnak (Berlin 7972).

5
The Late and Ptolemaic Periods

The Final Renaissance

26th Dynasty

The Royal Succession

26th Dynasty 664–525
PSAMETIK I
NEKAU II
PSAMETIK II
WAHIBRE
AHMOSE II
PSAMETIK III

(previous page) The gate of Ptolemy II at Philae, a complex founded during the Late Period, and the last stronghold of the Egyptian religion into late Roman times (see p. 264 ff.).

At least six separate graffiti are to be found on this rock-face in the Wadi Gasus in the Eastern Desert. The main one, on the lower left, shows Psametik I offering to Amun-Min. Behind him stand his daughter, the Adoratrix Nitokris I, and her adoptive grandmother, the God's Wife Shepenwepet II, daughter of Piye. At the top right-hand corner are the cartouches of Amenirdis I and Shepenwepet I, accompanied by the apparently corresponding regnal years of their respective ruling brothers, Piye and Rudamun.

Historical Background

During the conflict between Taharqa and Assurbanipal, a number of Delta princes sided with the Assyrians, in particular the rulers of Sais who were probably descended from the Kushites' old foe, Tefnakhte of the 24th Dynasty. As a result, the Saite prince Nekau I and his son, Psametik, were rewarded with rule of the western Delta, along with Memphis. The former was killed when Tanutamun made his comeback, but Psametik (I) fled to Nineveh, to return when Assurbanipal's army finally drove Tanutamun back into the far south.

Psametik I was to all appearances a loyal subject of Assurbanipal, even possessing an alternate Assyrian name, Nabushezibanni. However, as Assyrian power withered – beset by the threat of a resurgent Babylon to their south – he was able to assert himself over other vassal rulers in the country and become ruler of a united, independent Egypt.

The adhesion of Thebes, the first and last stronghold of Kushite influence in Egypt, was marked in year 9 by the adoption of Psametik I's daughter Nitokris as the ultimate successor of the current (Kushite) God's Wife of Amun, Shepenwepet II, and her heir Amenirdis II. The remaining four decades of the reign were concerned with the consolidation of power, within a country that had not seen true central control for very many years. Building work was carried out on a scale only possible in the context of a unified state.

Foreign affairs were essentially focused on maintaining the country's independence, hence an expedition into Lower Nubia, perhaps to discourage any thoughts the Kushite king might have had of staging a comeback in the north. In the north-east, the troubles of Assyria were such that Egypt became her ally in an attempt to hold back the power of Babylon. Through this, Egypt obtained control of the Palestinian coast and fought on the side of her former conqueror in the last years of Psametik I's reign. Action was also required on

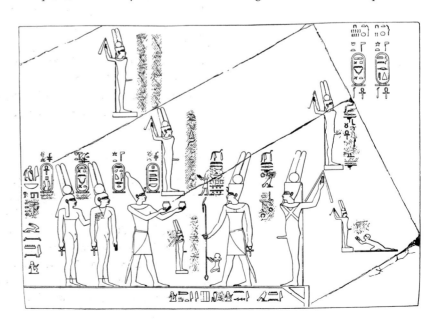

the Libyan frontier against the threat of fugitive Delta princes; indeed, at various potentially sensitive points, garrisons were installed to guarantee security, including a major fort-building programme in the Delta.

Nekau II followed his father's policy of intervening in Syria–Palestine in aid of the Assyrians, and doubtless also so as to extend his own sphere of influence. Despite managing at one point to push as far north as the Euphrates, he was later pushed back and left with his border at Gaza. His short-lived successor, Psametik II, is best known for a campaign into Nubia against the still-powerful Kushites; he was additionally responsible for the desecration of many of the standing monuments of the 25th Dynasty. In Syria–Palestine he undertook an expedition which seems to have been intended to mark Egypt's continued concern for the region in the face of the persistent Babylonian threat.

Wahibre (Apries) sustained this interest in the north-east, and undertook campaigns by land and sea against the Levantine coast. He was also, however, concerned with Libya, and mounted a campaign which was to end in military failure. This was blamed on the king himself, who was at length overthrown by one of his own Egyptian generals, who became King Ahmose II (Amasis), in spite of a final attempt by Wahibre to regain his throne with Babylonian aid.

Greeks had played a prominent part in the civil war, as well as in Egypt's commerce, with Aegean settlement encouraged by Psametik I in the Delta area of Naukratis. Ahmose II took this a step further by concentrating all Greek trade on that city, which thus took upon itself a largely Hellenic appearance. Ahmose II was particularly active in cultivating the states of the Aegean and exchanged gifts with many of them. This northern dimension to the king's policy doubtless had much to do with maintaining allies against the threat from the east, posed by Babylon and the rapidly expanding Persians.

At home, Ahmose II was a builder of some note, but his last years were clouded by the steady advance of the Persians, who had disposed of Babylon, conquered the Greek states of Asia and were now the sole great power of that continent. Led by Cambyses, they marched on Egypt, reaching the frontier almost at the moment of Ahmose II's death. The reign of the new king, Psametik III, was short; he attempted to resist the invasion but was forced to surrender at Memphis. Taken prisoner, he was at first allowed to live on at the Persian court, but, when found to be plotting a return to the throne, was then put to death.

The Royal Family

With this dynasty, Greek sources, particularly that of Herodotus, become useful. As far as the genealogy of the royal line is concerned, Herodotus explicitly states that the royal succession was from father to son until the deposition of Wahibre. Concerning the ancestry of the dynastic founder, **Psametik I**, Herodotus states that he was the son of Nekau I. The identity and paternity of his wife, Mehytenweskhet C, is provided by the monuments of their (elder?) daughter, Nitokris I. Another daughter, Meryetneith B, is known from an inscription dated to Psametik's 38th year. The queen's father

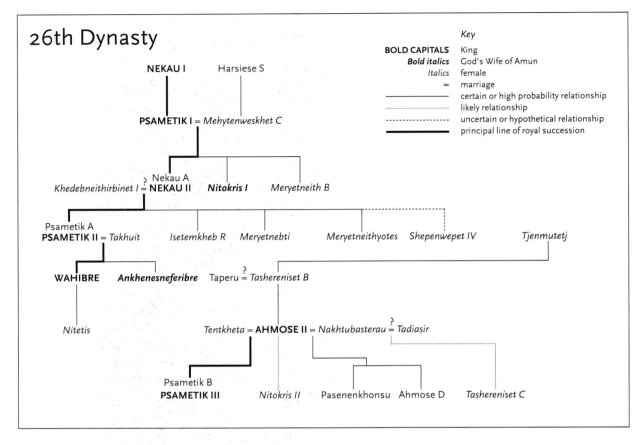

26th Dynasty

Key

BOLD CAPITALS	King
Bold italics	God's Wife of Amun
Italics	female
=	marriage
————	certain or high probability relationship
··········	likely relationship
- - - - -	uncertain or hypothetical relationship
▬▬▬	principal line of royal succession

NEKAU I — Harsiese S

PSAMETIK I = *Mehytenweskhet C*

Nekau A
Khedebneithirbinet I = NEKAU II — ***Nitokris I*** — *Meryetneith B*

Psametik A
PSAMETIK II = *Takhuit* — *Isetemkheb R* — *Meryetnebti* — *Meryetneithyotes* — *Shepenwepet IV* — *Tjenmutetj*

WAHIBRE — ***Ankhenesneferibre*** — Taperu = *Tashereniset B*

Nitetis

Tentkheta = AHMOSE II = *Nakhtubasterau* = *Tadiasir*

Psametik B
PSAMETIK III — *Nitokris II* — Pasenenkhonsu — Ahmose D — *Tashereniset C*

The college of the God's Wife of Amun around the end of the reign of Psametik I: at either end are repeated the Adoratrix, Shepenwepet IV, and the High Steward, Pedihorresnet; in the central part we have on the right the God's Wife Nitokris I, and on the left the God's Hand Amenirdis II; from a lintel, probably once part of the temple of Osiris Pededankh at North Karnak (CM JE29254B).

is identified in an inscription in her funerary chapel as the High Priest of Heliopolis, Harsiese (S).

The wife of **Nekau II** has been identified as Khedebneithirbinet I on the basis that the typology of her sarcophagus places her in the 26th Dynasty, that there is no directly attested wife of the king, and that her titles fit.[160] Apart from his successor, Psametik II, three daughters of Nekau II are known from a statue of their tutor in Cairo; another may have been the Shepenwepet IV who seems to have been adopted by Nitokris I as her heir.[161]

Psametik II's wife, Takhuit, is named by the couple's daughter Ankhenesneferibre on her sarcophagus. She was also presumably the mother of the

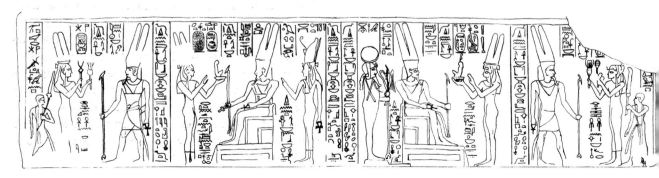

Black basalt lid of Ankhenesneferibre's sarcophagus; from Deir el-Medina, where it had been reused by a man named Pymentu (BM EA32).

king's son and successor, **Wahibre**, whose paternity is recorded in the stela recording the installation of his sister, Ankhenesneferibre, as God's Wife of Amun. Nothing is known of his family, except that Herodotus attributes to him a daughter, Nitetis.

The usurper, **Ahmose II**, has his maternity indicated by a statue of his mother, and a block from Mehallet el-Kubra, which also seems to name his grandmother. His father may have been a man named Taperu, if a libation basin in Paris naming an official Ahmose (C)-sineith-Wahibre does indeed refer to Ahmose II before coming to the throne, and not some completely separate individual. Two wives are mentioned on stelae from the Serapeum, with one, Nakhtubasterau, buried with her son Ahmose D at Giza. A princess Tashereniset C, known from a statue in London, is generally attributed to Ahmose II's reign, but this remains unproven; Nitokris II also appears to have been a child of Ahmose II.

Brief Lives ●

*Males in **bold**, females in **bold italic**.*

Ahmose D (KSon; Gen)
Son of Ahmose II and Nakhtubasterau,
buried in Giza tomb LG83. His
sarcophagus is in St Petersburg, and
shows the erasure of his titles, but not his
name.

*(above) The sarcophagus of Prince Ahmose
D; from Giza tomb LG83 (St Petersburg 766).*

Ankhenesneferibre (KDB; GS; HPA; GWA:
  prenomen **Hekatneferumut**)
Daughter of Psametik II, probably
renamed at his accession. Her adoption by
Nitokris I is recorded on a stela from
Karnak: she arrived at Thebes soon after
her father's accession, at which point she
was formally adopted and given the title of
High Priest of Amun – a role apparently
vacant since the end of the pontificate of
Harkhebi, back in the middle of Psametik
I's reign. Eight years later, in year 4 of her
brother Wahibre's reign, Ankhenesneferibre became God's Wife, on the
demise of Nitokris I. She continued in
office until the end of the dynasty, if not
beyond, amounting to over 60 years'
service. She is depicted in a number of
chapels on the north side of the temple at
Karnak. A statue is in the Nubian
Museum (Aswan) and her tomb-chapel
probably once lay at Medinet Habu. The
sarcophagus from this was reused in a

*(above) The God's Wife of Amun,
Ankhenesneferibre; from Karnak (Nubian
Museum, ex-CG42205).*

Ptolemaic tomb at Deir el-Medina, and is
now in the British Museum.

Harsiese S (HPH)
Father of Mehytenweskhet C. Possibly
identical with the Vizier Harsiese R who is
given the titles of a Heliopolitan High
Priest on the coffin of a daughter, as well
as other titles relating to cults at Memphis
and Letopolis.

Isetemkheb R (KD)
Daughter of Nekau II, shown with her
siblings on a statue of their tutor
Neferibre-nefer, now in Cairo.

Khedebneithirbinet I (KW; KM)
Probably wife of Nekau II and mother of
Psametik II. Possibly buried at
Sebennytos, if the provenance given for
her sarcophagus lid, found in 1807 and
now in Vienna, is correct.

Mehytenweskhet C (KGW)
Wife of Psametik I and mother of Nitokris
I and Meryetneith B; named on Nitokris'
sarcophagus and buried in the same
daughter's funerary chapel at Medinet
Habu. Her name also appears on a pillar
in the 18th Dynasty temple at the site.

*(below) The stone sarcophagus of
Khedebneithirbinet I, wife of Nekau II and
mother of Psametik II; probably from
Sebennytos (Vienna ÄOS3).*

Meryetnebti (KD)
Daughter of Nekau II, shown with her siblings on a statue of their tutor, Neferibre-nefer, now in Cairo.

Meryetneith B (KD)
Daughter of Psametik I, mentioned in an inscription.

Meryetneithyotes (KD)
Daughter of Nekau II, shown with her siblings on a statue of their tutor, Neferibre-nefer, now in Cairo.

Nakhtubasterau (KW)
Wife of Ahmose II and mother of Pasen-enkhonsu and Ahmose D; mentioned on a stela from the Serapeum, and buried with her second son in Giza tomb LG83. Her sarcophagus is in St Petersburg.

Nekau A (KSon)
Son of Psametik I and later king as **NEKAU II**. A privately owned statuette of the goddess Neith bears a New Year wish in his favour.

Nitokris I Shepenwepet III (KD; KSis; HPA; GWA: prenomen **Nebetneferumut**)
Daughter of Psametik I. In year 9 of her father she was adopted by Amenirdis II (as recorded in her Adoption Stela from Karnak), heir of the current God's Wife of Amun, Shepenwepet II. She is shown with the latter and her father in a relief in the Wadi Gasus. It is unknown at what date she succeeded as God's Wife, but she held the office until her death in year 4 of Wahibre, nearly 70 years since her adoption. During that period she was involved with building work around Karnak, Luxor and Abydos. She was buried in her tomb-chapel at Medinet Habu, which she shared with her natural mother and adoptive grandmother. Her sarcophagus was reused in a Ptolemaic tomb at Deir el-Medina, and is now in the Cairo Museum.

Nitokris II (HPA)
Daughter of Ahmose II, and Ankhenesneferibre's intended successor, but she is unlikely to have served, since the office of God's Wife of Amun seems to have been terminated following the Persian invasion.

Nitetis
Daughter of Wahibre. Known only from the writings of Herodotus, who states that she was sent in lieu of a daughter of Ahmose II to marry Cambyses II of Persia.

Pasenenkhonsu (KSon)
Son of Ahmose II and Nakhtubasterau; dedicator of a stela from the Serapeum.

Psametik A (KSon)
Son of Nekau II, and later king as **PSAMETIK II**. Shown with his siblings on a statue of their tutor, Neferibre-nefer, now in Cairo.

Psametik B (KSon)
Son of Ahmose II and Tentkheta; appears on a stela from the Serapeum and later king as **PSAMETIK III**.

Shepenwepet IV (Ador)
Perhaps a daughter of Nekau II. Heir to the God's Wife of Amun around the end of the reign of Psametik I; shown in a relief with Nitokris I, Amenirdis II and the High Steward of the Adoratrix, Pedihorresnet, but died prematurely.

Tadiasir
Mother of Tashereniset B, and probably wife of Ahmose II; named on the canopic jars of her daughter.

Takhuit (KGW)
Wife of Psametik II; named on the sarcophagus of Ankhenesneferibre; buried at Athribis, in a tomb found intact in 1950.

Taperu
Potentially the father of Ahmose II, if a libation basin in Paris really names Ahmose before he was made king.

Tashereniset B (KM)
Mother of Ahmose II, named on a block from Mehallet el-Kubra and depicted by the bust of a statue in the British Museum. Probably the owner of a set of canopic jars in the Vatican.

Tashereniset C (KD)
Daughter of Tadiasir, and probably Ahmose II; owner of canopic jars in St Petersburg, Oxford, Leiden and Leeuw St Pierre.

Tentkheta (KW)
Wife of Ahmose II and mother of Psametik III; mentioned on a stela from the Serapeum.

Tjenmutetj
Grandmother of Ahmose II; named on a block from Mehallet el-Kubra.

(below) Statue of Tashereniset B, mother of Ahmose II (BM EA775).

The Persian Pharaohs

27th and 31st Dynasties

The Royal Succession

27th Dynasty 525–342
CAMBYSES II
DARIUS I
XERXES I
ARTAXERXES I
XERXES II
DARIUS II
ARTAXERXES II

31st Dynasty 342–332
ARTAXERXES III
ARSES (ARTAXERXES IV)
DARIUS III

The tomb attributed to Xerxes I at Nashq-i Rastam, Iran.

Historical Background

Cambyses' triumph resulted in Egypt's incorporation into the Persian Empire, a situation which prevailed for over a century, and was renewed for a further decade before the final extinction of the empire and the onslaught of Alexander the Great.[162] From the outset, the Persian kings took the role of Egyptian pharaohs – Cambyses II having an Egyptian titulary composed for him by the native official, Udjahorresneith.[163] The reality of the situation is, however, obscured by later propagandistic accounts which ascribed to Cambyses II such crimes as the killing of the sacred Apis bull, the desecration of Ahmose II's tomb and the profanation of Egyptian temples.[164] It is probable that much of the resentment ultimately sprang from the sequestration of assets belonging to temples, a practice which seems to have occurred under both Cambyses II and Xerxes I.

Egypt was ruled from Memphis by a governor, known as a 'Satrap', one of whom – Akhemenes – was a brother of Xerxes I. Apart from Cambyses II and Darius I, the Persian kings did not visit Egypt, the later kings apparently not even adopting the full pharaonic titularies used by the earlier pair. Thus the Satrap was the actual ruler for most of the 27th Dynasty (as the first Persian dominion is called), but relatively little is known about individual Satraps, and they do not seem to appear on Egyptian monuments. Below them, there is some evidence of grouping the nomes into larger administrative units, but each nome continued to be ruled by its own groups of officials. Also of great import were the military forces, generally headed by Persians but containing various nationalities, including Egyptians. These forces reflected the cosmopolitan nature of the country under Persian rule, with a number of Persians shown being treated to Egyptian funerary rites.[165]

Under Darius I, the task of codifying Egyptian laws was carried out as part of a project covering the whole empire, and he visited Egypt on no fewer than three occasions. The same king's reign also saw considerable attention paid to the sacred sites of Egypt, including major modifications to the Serapeum of Saqqara, completion of the temple of Hibis at Kharga, and inscriptions at Karnak and elsewhere. Darius I was also responsible for completing the first canal through the isthmus of Suez, joining the eastern Delta with the Red Sea, and commemorating the fact with a series of stelae along its course.

At the end of Darius' reign an Egyptian rebellion arose that was only quelled a year into the rule of Xerxes I, who spent most of his reign fighting, particularly in Greece. This Greek campaign culminated in the Battle of Salamis, in which one of his brothers was killed. In contrast to his father, only a few mentions of Xerxes' name are found in hieroglyphs. Subsequent to Darius' reign, very little in the way of monumental construction can be identified, although as far as private monuments are concerned this may be due more

Cylinder seal of Darius I, said to have been found at Thebes, and presumably used by a high official. It shows the king hunting lions in a palm plantation and is inscribed with his name in Persian (BM).

to the poor modern dating of known structures than an actual lack of monuments.[166] A handful of Egyptian mentions are found of Artaxerxes I – most, like those of Xerxes I, coming from quarrying inscriptions – but none for his successors Xerxes II, Darius II and Artaxerxes II. These three reigns saw more revolts, in particular the uprising of a certain Inaros (460–454), during which the Satrap Akhemenes lost his life. Early in the reign of Artaxerxes II another revolt led to a Persian withdrawal from Egypt, and the seizure of power by King Amyrtaios of Sais (28th Dynasty).

Egypt remained free of Persian control for half a century, until Artaxerxes III captured the country once again. The king's reputation speaks of various cruelties, including the killing of the Apis bull, although as with Cambyses II, anti-Persian propaganda may distort the picture. Few monuments derive from the second Persian domination of Egypt, one exception being a stela of Darius III in the tomb of the sacred Buchis bull at Armant. Ultimately, the campaigns of Alexander III of Macedon resulted in the steady destruction of the Persian Empire and, with the murder of the fugitive Darius III, the land of the Nile passed into Macedonian hands.

The Royal Family

The Persian royal family, the Achaemenids, descended from a line of local kings who are listed on the Cyrus Cylinder in the British Museum.[167] The conqueror of Egypt, **Cambyses II**, was the son of Cyrus II, with Herodotus recording an alleged Egyptian claim that Cambyses was the son of Nitetis, who had actually married Cyrus, rather than Cambyses II (cf. p. 247 above). Herodotus remains the key source for the various members of

27th and 31st Dynasties

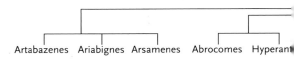

Artabazenes Ariabignes Arsamenes   Abrocomes Hyperant

Key

BOLD CAPITALS	King
CAPITALS	Foreign monarch
Italics	female
=	marriage
———————	relationship
——————	principal line of royal succession

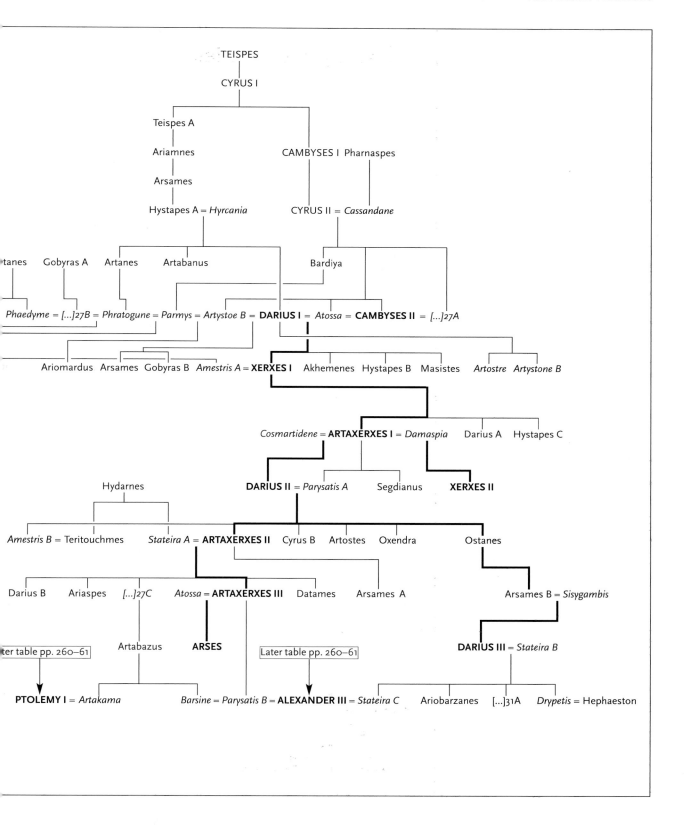

In the inscription above his own figure (third from left) in his great accession relief at Behistun in western Iran, Darius I traces his royal descent back to Teispes and Cyrus I, the founders of Achaemenid power.

the earlier Persian royal family and their relationships; given his closeness in time to these events he is likely to be accurate as to the basic picture, even if some of his stories are perhaps rather embroidered. Similarly, the writings of Ctesias, Thucydides, Xenophon and Plutarch are key for our knowledge of the empire's middle years.

Cambyses II married two of his sisters, seemingly hitherto a custom not known in Persia. At the end of his reign a man claiming to be the king's brother, Bardiya, rose in revolt against him and ruled for a brief period following Cambyses' accidental death; he was then killed by a group led by **Darius I**. It was claimed at the time that 'Bardiya' had already been killed, and that the rebel was actually Gaumata, an imposter. On the other hand, the story may have been invented by Darius to cover up his own murder of the real Bardiya.[168]

Darius I gives his genealogy in his accession inscription at Behistun in western Iran,[169] emphasizing his role as a member of the royal family. But since his father and grandfather were still alive at the time, it is clear that his *de jure* claim to the throne was in fact fairly remote. He married two daughters of Cyrus II (one of whom, Atossa, had been a wife of both Cambyses and Bardiya), a daughter of Bardiya himself, and one daughter of a comrade called Otanes; he had also previously been married to the daughter of another noble, Gobyras A.

Darius had twelve sons, his successor **Xerxes I** being the eldest offspring of Atossa, and thus born in the purple. However, Xerxes was murdered along with his heir Darius A, leaving a younger son, **Artaxerxes I**, to succeed him. The latter was ultimately followed by an illegitimate son, Ochus, who ascended the throne as **Darius II** after a dynastic struggle with his legitimate half-brother, **Xerxes II**, and another bastard, Segdianus.

Similarly, the accession of Darius II's son **Artaxerxes II** was disputed by his brother, Cyrus B, and yet more bloodletting accompanied **Artaxerxes III**'s assumption of power – three brothers, including the Crown Prince Darius B, died violently. In the same vein, Artaxerxes III's own reign ended with his being killed along with all his family, save his puppet-successor, **Arses**, who was also murdered two years' later. The final Achaemenid ruler, **Darius III**, was a great-nephew of Artaxerxes II. One of his daughters, Stateira C – captured at Issus along with Darius' wife, another daughter and six-year-old son – was later married to Alexander III.[170]

Brief Lives ●

Males in **bold**, *females in **bold italic**.*

Since the vast majority of the Persian royal family played no direct role in the running of Egypt, biographical notes are omitted with one exception:

Akhemenes (Hakhamanish)
Brother of Xerxes I; served as Satrap of Egypt from just after the accession of his brother (November 486) until his death at the Battle of Papremis in 459; led the Egyptian forces at the Battle of Salamis.

● ●

The Last Egyptian Pharaohs

28th to 30th Dynasties

The Royal Succession

28th Dynasty 409–399
AMYRTAIOS

29th Dynasty 399–380
NEFARUD I
PASHERENMUT
HAGAR
NEFARUD II

30th Dynasty 380–342
NAKHTNEBEF
DJEDHOR
NAKHTHORHEB

Historical Background

Weaknesses in the Persian regime allowed Egypt to secede from the empire at the end of 405 BC, under the leadership of Amyrtaios (Amenirdis) of Sais, the sole king of the 28th Dynasty. However, within a few years he had been overthrown by Nefarud I of Mendes, and possibly executed at Memphis.

The 29th Dynasty founded by Nefarud was itself soon wracked by dissension, a struggle for the throne breaking out on his death, and burial in a tomb at Mendes. The winner was Pasherenmut (Psammuthis), but he ruled for only a year, being himself supplanted by Hagar (Akhoris). The latter had a substantial reign, during which he undertook a fair amount of building and bolstered Egypt's strategic position through an alliance with Evagoras of Salamis (Cyprus). He was successful in repulsing a series of Persian attacks, aided by the presence within his army of Greek troops.

Akhoris' successor Nefarud II was short-lived, soon being overthrown by Nakhtnebef (Nectanebo I), first king of the 30th Dynasty, who originated from Sebennytos (Samannud), 30 kilometres west of Mendes. Within five years he faced yet another Persian attack, foiled only by the timely arrival of the inundation and squabbling between the Persians and their Athenian associates. Following this, there was a lengthy period of peace, during which the king built extensively, including the earliest surviving parts of the temples of Philae. Towards the end of the reign, an attempt was made to renew old alliances between Egypt and the Hellenic powers of Athens and Sparta, with a view to opposing the next move by the Persians, who were certain not to abandon what they continued to regard as a rebellious province.

Nakhtnebef was succeeded by his son Djedhor (Takhos), who had played a major role in his father's last few years on the throne, latterly as co-regent for two years. He went on the offensive against Persia, leaving Egypt in the hands of his brother Tjahapimu. However, high taxation to finance the war was used as a pretext by Tjahapimu to revolt and have his own son, Nakhthorheb (Nectanebo II), declared king in his place.

Sphinx of Nefarud I (Louvre A26).

A brief civil war against a Mendesian loyalist was followed by the last substantial period of native rule in Egypt. Extensive building works were carried out, including a major construction at Saqqara where the Serapeum was enlarged and major complexes established for a range of sacred animal cults. Ultimately, a successful Persian invasion caused Nakhthorheb to withdraw into the south, maintaining a regime around Edfu for at least two more years before finally retreating into Nubia.

Egypt was reincorporated into the Persian Empire although, at some point during the ensuing decade, one Khabbash held power at Memphis for long enough to bury an Apis bull (the only recorded event of his reign). With him passed the last native ruler of Egypt: henceforth the country's fate would be in the hands of foreigners.

The Royal Family

The final dynasties of Egyptian independence present a number of problems as far as their relationships are concerned. Nothing is known concerning the 28th Dynasty, but some material is available in the papyrus 'Demotic Chronicle', a curious pseudo-prophecy written in Ptolemaic times but purportedly composed under Djedhor. It contains various oracles and commentaries which relate to the history of the last three native dynasties and their aftermath. One of its tenets is that those kings whose sons were not destined to succeed them were thus being punished for some sinful behaviour. A number of relationships are therefore provided by the text, although its obscure and tortuous wording has led to misinterpretations, including one that made Nakhtnebef a 'son' of Nefarud, which he was certainly not (and which is not actually stated in the papyrus if properly translated).

Nefarud I is said to have been succeeded by his son, who was presumably **Pasherenmut**, although one interpretation of the papyrus has been that this son was rather an ephemeral ruler called 'Muthis', who appears in one redaction of Manetho's king list. Muthis' very existence, however, remains unattested by any other source. **Hagar** was certainly not the son of Pasherenmut, whom he deposed and, although one would assume that they were in some way related, no evidence exists. According to the Chronicle, Hagar's son **Nefarud II** succeeded him, before being overthrown by **Nakhtnebef.**

The sarcophagus lid of Nakhtnebef's great-nephew, also a Nakhtnebef (A), provides the

Head-end of the lid of the sarcophagus of Nakhtnebef A, a member of the 30th Dynasty royal family who served under the Macedonian regime of Ptolemy I (Berlin 7).

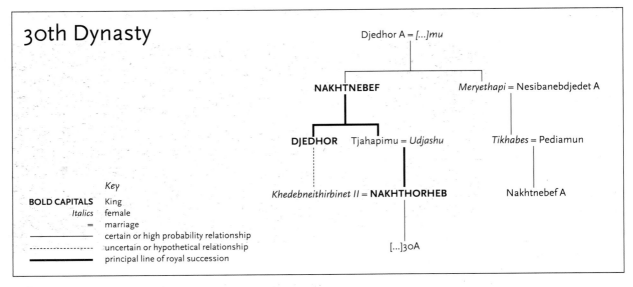

30th Dynasty

Djedhor A = [...]mu

NAKHTNEBEF   Meryethapi = Nesibanebdjedet A

DJEDHOR   Tjahapimu = Udjashu   Tikhabes = Pediamun

Khedebneithirbinet II = NAKHTHORHEB   Nakhtnebef A

[...]30A

Key

BOLD CAPITALS	King
Italics	female
=	marriage
————————	certain or high probability relationship
- - - - - - - - - - -	uncertain or hypothetical relationship
▬▬▬▬▬	principal line of royal succession

latter's genealogy and names his father as Djedhor (A). The king's sister, Meryethapi, appears in a now-lost inscription alongside their mother, [...]mu, the first part of her name now missing. A fascinating possibility suggested by a Ptolemaic inscription in the rock-temple of Ay at Akhmim, that Nakhtnebef may have married a Greek lady named Ptolemaïs,[171] has now been proved a misinterpretation, leaving Nakhtnebef without a known spouse. As far as offspring of the king are concerned, the Demotic Chronicle makes it clear that his successor, **Djedhor**, was a son. Djedhor's own successor was Nakhthorheb, the son of Tjahapimu, as indicated by the cult of the two men being linked on the sarcophagus of Wennefer in New York. On a statue from Memphis, Tjahapimu is called 'the brother and father of kings', who can only respectively be Djedhor and Nakhthorheb. Finally, Tjahapimu is shown to be the son of a king by a bronze seal giving him that title.

Tjahapimu's wife, and the mother of **Nakhthorheb**, was almost certainly the 'King's Mother' Udjashu, whose sarcophagus is of a similar design to her putative son's, and who significantly lacks any title making her the wife of a king. A final royal lady, Khedebneithirbinet II, may have been a wife of Nakhthorheb – on the basis of one of his *shabtis* being discovered in her burial at Saqqara. The fact that she was buried in the tomb of officials of the 26th Dynasty is consistent with interment there some time after Nakhthorheb had fled his throne, leaving the remains of the royal family somewhat in limbo. The king of whom she was daughter could have been Nakhtnebef or Djedhor – we have no basis for deciding.

Apart from the queen and his distant cousin Nakhtnebef A, Nakhthorheb's eldest son may also have lived and served under Alexander the Great or the Ptolemies, on the basis of a now-nameless statue. Thus, further descendants of the 30th Dynasty may have survived, perhaps providing ancestors for some of the Egyptian rebel kings of Ptolemaic times, but no evidence for this survives.

Brief Lives ●

Males in **bold,** *females in* **bold italic.**

Djedhor A (KF)
Father of Nakhtnebef A. Named on the sarcophagus of Nakhtnebef.

Khedebneithirbinet II (KD; KW)
Probable wife of Nakhthorheb, and daughter of one of his predecessors. Known from her burial at Saqqara, from which survive her canopic jars and some *shabtis* (Cairo Museum). On these she lacks a cartouche, although another *shabti*, in the Petrie Museum, does have one. On the other hand, this piece could belong to Khedebneithirbinet I.

Meryethapi (KSis)
Sister of Nakhtnebef. Named on the sarcophagus of Nakhtnebef A.

Nakhtnebef A (Genmo)
Great-nephew of Nakhtnebef who served under Ptolemy I, both as mayor of Sile (eastern Delta) and as a senior Generalissimo. His sarcophagus lid is in Berlin.

Nesibanebdjedet A
A palace official and brother-in-law of Nakhtnebef. Named on the sarcophagus of Nakhtnebef A.

Pediamun
Husband of the niece of Nakhtnebef. Named on the sarcophagus of Nakhtnebef A.

Tikhabes
Niece of Nakhtnebef. Named on the sarcophagus of Nakhtnebef A.

(right) Statue of Tjahapimu, father of Nakhthorheb; from Memphis (MMA 08.205.1).

(above) The sarcophagus of Queen Udjashu; from Masara (CM JE40645=CG29317).

Tjahapimu (KB&F)
Brother of Djedhor and father of Nakhthorheb. Revolted against his brother, leading to his son's accession to the throne. Owner of a statue from Memphis (now in New York).

Udjashu (GS; KM)
Probably wife of Tjahapimu and mother of Nakhthorheb; broken sarcophagus was found at Masara in the northern Delta and is now in Cairo, as is one of her *shabtis.*

[...]mu
Mother of Nakhtnebef. Named alongside her daughter, Meryethapi, in a now-lost inscription.

[...]30A (GKSon; Genmo)
Son of Nakhthorheb, who apparently lived on into the Ptolemaic Period. Owner of a statue missing the head and lower part of the legs and base; the name was lost with the destruction of the latter. His fragmentary autobiography speaks of his dealings with 'foreigners', but whether these were the Persians or Macedonians remains unknown.

Macedon

Argaeid Dynasty

The Royal Succession

Argaeid Dynasty 332–310
ALEXANDER III (*'the Great'*)
PHILIP III ARRHIDAEUS
ALEXANDER IV

Historical Background

There was a long and bitter history between the throne of Persia and the Hellenic peoples that approached its peak under Philip II of Macedon, who forcibly unified the Greeks under his leadership. After his murder, however, his son Alexander III ('the Great') took the war to the Persians. The Battle of Issus in 333 would be a turning point for Macedon, Persia and the Persian provinces – including Egypt.

Following his victory, rather than pursue the fleeing Darius III, Alexander set about consolidating what he now controlled, something that could only take place by uniting the territory with the economic base of Egypt's grain surplus.[172] Cyprus was ceded to him by its king and Phoenicia fell under Alexander's control after the seven-month siege of Tyre. From there he moved through Palestine towards Egypt, with an army of 40,000 Macedonians and Greeks. Once within the country he made his way to Heliopolis and Memphis, where he made sacrifices to the local gods – Ptah in particular – to give credence to his authority as the new monarch and legitimate successor to the native pharaohs. By the start of the following year he was travelling along the Canopic branch of the Nile and ordering the creation of a new city, Alexandria, which would become the capital, and which he is said to have laid out himself. One well-attested journey of Alexander's was made to pay his respects to the oracle of Amun at Siwa Oasis.

The king rearranged the administration of the country before leaving to continue his campaign eastwards. He left two governors: Doloaspis, who might previously have served under Darius; and Peteisis, an Egyptian who quickly resigned, leaving the former in charge of civil matters. Military matters came under two Macedonian generals (*strategoi*), with another Egyptian, Kleomenes of Naucratis, swiftly promoted to the office of Satrap.

Within ten years Alexander was dead, leaving a pregnant wife and a less-than-able half-brother, Philip. The empire was divided into a number of provinces, each under the rule of a Satrap, with a triumvirate in Macedonia in overall command, acting in the name of the feeble-minded new king Philip III and his as-yet-unborn co-ruler, Alexander IV. The triumvirs were Perdiccas, Antipater and Craterus, the latter two rapidly dissenting from Perdiccas' dictatorial approach. The rule of Egypt now fell to Ptolemy, son of Lagus, who allied himself with Antipater in the ensuing hostilities and reinforced his position by 'kidnapping' Alexander III's corpse, which he ultimately buried at Alexandria. He also undertook building work in the name of Philip, in particular at Karnak and Hermopolis.

Perdiccas tried to invade Egypt but was murdered by his own officers in the attempt, while Craterus had been killed in action against Perdiccas' allies in Syria. Antipater was thus left as sole ruler of the empire but, on his death soon afterwards, his successor Polyperchon was unable to secure the loyalty of the Satraps. This led to the Second War of the Successors, resulting in Polyperchon's deposition and the assumption of the regency of Cassander; Olympias then murdered Philip III. Ptolemy was able to add Syria and Phoenicia to his domain.

(opposite) Alexander III offers to Amun-Min in the temple of Luxor.

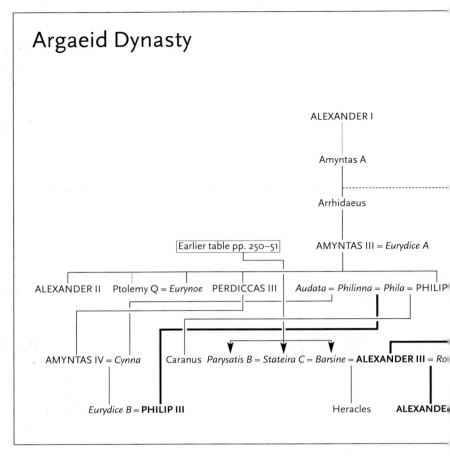

Argaeid Dynasty

Three years later, the Third War of the Successors began, by the end of which Ptolemy had lost Syria, but acquired Cyprus. In the name of Alexander IV, now in Cassander's control, Ptolemy added to the temple of Khnum at Elephantine. To this period also dates the institution of the cult of Serapis.

Within two years – in 310 or 309 – Alexander IV was dead at the hands of Cassander, although his reign continued until 306. Ptolemy initially remained as Satrap, but dissension within the empire continued, Ptolemy losing Cyprus in 306. The assumption of kingly titles by Ptolemy's Cypriot opponents, Antigonus and Demetrius Poliorcetes, led directly to the taking of crowns by Ptolemy in Egypt, Cassander in Macedon, Seleucus (I) in Syria and Lysimachus (A) in Thrace. The empire of Alexander the Great was at an end.

The Royal Family [173]

The Argaeid Dynasty allegedly went back to Heracles, their descent being traced initially by Satyrus, and from the 7th century onwards by Herodotus. Arsinoe A, the ancestress of the Ptolemaic Dynasty, is said by the former tradition to trace her descent via a son, grandson and great-grandson of Alexander I.

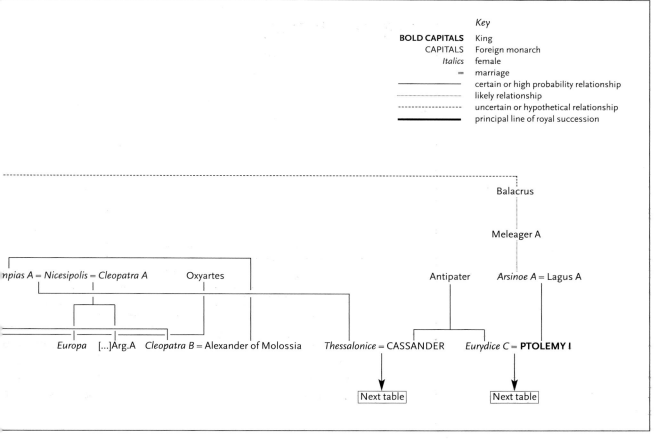

Key

BOLD CAPITALS	King
CAPITALS	Foreign monarch
Italics	female
=	marriage
———————	certain or high probability relationship
····················	likely relationship
- - - - - - - - - -	uncertain or hypothetical relationship
▬▬▬▬▬	principal line of royal succession

Balacrus

Meleager A

npias A = *Nicesipolis* = *Cleopatra A*   Oxyartes   Antipater   *Arsinoe A* = Lagus A

Europa   [...]*Arg.A*   *Cleopatra B* = Alexander of Molossia   *Thessalonice* = CASSANDER   *Eurydice C* = **PTOLEMY I**

Next table   Next table

A key source for the history of the royal family during the Argaeids' rule of Egypt is Plutarch's *Life* of **Alexander III**, together with the works of such writers as Arrian and Justin.[174] Alexander and his father Philip II both contracted multiple marriages, leading to various fratricidal jealousies that contributed fundamentally to the extinction of the dynasty. An early example was Philip's marriage to Cleopatra A, a lady of purer Macedonian blood than Alexander's mother, Olympias (A). Just before Philip's assassination, Cleopatra had given birth to a son: both were subsequently murdered, allegedly by Olympias as a threat to the position of the new king, Alexander III. Another killing was that of the son borne to Philip II by Phila.

Alexander himself acquired his four wives – Parysatis B, Barsine, Stateira C and Roxane – during his campaigns in Persia and the East. Barsine, the widow of a Greek general in Persian service and a great-granddaughter of Artaxerxes II, was captured at Damascus. The third was espoused at the same time as other distinguished Persian ladies were married by Macedonians in a mass ceremony at Susa. His final wife was Roxane, the daughter of a Bactrian prince who had surrendered to Alexander in 327.

After Alexander's death, family bloodshed began immediately with Stateira's killing by Roxane. The latter became the mother of the king's

(right) Philip III Arrhidaeus, as depicted on the bark-shrine of Amun-Re at Karnak.

posthumous son, **Alexander IV**, who joined his uncle, **Philip III**, as joint ruler of the empire. This arrangement was soon caught up in the rivalry between Philip's wife, Eurydice B, and Olympias A. An attempt by the former to replace regent Polyperchon with Cassander resulted in Philip and Eurydice's capture and death at the hands of Olympias, thus leaving her grandson, Alexander IV, as sole king. However, shortly afterwards, Olympias was condemned to death at the bidding of Cassander, and Alexander and Roxane were taken into custody. They were killed by Cassander as Alexander approached adulthood, as was Heracles – Alexander III's other son. The direct Argaeid line was thus extinct.

Brief Lives ●

Males in **bold**, *females in* ***bold italic***.
m. *married*; b. *born*; fl. *floruit*.

Alexander (King of Molossia)
Uncle and brother-in-law of Alexander III.

Alexander I (King of Macedon, *c.* 489–454)
Great-great-great-grandfather of Alexander III.

Alexander II (King of Macedon, 370–367)

Uncle of Alexander III; assassinated by Eurydice A and Ptolemy Q.

Amyntas III (King of Macedon, 393–370)
Grandfather of Alexander III.

Amyntas IV (King of Macedon?, 359)
Cousin of Alexander III and father-in-law of Philip III; it is uncertain whether he ever reigned, and if he did so it was only very briefly before being set aside; finally executed in 336.

Amyntas A
Allegedly youngest son of Alexander I, great-great-grandfather of Alexander III and ancestor of Arsinoe A.

Arsinoe A
See next section.

Antipater
See next section.

Arrhidaeus
Great-grandfather of Alexander III.

Audata
Illyrian wife of Philip II (m. *c.* 358) and grandmother-in-law of Philip III.

Balacrus
Allegedly grandfather of Arsinoe A.

Barsine A
Persian wife of Alexander III (m. *c.* 333); previously married to Rhodian mercenary commander Memnon. She retired to Pergamum prior to Alexander's death.

Caranus
Alleged son of Philip II and Phila; killed as a child soon after Alexander III's accession in 335.

Cassander
See next section.

Cleopatra A
Wife of Philip II (m. 337); murdered by Olympias in 335 – allegedly by roasting or hanging – and probably buried in the antechamber of Tomb II at Vergina.

Cleopatra B
Daughter of Philip II, and sister and aunt of Alexander III; murdered 310 or 309.

Cynna
Daughter of Philip II and mother-in-law of Philip III.

Europa
Infant daughter of Philip II and Cleopatra A; murdered with her mother in 335.

Eurydice A
Grandmother of Alexander III; buried in the Vaulted Tomb at Vergina.[175]

Eurydice B
Granddaughter of Philip II and wife of Philip III; forced to commit suicide in 317.

Eurydice C
See next section.

Eurynoe
Aunt of Alexander III.

Heracles
Son of Alexander III and Barsine (b. *c.* 327); murdered 309.

Lagus A
See next section.

Meleager A
Allegedly father of Arsinoe A and a descendant of Alexander I.

Nicesipolis
Thessalian wife of Philip II (m. 358 or 357) and mother-in-law of Cassander.

Olympias A
Wife of Philip II (m. 357) and mother of Alexander III, from Epirus. Allegedly responsible for the disability of Philip III and later his murder, she had also previously murdered Cleopatra A and [...]Arg.A. Condemned to death by a military assembly early in 315.

Oxyartes
Father-in-law of Alexander III; a Bactrian prince who had fought against Alexander until his surrender in 327.

Parysatis B
Daughter of Artaxerxes III and wife of Alexander III (m. 324).

Perdiccas III (King of Macedon, 367–359)
Uncle of Alexander III; killed during his conflict with Eurydice A.

Phila
Wife of Philip II.

Philinna
Thessalian wife of Philip II (m. 358 or 357) and mother of Philip III.

Philip II (King of Macedon, 359–336)
Father of Alexander III; deposed Amyntas IV, consolidated the Macedonian state and created the Corinthian League to unite Greece against the Persians. Assassinated during the wedding of Cleopatra B in October 336 by one Pausanias. Buried in Tomb II at Vergina, found intact and containing the king's cremated remains.

Ptolemy Q (of Alorus)
Uncle of Alexander III and possible half-brother of Alexander II, whom he murdered; regent for Perdiccas III until his death at the hands of Perdiccas in 365.

Roxane
Wife of Alexander III and mother of Alexander IV; murdered with her son in 310 or 309.

Stateira C
Also referred to as **Barsine (B)**; daughter of Darius III and wife of Alexander III (m. 324). Murdered by Roxane in 323, following Alexander's death, together with her sister Drypetis.

Thessalonice
Daughter of Philip II and Nicesipolis; wife of Cassander (m. 316).

[ ]Arg.A
Infant son of Philip II and Cleopatra A; murdered with his mother.

The House of Ptolemy

Ptolemaic Dynasty

The Royal Succession

Ptolemaic Dynasty 310–30 BC

PTOLEMY I (SOTER I)
PTOLEMY II (PHILADELPHUS)
PTOLEMY III (EUERGETES I)
PTOLEMY IV (PHILOPATOR)
PTOLEMY V (EPIPHANES)
PTOLEMY VI (PHILOMETOR)
PTOLEMY VI
PTOLEMY VIII (EUERGETES II)
(co-regent)

PTOLEMY VI (again)
PTOLEMY VIII (again)
PTOLEMY IX (SOTER II)
PTOLEMY X (ALEXANDER I)
PTOLEMY IX (again)
PTOLEMY XI (ALEXANDER II)
BERENICE III (co-regent)
PTOLEMY XII (NEOS DIONYSOS)
CLEOPATRA VI
BERENICE IV (co-regent)
PTOLEMY XII (again)
CLEOPATRA VII
PTOLEMY XIII (co-regent)
CLEOPATRA VII
PTOLEMY XIV (co-regent)
CLEOPATRA VII
PTOLEMY XV (CAESAR) (co-regent)

In year 7 of Alexander IV, the Satrap of Egypt, Ptolemy (I) son of Lagus, erected a stela celebrating his successes; although dated by the reign of the young king, the cartouches in the scene at the top are blank, perhaps a constructive ambiguity indicating Ptolemy's drift towards kingship (CM CG22181).

Historical Background

In 304 Ptolemy I was formally crowned as pharaoh. During the struggles of the time, he lent support to various factions fighting Demetrius Poliorcetes in Macedon, acquiring Cyprus in the process. In Egypt itself a certain amount of building took place, particularly in areas being settled by Greeks. After Ptolemy I's death, the second Ptolemy expanded Egyptian power into parts of Asia Minor and the Aegean islands, as well as carrying out considerable amounts of building at Karnak and Philae, together with many other sites.

Under Ptolemy III, the Ptolemaic Empire reached its greatest extent, embracing both Libya and Syria, as well as the previously acquired northern part of Nubia, and areas around the Aegean. However, the Syrian campaign was interrupted by what was to be the first in a series of revolts by the native Egyptians against their Macedonian and Greek overlords. In spite of the placement of a number of his own *strategoi* as heads of nome administrations, these uprisings continued into the reign of Ptolemy IV. Indeed, a counter-pharaoh, Harwennefer, ruled in the Thebaid from 205, thus also enabling the Kushites to return to northern Nubia. Nevertheless, Ptolemy IV completed the naos of the Edfu temple, built the temple at Deir el-Medina, and added to a considerable number of other sanctuaries.

The premature death of Ptolemy IV – and subsequent murder of his wife – left his six-year-old son, Ptolemy V, in the hands of a series of regents. This

The temple of Horus at Edfu, one of the greatest monuments of the Ptolemaic Dynasty, begun by Ptolemy IV and completed by Ptolemy XII.

young king inherited the continuing native revolt along with a new (or merely renamed?) counter-pharaoh, Ankhwennefer, who took over in 199; it was not until 186 that nationwide Ptolemaic control was finally reasserted and an amnesty declared. Outside the borders of Egypt parts of Syria and Thrace were lost, although a marriage-alliance between Egypt and the Seleucid Syria was later cemented with the arrival of Cleopatra I.

The murder of Ptolemy V left Ptolemy VI under the regency of his Syrian mother and then, after her death, in the care of courtiers. From 170 onwards, the king shared his throne with his sister-wife Cleopatra II and their brother, Ptolemy VIII; a Syrian invasion by Antiochus IV soon afterwards was only prevented from taking Alexandria by the intervention of a Roman envoy. In the aftermath of this humiliation, and widespread revolts and disturbances, the royal triumvirate began to collapse, with Ptolemy VIII briefly holding

Ptolemaic Dynasty part 1

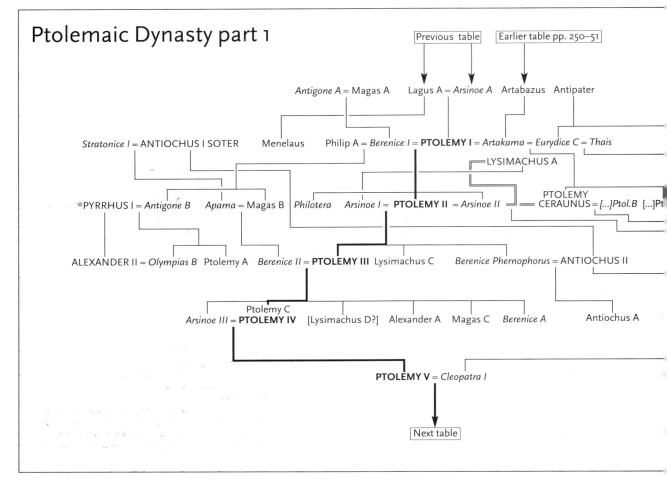

Previous table

Earlier table pp. 250–51

supreme power, followed by his siblings. Ultimately, Ptolemy VIII was granted the rule of Libya and left Egypt.

With Ptolemy VI's return to power, building work was carried out throughout northern Nubia, which was progressively regained by the Egyptian crown, as well as at numerous sites in Egypt proper. The last five years of the reign were occupied by war in Syria, culminating in the king's death in battle against Alexander I Balas.

The return of Ptolemy VIII was marked by a reversal of his brother's favourable treatment of the Jews, as well as harsh measures against his Alexandrine opponents. Having established a tripartite rule with his wives Cleopatra II and III, a civil war ensued, with Ptolemy and Cleopatra III fleeing to Cyprus. A new counter-pharaoh, Harsiese (II), took the opportunity to raise another Theban revolt, which was not ended until after the return of Ptolemy VIII in 130. Within two years, the failure of intervention on behalf of Cleopatra II by Syria's Demetrius II saw her escape to Syria, although a reconciliation between the triumvirate finally occurred in 124; a general amnesty came about six years later.

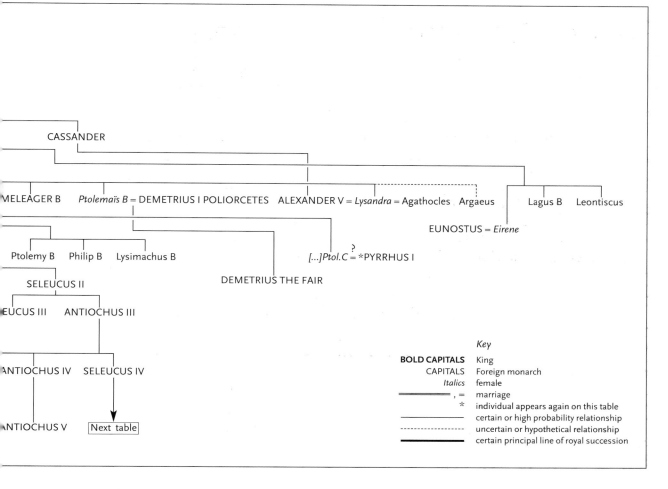

CASSANDER

MELEAGER B   *Ptolemaïs B* = DEMETRIUS I POLIORCETES   ALEXANDER V = *Lysandra* = Agathocles   Argaeus   Lagus B   Leontiscus

EUNOSTUS = *Eirene*

Ptolemy B   Philip B   Lysimachus B   [...]*Ptol.C* = *PYRRHUS I ?

SELEUCUS II   DEMETRIUS THE FAIR

EUCUS III   ANTIOCHUS III

ANTIOCHUS IV   SELEUCUS IV

ANTIOCHUS V   Next table

Key

BOLD CAPITALS	King
CAPITALS	Foreign monarch
Italics	female
═══ , =	marriage
*	individual appears again on this table
────	certain or high probability relationship
--------	uncertain or hypothetical relationship
▬▬▬	certain principal line of royal succession

Scene on the 'Raphia Stela', showing a mounted Ptolemy VI slaying a (missing) figure of Antiochus III. Behind the king is Arsinoe III; from Memphis (CM CG31088).

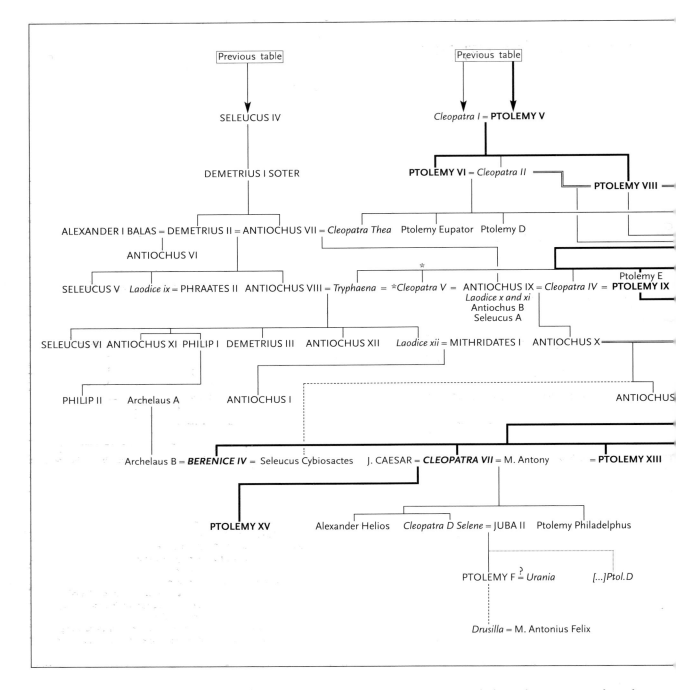

Ptolemy VIII undertook construction work throughout Egypt and north-ern Nubia. After his death, a short-lived triumvirate of Ptolemy IX with Cleopatra II and III ended with the death of the elder Cleopatra. Disputes between the king and surviving queen resulted in civil war, with Ptolemy leaving for Cyprus in 107, to be replaced by Ptolemy X. Ptolemy IX returned in 88 and continued to rule with his daughter Berenice III until his death,

Ptolemaic Dynasty part 2

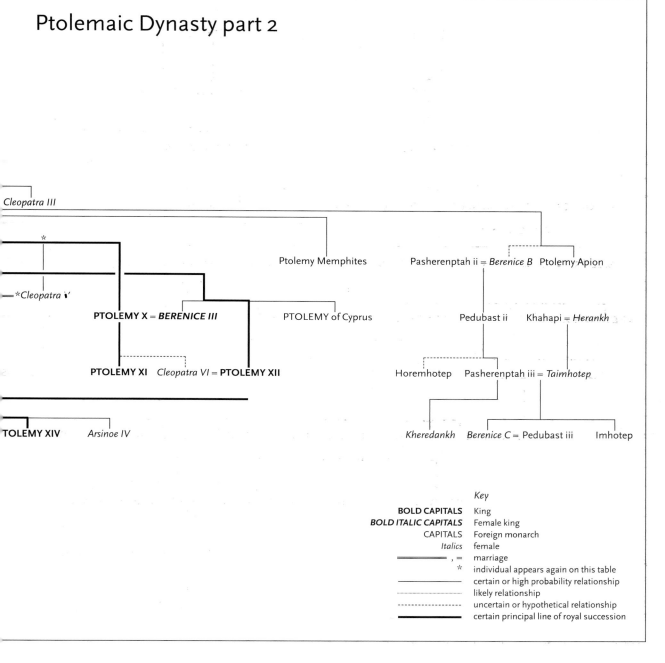

Cleopatra III

Ptolemy Memphites   Pasherenptah ii = *Berenice B*   Ptolemy Apion

*Cleopatra v

PTOLEMY X = ***BERENICE III***   **PTOLEMY** of Cyprus   Pedubast ii   Khahapi = *Herankh*

PTOLEMY XI   *Cleopatra VI* = **PTOLEMY XII**   Horemhotep   Pasherenptah iii = *Taimhotep*

TOLEMY XIV   *Arsinoe IV*   Kheredankh   *Berenice C* = Pedubast iii   Imhotep

Key

BOLD CAPITALS	King
BOLD ITALIC CAPITALS	Female king
CAPITALS	Foreign monarch
Italics	female
═══ , =	marriage
*	individual appears again on this table
────	certain or high probability relationship
··········	likely relationship
- - - - -	uncertain or hypothetical relationship
▬▬▬	certain principal line of royal succession

and Ptolemy X, who was killed in 87, willed the Egyptian Empire to the Romans; but they declined to execute the bequest.

Berenice III was left in power but forced to marry Ptolemy XI, who had returned from Italy. Having murdered the queen, Ptolemy was then killed by the Alexandrine mob. It was with the next king, Ptolemy XII, that the final decay of the Ptolemaic Empire began. First, Cyprus was given to the king's

(above) Clay sealing showing Ptolemy IX Soter II; from Edfu (ROM).

(above right) Clay sealing showing Ptolemy X Alexander I; from Edfu (ROM).

brother, and later taken by the Romans in partial fulfilment of Ptolemy X's will. This will placed the king permanently in thrall to the Romans, although Julius Caesar confirmed Ptolemy XII's right to the throne in 59. Following Rome's annexation of Cyprus in 58, the king's position became untenable and he was exiled to Rome. Three years later, Ptolemy was replaced on the throne by a Roman military force, and on his death made the Romans guarantors of his will, by which the throne passed to Cleopatra VII and Ptolemy XIII.

In good Ptolemaic tradition the siblings soon fell out, Cleopatra being exiled in 49. The same year saw the start of the Roman Civil War and, despite Pompey's support of the pharaoh, Ptolemy had him murdered on his arrival in Egypt in 48. Caesar arrived shortly afterwards and, using the Roman guarantee of Ptolemy XII's will as a legal basis, proceeded to impose a settlement on the warring siblings. Ptolemy XIII's supporters, however, then initiated an unsuccessful war against Caesar in which their king was ultimately killed.

Rule was handed over to Cleopatra VII, with her younger brother – Ptolemy XIV – as a junior co-ruler. The two spent 46–44 in Rome as Caesar's guests, but after his assassination they returned to Egypt, where Ptolemy was murdered. He was replaced as co-ruler by Cleopatra's son Ptolemy XV. Following the war that resulted from Caesar's murder, Cleopatra succeeded in obtaining the favour of Mark Antony (Marcus Antonius), in spite of the Egyptian-based Roman legions going over to the assassins' cause. The Ptolemaic Empire was greatly enhanced during the ensuing reorganization of the eastern Roman Empire by Antony – the eastern Mediterranean lands becoming in effect the joint dominion of queen and Roman general.

However, tensions rapidly grew between the new entity and the Roman west, opposition centring on Octavian, Caesar's adopted son, and resulting in war. At length, Antony's fleet was defeated at Actium on the west coast of Greece on 2 September 31. This led to a rapid crumbling in the Antonian-Egyptian position, with control reduced by the following spring to Egypt alone; Egypt itself was then lost with Octavian's entry into Alexandria on 1 August 30. The successive suicides of Antony and Cleopatra, and the murder of Ptolemy XV by Octavian, subsequently confirmed the extinction of the Egyptian state. Egypt was annexed to the Roman Empire as the province of Aegyptus with effect from the entry into Alexandria by Octavian – soon to be the Emperor Augustus.

The Royal Family [176]

The mother of **Ptolemy I** was Arsinoe (A), daughter of Meleager and an unknown mother, and a scion of the Macedonian royal house. Her ancestry is provided by Satyrus (in the time of Ptolemy IV) and quoted by Theophilus, although a number of earlier writers had noted her royal connections. The paternity of Ptolemy I is somewhat problematic, his 'official' father Lagus A being of unknown origins, with a possibility that he may have married Arsinoe while she was pregnant by another; indeed, some tales have Ptolemy as a son of Philip II, although these all seem to date to after Ptolemy's death.[177] Ptolemy I had at least one brother (or half-brother), Menelaus, as recorded from a number of sources, including Plutarch, Diodorus and Justin.

A head, probably of Arsinoe II (MMA 38.10).

Four or five women are known to have been Ptolemy's wives or mistresses, beginning with Thais according to Athenaeus, who also supplies details of Ptolemy's sons by her: Lagus and Leontiscus, and daughter Eirene. A second wife, Artakama, a descendant of Artaxerxes II, is recorded by Arrian, with a third lady Eurydice (daughter of Antipater) and her offspring being mentioned by Pausanias and other writers. Eurydice became the mother of a number of children: Ptolemy Ceraunus, said by Justin to have had a daughter, who married Pyrrhus; Meleager B (noted by Porphyry); an unknown male; Lysandra and Ptolemais B (according to Plutarch); and Argaeus may also have been her son.

Ptolemy I's fourth wife was Berenice I, a major source of information again being Pausanias, who also provides data on her offspring. She bore him three children: Ptolemy II, Arsinoe II and Philotera. **Ptolemy II** married twice – first to Arsinoe I, with whom he had three children: Ptolemy III, Lysimachus (C) and Berenice Phernophorus (as recorded in a commentary on Theocritus). Ptolemy II's second spouse was his sister, Arsinoe II, but the union proved childless; although she had borne children to her first husband, Lysimachus A, she had not to her second, Ptolemy Ceraunus. In addition to his legitimate descendants, Ptolemy II probably had a son – Ptolemy Andromachou – by Bilistiche, one of many mistresses.

Ptolemy III married but once, to Berenice II, whose parentage is preserved in the work of Justin and Polybius. It is assumed that all six of the king's known children were hers, as listed on the Exedra of Thermos, a U-shaped monument in north-western Greece. This originally preserved names and statues of the royal family,[178] information also documented in other texts. Of the children shown, **Ptolemy C** became the fourth king of the name; he married his sister Arsinoe III with whom he had a single child, Ptolemy V, plus a possible child by his mistress, Agathoclea.

(right) Ptolemy VIII and one of the two Cleopatras (II and III, mother and daughter) whom he espoused; from the East Temple at Karnak (Berlin 2116).

(below) Reconstruction of the Exedra of Thermos in north-west Greece, on the shore of Lake Trikhonis, the spiritual centre of the ancient Aetolian League. It commemorates an alliance between them and Ptolemy III, either the known example towards the end of the reign, or an earlier one, given the appearance on it of Berenice A. It formerly had a series of statues of the royal family in front of it, but only their names now survive; the right wing of the structure is entirely lost.

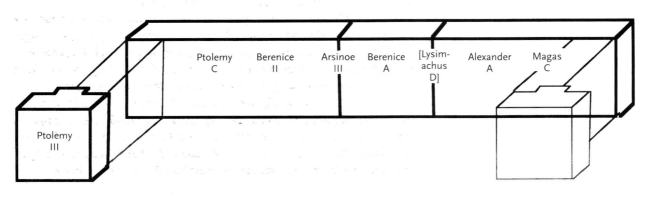

Ptolemy III · Ptolemy C · Berenice II · Arsinoe III · Berenice A · [Lysimachus D] · Alexander A · Magas C

Ptolemy V married Cleopatra I, a union attested by a range of sources and which probably produced Ptolemy's three children. The two sons were certainly borne by Cleopatra, according to a number of ancient writers, whereas the parentage of Cleopatra II is implied but never spelt out. **Ptolemy VI** became the first husband of this Cleopatra, who bore him at least one son, Ptolemy Eupator. He was at one time reckoned to be 'Ptolemy VII' and the ephemeral successor of Ptolemy VI – as a result of his appearance in the lists of dynastic cults between the latter and Ptolemy VIII – but seems in fact never to have been a co-regent, and certainly not an independent king.[179] A younger son is known, from a papyrus in Cologne,[180] and there were also two daughters, Cleopatra III and Cleopatra Thea.

Subsequently, Cleopatra II married her second brother, **Ptolemy VIII**, and bore him a son, Ptolemy Memphites; the king also had another son, Ptolemy Apion, by an unknown concubine, and a daughter, also by an unknown lady. This daughter, Berenice B, is apparently stated on the stela of her son to have been 'the [?younger sister] of King Ptolemy whom men call Alexander';[181] the latter was presumably Ptolemy X and, if the implication is that Berenice was his full sister, her mother will have been Cleopatra III who became Ptolemy VIII's wife in parallel with her mother. By Cleopatra III, he had five children, for whose parentage Justin is a main source, although it has been suggested that Ptolemy IX might actually have been borne by the second Cleopatra.

Ptolemy IX had two marriages; an assertion that he also espoused his daughter Berenice III appears highly unlikely. The first wife was his sister Cleopatra IV, and whether they had children remains a moot point. Ptolemy IX's offspring Ptolemy XII and Ptolemy of Cyprus are generally regarded as illegitimate, perhaps borne by an Egyptian. They may be identifiable with two sons mentioned by Justin, and be reflected by the description of Ptolemy XII as a 'bastard' by Pompeius Trogus, and a statement by Pausanias that Berenice III was his only legitimate child. The maternity of the latter is also uncertain: having divorced Cleopatra IV, Ptolemy had married his younger sister Cleopatra Selene, who may have been Berenice's mother.

Ptolemy X first married an unknown individual (possibly his sister Cleopatra Selene), by whom he had a son, Ptolemy XI. Ptolemy X's next wife was Berenice III, who may have borne Cleopatra VI, but no data provides definite information on Cleopatra's ancestry. **Berenice**'s brief and fatal second marriage was to **Ptolemy XI**, and inevitably childless.

Ptolemy XII – son of Ptolemy IX – married Cleopatra VI, whose ancestry is nowhere stated but was presumably his sister or cousin, perhaps a daughter of Ptolemy X and Berenice III. He may have had a second wife, as at least three of the king's children were born after Cleopatra's disappearance from the record in late 69, but there is no positive evidence to affirm this.

At least four, and probably five, children of Ptolemy XII can be traced (it is sometimes argued that Cleopatra Tryphaena was an additional daughter, rather than being identical to Ptolemy's wife, **Cleopatra VI**). These five were Berenice IV, Cleopatra VII, Arsinoe IV, Ptolemy XIII and Ptolemy XIV. Apart from the first, there is no evidence as to the identity of their mother(s).

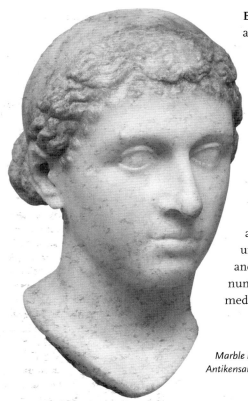

Berenice IV had two childless marriages, first to Seleucus Cybiosactes and then to Archelaus B. **Cleopatra VII** then married **Ptolemy XIII** and **Ptolemy XIV** in turn and had a child with Julius Caesar, before marriage to Mark Antony and a further three children by him. All these relationships are well documented.

After the fall of the dynasty in Egypt, the blood of the Ptolemies can be detected in a number of lines. While traceable with certainty for only a few generations, Cleopatra VII's likely great-granddaughter may have married into the royal family of Emesa. If so, some of the Severan emperors may have had Ptolemaic blood, as might Zenobia, queen of Palmyra – a line which continues at least until the end of the 5th century AD. Rather more certain is the genealogy of Cleopatra Thea, whose descendants are to be found into the 2nd century AD as a result of Laodice Thea's union with the king of Commagene. She was probably thus an ancestress of the kings of Emesa, Media, Parthia and Armenia and their numerous connections, which is in some cases potentially traceable into medieval Europe and beyond.

Marble head identified as Cleopatra VII (Berlin, Antikensammlung 1976.10).

Brief Lives ●

Males in **bold**, *females in* ***bold italic***.
m. *married*; b. *born*; fl. *floruit*

Agathocles
Son-in-law of Ptolemy I; son and heir of Lysimachus A, and executed by his father *c.* 283/282.

Alexander A
Son of Ptolemy III and Berenice II; born 242 and probably died naturally or in a purge before 221. Commemorated in the Exedra of Thermos.

Alexander Helios
Son of Cleopatra VII and Mark Antony; born 40 (twin of Cleopatra D Selene). Declared king of Armenia and King of Kings of Media and Parthia in autumn 34. After his parents' deaths he was placed under the guardianship of Augustus' sister, Octavia, and then with Cleopatra Selene in

20 (BC). His ultimate fate is unknown.

Alexander I Balas (King of Syria, 150–145)
First husband of Cleopatra Thea; died in battle against Demetrius II.

Alexander II (King of Epirus, 272–240)
Son of Pyrrhus I, husband of Olympias B.

Alexander V (King of Macedon, 297–294)
Son-in-law of Ptolemy I; assassinated by Demetrius I Poliorcetes in spring or summer 294.

Antigone A
Mother of Berenice I and a cousin of Eurydice C.

Antigone B
Daughter of Philip A and Berenice I; wife of Pyrrhus I (m. 299/298). Born before 317 and died 295, possibly in childbirth.

Antiochus I (King of Commagene, ?69–?32)
Great-grandson of Ptolemy VIII.

Antiochus I Soter (King of Syria, 292–261)
Father-in-law of Magas B; assassinated.

Antiochus II Theos (King of Syria, 261–246)
Son-in-law of Ptolemy II.

Antiochus III (King of Syria, 223–187)
Father of Cleopatra I; born 242.

Antiochus IV Epiphanes (King of Syria, 176–163)
Son of Antiochus III; born *c.* 215.

Antiochus V Eupator (King of Syria, 163–162)
Son of Antiochus IV; born 173 and murdered by Demetrius I Soter.

Antiochus VI Epiphanes Dionysius
(King of Syria, 145–142)
Grandson of Ptolemy VI and son of
Alexander Balas and Cleopatra Thea;
co-ruler with Demetrius II, who may have
killed him.

Antiochus VII Sidetes (King of Syria,
139–129)
Third husband of Cleopatra Thea (m. 138
– while Demetrius II was in captivity);
died in battle in Babylonia against the
Parthians.

Antiochus VIII Philometor (King of Syria,
125–96)
Grandson of Ptolemy VI and younger
son of Demetrius II and Cleopatra Thea;
son-in-law of Ptolemy VIII.

Antiochus IX Cyzikenos (Pretender to
throne of Syria, 115–95)
Grandson of Ptolemy VI; son of
Antiochus VII and Cleopatra Thea; and
husband of Cleopatra IV and Cleopatra V.
Killed by Seleucus VI.

Antiochus X Eusebes Philopator (King of
Syria, 95–92)
Son of Antiochus IX and probably
Cleopatra IV; son-in-law of Ptolemy VIII.
Killed fighting against the Parthians
while opposing Demetrius III and
Philip I Epiphanes.

Antiochus XI Epiphanes Philadelphus
(King of Syria, 92)
Great-grandson of Ptolemy VIII and twin
son (with Philip I) of Antiochus VIII and
Tryphaena. Killed while fighting against
Antiochus X.

Antiochus XII Dionysos (King of Syria,
87–84)
Great-grandson of Ptolemy VI; son of
Antiochus VIII and probably Tryphaena.

Antiochus XIII (King of Syria, 69–64)
Great-grandson and grandson of Ptolemy
VIII; son of Antiochus X and Cleopatra V.
Deposed by Pompey when Syria became a
Roman province and murdered shortly
afterwards by the Arab potentate,
Sampsiceramos.

Antiochus A
Son of Berenice Phernopherus and
Antiochus II. Murdered with his mother
in 246.

Antiochus B
Son of Antiochus VII and Cleopatra Thea.
Died of disease along with sisters Laodice
x and xi.

Antipater (Regent of Macedonia,
334–319/8).
Father-in-law of Ptolemy I and father of
King Cassander.

Apama
Daughter of Antiochus I Soter and wife of
Magas B; almost certainly identical to his
'second wife', Arsinoe B.

Archelaus A
Father-in-law of Berenice IV; a general of
Mithridates VI of Pontus.

Archelaus B (High Priest of Bellona at
Comana)
Husband of Berenice IV and son of
Archelaus A; possibly made co-regent on
marriage, but killed in battle against the
forces of A. Gabinius, Roman governor
of Syria, in January/February 55. By a
previous marriage, he became an ancestor
of a king of Cappadocia and kings of
Armenia.

Argaeus
Probably a son of Ptolemy I and Eurydice
C; executed by Ptolemy II for plotting
rebellion c. 282/281.

Arsinoe I
Wife of Ptolemy II; daughter of
Lysimachus A (m. 284/281). Exiled to
Koptos for plotting against her husband in
the 270s.

Arsinoe II (GM; KGW; KSis; Exec)
Daughter of Ptolemy I and Berenice I;
married first Lysimachus A in 300/299,
and then Ptolemy Ceraunus, whom she
married at Cassandrea in 281/280. She
then became sister-wife of Ptolemy II (m.
c. 273/272). Born c. 316 and died 25 July
270 or 1/2 July 268; posthumously given

the prenomen 'Khnemibenmaat-
merynetjeru'.

Arsinoe III (GM; KGW; SWSR; KSis; KD)
Daughter of Ptolemy III and Berenice II;
sister-wife of Ptolemy IV (m. before
October/November 220). Born 246/245;
perhaps repudiated by husband in 204
and dying later that year, possibly in a
palace fire set deliberately to kill her.
Commemorated in the Exedra of
Thermos.

Arsinoe IV
Daughter of Ptolemy XII and Cleopatra
VI; born 68/62. Possibly co-regent with
Ptolemy XIII 50/49, and joint ruler of
Cyprus with Ptolemy XIV in August 48.
Ruler of Egypt in opposition to Ptolemy
XIII and Cleopatra VII early September
48, and then altered allegiance in early
October to be an ally of Ptolemy XIII in
opposition to Cleopatra VII. Captured by
Julius Caesar in January 47 and taken to
Rome for his triumph (July 46), after
which she was exiled to Ephesus and
finally executed there by Mark Antony in
41. It has been suggested that she was
buried at Ephesus, on the basis of the date
and scale of a large tomb found there
containing the body of a woman in her
20s.[182]

Arsinoe A
Mother of Ptolemy I and daughter of
Meleager A.

Artabazus (Satrap)
Father-in-law of Ptolemy I and grandson
of Artaxerxes II. Satrap of Daskyleion
under the 31st Dynasty and of Bactria
under Alexander III.

Artakama
Wife of Ptolemy I (m. April 324); great-
granddaughter of King Artaxerxes II.

Berenice I (GM)
Wife of Ptolemy I (m. c. 317); born c. 340
and died before 268. She had previously
been married to Philip A.

Berenice II (KM; GM; SWSR)
Wife of Ptolemy III (m. 246) and

Berenice III; rear wall of Edfu temple.

daughter of Magas B; born *c.* 267/266 and died early 221, possibly poisoned. She had previously been engaged or married to Demetrius the Fair, an alliance terminated when he was found in intimacy with Berenice's own mother.

Berenice III Cleopatra Philopator (KW; KSis; L2L)

Daughter of Ptolemy IX, probably by Cleopatra V; married Ptolemy X in October 101 and later Ptolemy XI (m. early 80); born 115/114. Fled Alexandria with Ptolemy X in 88, returning before 81/80, and was sole ruler for a short while before becoming co-regent with Ptolemy XI, who killed her shortly afterwards.

Berenice IV Cleopatra Epiphaneia

Daughter of Ptolemy XII by Cleopatra VI, and wife successively of Seleucus Cybiosactes and then Archelaus B (m. mid 56); probably born *c.* 79–75. Co-ruler with her mother in 58, and possibly also co-ruler with Archelaus in the summer of 56. Deposed by Ptolemy XII in January/February 55 and executed soon afterwards.

Berenice A

Daughter of Ptolemy III and Berenice II; born 239 and died February 238. Commemorated in the Exedra of Thermos and the Canopus Decree.

Berenice B

Probable daughter of Ptolemy VIII and wife of Pasherenptah ii (m. before 122/121); mentioned on the Vienna stela of her son, Pedubast ii.

Berenice C

Probably great-great-granddaughter of Ptolemy VIII; lived 56–33 and appears to have died in childbirth. Known from a stela in the British Museum.

Berenice Phernophorus

Daughter of Ptolemy II and Arsinoe I; wife of Antiochus II (m. 252). Murdered with her son at Daphne near Antioch by agents of Seleucus II and his wife Laodice ii, *c.* September/October 246.

Cassander (King of Macedon, 305–297) Brother-in-law of Ptolemy I; born 358 and murderer of Alexander IV.

Cleopatra I (GM; SWSR; L2L)

Wife of Ptolemy V (m. 194/193); daughter of Antiochus III. Senior co-ruler with her son Ptolemy VI from September 180, and died September/October 177.

Cleopatra II (SWSR; L2L)

Daughter of Ptolemy V, presumably by Cleopatra I; sister-wife of Ptolemy VI (m. 175). Born *c.* 185/184 and became co-ruler with Ptolemy VI and Ptolemy VIII in 170. She remained with Ptolemy VIII after the departure of Ptolemy VI in 169, negotiating the latter's return.

Ptolemy VIII with Cleopatra II and III; temple of Sobk and Harouris, Kom Ombo.

Subsequently, she sided with Ptolemy VI and ruled with him until his death, then ruling alongside Ptolemy VIII. After Cleopatra III joined the rulership, Cleopatra II took the epithet of Adelphos ('the Sister'). Following the rebellion against Ptolemy VIII in 132/131 she was ruler in Alexandria until *c.* 127, when she fled to Syria. Cleopatra returned and once again ruled alongside Ptolemy VIII and Cleopatra III from *c.* 124, and then as senior ruler jointly with Cleopatra III and Ptolemy IX from 116 until her own death sometime before April 115.

Cleopatra III (L2L)

Daughter of Ptolemy VI and Cleopatra II, probably born around 160/155; wife of Ptolemy VIII (m. 141/140). Went to Cyprus with Ptolemy VIII in 130 and returned with him to Egypt *c.* 127; ruled alongside

Cleopatra VI receiving 'life' from Hathor; Edfu.

Ptolemy IX following the death of Cleopatra II, but soon afterwards expelled him in 116/115. Then reigned with Ptolemy X until she was killed by him in 101.

Cleopatra IV (L2L)
Daughter of Ptolemy VIII and Cleopatra III; wife of Ptolemy IX (as prince: m. 119/118) and then Antiochus IX (m. *c.* 114). Born *c.* 138/135; murdered in the sanctuary of Daphne near Antioch on the orders of Tryphaena in 112.

Cleopatra V Selene
Daughter of Ptolemy VIII and Cleopatra III; married Ptolemy IX in 115, and then possibly Ptolemy X (m. *c.* 107). Her next husband was Antiochus VIII (m. 103/102), followed by Antiochus IX in 96 and finally Antiochus X the following year. Born *c.* 135/130, she was executed at Seleucia by the Armenian King Tigranes in 69.

Cleopatra VI Tryphaena (L2L)
Possibly daughter of Ptolemy X and

Berenice III; wife of Ptolemy XII (m. before 17 January 79), with whom she was co-regent until late 69; ruled alongside Berenice IV *c.* June 58 and died about a year later.

Cleopatra VII Philopator (GS; Exec; MULE)
Daughter of Ptolemy XII and probably by Cleopatra VI; mistress of Julius Caesar and Mark Antony (whom she may have married), and probably nominal wife of successively Ptolemy XII and XIII; born 70/69. Became senior ruler alongside Ptolemy XIII in spring 51, who expelled her from Egypt mid 48. Restored by Julius Caesar late August 48 and associated as senior ruler with Ptolemy XIV late January 47; became senior ruler with Ptolemy XV September 44. Committed suicide in Alexandria *c.* 12 August 30.

Cleopatra C Thea Eueteria
Daughter of Ptolemy VI and Cleopatra II; wife of Alexander I Balas (m. 150), then Demetrius II (m. 148/147) and finally

Antiochus VII (m. *c.* 137). Ruled Phoenician portion of Syria after 125 in co-regency with Antiochus VIII, who poisoned her in 121/120.

Cleopatra D Selene
Daughter of Cleopatra VII and Mark Antony; wife of Juba II. Born 40 (twin of Alexander Helios). Declared queen of Cyrene in autumn 34. After her parents' deaths she was placed under the guardianship of Augustus' sister, Octavia, until her marriage. Probably died *c.* 5 (BC).

Demetrius I Poliorcetes (King of Macedon, 294–288)
Son-in-law of Ptolemy I.

Demetrius I Soter (King of Syria, 162–150)
Father-in-law of Cleopatra Thea, born *c.* 197. Killed by Alexander I Balas.

(opposite) The very last pharaohs: Cleopatra VII and Ptolemy XV Caesar at Dendara.

Demetrius II Nicator (King of Syria, 145–139 and 129–125)
Second husband of Cleopatra Thea; captive of the Parthians from 139–129, and ultimately assassinated at Tyre on the orders of Cleopatra Thea.

Demetrius III Eucarius Philopator Soter (King of Syria, 95–88)
Son of Antiochus VIII and probably Tryphaena. Spent latter part of his life in Parthian captivity.

Demetrius the Fair (King of Cyrene, *c.* 250)
Grandson of Ptolemy I and fiancé of Berenice II; became lover of Arsinoe I (Berenice's mother) and was killed when found with her.

Drusilla
Probably great-granddaughter of Cleopatra VII; wife of M. Antonius Felix.

Eirene
Daughter of Ptolemy I and Thais, and wife of Eunostus.

Eunostus (King of Soli in Cyprus, *c.* 320–311)
Son-in-law of Ptolemy I; probably a son of Pasicrates (King of Soli, fl. 331–321).

Eurydice B
See previous section.

Eurydice C
Wife of Ptolemy I (m. *c.* 320/319); daughter of Antipater. Attended the marriage of Ptolemais B in Miletus in 287, and may have accompanied Ptolemy Ceraunus to Macedon in 280.

Herankh (Sistrum-player)
Mother of Taimhotep.

Horemhotep (PPtah)
Probably great-grandson of Ptolemy VIII.

Imhotep/Pedubast iv (HPM, 39–30)
Great-great-grandson of Ptolemy VIII; lived 46–30 (BC). Died shortly before the fall of Alexandria to Octavian (perhaps on

1 August 30) and was not formally buried for seven years, suggesting an unnatural death.

Juba II (King of Mauretania, 25– AD 23)
Husband of Cleopatra D Selene (m. 20).

(Caius) Julius Caesar
Lover of Cleopatra VII and father of Ptolemy XV; born 12/13 July 100 and assassinated in Rome on 15 March 44.

Khahapi (Sem-Priest of Letopolis)
Father of Taimhotep.

Kheredankh (Sistrum-player)
Probably great-great-granddaughter of Ptolemy VIII; lived 65–43; known from a stela in the British Museum.

Lagus A
Father of Ptolemy I.

Lagus B
Son of Ptolemy I and Thais; winner of a chariot race at the Lycaean festival in Arcadia in 308/307.

Laodice ix
Daughter of Demetrius II and Cleopatra Thea; captured by Parthians and while in captivity married Phraates II (129).

Laodice x
Daughter of Antiochus VII and Cleopatra Thea; died of disease along with Antiochus B and Laodice xi.

Laodice xi
Daughter of Antiochus VII and Cleopatra Thea; died of disease along with Antiochus B and Laodice x.

Laodice xii Thea Philadelphus
(Great-)granddaughter of Ptolemy VIII, and daughter of Antiochus VIII and (probably) Tryphaena; wife of Mithridates I of Commagene.

Leontiscus
Son of Ptolemy I and Thais; captured by Demetrius Poliorcetes at the Battle of Salamis in Cyprus in 306 and returned by him to Egypt.

Lysandra
Daughter of Ptolemy I and Eurydice C; wife of Alexander V and then Agathocles. After the latter's execution, she moved to the court of Seleucus I.

Lysimachus A (King of Thrace, 305–281 and Macedon, 285–281)
Father-in-law and brother-in-law of Ptolemy II; killed in battle.

Lysimachus B
Son of Lysimachus A and Arsinoe II; born *c.* 296 and killed by Ptolemy Ceraunus at Cassandrea in 280.

Lysimachus C
Son of Ptolemy II and Arsinoe I; murdered by Sosibios at the orders of Ptolemy IV *c.* 221.

[Lysimachus D?]
Son of Ptolemy III and Berenice II; born 243 and probably died in a purge before 221. Commemorated in the Exedra of Thermos.

Magas A
Father of Berenice I.

Magas B (Governor of Cyrene, *c.* 300; King of Cyrene, *c.* 282/270–250)
Son of Philip A and Berenice I, and father-in-law of Ptolemy III.

Magas C
Son of Ptolemy III and Berenice II; born 241 and scalded to death in his bath by an agent of Ptolemy IV in 222/221. Commemorated in the Exedra of Thermos.

Marcus Antonius (Mark Antony)
Lover and possibly husband of Cleopatra VII; born *c.* 82 and committed suicide 3 August 30.

Marcus Antonius Felix (Procurator of Judaea)
Husband of Drusilla (m. *c.* AD 52). Served under Claudius. His name may actually have been Tiberius Claudius Felix.

Meleager B (King of Macedon, 279)
Son of Ptolemy I and Eurydice C; succeeded Ptolemy Ceraunus, but soon

deposed by Antipater Etesias. Possibly identical with [...]Ptol.A.

Menelaus (King of Salamis and Strategos of Cyprus 310/309–306)
Brother of Ptolemy I; defeated and captured by Demetrius Poliorcetes in 306. Back in Egypt he was still alive as Eponymous Priest[183] in 284/283.

Mithridates I (King of Commagene)
Grandson-in-law of Ptolemy VIII.

Olympias B
Daughter of Pyrrhus I and, probably, Antigone B. Wife of her half-brother Alexander II of Epirus, and mother of kings Pyrrhus II and Ptolemy of Epirus, and of Phthia, second wife of Demetrius II of Macedon.

Pasherenptah ii (HPM)
Probably son-in-law of Ptolemy VIII.

Pasherenptah iii (HPM, 76–41)
Probably great-grandson of Ptolemy VIII; born 90.

Pedubast ii (HPM, 104/103–76)
Probably grandson of Ptolemy VIII; born 21 November 121. Died 15 February 76, his funerary stela is now in Vienna.

Pedubast iii
Husband of Berenice C.

Philip I Epiphanes Philadelphus (King of Syria, 92–83)
Twin son (with Antiochus XI) of Antiochus VIII and Tryphaena; killed in Cilicia by Tigranes of Armenia.

Philip II Philoromaeus (King of Syria, ?66–63)
Great-grandson of Ptolemy VIII; last king of Syria, who lost his kingdom to the Romans.

Philip A
A Macedonian nobleman and the first husband of Berenice I.

Philip B
Son of Lysimachus A and Arsinoe II;
born c. 293 and killed by Ptolemy Ceraunus at Cassandrea in 280.

Philotera (KSis; KD)
Daughter of Ptolemy I and Berenice I; born c. 315/309; died 282/268. Named on the monuments of members of her priesthood from Saqqara: the stela of the HPM Nesisut in the British Museum, and a statue of Heresankh in the Louvre.

Phraates II (King of Parthia, 138–128)
Son-in-law of Cleopatra Thea; assassinated.

Ptolemaïs B
Daughter of Ptolemy I and Eurydice; wife of Demetrius Poliorcetes (m. 287/286).

Ptolemy A
Son of Pyrrhus I and Antigone B.

Ptolemy B
Son of Lysimachus A and Arsinoe II; born c. 299/298 and claimed to the throne of Macedon during 281/276. Possibly ruler of Telmessos from c. 259/256, and also tentatively identified as Ptolemy Nios (the son), Ptolemy II's co-regent during 268/267–259; died after 240.

Ptolemy C
Son of Ptolemy III and Berenice II; depicted on the Exedra of Thermos and later king as **PTOLEMY IV**.

Ptolemy D
Son of Ptolemy VI and Cleopatra II; probably born before 5 April 152. Attested as an Eponymous Priest in 144/143, but probably died (perhaps murdered by Ptolemy VIII) before August 142. He has on occasion been equated with the mysterious 'Ptolemy (VII) Neos Philopator'.

Ptolemy E
Son of Ptolemy VIII and Cleopatra III; probably born in 143/142 and Eponymous Priest in 135/134. Governor of Cyprus c. 118; king from June 116 as **PTOLEMY IX**.

Ptolemy F (King of Mauretania, AD 21–40)

Ptolemy VIII with Cleopatra II and Ptolemy Memphites receive jubilee symbols from Thoth; Edfu.

Grandson of Cleopatra VII; executed by Caligula.

Ptolemy Apion (King of Cyrene, 105/101–96)
Son of Ptolemy VIII by an unknown concubine.

Ptolemy Ceraunus (King of Macedon)
Son of Ptolemy I and Eurydice C, born c. 319/318; left Egypt after the selection of Ptolemy II as heir to the throne, and killed **Seleucus I** in c. 283/282. Became king of Macedon September 281. Wounded and captured in battle against invading Gauls, then beheaded by them in 279.

Ptolemy of Cyprus (King of Cyprus)
Son of Ptolemy IX and perhaps Cleopatra IV; born 116. Went to Cos in 103, and was captured there by Mithridates VI of Pontus in 88. Returned to Egypt in 80 and was made king of Cyprus; committed suicide by poison in 58.

Ptolemy Eupator
Son of Ptolemy VI and Cleopatra II; probably

born 15 October 166. Mentioned on a demotic papyrus in the British Museum as an Eponymous Priest in 158/157, and co-regent with his father in 152, but probably died before the end of August that year. Included in the lists of deified Ptolemies.

Ptolemy Memphites

Son of Ptolemy VIII and Cleopatra II, born 144/142, and proclaimed Crown Prince in 142. Went to Cyprus, where Ptolemy VIII was then exiled in 130, and was murdered by his father shortly afterwards. Depicted in the Edfu temple and perhaps identical with the king known as 'Ptolemy (VII) Neos Philopator' in the Ptolemaic dynastic cult lists.

Ptolemy Nios

Co-regent with Ptolemy II during 268/267–259; possibly identical with Ptolemy B.

Ptolemy Philadelphus

Son of Cleopatra VII and Mark Antony; born *c.* 36. Declared king of Phoenicia, Syria and Cilicia in autumn 34. After his parents' deaths he was placed under the guardianship of Augustus' sister, Octavia,

followed by Cleopatra D Selene in 20 (BC). His ultimate fate is unknown.

Pyrrhus I (King of Epirus, 307– *c.* 302 and 297–272)
Son-in-law of Berenice I; born 319 and killed in a skirmish in Argos in 272.

Seleucus II Callinicus (King of Syria, 246–225)
Grandfather-in-law of Ptolemy V.

Seleucus III Soter (King of Syria, 225–223)
Elder brother of Antiochus III; assassinated.

Seleucus IV Philopator (King of Syria, 187–175)
Son of Antiochus III, born *c.* 217; assassinated.

Seleucus V (King of Syria, 125)
Grandson of Ptolemy VI, and elder son of Demetrius II and Cleopatra Thea; captured by Parthians in 123, but returned as a puppet king who was soon killed by his mother.

Seleucus VI Epiphanes Nicator (King of Syria, 96–95)
Great-grandson of Ptolemy VIII, and son

of Antiochus VIII and Tryphaena; deposed by Antiochus X and killed in Cilicia.

Seleucus A

Possibly son of Antiochus VII and Cleopatra Thea, although conceivably identical with Seleucus V.

Seleucus Cybiosactes

Husband of Berenice IV, and probably the younger son of Antiochus X and Cleopatra V. Strangled on his wife's orders after a few days of marriage.

Stratonice I

Mother-in-law of Magas B.

Taimhotep

Daughter of Khahapi (Sem-Priest of Letopolis) and the sistrum-player Herankh.

Thais (Athenian hetaera)

Wife of Ptolemy I (m. *c.* 335) and mother of Lagus B, Leontiscus and Eirene.

Tryphaena

Daughter of Ptolemy VIII and Cleopatra III; wife of Antiochus VIII (m. 124). Probably born 141/140; captured and executed by Antiochus IX *c.* 112/111.

Urania

Probably wife of Ptolemy F, known from the funerary inscription of a freedwoman.

[...]Ptol.A

Son of Ptolemy I and Eurydice, possibly identical with Meleager; executed by Ptolemy II for plotting rebellion in Cyprus *c.* 282/281.

[...]Ptol.B

Wife of Ptolemy Ceraunus (m. *c.* 300/295).

[...]Ptol.C

Daughter of Ptolemy Ceraunus; said to have married Pyrrhus I, king of Epirus, 281/280.

[...]Ptol.D

Probably a granddaughter of Cleopatra VII; dedicated in an Athenian inscription as 'daughter of King Juba'.

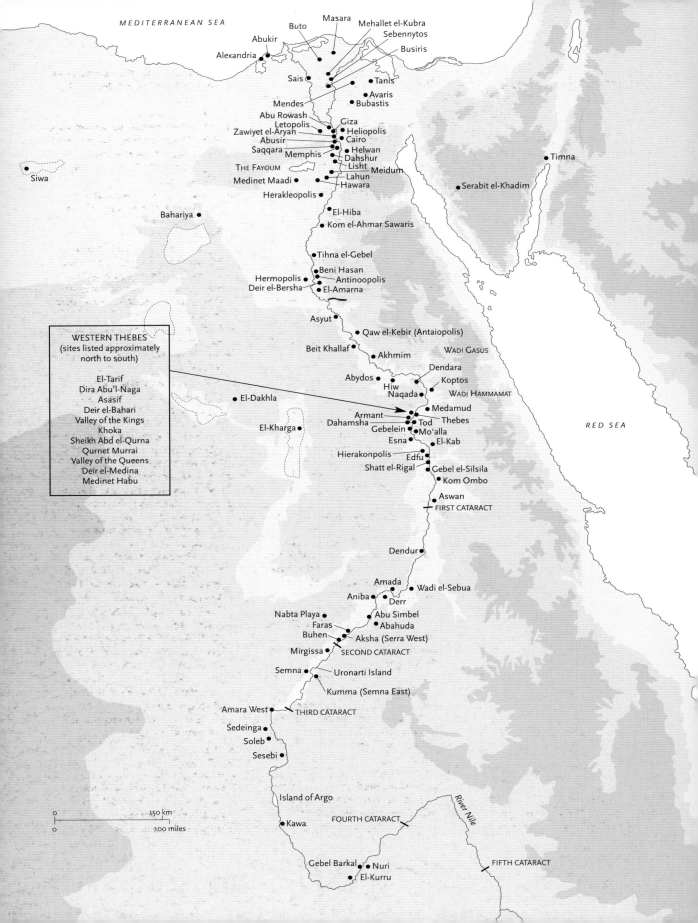

MEDITERRANEAN SEA

Abukir
Alexandria
Buto
Masara
Mehallet el-Kubra
Sebennytos
Busiris
Sais
Tanis
Mendes
Avaris
Bubastis
Abu Rowash
Letopolis
Giza
Heliopolis
Zawiyet el-Aryan
Cairo
Abusir
Saqqara
Helwan
Memphis
Dahshur
Lisht
Meidum
THE FAYOUM
Medinet Maadi
Lahun
Hawara
Herakleopolis
El-Hiba
Kom el-Ahmar Sawaris
Timna
Serabit el-Khadim
Siwa
Bahariya
Tihna el-Gebel
Beni Hasan
Antinoopolis
Hermopolis
Deir el-Bersha
El-Amarna
Asyut
Qaw el-Kebir (Antaiopolis)
Beit Khallaf
WADI GASUS
Akhmim
Dendara
Koptos
Abydos
Hiw
Naqada
WADI HAMMAMAT
RED SEA
El-Dakhla

WESTERN THEBES
(sites listed approximately
north to south)

El-Tarif
Dira Abu'l-Naga
Asasif
Deir el-Bahari
Valley of the Kings
Khoka
Sheikh Abd el-Qurna
Qurnet Murrai
Valley of the Queens
Deir el-Medina
Medinet Habu

El-Kharga
Medamud
Armant
Tod
Thebes
Dahamsha
Mo'alla
Gebelein
Esna
El-Kab
Hierakonpolis
Edfu
Shatt el-Rigal
Gebel el-Silsila
Kom Ombo
Aswan
FIRST CATARACT

Dendur

Amada
Wadi el-Sebua
Aniba
Derr
Nabta Playa
Abu Simbel
Faras
Abahuda
Buhen
Aksha (Serra West)
Mirgissa
SECOND CATARACT
Semna
Uronarti Island
Kumma (Semna East)
Amara West
THIRD CATARACT
Sedeinga
Soleb
Sesebi

Island of Argo
River Nile
Kawa
FOURTH CATARACT
FIFTH CATARACT

Gebel Barkal
Nuri
El-Kurru

0   150 km
0   100 miles

Notes to the Text

1 E.g. Dodson 1988a; 1990; 1995; 2000; Dodson and Janssen 1989.

2 For those of the latter who need to delve deeper in the future, Chris Bennett's mammoth world-wide-web project is intended to provide fully annotated genealogies of a kind that no printed book could ever contemplate. At www.geocities.com/christopherjbennett/, the parts thus far available have been of the greatest help in preparing our Ptolemaic sections and the site promises much.

3 It appears that on one level *nsw* designated the 'eternal' aspect of the pharaonic kingship, while *bity* was a more earthly facet. The same issue concerns the White and Red crowns associated with each of these titles.

4 Brunner 1964.

5 Deir el-Bahari (Naville 1894–1908: II, pl. XLVII–LVI).

6 Luxor Temple (Campbell 1912: 1–95).

7 Fragments found at Medinet Habu (Habachi 1969).

8 Papyrus Berlin 3033, acquired by Lepsius from Henry Westcar in 1838/39. A complete translation is given in Simpson (ed.) 1973: 15–30.

9 For the *ka*, see Bolshakov 2001.

10 Respectively in the temple at Deir el-Bahari and the temple of Sety I at Abydos.

11 It has long been recognized that the Hatshepsut text is a fictional retrospective justification for her seizure of royal titles; however, the very fact that she took this approach implies that the scenario was a well-known, conventional one.

12 In the temple of Karnak, on the south wall of the complex directly south of the sanctuary.

13 Mertz 1978b: 61–63.

14 Ruffer 1921: 322–57.

15 'Certain Titles of the Egyptian Queens and the Bearing on the Hereditary Right to the Throne', unpublished, but with her conclusions included in her popular books (Mertz 1978a: 206–09 and 1978b: 61–67).

16 Robins 1983.

17 Gardiner 1953b.

18 In the Great Harris Papyrus, written three decades after Setnakhte's death, the only person mentioned in these years was an 'upstart Syrian', probably the Chancellor Bay, the 'kingmaker' of the period: see further below, p. 285, with n. 123.

19 Bryan 1991: 144–56.

20 Good summaries and bibliographies of the subject are given by Quirke 2001, Pardey 2001, Warburton 2001 and Trigger, Kemp, O'Connor and Lloyd 1983: 204–18.

21 Although, of course, it is quite likely that some later Viziers may have been of royal descent.

22 Van den Boorn 1988.

23 A good overview of Graeco-Roman Egypt is provided by Bowman 1986.

24 The continued service of Egyptians under the early Ptolemies is now being recognized, against the usual received wisdom.

25 On the administration of temples, see Haring 2001.

26 On the priesthood in Egypt, see Schafer (ed.) 1997: 1–18.

27 Ptah was patron of craftsmen.

28 This title was generally held by the High Priest of Amun or the Vizier during the New Kingdom.

29 Caminos 1964; Dodson 2002b; Gitton 1981; 1984; Graefe 2003; Leahy 1996; Leclant 1965: 353–86.

30 For an overview of Egyptian military matters, see Gnirs 2001 and Shaw 1991.

31 One probable exception is the 19th Dynasty Viceroy, Messuy, apparently the grandson of Merenptah at the time of his appointment, and later a rebel against his father, Sety II (see pp. 179–82). In addition, Arielle Kozloff proposed at the 2004 meeting of the American Research Center in Egypt that Amenhotep D (the future Amenhotep III) might actually be identical with the Viceroy Amenhotep, known from the last years of Thutmose IV; she also queried whether Amenhotep III's Viceroy, Merymose, could also have been a real royal son.

32 Cf. Radwan 1969.

33 For a comprehensive listing of royal ladies titles, see Troy 1986: 151–97.

34 Cf. p.11, above, with n. 3.

35 Perdu 1977.

36 A scarab which has been used to suggest that the 'Great Wife' title went back to Ashayet of the 11th Dynasty is unlikely to be that early.

37 Discussed in detail in Troy 1986.

Map of Egypt and Nubia, showing the principal locations mentioned in the text.

38 Particular examples are Tiye A, Nefertiti and Nefertiry D.

39 For example, one may compare the titulary of Osorkon II of the 22nd Dynasty with that of Psametik I of the 26th:

OSORKON II:

Horus	Ka-nakht-merymaet-sekha-su-re-em-nesu-er-seped-tawi
Nebty	Sema-pesesheti-mi-sieset-demedjef-sekhemty-em-hetep
Bik-nub	Werpehty-huy-Mentu
Prenomen	User-maetre-meryamun
Nomen	Osorkon-sibast-meryamun

PSAMETIK I:

Horus	Aib
Nebty	Neba
Bik-nub	Qenu
Prenomen	Wahibre
Nomen	Psametik

40 Baud 1996.

41 For example, Ahmes-Nefertiry is given the title of King's Mother at least three years before her husband's death, implying a co-regency between him and their son: Vittmann 1974.

42 For the confusion this has caused some scholars, see pp. 187 ff., below.

43 In particular Henttawy Q.

44 Tomb of Sobknakhte (El-Kab 10: 13th Dynasty).

45 Tetiky (TT15).

46 Kitchen 1972; 1982b.

47 Gardiner 1953a: 10–11.

48 The innovation coincides with the increasing use of the nomen to identify a king, rather than the usually more specific prenomen; however the effect of this is reduced by the frequent recycling of prenomina during the 3rd Intermediate Period, contrasting with the situation for most other periods of Egyptian history.

49 Found in the Old Kingdom and the 18th Dynasty only.

50 Dodson 1987: 227, against the views of Van Siclen 1974 and Grist 1985: 79–80.

51 sn-nsw was later used in the Ptolemaic Period as an Egyptian equivalent of the Greek court title 'Adelphos' (Ranke 1953).

52 Cf. the issues surrounding Henutmire during the reign of Ramesses II, p.164.

53 Cf. the problem of Ahmes B, wife of Thutmose I.

54 For a summary of most of the facts, see Gardiner 1947: I, 47*–52*.

55 Habachi 1958.

56 Apart from the father of Nakthorheb, as already noted above.

57 Brunner 1961.

58 Haslauer 2001.

59 Wilkinson 2000.

60 For this cemetery, see Saad 1957.

61 Quibell 1923: 22.

62 Emery 1962.

63 The best single source of information and references for Old Kingdom genealogies is Harpur 1987: 240–52. An earlier treatment of the 4th Dynasty, with perhaps rather too many assumptions, is Reisner 1931: 239–59.

64 Lichtheim 1973, I: 215–22.

65 Drioton 1954.

66 Edwards 1994. The old dating of the pyramid to the 3rd Dynasty is now generally agreed to be impossible.

67 Lehner 1985.

68 Cf. Mertz 1978: 97–98.

69 Reisner and Smith 1955: 8.

70 Lichtheim 1973, I: 215–22.

71 Although the 1st and 3rd Dynasty kings referred to by this name in later sources cannot be ruled out.

72 Lichtheim 1973, I: 97–109.

73 Although the use of God's Father to denote an actual king, rather than a non-ruling ancestor, is highly unusual, it certainly seems the best explanation here – see Gardiner 1956. Earlier ideas that he might be an otherwise-unknown heir of Mentuhotep II, granted royal titles while his father yet lived, seem much less likely.

74 An old suggestion that the God's Father Senwosret A (see next section) was his son is highly unlikely.

75 This seems a far more realistic solution than earlier suggestions that Senwosret might have been a prematurely deceased son of Mentuhotep III.

76 Similarly, the 18th Dynasty was dominated by two names – Amenhotep and Thutmose – and the 22nd/23rd by three – Shoshenq, Osorkon and Takelot.

77 There is no real evidence for making her identical with Neferet Q, and thus the latter's mother, Didit, a further wife of Amenemhat I; see p. 99.

78 Fay 1996: 43–47.

79 Cf. Dodson 1988a.

80 It is not impossible that she could have been identical with Khnemetneferhedjet I, although as the latter lacks the title of King's Daughter this is less likely.

81 It is possible that the papyrus may actually refer to the family of Senwosret III, but the balance is probably in favour of the earlier generation.

82 It is possible that Sithathor A could have been Senwosret II's sister, as her jewellery included a pectoral of Senwosret II.

83 Much of this section is derived from the conclusions of Ryholt 1997, subject to the reservation expressed in Dodson 2000d.

84 Cf. Dodson 2000d.

85 On the basis of an architrave bearing the Horus name of Hor plus another which is most likely to have been that of Reniseneb, arranged in such a way to imply that they were reigning together (Dodson 2000d: 50).

86 An apparently funerary statue of Prince Sihathor exists, dedicated by Sobkhotep IV, which would suggest that he was never an actual king (Davies 1998).

87 Bietak 1996.

88 Ryholt 1997.

89 Ryholt 1997; he argues that many of the 14th Dynasty kings are listed in the Turin Canon, with others known from various seals. However, only a handful of monuments are known, and it seems pointless listing what in many cases are severely broken names of which only one or two letters survive: see Ryholt 1997: 359–83.

90 See Ryholt 1997: 251–56, including the possibility of intermarriage between the 14th Dynasty and the rulers of Kush.

91 See Ryholt 1997.

92 This designation for the immediately post-Hyksos Theban kings was employed by Winlock in 1947, but not generally used until revived in Ryholt 1997; otherwise, the whole group has usually been called the 17th Dynasty, ignoring the break during which the Hyksos occupied Thebes.

93 Rather than Mentuhotep V, as suggested by Ryholt 1997: 236–37.

94 Ryholt 1997: 270–71.

95 See p. 201, below.

96 She was confounded with

Meryetamun C in Winlock 1932; for confirmation of the date of her tomb, see Wysocki 1984.

97 Dorman 1988: 78–79.

98 With the possible exception of a re-carved stela that may originally date to Amenhotep II's reign: Bryan 1991: 96–97.

99 He will probably have had another constructed earlier, under Amenhotep II, but this is now unidentifiable: the building of such 'bigger and better' tombs by long-lived officials is not uncommon.

100 On the assumption that all the figures were male.

101 Dodson and Janssen 1989.

102 She was 'Great Beloved Wife' (not 'King's ... Wife', except by implication), but it is important to note that the word translated as 'great' is ꜥꜣt, not wrt, which is the distinctive element of the 'King's Great Wife' title; similarly, 'beloved' is an integral part of Kiya's title, rather than the 'his beloved' that sometimes follows the 'Great Wife' title. The two tags are thus unrelated, the inferior status of Kiya being shown by her lack of the cartouche, used by Akhenaten's other wife, Nefertiti.

103 Speculation in the past that she might be a daughter of Amenhotep III was based on assumptions surrounding the ill-starred 'Heiress Theory' (p. 16 ff.), and is thus groundless.

104 The nḏm and bnr signs are very similar, and it is not possible to be definitive as to which one is correct in this case.

105 A scene in the tomb of Huya at Amarna, where Akhenaten's family is shown on one side, and Amenhotep III, Tiye and Beketaten on the other; the latter is simply entitled 'King's Daughter', but the offspring of Nefertiti are called 'King's Daughter ... NAME, born of the King's Great Wife Neferneferuaten-Nefertiti'. Aldred's impression was that 'while the father remains the same, the identity of the mother has to be defined in the case of Nefert-iti since she was the junior queen [vis-à-vis Tiye]'. (Aldred 1972: 104).

106 This was picked up by Immanuel Velikovsky (1960), who went so far as to propose that Akhenaten and Oedipus were one and the same, with Tiye as Jocasta and Beketaten as Antigone!

107 Gabolde 1998: 118–21; for other reconstructions of the text, generally implying that Nefertiti is the grandmother of the infant, see Martin 1989: 44.

108 Gabolde 1998: 122–23.

109 Meyer 1984; alternatively, one, or both, could have been the offspring of Smenkhkare and Meryetaten.

110 Gabolde 1998: 118–23. Martin (1989: 40) also suggests that Tutankh(u)aten is shown in the tomb, but only in the chamber 'alpha' death scene, which he interprets as depicting Tutankh(u)aten's unknown mother dying in childbirth. Gabolde's interpretation of the baby in both scenes as simply the youngest child of Nefertiti dispenses with the need to relate the scenes to deaths in childbirth.

111 Definitive evidence as to Neferneferuaten's gender was revealed by James Allen of the Metropolitan Museum of Art at the April 2004 meeting of the American Research Center in Egypt. He reported that examination of palimpsest inscriptions of Neferneferuaten on objects reused in Tutankhamun's tomb (on a pectoral and on the canopic coffinettes) have shown conclusively that one the former used the epithet ꜣḫ-n-ḥ.s, 'effective for her husband'. This makes impossible the reconstruction put forward in Dodson 2003, which viewed Smenkhkare and Neferneferuaten as one and the same. Debate will continue as to whether Neferneferuaten should be identified with Nefertiti, Meryetaten, or even another lady. See now Dodson 2009a.

112 A recent theory (Gabolde 1998) has made him the Hittite prince, Zannanza, summoned not by Ankhesenamun, but Nefertiti; this seems extremely unlikely on multiple grounds.

113 Given that he will have become co-regent within a year or two of Meketaten's death.

114 Desroches-Noblecourt's theory (1962: 252–54) that they were part of the equipment placed in the tomb to help towards the king's rebirth is without any corroboration from other sources.

115 It is not impossible that the queen referred to might rather be Tiye A, on the basis of the spelling of the name. However, taking into account the dating of the statue, it seems most likely that Ay B's aunt was the contemporary queen, i.e. Tey – unless the Ay cartouche is actually secondary (cf. Freed, Markowitz and D'Auria (eds.) 1999: 279).

116 Gardiner 1953b: 14, 16, 21.

117 Conceivably to be read 'Mutbenret': see above, n. 104.

118 Germer 1984.

119 Martin 1997: 60–62.

120 Sourouzian 1983.

121 See pp. 144–45, above.

122 It has been suggested that this Siptah was the future king of the name, and his mother thus the wife of a later king; this seems unlikely.

123 The Huy mentioned at Silsila and called a son by early writers was in fact unrelated to Prince Khaemwaset, his title having been misread.

124 There is no evidence for his frequently proposed burial in the Serapeum at Saqqara, his 'mummy' actually being that of a sacred bull; see Dodson 1995a.

125 Unlike other Ramesside princes' names, the first part of this one comprises the nomen-cartouche of Ramesses II, rather than the simple name 'Ramesses'. It thus has the essential meaning 'King Ramesses II is lord of sunshine'; such 'basilophorous' are found at various periods, often as additional names taken by high officials, but are only rarely found as the given names of members of the royal family.

126 Grandet 2000.

127 This source, the Great Harris Papyrus, has often been taken as referring to an interregnum during which Bay held power, perhaps in the south. If he was indeed executed under Siptah, the allusion must refer to his (allegedly malign) role as 'power behind the throne' in the period following the death of Sety II.

128 These reliefs were for many years misattributed to Ramesses II, and

Khaemwaset confounded with Khaemwaset C: see Yurco 1978.

129 Assumptions that have made her a royal daughter are baseless, as Tawosret nowhere bears the appropriate title.

130 Contrary to what has often been asserted, the Queen Baketwernel depicted in the tomb of Amenmesse, KV10, cannot have been a wife of his. The reliefs in question are secondary, carved in plaster over the mutilated decoration of the king, reflecting later usurpation of the sepulchre, probably in the 20th Dynasty – see p. 192, below.

131 It has often been assumed that he was actually married to Tawosret, but since she had already acquired queenly titles through her union with Sety II there is no way of being certain one way or the other.

132 A mummy found in the coffin lid of Setnakhte when cached in KV35 has often been attributed to Tawosret, but there is no evidence for this identification.

133 One of the trials is recorded in the Turin Judicial Papyrus: De Buck 1937.

134 Taylor 1998.

135 The record of her own trial does not survive.

136 The foetus currently displayed in the tomb has nothing to do with the prince: it was found without context elsewhere in the Valley.

137 Taylor 1998.

138 For this reconstruction, see Dodson 1987b; 2000e; 2001a.

139 As noted on p. 186, the relative order of the last two High Priests of that period, Piankh and Hrihor, is uncertain; this affects the potential relationships at the beginning of the chain. The present work follows the view that Hrihor was the later, with relationships as suggested in Taylor 1998.

140 Thijs 1998.

141 Written there in an alternate form, Nedjemmut.

142 A grandson might be suggested by the marked old-age exhibited by Amenemopet's mummy.

143 1 Kings 14: 25–26; 2 Chronicles 12: 3–4.

144 That two separate campaigns are involved is clear, owing to significant differences in the itineraries of the campaigns described in the Bibleon on one hand, and at Karnak on the other.

145 See Dodson 2009b.

146 Harsiese A was long thought to be the son of Shoshenq Q, but it now seems much more likely that he was a son of Nesibanebdjedet III (see Jansen-Winkeln 2006: 241 n. 64); the known son of Shoshenq Q named Harsiese was more probably Harsiese B.

147 Aston 1989, and next section.

148 Not as unlikely an event as it might seem: Shoshenq IV was only recognized in 1993 (see below).

149 Shoshenq IV's existence was first demonstrated in Dodson 1993b; formerly, it was believed that Pimay had followed Shoshenq III directly.

150 Considerable debate continues as to the nature of the 23rd Dynasty, which one school of thought regards as a Delta line, albeit one to which Thebes owed allegiance (as enshrined in Kitchen 1995). However, other researchers interpret it as a wholly Thebes-based regime, headed by Takelot II, previously viewed as a king of the 22nd Dynasty, succeeding Osorkon II (see Aston 1989); the present work follows the latter approach.

151 Previously known as Shoshenq IV, prior to the latter's identification in the 1990s (see n. 149, above).

152 For similar evidence concerning the former status of Pasebkhanut II, see n. 138, above.

153 For the whole family of Takelot III, see Aston and Taylor 1990.

154 Kitchen 1995: 138–43.

155 Yoyotte 1960.

156 The reconstruction shown here broadly follows the views of Morkot 1999 and 2000, rather than older ones, such as enshrined in Kitchen 1995, following such earlier researchers as Dows Dunham and M.F. Laming Macadam. On the history of the debate, see Morkot 1999.

157 Eide, Hägg, Holton Pierce and Török (eds.) 1994: 244–52.

158 Leclant 1961: 264–65.

159 See Dodson 2002b.

160 Khedebneithirbinet I has been confused with a 30th Dynasty queen of the same name, and had her sarcophagus misattributed to Khedebneithirbinet II's tomb at Saqqara: see Vittmann 1974.

161 Dodson 2002b.

162 Ray 1988; Bresciani 2001a; 2001b.

163 Lloyd 1982.

164 Devauchelle 1995.

165 Mathieson, Bettles, Davies and Smith 1995.

166 Cf. Aston 1999.

167 Kuhrt 1995: 602–03.

168 Kuhrt 1995: 664–65.

169 Stronarch and Zournatzi 1997.

170 The other daughter married Alexander's companion, Hephaeston.

171 Kuhlmann 1981.

172 Hölbl 2001: 9.

173 The key recent study of the family is Ogden 1999.

174 A good summary of sources is given by Hornblower 1983: 314–16.

175 Andronikos 1987; Hammond 1991.

176 The key recent sources for the family are Ogden 1999 and Bennett 2001–02; it should be noted that even for this relatively recent period there are major differences in their reconstructions.

177 Collins 1997.

178 Huss 1975.

179 Chauveau 1990; 2000; Mooren 1988.

180 Chauveau 2000.

181 Reymond 1981: 132 and 127(9).

182 Thür 1990.

183 In Classical antiquity, years were generally named after one of the year's magistrates – e.g. the Consuls of Rome. Although the Hellenistic monarchies – such as Ptolemaic Egypt – used a regnal-year dating system, the Greek centres of Alexandria and Ptolemaïs named years after priests and priestesses of Alexander III and the deified Ptolemies (Fraser 1972: 213–16). From the 2nd century onwards, the royal family itself began to hold the Eponymous Priesthood. First it was such Crown Princes as Ptolemy Eupator and Ptolemy E, but later the ruler himself/herself held office; Cleopatra III did so, while Ptolemy IX effectively made it part of the king's role. Ptolemy X also held the priesthood for many years.

Chronological Tables

A Note on Egyptian Chronology

The scheme used by modern scholars for structuring the chronology of historic ancient Egypt is based upon one drawn up by the Egyptian priest Manetho, around 300 BC. He divided the succession of kings into a series of numbered 'dynasties', corresponding to our idea of royal 'houses' (e.g. Plantagenet, Windsor, Bourbon, Hapsburg, Hohenzollern). These broadly fit in with our knowledge of changes in the ruling family, but in some cases the reason for a shift is unclear. Historians of ancient Egypt have refined this structure by grouping dynasties into 'Kingdoms' and 'Periods', during which constant socio-political themes can be identified.

Ancient dating was by means of regnal years, rather than the kind of 'era' dating used today (e.g. BC, AD and AH). Thus absolute dates, in terms of years BC, have to be established through various indirect methods. Some reigns can be fixed by relation to events linked to better-dated cultures, while others can be placed by reference to mentions of various astronomical phenomena. These allow the extent of other reigns to be calculated by dead-reckoning. Nevertheless, there remain many areas of uncertainty and, while dating is solid back to 663 BC, margins of error before then may run in excess of century.

Brackets around an entry denote a co-regency.

	Horus or Throne name	Personal name	Conjectural dates	Regnal years
Predynastic Period	Badarian Culture		5000–4000 BC	
	Naqada I (Amratian) Culture		4000–3500 BC	
	Naqada II (Gerzian) Culture		3500–3150 BC	
	Naqada III Culture		3150–3000 BC	
Early Dynastic Period	**1st Dynasty**			
	Horus NARMER	**MENES?**	3150–	
	Hor-AHA		:	
	Horus DJER	**ITIT**	:	
	Horus DJET	**ITI**	:	
	Horus DEN	**SEMTI**	:	
	Horus ADJIB	**MERPIBIA**	:	
	Horus SEMERKHET	**IRINETJER**	:	
	Horus QAA	**QEBH**	:	
	2nd Dynasty			
	Horus HOTEPSEKHEMWY	**BAUNETJER**	:	
	Horus NEBRE	**KAKAU**	:	
	Horus NINETJER	**NINETJER**	:	
	?	**WENEG**	:	
	?	**SENED**	:	
	Horus SEKHEMIB/ SETH PERIBSEN	**PERIBSEN**	:	
	?	**NEFERKARE**	:	
	?	**NEFERKASOKAR**	:	
	?	?	–2611	
	Horus and Seth KHASEKHEMWY	**NEBWYHETEPIMYEF**	2611–2584	27
Old Kingdom	**3rd Dynasty**			
	Horus NETJERKHET	**DJOSER**	2584–2565	19
	Horus SANAKHT	**NEBKA**	2565–2556	9
	Horus SEKHEMKHET	**DJOSER-TI**	2556–2550	6
	Horus KHABA	**TETI?**	2550–2544	6
	Horus QAHEDJET?	**HUNI**	2544–2520	24
	4th Dynasty			
	Horus NEBMAET	**SENEFERU**	2520–2470	50

	Horus or Throne name	Personal name	Conjectural dates	Regnal years
	Horus MEDJEDU	KHUFU	2470–2447	23
	Horus KHEPER	DJEDEFRE	2447–2439	8
	NEBKARE	SET?KA	2439–2437	
	Horus USERIB	KHAFRE	2437–2414	23
	Horus KAKHET	MENKAURE	2414–2396	18
	Horus SHEPSESKHET	SHEPSESKAF	2396–2392	4
	5th Dynasty			
	Horus IRIMAET	USERKAF	2392–2385	7
	Horus NEBKHAU	SAHURE	2385–2373	12
	NEFERIRKARE	KAKAI	2373–2363	10
	SHEPSESKARE	ISI	2363–2362	1
	HORUS NEFERKHAU	NEFEREFRE	2362–2359	3
	NIUSERRE	INI	2359–2348	11
	MENKAUHOR	IKAUHOR	2348–2340	8
	DJEDKARE	ISESI	2340–2312	28
	HORUS WADJTAWY	UNAS	2312–2282	30
	6th Dynasty			
	HORUS SEHETEPTAWY	TETI	2282–2270	12
	USERKARE		2270–2265	
	NEFERSAHOR/MERYRE	PEPY I	2265–2219	46
	MERENRE	NEMTYEMSAF I	2219–2212	7
	NEFERKARE	PEPY II	2212–2118	94
	MERENRE?	NEMTYEMSAF II	2118–2117	1
1st Intermediate Period	**7th and 8th Dynasties**			
	NETJERKARE	?	–	
	MENKARE	?	:	
	NEFERKARE	?	:	
	NEFERKARE	NEBY	:	
	DJEDKARE	SHEMAY	:	
	NEFERKARE	KHENDU	:	
	MERENHOR	?	:	
	NIKARE	?	:	
	NEFERKARE	TERERU	:	
	NEFERKAUHOR	?	:	
	NEFERKARE	PEPYSONBE	:	
	NEFERKAMIN	ANU	:	
	QAKARE	IBI	:	4
	NEFERKAURE	?	:	
	NEFERKAUHOR	KHUIHAPY	:	
	NEFERIRKARE	?	–	
	9th and 10th Dynasties			
	MERYIBRE	AKHTOY I	–	
	NEFERKARE	?	:	
	WAHKARE	AKHTOY II	:	
	?	SENENEN [...]	:	
	NEFERKARE	AKHTOY III	:	
	MERY...	AKHTOY IV	:	
	(Various)	(Various)	:	
	?	MERYHATHOR	:	
	NEBKAURE	AKHTOY V	:	
	MERYKARE	?	:	
	?	?	–2040	
	Dynasty 11a			
	HORUS TEPYA	MENTUHOTEP I	2160–	

	Horus or Throne name	Personal name	Conjectural dates	Regnal years
	HORUS SEHERTAWY	**INYOTEF I**	−2123	
	HORUS WAHANKH	**INYOTEF II**	2123–2074	49
	HORUS NAKHTNEBTEPNEFER	**INYOTEF III**	2074–2066	8
Middle Kingdom	**Dynasty 11b**			
	NEBHEPETRE	**MENTUHOTEP II**	2066–2014	52
	SANKHKARE	**MENTUHOTEP III**	2014–2001	13
	NEBTAWYRE	**MENTUHOTEP IV**	2001–1994	7
	12th Dynasty			
	SEHETEPIBRE	**AMENEMHAT I**	1994–1964	30
	KHEPERKARE	**SENWOSRET I**	1974–1929	45
	NUBKHAURE	**AMENEMHAT II**	1932–1896	36
	KHAKHEPERRE	**SENWOSRET II**	1900–1880	20
	KHAKAURE	**SENWOSRET III**	1881–1840	41
	NIMAETRE	**AMENEMHAT III**	1842–1794	48
	MAEKHERURE	**AMENEMHAT IV**	1798–1785	13
	SOBKKARE	**SOBKNEFERU**	1785–1781	4
	13th Dynasty			
	SEKHEMRE-KHUTAWI	**SOBKHOTEP I**	1781–	3
	SEKHEMKARE	**SONBEF**	:	3
	NERIKARE	**?**	:	1
	SEKHEMKARE	**AMENEMHAT V**	:	3
	SEHETEPIBRE	**QEMAU**	:	2
	SANKHIBRE	**AMENEMHAT VI**	:	
	SMENKARE	**NEBNUNI**	:	
	?	**IUFENI**	:	
	HOTEPIBRE	**SIHORNEDJHIRYOTEF**	:	
	SWADJKARE	**?**	:	
	NEDJEMIBRE	**?**	:	
	KHAANKHRE	**SOBKHOTEP II**	:	
	SEKHEMRE-KHUTAWI	**RENISENEB**	:	
	AUIBRE	**HOR**	:	
	SEDJEFAKARE	**AMENEMHAT VII**	:	
	KHUTAWIRE	**WEGAF**	:	
	USERKARE/ NIKHANIMAETRE	**KHENDJER**	:	
	SMENKHKARE	**IMYROMESHA**	:	
	SEHOTEPKARE	**INYOTEF IV**	:	
	MERYIBRE	**SET(Y)**	:	
	SEKHEMRE-SWADJTAWI	**SOBKHOTEP III**	:	3
	KHASEKHEMRE	**NEFERHOTEP I**	:	11
	MENWADJRE (?)	**SIHATHOR**	:	?
	KHANEFERRE	**SOBKHOTEP IV**	:	
	MERHOTEPRE	**SOBKHOTEP V**	:	
	KHAHETEPRE	**SOBKHOTEP VI**	:	4
	WAHIBRE	**IAIB**	:	10
	MERNEFERRE	**AYA**	:	23
	MERHETEPRE	**INI I**	:	2
	SANKHENRE	**SEWADJTU**		
	MERSEKHEMRE	**INED**		
	SEWADJKARE	**HORI**		
	MERKAURE	**SOBKHOTEP VII**	:	
	MERSHEPSESRE	**INI II**	:	
	MERSEKHEMRE	**NEFERHOTEP II**	:	
	[5 unknown kings]		:	

	Horus or Throne name	Personal name	Conjectural dates	Regnal years
	MER[...]RE	?	:	
	MERKHEPERRE	?	:	
	MERKARE	?	:	
	?		:	
	SEWADJARE	MENTUHOTEP V	:	
	[...]MESRE?	?	:	
	[...]MAETRE	IBI II	:	
	[...]WEBENRE	HOR[..]	:	
	SE[...]KARE	?	:	
	SEHEQAENRE	SANKHPTAHI	:	
	SEKHAENRE	[...]S	:	
	SEWAHENRE	SENEBMIU	−1650	
2nd Intermediate Period	**15th Dynasty**			
		SEMQEN	1650−	
		APER-ANATI		
		SAKIRHAR	:	
	SEUSERENRE	KHYAN	:	
	NEBKHEPESHRE/ AQENENRE/AUSERRE	APEPI	1585−1545	40
	?	KHAMUDY	1545−1535	
	16th Dynasty			
	?	?	1650−	
	SEKHEMRE-SMENTAWI	DJEHUTY	:	
	SEKHEMRE-SEWOSERTAWI	SOBKHOTEP VIII	:	
	SEKHEMRE-SEANKHTAWI	NEFERHOTEP III	:	
	SANKHENRE	MENTUHOTEPI	:	
	SWADJENRE	NEBIRIAU I	:	
	NEFERKARE?	NEBIRIAU II	:	
	SEMENRE	?	:	
	SEUSERENRE	BEBIANKH	:	
	SEKHEMRE-SHEDWASET	?	:	
	DJEDHOTEPRE	DEDUMOSE I	:	
	DJEDNEFERRE	DEDUMOSE II	:	
	DJEDANKHRE	MENTUEMSAF	:	
	MERANKHRE	MENTUHOTEP VI	:	
	SENEFERIBRE	SENWOSRET IV	−1590	
	17th Dynasty			
	SEKHEMRE-WAHKHAU	RAHOTEP	1585−	
	SEKHEMRE-SHEDTAWI	SOBKEMSAF I	:	
	SEKHEMRE-WEPMAET	INYOTEF V	:	
	NUBKHEPERRE	INYOTEF VI	:	
	SEKHEMRE-HERUHIRMAET	INYOTEF VII	:	
	SEKHEMRE-WADJKHAU	SOBKEMSAF II	:	
	SENAKHTENRE	TAA I	:	
	SEQENENRE	TAA II	:	
	WADJKHEPERRE	KAMOSE	−1545	
New Kingdom	**18th Dynasty**			
	NEBPEHTIRE	AHMOSE I	1545−1520	25
	DJESERKARE	AMENHOTEP I	1520−1499	21
	AKHEPERKARE	THUTMOSE I	1499−1489	10
	AKHEPERENRE	THUTMOSE II	1489−1479	10
	MENKHEPER(EN)RE	THUTMOSE III	1479−1425	54
	(MAETKARE	HATSHEPSUT	1472−1457)	
	AKHEPERURE	AMENHOTEP II	1425−1399	26

Horus or Throne name	Personal name	Conjectural dates	Regnal years
MENKHEPERURE	**THUTMOSE IV**	1399–1389	10
NEBMAETRE	**AMENHOTEP III**	1389–1349	40
NEFERKHEPERURE-WAENRE	**AMENHOTEP IV/**		
	AKHENATEN	1349–1333	16
(ANKHKHEPERURE	**SMENKHKARE**	1337–1336)	
(ANKHKHEPERURE-			
MERWAENRE	**NEFERNEFERUATEN**	1336–1329)	
NEBKHEPERRE	**TUTANKHAMUN**	1333–1324	9
KHEPERKHEPERURE	**AY**	1324–1320	4
DJESERKHEPERURE-			
SETPENRE	**HOREMHEB**	1320–1291	29
19th Dynasty			
MENPEHTIRE	**RAMESSES I**	1291–1289	2
MENMAETRE	**SETY I**	1289–1279	10
USERMAETRE-SETPENRE	**RAMESSES II**	1279–1212	67
BANENRE	**MERENPTAH**	1212–1202	10
USERKHEPERURE	**SETY II**	1202–1196	6
(MENMIRE-SETPENRE	**AMENMESSE**	1202–1198	4)
SEKHAENRE/AKHEPERRE	**SIPTAH**	1196–1190	6
SITRE-MERENAMUN	**TAWOSRET**	1190–1188	2
20th Dynasty			
USERKHAURE	**SETNAKHTE**	1190–1186	4
USERMAETRE-MERYAMUN	**RAMESSES III**	1186–1154	32
USER/HEQAMAETRE-			
SETPENAMUN	**RAMESSES IV**	1154–1148	6
USERMAETRE-	**RAMESSES V**		
SEKHEPERENRE	**AMENHIRKOPSHEF I**	1148–1143	5
NEBMAETRE-MERYAMUN	**RAMESSES VI**		
	AMENHIRKOPSHEF II	1143–1135	8
USERMAETRE-SETPENRE-			
MERYAMUN	**RAMESSES VII ITAMUN**	1135–1128	7
USERMAETRE-	**RAMESSES VIII**		
AKHENAMUN	**SETHIRKOPSHEF**	1128–1127	1
NEFERKARE-SETPENRE	**RAMESSES IX KHAEMWASET I**	1127–1107	20
KHEPERMAETRE-SETPENRE	**RAMESSES X**		
	AMENHIRKOPSHEF III	1107–1103	4
MENMAETRE-SETPENPTAH	**RAMESSES XI**		
	KHAEMWASET II	1103–1073	30
(HEMNETJERTEPYENAMUN	**HRIHOR**	c. 1070)	

3rd Intermediate Period

21st Dynasty			
HEDJKHEPERRE-SETPENRE	**NESIBANEBDJEDET I**	1073–1049	24
NEFERKARE-HEQAWASET	**AMENEMNISU**	1049–1046	3
(KHEPERKHARE-			
SETPENAMUN	**PINUDJEM I**	1058–1037	21)
AKHEPERRE-SETPENAMUN	**PASEBKHANUT I**	1046–998	48
USERMAETRE-			
SETPENAMUN	**AMENEMOPET**	998–989	9
AKHEPERRE-SETPENRE	**OSORKON THE ELDER**	989–983	6
NETJERKHEPERRE-			
MERYAMUN	**SIAMUN**	983–964	19
(TYETKHEPERURE-			
SETPENRE	**PASEBKHANUT II**	964–948	6)

	Horus or Throne name	Personal name	Conjectural dates	Regnal years
	22nd Dynasty			
	HEDJKHEPERRE-SETPENRE	**SHOSHENQ I**	948–927	21
	SEKHEMKHEPERRE-SETPENRE	**OSORKON I**	927–892	35
	(HEQAKHEPERRE-SETPENRE	**SHOSHENQ II**	895–895)	
	HEDJKHEPRRE-SETPENRE	**TAKELOT I**	892–877	15
	USERMAETRE-SETPENAMUN	**OSORKON II**	877–838	39
	USERMAETRE-SETPENRE	**SHOSHENQ III**	838–798	40
	HEDJKHEPERRE-SETPENRE	**SHOSHENQ IV**	798–786	12
	USERMAETRE-SETPENAMUN	**PIMAY**	786–780	6
	AKHEPERRE	**SHOSHENQ V**	780–743	37
	SEHETEPIBENRE	**PEDUBAST II**	743–733	10
	AKHEPERRE-SETPENAMUN	**OSORKON IV**	733–715	18
	23rd Dynasty			
	HEDJKHEPERRE-SETPENAMUN	**HARSIESE**	867–857	10
	HEDJKHEPERRE-SETPENRE	**TAKELOT II**	841–815	26
	USERMAETRE-SETPENAMUN	**PEDUBAST I**	830–805	25
	(?	**IUPUT I**	815–813)	
	USERMAATRE-MERYAMUN	**SHOSHENQ VI**	805–796	
	USERMAETRE-SETPENAMUN	**OSORKON III**	796–769	30
	USERMAETRE	**TAKELOT III**	774–759	15
	USERMAETRE-SETPENAMUN	**RUDAMUN**	759–739	20
	?	**INY**	739–734	5
	NEFERKARE	**PEFTJAUAWYBAST**	734–724	10
	24th Dynasty			
	SHEPSESRE	**TEFNAKHTE**	735–727	8
	WAHKARE	**BAKENRENEF**	727–721	6
	25th Dynasty			
	SENEFERRE	**PIYE**	752–721	30
	NEFERKARE	**SHABAKA**	721–707	14
	DJEDKARE	**SHABATAKA**	707–690	16
	KHUNEFERTUMRE	**TAHARQA**	690–664	26
	BAKARE	**TANUTAMUN**	664–656	8

Saite Period	**26th Dynasty**			
	WAHIBRE	**PSAMETIK I**	664–610	54
	WEHEMIBRE	**NEKAU II**	610–595	15
	NEFERIBRE	**PSAMETIK II**	595–589	6
	HAAIBRE	**WAHIBRE**	589–570	19
	KHNEMIBRE	**AHMOSE II**	570–526	44
	ANKHKA(EN)RE	**PSAMETIK III**	526–525	1
Late Period	**27th Dynasty**			
	MESUTIRE	**CAMBYSES II**	525–522	3
	SETUTRE	**DARIUS I**	521–486	35
	?	**XERXES I**	486–465	21
	?	**ARTAXERXES I**	465–424	41
	?	**XERXES II**	424	1
	?	**DARIUS II**	423–405	18
		ARTAXERXES II???		
	28th Dynasty			
	?	**AMYRTAIOS**	404–399	5

Horus or Throne name	Personal name	Conjectural dates	Regnal years
29th Dynasty			
BAENRE-MERYNETJERU	**NEFARUD I**	399–393	6
USERMAETRE-SETPENPTAH	**PASHERENMUT**	393	1
KHNEMMAETRE	**HAGAR**	393–380	13
?	**NEFARUD II**	380	1
30th Dynasty			
KHEPERKARE	**NAKHTNEBEF**	380–362	18
IRIMAETENRE	**DJEDHOR**	365–360	2
SENEDJEMIBRE-SETPENANHUR	**NAKHTHORHEB**	360–342	18
31st Dynasty			
	ARTAXERXES III OKHOS	342–338	5
	ARSES (ARTAXERXES IV)	338–336	2
	DARIUS III	335–332	3

Hellenistic Period

Horus or Throne name	Personal name	Conjectural dates	Regnal years
Dynasty of Macedonia			
SETPENRE-MERYAMUN	**ALEXANDER III**	332–323	9
SETEPKAENRE-MERYAMUN	**PHILIP III ARRHIDAEUS**	323–317	5
HAAIBRE	**ALEXANDER IV**	317–310	7
Dynasty of Ptolemy			
SETPENRE-MERYAMUN	**PTOLEMY I (SOTER I)**	310–282	28
USERKA(EN)RE-MERYAMUN	**PTOLEMY II (PHILADELPHUS)**	285–246	36
IWAENNETJERWYSENWY-SETPENRE-SEKHEMANKHEN-AMUN	**PTOLEMY III (EUERGETES I)**	246–222	24
IWAENNETJERWYMENEKHWY-SETPENPTAH-USERKARE-SEKHEMANKHENAMUN	**PTOLEMY IV (PHILOPATOR)**	222–205	17
IWAENNETJERWY-MERWYYOT-SETPENPTAH-USERKARE-SEKHEMANKHENAMUN	**PTOLEMY V (EPIPHANES)**	205–180	25
IWAENNETJERWYPERWY-SETPENPTAHKHEPRI-IRIMAETAMUNRE	**PTOLEMY VI (PHILOMETOR)**	180–164	16
IWAENNETJERWYPERWY-SETPENPTAH-IRIMAETRE-SEKHEMANKENAMUN	**PTOLEMY VIII (EUERGETES II)**	170–163	7
	PTOLEMY VI (again)	163–145	18
	PTOLEMY VIII (again)	145–116	29
IWAENNETJERMENEKH-NETJERETMERYMUTESNEDJET-SEPENPTAH-MERYMAETRE-SEKHEMANKHAMUN	**PTOLEMY IX (SOTER II)**	116–110	6
IWAENNETJERMENEKH-NETJERETMENEKHSATRE-SETPENPTAH-IRIMAETRE-SENENANKHENAMUN	**PTOLEMY X (ALEXANDER I)**	110–109	1
	PTOLEMY IX (again)	109–107	2
	PTOLEMY X (again)	107–88	19
	PTOLEMY IX (again)	88–80	8
(?	**PTOLEMY XI (ALEXANDER II)**	80)	
(	**BERENICE III**	80)	

	Horus or Throne name	Personal name	Conjectural dates	Regnal years
	IWAENPANETJERENTINEHEM-SETPENPTAH-MERYMAETENRE-SEKHEMANKHAMUN	**PTOLEMY XII (NEOS DIONYSOS)**	80–58	22
		PTOLEMY XII (again)	55–51	4
	(?	**BERENICE IV**	56)	
		CLEOPATRA VII PHILOPATOR	51–30	21
	(?	**PTOLEMY XIII**	51–47	4)
	(?	**PTOLEMY XIV**	47–44	3)
	(IWAENPANETJERENTINEHEM-SETPENPTAH-IRIMERYRE-SEKHEMANKHAMUN	**PTOLEMY XV (CAESAR)**	41–30	11)

Roman Period		30 BC–AD 395
Byzantine Period		395–640
Arab Period		640–1517
Ottoman Period		1517–1805
Khedeval Period		1805–1914
British Protectorate		1914–1922
Monarchy		1922–1953
Republic		1953–present

Bibliography

List of Abbreviations

AL	*Amarna Letters* (San Francisco/Sebastopol: KMT Communications).
AncSoc	*Ancient Society* (Louvain: Katholeieke Universiteit).
AR	*Amarna Reports* (London: EES).
ASAE	*Annales du Service des Antiquités de l'Égypte* (Cairo).
ATut	*After Tut'ankhamun* (ed. C.N. Reeves) (London: Kegan Paul International, 1992).
AUC	American University in Cairo.
A6CIE	*Atti del VI Congresso Internazionale di Egittologia* (Turin, 1992).
BES	*Bulletin of the Egyptological Seminar* (New York).
BIFAO	*Bulletin de l'Institut Français d'Archéologie Orientale du Caire* (Cairo).
BioAnth	*Biological Anthropology and the Study of Ancient Egypt* (eds. W.V. Davies and R. Walker) (London: British Museum Press, 1993).
BiOr	*Bibliotheca Orientalis* (Leiden: Nederlands Instituut voor het Nabije Oosten).
BM	British Museum, London.
BMA	Brooklyn Museum of Art.
BMFA	*Bulletin of the Museum of Fine Arts* (Boston).
BMMA	*Bulletin of the Metropolitan Museum of Art* (New York).
BSA	*Annual of the British School at Athens* (London).
BSAA	*Bulletin Société Archéologique d'Alexandrie* (Alexandria).
BSFE	*Bulletin de la Societé Française d'Egyptologie* (Paris).
CAH	*Cambridge Ancient History* (Cambridge).
CdE	*Chronique d'Egypte* (Brussels).
CCG	*Catalogue Général des Antiquités Egyptiennes du Musée du Caire.*
CM	Egyptian Museum, Cairo.
CUP	Cambridge University Press.
DE	*Discussions in Egyptology* (Oxford: DE Publications).
EEF/S	Egypt Exploration Fund/Society.
EEFAR	*Egypt Exploration Fund Archaeological Report* (London: EEF).
ERA	Egyptian Research Account.
Études Lauer	*Études sur l'Ancien Empire et la nécropole de Saqqâra dédiées à Jean-Phillipe Lauer* (eds. C. Berger and B. Mathieu) (Montpellier: Université Paul Valéry, 1997).
GM	*Göttinger Miszellen* (Göttingen).
Homm. Leclant	*Hommages à Jean Leclant* (eds. C. Berger, G. Clerc and N. Grimal) (Cairo: IFAO).
IFAO	Institut Français d'Archéologie Orientale.
JAOS	*Journal of the American Oriental Society.*
JARCE	*Journal of the American Research Center in Egypt* (New York, etc.).
JE	Journal d'Entree (CM).
JEA	*Journal of Egyptian Archaeology* (London: EEF/S).
JMFA	*Journal of the Museum of Fine Arts, Boston* (Boston).
JNES	*Journal of Near Eastern Studies* (Chicago: Chicago University Press).
JOAI	*Jahreshefte des Österreichischen Archaologischen Institutes* (Vienna).
JSSEA	*Journal of the Society for the Study of Egyptian Antiquities* (Toronto).
Kmt	*Kmt: A Modern Journal of Egyptology.*
LÄ	*Lexikon der Ägyptologie* (Wiesbaden: Otto Harrassowitz, 1975 ff.).
MDAIK	*Mitteilungen des Deutschen Archäologischen Instituts, Kairo* (Mainz: Philipp von Zabern).
MelMasp	*Melanges Maspero* (Cairo: IFAO 1935–53).
MFA	Museum of Fine Arts, Boston.
MKS	*Middle Kingdom Studies* (ed. S. Quirke) (New Malden: Sia, 1991).
MMA	Metropolitan Museum of Art, New York.
MMJ	*Metropolitan Museum Journal* (New York).
Mnemosyne	*Mnemosyne* (Leiden: Brill).
NARCE	*Newsletter of the American Research Center in Egypt* (New York/Atlanta).
OEAE	*Oxford Encyclopedia of Ancient Egypt* (ed. D.B. Redford) (New York: Oxford University Press).
OEANE	*Oxford Encyclopedia of Archaeology in the Near East* (E.M. Meyers) (New York: Oxford University Press).
OMRO	*Oudheidkundige Mededelingen uit het Rijksmuseum van Oudheden te Leiden* (Leiden).
OUP	Oxford University Press.
PM	*Topographical Bibliography of Ancient Egyptian Hieroglyphic Texts, Reliefs and Paintings* (B. Porter and R.B. Moss) (Oxford: Griffith Institute).
P7ICE	*Proceedings of the Seventh International Congress of Egyptologists* (ed. C.J. Eyre) (Leuven: Peeters, 1998).
PSBA	*Proceedings of the Society for Biblical Archaeology* (London).
RdE	*Revue d'Egyptologie* (Leuven: Peeters).

REG	*Revue des Études Grecques.*
RMO	Rijksmuseum van Oudheden, Leiden.
RMS	Royal Museum of Scotland, Edinburgh.
SAK	*Studien zur altägyptschen Kultur* (Hamburg).
SOAS	School of Oriental and African Studies, University of London.
SR	Special Register (CM).
Stud. F.Ll.G.	*Studies Presented to F.Ll. Griffith* (London: EES).
Stud. Smith	*Studies on Ancient Egypt in Honour of H.S. Smith* (eds. A. Leahy and W.J. Tait) (London).
TAE	*Temples in Ancient Egypt* (ed. B.E. Schafer) (London: I.B. Tauris, 1998).
TR	Temporary Register (CM).
UC	Petrie Museum, University College London.
UP	University Press.
U. Reed	*The Unbroken Reed: Studies in the Culture and Heritage of Ancient Egypt In Honour of A.F. Shore* (eds. C. Eyre, A. Leahy and L.M. Leahy) (London: Egypt Exploration Society, 1994).
VA	*Varia Aegyptiaca* (San Antonio, TX: Van Siclen Books).
VSK	*Valley of the Sun Kings: New Explorations in the Tombs of the Pharaohs* (ed. R.H. Wilkinson) (Tucson, AZ, 1995).
ZÄS	*Zeitschrift für Ägyptische Sprache und Altertumskunde* (Leipzig, Berlin).
ZPE	*Zeitschrift für Papyrologie und Epigraphik* (Bonn: Habet).

Section-by-Section Bibliography

The Founders (pp. 44–49) Roth 2001; Schmitz 1976; Seipel 1980; Troy 1986; Wilkinson 1999; 2000.

The Great Pyramid Builders (pp. 50–61) Alexanian 1999; Bolshakov 1995; Callender and Jánosi 1997; Harpur 1987; 2001; Hassan 1997; Jánosi 1997; Johnson 1996–97; Lesko 1998; Porter and Moss 1934; 1974–81; Reisner 1942; Roth 2001; Schmitz 1976; Seipel 1980; Stadelmann 1984; Strudwick 1985; Troy 1986.

Children of the Sun-God (pp. 62–69) Baud 1996; Labrousse 1997; Maragioglio and Rinaldi 1964–77: VI; Munro 1993; Porter and Moss 1974–81; Roth 2001; Schmitz 1976; Seipel 1980; Troy 1986; Verner 1982; 1994; 1995; Verner and Callender 1997.

The House of Teti and Pepy (pp. 70–78) Baud and Dobrev 1995; Dobrev 1996; Dobrev, Labrousse and Mathieu 2000; Dobrev and Leclant 1997; Dodson 1992; Eyre 1994; Habachi 1983; Labrousse 1994; 1999; Malek 1980; Munro 1993; Roth 2001; Schmitz 1976; Seipel 1980; Stadelmann 1994; Strudwick 1982; Troy 1986; Verner 1978; 1980; 1988; 1994; 1997.

The House of Akhtoy (pp. 80–81) Habachi 1958; Shaw (ed.) 1999: 118–47; Von Beckerath 1966.

The Head of the South (pp. 82–89) Gardiner 1956; Habachi 1958; Newberry 1936; Roth 2001; Schmitz 1976: 180–202; Troy 1986; Winlock 1942; 1943; 1947.

Seizers of the Two Lands (pp. 90–99) Arnold 2002; Arnold and Oppenheim 1995; Brunton 1920; Callender 1998a; 1998b; De Morgan 1895; 1903; Dodson 1988a; Fay 1996: 30–32, 43–47; Farag and Iskander 1971; Habachi 1958; Mace 1914; 1921; 1922; Perdu 1977; Petrie 1890; 1891; Petrie, Brunton and Murray 1923; Roth 2001;

Ryholt 1997: 209–14; Sabbahy 2003; Schmitz 1976: 180–202; Troy 1986; Valoggia 1969.

Kings and Commoners (pp. 100–113) De Morgan 1895; Franke 1984; Gauthier 1912; Jéquier 1938; Macadam 1951; Roth 2001; Ryholt 1997; Schmitz 1976; Troy 1986.

Rulers of Foreign Countries (pp. 114–15) Ryholt 1997.

The Southern Kingdom (pp. 116–20) Bennett 2002; Dodson 1991c; Habachi 1984; Parkinson and Quirke 1992; Ryholt 1997; Schmitz 1976; Troy 1986.

The Taosids (pp. 122–29) Bennett 1994; 2002; Dodson 1991c; Gitton 1981; Ryholt 1997; Schmitz 1976; Snape 1985; Troy 1986; Winlock 1924.

The Power and the Glory (pp. 130–41) Baligh 2003; Bryan 1991; Berg 1987; D'Auria 1983; Dodson 1990; n.d.; Dodson and Janssen 1989; Dorman 1988; El-Bialy 1990; Habachi 1968; Hassan 1953; Lilyquist 2003; Manuelian 1987: 172–90; Newberry 1928; Radwan 1969; Redford 1965; Robins 1978; 1999; Schmitz 1976; Troy 1986; Van Siclen 1995; Winlock 1929; 1948; Zivie 1976.

The Amarna Interlude (pp. 142–57) Aldred 1968; 1988; Arnold, Do. 1996; Brock 1999; Dodson 1990; 1994; 2002a; 2009a; Freed, Markowitz and D'Auria (eds.) 1999; Gabolde 1998; Gardiner 1953b; Gauthier 1912; Giles 2001; Martin 1991; O'Connor and Cline (eds.) 1998; Raven 1994; Redford 1984; Reeves 1988; 2001; Schaden 1982; Smith and Redford 1977: 83–94; Van de Walle 1968; Ziegler 1994.

The House of Ramesses (pp. 158–75) Berlandini 1997: 101–04; Brand 2000; Brock 2003; Cruz-Uribe 1977; 1978; Fisher 2001; Gomaà 1973; Habach 1974; Habachi 1969; Kitchen 1982a; 1996; Kitchen and Gaballa 1968; Martin 1997; Maystre 1948;

Moursi 1972; Schmidt and Willeitner 1994; Sourouzian 1983; Weeks 1998; 2000.

The Feud of the Ramessides (pp. 176–83) Aldred 1963; Brock 2003; Cruz-Uribe 1977; Dodson 1987b; 1997b; 2002a; Gardiner 1954; 1958; Krauss 1976; 1977; 1997; 2000; Sourouzian 1989; Yurco 1978; 1979.

The Decline of the Ramessides (pp. 184–94) Altenmüller 1994a; 1994b; Dodson 1987b; 1997a; Grist 1985; Kitchen 1972; 1982b; Moursi 1972; Redford 2002.

Of Kings and Priests (pp. 196–209) Blackman 1941; Goyon 1982; Gunn 1955; Hayes 1948; Kitchen 1995; Niwinski 1979; 1988; Taylor 1998; Troy 1986.

The Rise and Fall of the House of Shoshenq (pp. 210–23) Aston 1989; Aston and Taylor 1990; Bierbrier 1975; Dodson 1993b; 2001a; 2009b; Gauthier 1914; Hayes 1948; Jacquet-Gordon 1967; Jansen-Winkeln 2006; Kitchen 1995; Lecuyot et al. 1990; Tresson 1935–38.

The Independence of Thebes (pp. 224–31) Aston 1989; Aston and Taylor 1990; Bierbrier 1975; Dodson 1993b; 2001a; Kitchen 1995; Peterson 1967.

The Princes of the West (pp. 232–33) Kitchen 1995.

Lords of the Holy Mountain (pp. 234–40) Caminos 1964; 1994; Dodson 2002; Dunham and Macadam 1949; Eide, Hägg, Holton Pierce and Török (eds.) 1994; Kitchen 1995; Leahy 1984; Leclant 1965; Morkot 1999; 2000.

The Final Renaissance (pp. 242–47) Adam 1958; Caminos 1964; De Meulenaere 1968; Dodson 2002b; El-Sayed 1974: 35; Kienitz 1953; Leahy 1996; Troy 1986; Vittmann 1974a; 1975; Yoyotte 1982–83.

The Persian Pharaohs (pp. 248–53) Balcer 1993; Brosius 1996.

The Last Egyptian Pharaohs (pp. 254–57)

Cléré 1951; De Meulenaere 1963; Grimal 1992: 372–81; Johnson 1974; Kienitz 1953; Kuhlmann 1981; Ray 2001; Traunecker 1979; Vittmann 1974a.

Macedon (pp. 258–63) Andronikos 1984; Berve 1926; Hölbl 2001; Ogden 1999; Prag and Neave 1997: 53–84.

The House of Ptolemy (pp. 264–81) Austin 1981; Bakry 1972; Bennett 1997; 2001–02; Bouché-Leclercq 1903–07; Burstein 1982; Chanler 1934; Clarysse and Van der Veken 1983; Collins 1997; Ellis 1994; Fraser 1972; Grainger 1997; Grant 1972; Hammond and Griffith 1979; Hammond and Walbank 1988; Hölbl 2001; Huss 1975; 1994a; 1994b; 1998, 2001; Lindsay 1971; Macurdy 1932; Mooren 1988; Ogden 1999; Quaegebeur 1978; 1980; Reymond 1981; Samuel 1962; Skeat 1969; Thompson 1988; Tunny 2000; Whitehorne 1994.

Addenda (p. 304) Arnold 2002; Weeks (ed.) 2001: 275, 280.

List of Works Cited and General Bibliography

ABITZ, F. 1986. *Ramses III. in den Gräbern seiner Söhne* (Freibourg Universitätsverlg/Göttingen: Vandenhoeck und Ruprecht).

ADAM, S. 1958. 'Recent discoveries in the eastern Delta (Dec. 1950–May 1955)', *ASAE* 55: 301–24.

ALDRED, C. 1963. 'The parentage of King Siptah', *JEA* 49: 41–48.

— 1972. *Akhenaten, King of Egypt* (London: Sphere Books).

— 1988. *Akhenaten, Pharaoh of Egypt* (London and New York: Thames & Hudson).

ALEXANIAN, N. 1999. *Dahschur II: Das Grab des Prinzen Netjer-aperef. Die Mastaba II/1 in Dahschur* (Mainz: Philipp von Zabern).

ALTENMÜLLER, H. 1983. 'Das Grab des Königin Tausret im Tal des Könige von Theben', *SAK* 10: 1–24.

— 1994a. 'Prinz Mentu-her-chopeschef aus der 20. Dynastie', *MDAIK* 50: 1–12.

— 1994b. 'Dritter Vorbericht in die Arbeiten des Archäologischen Instituts der Universität Hamburg am Grab des Bay (KV 13) im Tal der Könige von Theben', *SAK* 21: 1–18.

AMÉLINEAU, E. 1899. *Mission Amélineau: Les Nouvelles Fouilles d'Abydos 1895–1896. Compte Rendu in Extenso des Fouilles, Description des Monuments et Objets Découverts* (Paris: E. Leroux).

ANDRONIKOS, M. 1984. *Vergina: The Royal Tombs and the Ancient City* (Athens: Ekdotike Athenon).

— 1976. *Gräber des Alten und Mittleren Reiches in El-Tarif* (Mainz: Philipp von Zabern).

— 1979a. *The Temple of Mentuhotep at Deir el-Bahri* (New York: MMA).

— 1979b. 'Das Labyrinth und seine Vorbilder', *MDAIK* 35: 1–9.

— 1987a. 'Some reflections on the Macedonian tombs', *BSA* 82: 1–16.

— 1987b. *Der Pyramidbezirk des Königs Amenemhet III in Dahschur* I: *Die Pyramide* (Mainz: Philipp von Zabern).

— 1988. *The Pyramid of Senwosret* I (New York: MMA).

— 1992. *The Pyramid Complex of Senwosret* I (New York: MMA).

ARNOLD, D. 2002 *The Pyramid Complex of Senwosret III at Dahshur: Architectural Studies* (New York: MMA).

ARNOLD, Di. and A. OPPENHEIM 1995. 'Re-excavating the Senwosret III Pyramid Complex at Dahshur', *Kmt* 6/2: 44–56.

ARNOLD, Do. 1991. 'Amenemhat I and the early Twelfth Dynasty at Thebes', *MMJ* 26: 5–48.

— 1996. *The Royal Women of Amarna: Images of Beauty from Ancient Egypt* (New York: MMA).

ASSOCIATION FRANÇAISE D'ACTION ARTISTIQUE 1987. *Tanis: L'or des Pharaons* (Paris: Association Française d'Action Artistique).

ASTON, D.A. 1989. 'Takeloth II – A king of the 'Theban Twenty-third Dynasty'?', *JEA* 75: 139–53.

— 1999. 'Dynasty 26, Dynasty 30, or Dynasty 27? In search of the funerary archaeology of the Persian Period', *Stud. Smith*: 17–22.

ASTON, D.A. and J.H. TAYLOR 1990. 'The family of Takeloth III and the 'Theban' Twenty-third Dynasty', in A. Leahy (ed.) *Libya and Egypt c. 1300–750 BC* (London: SOAS): 131–54.

AUSTIN, M.M. 1981. *The Hellenistic World from Alexander to the Roman Conquest* (Cambridge: CUP).

BADAWI, A. 1957. 'Das Grab des Kronprinzen Scheschonk, sohnes Osorkon's II und Hohenpriesters von Memphis', *ASAE* 54: 153–77.

BALCER, J.M. 1993. *A Prosopographical Study of the Ancient Persians Royal and Noble C. 550–450 BC* (Lewiston/Queenstown/Lampeter: Edwin Mellen Press).

BALIGH, R. 2003. 'Reflections on the genealogy of Tuthmosis I and his family', in N. Grimal, A. Kamel and C. May-Sheikholeslami, *Hommages Fayza Haikel* (Cairo: IFAO): 45–50.

BARSANTI, A. 1902. 'Rapport sur la fouille de Dahchour', *ASAE* 3: 198–205.

BAINES, J. and J. MÁLEK 1980. *Atlas of Ancient Egypt* (New York and Oxford: Facts on File).

BAKRY, H. S. K. 1972. 'A family of High Priests of Alexandria and Memphis', *MDAIK* 28: 75–77.

BAUD, M. 1995. 'La tombe de la reine-mère Ḫˁ-mrr-Nbtj Ier', *BIFAO* 95: 11–19.

— 1996. 'Les formes du titre de "mère royale" à l'Ancien Empire', *BIFAO* 96: 51–71.

— 1997. 'Aux pieds de Djoser: les mastabas entre fosse et enceinte de la partie nord du complexe funéraire', *Études Lauer*: 69–87.

BAUD, M. and V. DOBREV 1995. 'De nouvelles annales de l'Ancien Empire Égyptien. Une "Pierre de Palerme" pour la VIe dynastie', *BIFAO* 95: 23–92.

BAUD, M. and E. DRIOTON 1928. *Le Tombeau de Rôy (tombeau 255)* (Cairo: IFAO).

BENNETT, C.J. 1994. 'Thutmosis I and Ahmes-Sapaïr', *GM* 141: 35–37.

— 1997. 'Cleopatra V Tryphaena and the Genealogy of the Later Ptolemies', *AncSoc* 28: 39–66.

— 2001–02. *Royal Genealogies: Ptolemaic Dynasty* (http://www.geocities.com/christopherjbennett/ptolemies/ptolemies.htm).

— 2002. 'A genealogical chronology of the Seventeenth Dynasty', *JARCE* 39: 123–55.

BERG, D. 1987. 'The Vienna Stela of Meryre', *JEA* 73: 213–16.

BERVE, H. 1926. *Alexanderreich auf prosopographischer Grundlage* (Munich: Beck).

BEVAN, E.R. 1927. *A History of Egypt under the Ptolemaic Dynasty* (London: Methuen).

BERLANDINI, J. 1997. 'Contribution aux "Princes du Nouvel Empire à Memphis", le prince Thoutmès, fils d'Amenhotep III. Le prince Senakhtenamon, fils de Ramsès II', in *Études Lauer*: 55–68.

BIANCHI, R.S. 1988. *Cleopatra's Egypt: Age of the Ptolemies* (Brooklyn: Brooklyn Museum).

BIERBRIER, M.L. 1975. *The Late New Kingdom in Egypt (c. 1300–664 BC): A Genealogical and Chronological Investigation* (Warminster: Aris and Phillips).

BIETAK, M. 1996. *Avaris: The Capital of the Hyksos* (London: British Museum Press).

BLACKMAN, A.M. 1941. 'The stela of Shoshenk, Great Chief of the Meshwesh', *JEA* 27: 83–95.

BORCHARDT, L. 1898. 'Das Grab des Menes', *ZÄS* 36: 87–105.

— 1907. *Das Grabdenkmal des Königs Ne-user-rˁ* (Leipzig: Heinrichs).

— 1910–13. *Das Grabdenkmal des Königs Sˁaȝhu-rˁ* (Leipzig: Heinrichs).

BOLSHAKOV, A.O. 1995. 'Princes who became kings: where are their tombs?', *GM* 146: 11–22.

— 2001. 'Ka', *OEAE* II: 215–17.

BOUCHÉ-LECLERCQ, A. 1903–07. *Histoire des Lagides*, 4vv. (Paris: Leroux).

BOWMAN, A,K. 1986. *Egypt after the Pharaohs* (Oxford: OUP).

BRAND, P.J. 2000. *The Monuments of Seti I: Epigraphic, Historical and Art Historical Analysis* (Leiden: Brill).

BRESCIANI, E. 2001a. 'Achaemenids', *OEAE* I: 12.

— 2001b. 'Persia', *OEAE* 3: 35–37.

BRINKS, J. 1980. 'Mastaba', *LÄ* III: 1214–31.

BROCK, E.C. 1996. 'The sarcophagus of Queen Tiy', *JSSEA* 26: 8–21.

— 2003. 'The Sarcophagus Lid of Queen Takhat', *P8ICE* I: 97–102.

BROCK, L.P. 1999. 'Jewels in the Gebel: a preliminary report on the tomb of Anen', *JARCE* 36: 71–85.

BROSIUS, M. 1996. *Women in Ancient Persia* (Oxford: OUP).

BRUNNER, H. 1961. 'Der "Gottesvater" als Erzieher des Kronprinzen', *ZÄS* 86: 91–100.

— 1964. *Die Geburt des Gottkönigs* (Weisbaden: Harrassowitz).

BRUNTON, G. 1920. *Lahun* I: *The Treasure* (London: BSAE).

— 1947. 'The burial of Prince Ptah-Shepses at Saqqara', *ASAE* 47: 125–37.

BRYAN, B. 1991. *The Reign of Thutmose IV* (Baltimore: Johns Hopkins University Press).

BUDGE, E.A.W. 1885. *The Sarcophagus of Anchnesraneferab, Queen of Ahmes II, King of Egypt* (London: Whiting and Co.).

BURSTEIN, S.M. 1982. 'Arsinoe II Philadelphos: a revisionist view', in W.L. Adams & E.N. Borza (eds.) *Philip II, Alexander the Great and the Macedonian Heritage* (Washington: University Press of America): 197–212.

CALLENDER, V.G. 1998a. 'What sex was King Sobekneferu?', *KMT* 9/1: 45–56.

— 1998b. 'Materials for the Reign of Sebekneferu', *P7ICE*: 227–36.

CALLENDER, V.G. and P. JÁNOSI 1997. 'The tomb of Queen Khamerernebty II at Giza. A reassessment', *MDAIK* 53: 1–22.

CAMINOS, R. 1958. *The Chronicle of Prince Osorkon* (Rome: Pontificum Institutum Biblicum).

— 1964. 'The Nitocris Adoption Stela', *JEA* 50: 71–101.

— 1994. 'Notes on Queen Katimala's inscribed panel in the Temple of Semna', *Homm. Leclant* II: 73–80.

CAMPBELL, C. 1912. *The Miraculous Birth of King Amon-hotep III and Other Egyptian Studies* (Edinburgh: Oliver and Boyd).

CARTER, H. 1916. 'Report on the tomb of Zeser-ka-ra Amenhetep I', *JEA* 3: 147–54.

— 1917a. 'A tomb prepared for Queen Hatshepsuit discovered by the Earl of Carnarvon', *ASAE* 16: 179–82.

— 1916. 'Report on the tomb of Zeser-ka-Ra Amen-hetep I, discovered by the Earl of Carnarvon in 1914', *JEA* 3: 147–54.

— 1917b. 'A tomb prepared for Queen Hatshepsuit and other recent discoveries at Thebes', *JEA* 4: 107–18.

CHANLER, B. 1934. *Cleopatra's Daughter, the Queen of Mauritania* (London: Putnam).

CHAUVEAU, M. 1990 'Un été 145', *BIFAO* 90: 135–68.

— 2000. 'Encore Ptolémée "VII" et le dieu Néos Philopatôr?', *RdE* 51: 257–61.

CHEVRIER, H. and E. DRIOTON 1940–45. *Le Temple Reposoir de Séti II à Karnak* (Boulaq: Imprimerie Nationale).

CHRISTOPHE, L.-A. 1951. 'La carrière du Prince Merenptah et les trois regencies Ramessides', *ASAE* 51: 335–72.

— 1957. 'Les trois deriers grands majordomes de la XXVIe dynastie', *ASAE* 54: 83–100.

CLARYSSE, W. and G. VAN DER VEKEN 1983. *The Eponymous Priests of Ptolemaic Egypt: Chronological Lists of the Priests of Alexandria and Ptolemais with a Study of the Demotic Transcriptions of their Names* (Leiden: Brill).

CLÈRE, J.J. 1951. 'Une statuette du fils aîné du roi Nectanebo', *CdE* 6: 135–56.

COLLINS, N.L. 1997. 'The various fathers of Ptolemy I', *Mnemosyne* (ser. 4) 50: 436–76.

COMMISSION DES MONUMENTS D'ÉGYPTE 1809–22. *Description de l'Égypte, ou Recueil des Observations et des Recherches qui ont été faites en Égypte pendant l'Expédition de l'Armée Français: Antiquités (Planches)*, 9 + 10vv (Paris: Imprimerie Impériale).

CRUZ-URIBE, E. 1977. 'On the wife of Merenptah', *GM* 24: 23–29.

— 1978. 'The father of Ramses I', *JNES* 37: 237–44.

DARESSY, G. 1909. *Cercueils des Cachettes Royales* (Cairo: IFAO).

— 1917. 'Stèle du roi Pefnifdubast', *ASAE* 21: 138–34.

D'AURIA, S. 1983. 'The Princess Beketamun', *JEA* 69: 161–63.

DAVIES, W.V. 1998. 'A statue of the "King's Son, Sahathor", from Thebes', in H. Guksch and D. Polz (eds.), *Stationen. Beiträge zur Kulturgeschichte Ägyptens. Rainer Stadelmann gewidmet* (Mainz: Philipp von Zabern): 177–79.

DAVIS, T.M. et al. 1904. *The Tomb of Thoutmôsis IV* (Westminster: Archibald Constable).

— 1907. *The Tomb of Iouiya and Touiyou* (Westminster: Archibald Constable).

— 1908. *The Tomb of Siphtah; the Monkey Tomb and the Gold Tomb* (Westminster: Archibald Constable).

DE BUCK, A. 1937. 'The Judicial Papyrus of Turin', *JEA* 23: 152–64.

DE MEULENAERE, H. 1963. 'La famille royale de Nectanebo', *ZÄS* 90: 90–93.

— 1968. 'La famille du roi Amasis', *JEA* 54: 183–88.

DE MORGAN, J. 1895, 1903. *Fouilles à Dahchour* I, II (Vienna: Adolphe Holzhausen).

DE MORGAN, J., U. BOURIANT, G. LEGRAIN, G. JÉQUIER and A. BARSANTI 1894. *Catalogue des monuments et inscriptions de l'Egypte antique*, I:1 (Vienna: Adolphe Holzhausen).

DESROCHES-NOBLECOURT, C. 1962. *Tutankhamen: Life and Death of a Pharaoh* (London: Michael Joseph).

DEVAUCHELLE, D. 1995. 'Le sentiment anti-perse chez les anciens Égyptiens', *Transeuphratène* 9: 67–80,

DOBREV, V. 1996. 'Les marques sur pierres de construction de la nécropole de Pépi Ier. Étude prosopographique', *BIFAO* 96: 103–32.

DOBREV, V.A. LABROUSSE and B. MATHIEU 2000. 'La dixième pyramide à textes de Saqqâra: Ânkhesenpepy II. Rapport préliminaire de la campagne de fouilles 2000', *BIFAO* 100: 275–96.

DOBREV, V. and J. LECLANT 1997. 'Nedjeftet. Une nouvelle reine identifiée à Saqqara-Sud', *BIFAO* 97: 149–56.

DODSON, A.M. 1987. 'The Takhats and some other royal ladies of the Ramesside Period', *JEA* 73: 224–29.

— 1987b. '"Psusennes II." Revue d'Égyptologie 38 (1987): 49–54.

— 1988a. 'The tombs of the queens of the Middle Kingdom', *ZÄS* 115: 123–36.

— 1988b. 'Egypt's first antiquarians?' *Antiquity* 62/236: 513–17.

— 1988c. 'The tombs of the kings of the early Eighteenth Dynasty at Thebes', *ZÄS* 115, 110–23.

— 1990. 'Crown Prince Djhutmose and the royal sons of the Eighteenth Dynasty', *JEA* 76: 87–96.

— 1991a. *Egyptian Rock-Cut Tombs* (Princes Risborough: Shire Publications).

— 1991b. 'Two Who Might Have Been King', *Amarna Letters* I: 26–27.

— 1991c. 'On the internal chronology of the Seventeenth Dynasty', *GM* 120: 33–38.

— 1992. 'On the burial of Prince Ptahshepeses', *GM* 129: 49–51.

— 1993a. 'Psusennes II and Shoshenq I', *JEA* 79: 267–68.

— 1993b. 'A new King Shoshenq confirmed?', *GM* 137: 53–58.

— 1994. 'Kings' Valley Tomb 55 and the fates of the Amarna Kings', *AL* 3: 92–103.

— 1995a. 'Of bulls and princes: the early years of the Serapeum at Sakkara', *KMT* 6/1: 18–32.

— 1995b/2000. *Monarchs of the Nile* (London: Rubicon/Cairo: American University in Cairo Press).

— 1995c. 'Rise & Fall of the House of Shoshenq: the Libyan Centuries of Egyptian History', *KMT* 6/3: 52–67.

— 1997a. 'The Sons of Rameses III', *KMT* 8/1: 29–43.

— 1997b. 'Messuy, Amada and Amenmesse', *JARCE* 34: 41–48.

— 1997/8. 'The so-called Tomb of Osiris at Abydos', *KMT* 8/4: 37–47.

— 2000a. *After the Pyramids* (London: Rubicon).

— 2000c. 'Lahun and its treasure', *KMT* 11/1: 38–49.

— 2000d. Review of Ryholt 1997, *BiOr* LVII No. 1/2: 48–52.

— 2000e. 'Towards a minimum chronology of the New Kingdom and Third Intermediate Period', *BES* 14: 7–18.

— n.d. [2000] 'Amenhotep III: uncles, brothers, sons and the Serapeum', in *Amenhotep III y su tiempo: I Jornadas Temáticas* (Madrid: Fundación del Sur/Egeria): 35–51.

— 2000/1. 'The intact pyramid burial at Hawara of 12th Dynasty Princess Neferuptah', *KMT* 11/4: 40–47.

— 2001a. 'Third Intermediate Period', in *OEAE* III: 388–94.

— 2001b. Review of Peden 1994, *CdE* 76: 263–67.

— 2001c. 'The burial of members of the royal family during the Eighteenth Dynasty', in Z. Hawass & Lyla Pinch Brock (eds.) *Egyptology at the Dawn of the Twenty-First Century: Proceedings of the Eighth International Congress of Egyptologists, Cairo, 2000* (Cairo: AUC Press).

— 2002a. 'Divine queens in Nubia: Tiye at Sedeinga and Nefertari at Abu Simbel', *KMT* 13/2: 58–65.

— 2002b. 'The problem of Amenirdis II and the heirs to the office of God's Wife of Amun during the Twenty-Sixth Dynasty', *JEA* 88.

— 2004. 'An eternal harem: the tombs of the royal families of ancient Egypt, Part I', *KMT* 15: 2.

— 2003. 'Why did Nefertiti disappear?', in W. Manley (ed.), *Seventy Great Mysteries of Ancient Egypt* (London and New York: Thames & Hudson): 127–31.

— 2009a. *Amarna Sunset: Nefertiti, Tutankhamun, Ay, Horemheb and the Egyptian Counter-Reformation* (Cairo: American University in Cairo Press).

— 2009b. 'The Prophet of Amun Iuput and his Distinguished Ancestors', *JEA* 95.

DODSON, A.M. and J.J. JANSSEN, 1989. 'A Theban tomb and its tenants', *JEA* 75: 125–38.

DONADONI ROVERI, A.M. 1969. *I sarcofagi egizi dalle origini alla fine dell'Antico Regno* (Rome: Università degli Studi di Roma).

DORMAN, P.F. 1988. *The Monuments of Senenmut: Problems in Historical Methodology* (London: Kegan Paul International).

DRIOTON, É. 1954. 'Une liste de rois de la IVe Dynastie dans l'Ouadi Hamâmât', *BSFE* 16: 41–49.

DUNHAM, D. 1950. *Royal Cemeteries of Kush* I, *El Kurru* (Boston: MFA).

— 1955. *Royal Cemeteries of Kush* II, *Nuri* (Boston: MFA).

DUNHAM, D. and M.F.L. MACADAM 1949. 'Names and relationships of the royal family of Napata', *JEA* 35: 139–49.

DUNHAM, D. and W.K. SIMPSON 1974. *The Mastaba of Queen Mersyankh III* (Boston: MFA).

EATON-KRAUSS, M. 1991. 'The fate of Sennefer and Senetnay at Karnak temple and in the Valley of the Kings', *JEA* 85: 113–129.

EDGAR, C.C. and G. MASPERO 1907. 'The sarcophagus of an unknown queen', *ASAE* 8: 276–81.

EDWARDS, I.E.S. 1985. *The Pyramids of Egypt³* (Harmondsworth: Penguin).

— 1994. 'Chephren's place amongst the kings of the Fourth Dynasty', *U. Reed*: 97–105.

EIDE, T., T. HÄGG, R. HOLTON PIERCE and L. TÖRÖK (eds.) 1994. *Fontes Historiae Nubiorum* I (Bergen: Klassisk instituut, Universitetet i Bergen).

EL-BIALY, M. 1990. 'Une tombe de la XVIII dynastie découverte à Gournet Mourai, *Les Dossiers d'Archéologie* 149–50: 96.

EL-KHOULY, A. and G.T. MARTIN 1987. *Excavations in the Royal Necropolis at El-'Amarna 1984* (Cairo: EAO).

EL-SAYED, R. 1974. 'Quelques éclaircissements sur l'histoire de la XXVIᵉ Dynastie d'après la statue du Caire C.G. 658', *BIFAO* 74: 29–44.

ELLIS, W.M. 1994. *Ptolemy of Egypt* (London: Routledge).

EMERY, W.B. 1949–58. *Great Tombs of the First Dynasty* (Cairo: IFAO/London: EES).

EMERY, W.B. 1962. *A Funerary Repast in an Egyptian Tomb of the Archaic Period* (Leiden: Nederlands Instituut voor het Nabije Oosten).

EPIGRAPHIC SURVEY 1980. *The Tomb of Kheruef, Theban Tomb 192* (Chicago: Oriental Institute).

ERTMAN, E.L. 1993. 'A first report on the preliminary survey of unexcavated KV10 (the tomb of King Amenmesse)', *KMT* 4/2: 38–46.

EYRE, C.J. 1994. 'Weni's career and Old Kingdom historiography', *U. Reed*: 107–24.

FAKHRY, A. 1961. *The Pyramids*, 2nd ed. (Chicago: Chicago UP).

FARAG, N. and Z, ISKANDER 1971. *The Discovery of Neferwptah* (Cairo: General Organization for Government Printing Offices).

FAY, B. 1996. *The Louvre Sphinx and Royal Sculpture from the Reign of Amenemhat II* (Mainz: Philipp von Zabern).

FIRTH, C.M. and B. GUNN 1926. *The Teti Pyramid Cemeteries* (Cairo: IFAO).

FISHER, M.M. 2001. *The Sons of Ramesses II*, 2vv (Wiesbaden: Otto Harrassowitz).

FORBES, D.C. 1999. *Tombs; Treasures; Mummies: Seven Great Discoveries of Egyptian Archaeology* (San Francisco: KMT Communications).

— 2001. 'God's Wives of Amen: the Divine Adoratrixes', *KMT* 12/2: 60–65.

FRANKE, D. 1984. *Personendaten aus dem Mittleren Reiches* (Wiesbaden: Otto Harrassowitz).

FRASER, P.M. 1972. *Ptolemaic Alexandria*, 3vv. (Oxford: OUP).

FREED, R.E., Y.J. MARKOWITZ and S.H. D'AURIA (eds.) 1999. *Pharaohs of the Sun: Akhenaten; Nefertiti; Tutankhamen* (London: Thames & Hudson/Boston: MFA).

GABOLDE, M. 1998. *D'Akhenaton à Toutânkhamon* (Lyon: Université Lumiére-Lyon 2).

GARDINER, A.H. 1947. *Ancient Egyptian Onomastica*, 3vv (Oxford: OUP).

— 1953a. 'The tomb of the General Haremhab', *JEA* 39: 3–12.

— 1953b. 'The coronation of King Haremhab', *JEA* 39: 13–31.

— 1954. 'The tomb of Queen Twosre', *JEA* 40: 40–44.

— 1956. 'The first King Mentuhotep of the Eleventh Dynasty', *MDAIK* 14: 42–51.

— 1958. 'Only one King Siptah and Twosre not his wife', *JEA* 44: 12–22.

GAUTHIER, H. 1907, 1912, 1914, 1916, 1917. *Le Livre des Rois d'Égypte* I–V (Cairo: IFAO).

— 1921. 'Un tombeau de Tell Moqdam', *ASAE* 21: 21–27.

GAUTIER, J.É. and G. JÉQUIER 1902. *Mémoire sur les fouilles de Licht* (Cairo: IFAO).

GERMER, R. 1984. 'Die Angebliche Mumie der Teje: Probleme Interdisziplinärere Arbeiten', *SAK* 11: 85–90.

GILES, F.J. 2001. *The Amarna Age: Egypt* (Warminster: Aris and Phillips).

GITTON, M. 1981. *L'Épouse du Dieu Ahmes Néfertary*, 2nd ed. (Paris: Belles Lettres).

— 1984. *Les divines Épouses de la 18ᵉ Dynastie* (Besançon-Paris: Université de Besançon).

GNIRS, A.M. 2001. 'The military: an overview', *OEAE* II: 400–406.

GOMAÀ F. 1973. *Chaemwese, Sohn Ramses' II und Hoherpriester von Memphis* (Wiesbaden: Otto Harrassowitz).

GOYON, J.-C. 1982. 'Une dale aux noms de Menkheperrë, fils de Pinedjem I, d'Isetemkheb et de Smendes (CS X 1305), *Cahiers de Karnak* VII (Paris: Éditions Recherche sur les Civilizations): 275–80.

GRAEFE, E. 1981. *Untersuchungen zur Verwaltung und Geschichte der Institution der Gottesmahlin des Amun vom Beginn des Neuen Reiches bis zur Spätzeit* (Wiesbaden: Otto Harrassowitz).

— 1994. 'Der autobiographische Text des Ibi', *MDAIK* 50: 85–99.

— 2000. 'Vorbericht über die erste Kampagne einer Nachuntersuchung der königlichen *Cachette* TT 320 von Deir el Bahri', *MDAIK* 56: 215–21.

— 2003. 'Nochmals zum Gebrauch des Titels dw3t-ntr inder Spätzeit', *JEA* 89: 246–47.

GRAINGER, J.D.A. 1997. *Seleukid Prosopography and Gazeteer* (Leiden: Brill).

GRANDET, P. 2000. 'L'exécution du chancelier Bay: O.IFAO 1864', *BIFAO* 339–45.

GRANT, M. 1972. *Cleopatra* (London: Weidenfeld and Nicolson).

— 1992. *Readings in the Classical Historians* (New York: Charles Scribner's Sons).

GRDSELOFF, B. 1943a. 'Deux inscriptions juridiques de l'ancien Empire', *ASAE* 42: 25–70.

— 1943b. 'Notes sur deux monuments inédits de l'ancien Empire', *ASAE* 43: 107–25.

GRIFFITH, F.Ll. 1929. 'Scenes from a destroyed temple at Napata', *JEA* 15: 26–28.

GRIMAL, N. 1992. *A History of Ancient Egypt* (Oxford: Blackwell).

GRIST, J. 1985. 'The identity of the Ramesside Queen Tyti', *JEA* 71: 71–81.

GUNN, B. 1955. 'The decree of Amonrasonther for Neskhons', *JEA* 41: 83–99.

HABACHI, L. 1958. 'God's Fathers and the role they played in the history of the First Intermediate Period', *ASAE* 55: 167–90.

— 1968. 'Tomb no. 226 of the Theban Necropolis and its unknown owner', in W. Helck (ed.), *Festschrift für Siegfried Schott am seinem 70. Geburtstag* (Wiesbaden: Otto Harrassowitz): 69–70.

— 1974. 'Lids of the Outer Sarcophagi of Merytamen and Nefertari, Wives of Ramesses II', in *Festschrift zum 150 jährigen Bestehen der Berliner Ägyptologischen Museums, Staatliche Museen zu Berlin* (Berlin: Akademie-Verlag): 105–12.

— 1969. 'La reine Touy, femme de Séthi I et ses proches parents inconnus', *RdE* 21: 27–47.

— 1983. 'The tomb of the princess Nebt of the VIIIth Dynasty discovered at Qift', *SAK* 10: 205–13.

— 1984. 'The family of the Vizier Ibi' and his place among the viziers of the Thirteenth Dynasty', *SAK* 11: 113–26.

HAMMOND, N.G.L. 1991. *The Miracle That Was Macedonia* [Great Civilizations series] (London: Sidgwick & Jackson).

HAMMOND, N.G.L. and G.T. GRIFFITH 1979. *A History of Macedonia* II: 550–336 BC (Oxford: Clarendon Press).

HAMMOND N.G.L. and F.W. WALBANK 1988. *A History of Macedonia* III: 336–167 BC (Oxford: Clarendon Press).

HARING, B. 2001. 'Temple administration', *OEAE* I: 20–23.

HARPUR, Y. 1987. *Decoration of Private Tombs in the Old Kingdom* (London: Kegan Paul International).

— 2001. *The Tombs of Nefermaat and Rahotep at Maidum: Discovery, Destruction and Reconstruction* (Oxford: Oxford Expedition to Egypt).

HARRIS, J.E. and K.R. WEEKS 1973. *X-Raying the Pharaohs* (London: Macdonald/New York: Scribners).

HARRIS, J.E., E.F. WENTE et al. 1979. 'The identification of the "Elder Lady" in the tomb of Amenhotep II as Queen Tiye', *Delaware Medical Journal* 51/2: 39–93.

HASLAUER, E. 2001. 'Harem', *OEAE* II: 76–80.

HASSAN, A. 1997. *The Queens of the Fourth Dynasty* (Cairo: Supreme Council of Antiquities).

HASSAN, S. 1949. *The Sphinx: Its History in the Light of Recent Excavations* (Cairo: Government Press).

— 1953. *The Great Sphinx and its Secrets: Historical Studies in the Light of Recent Excavations* (Cairo: Government Press).

— 1975. *Mastabas of Princess Hemet-Re' and Others* (Cairo: General Organisation for Government Printing Offices).

HASSANEIN, F. 1985. 'Le problème historique du Seth-her-khepshef, fils de Ramses III: à propos de la tombe no. 43 de la Vallée des Reines', *SAK Beiheft* 4: 63–66.

HASSANEIN, F. and M. NELSON, 1976. *La Tombe du Prince Amon-(her)-khepchef* (Cairo: Centre d'Études et Documentation sur l'Ancienne Égypte).

HAYES, W.C. 1935. *Royal Sarcophagi of the XVIII Dynasty* (Princeton: Princeton UP).

— 1948. 'Writing palette of the High Priest of Amun, Smendes', *JEA* 34: 47–50.

— 1951. 'Inscriptions from the palace of Amunhotep III', *JNES* 10: 35–56, 82–111, 156–83, 231–42.

HÖLBL, G. 2001. *A History of the Ptolemaic Empire* (London: Routledge).

HÖLSCHER, U. 1954. *The Excavation of Medinet Habu, V: Post-Ramessid Remains* (Chicago: Chicago UP).

HORNBLOWER, S. 1983. *The Greek World*

479–323 (London: Methuen).

HUSS, W. 1975. 'Die zu Ehren Ptolemaios' III. und seiner Familie errichtete Statuengruppe von Thermos (IG IX I, I², 56)', *CdE* 50: 312–20.

— 1994a. 'Das Haus des Nektanebis und das Haus des Ptolemaios', *AncSoc* 25: 111–17.

— 1994b. 'Ptolemaios Eupator', in A. Bülow-Jacobsen (ed.), *Proceedings of the 20th International Congress of Papyrologists, Copenhagen, 23–29 August, 1992* (Copenhagen: Museum Tusculanum Press): 555–61.

— 1998. 'Ptolemaios der Sohn', *ZPE* 121: 229–50.

— 2001. *Ägypten in Hellenistischer Zeit 332–30 v. Chr.* (Munich: Beck).

IBRAHIM, M. 1993. 'Apropos du prince Khâemouas et sa mère Isetneferet. Nouveaux documents provenant du Sérapéum', *MDAIK* 49: 97–106.

IKRAM, S. 1989. 'Domestic shrines and the cult of the royal family at el-'Amarna', *JEA* 75: 89–101.

IKRAM, S. and A.M. DODSON 1998. *The Mummy in Ancient Egypt: Equipment for Eternity* (London and New York: Thames & Hudson/Cairo: American University in Cairo Press).

JACQUET-GORDON, H. 1967. 'A statue of Ma'et and the identity of the Divine Adoratress Karomama', *ZÄS* 94: 86–93.

JÁNOSI, P. 1996. *Die Pyramidenanlagen der Königinnen* (Vienna: Verlag der Österreichischen Akademie der Wissenschaften).

— 1997. 'Grab des Kronprinzen in der 4. Dynastie: "Kronprinz" Iunre', *GM* 158: 15–32.

JANSEN-WINKELN, K. 1987. 'Thronname und Begräbnis Takeloths I', *VA* 3: 253–58.

— 1995. 'Historische Probleme der 3. Zwischenzeit', *JEA* 81: 129–49.

— 2006. 'The Chronology of the Third Intermediate Period', in R. Krauss, E. Hornung and D. Warburton (eds.), *Handbook of Ancient Egyptian Chronology* (Leiden: Brill).

JEFFREYS, D.G. 1985. *The Survey of Memphis* (London: EES).

JÉQUIER, G. 1928. *Le Pyramide d'Oudjebten* (Cairo: IFAO).

— 1929. *Tombeaux de Particuliers Contemporains de Pepi II* (Cairo: IFAO).

— 1933. *Les Pyramides des Reines Neit et Apouit* (Cairo: IFAO).

— 1938. *Deux Pyramides du Moyen Empire* (Cairo: IFAO).

JOINT ASSOCIATION OF CLASSICAL TEACHERS 1984. *The World of Athens: An Introduction to Classical Athenian Culture* (Cambridge: CUP).

JOHNSON, J.H. 1974. 'The Demotic

Chronicle as an historical source', *Enchoria* 4: 1–17.

JOHNSON, G.B. 1996–97. 'Queen Meresankh III: her tomb and times', *KMT* 7/4: 44–59.

JOHNSON, W.R. 1996. 'Amenhotep III and Amarna: some new considerations', *JEA* 82: 65–82.

JORDAN, P. 1998. *Riddles of the Sphinx* (Stroud: Sutton Publishing).

KEMP, B.J. 1967. 'The Egyptian First Dynasty royal cemetery', *Antiquity* 41: 22–32.

KIENITZ, F.K. 1953. *Die politische Geschichte Ägyptens von 7. bis zum 4. Jahrhundert vor der Zeitwende* (Berlin: Akademie-Verlag).

KITCHEN, K.A. 1972. 'Ramesses VII and the Twentieth Dynasty', *JEA* 58: 182–94.

— 1982a. *Pharaoh Triumphant* (Warminster: Aris and Phillips).

— 1982b. 'The Twentieth Dynasty revisited', *JEA* 68: 116–25.

— 1984. 'Family relationships of Ramesses IX and the late Twentieth Dynasty', *SAK* 11: 127–34.

— 1995. *The Third Intermediate Period in Egypt (1100–650 BC)*, 3rd ed. (Warminster: Aris and Phillips).

— 1996. '"As arrows in his quiver": the sons of Rameses II', *KMT* 7/1: 40–51.

KITCHEN, K.A. and G.A. GABALLA 1968. 'The ancestry of Ramesses II', *CdE* 43/86: 259–63.

KOZLOFF, A. and B.M. BRYAN 1992. *Egypt's Dazzling Sun: Amenhotep III and his World* (Cleveland, OH: Cleveland Museum of Art/Indiana University Press).

KRAUSS, R. 1976. 'Untersuchungen zu König Amenmesse (1. Teil)', *SAK* 4: 161–99.

— 1977. 'Untersuchungen zu König Amenmesse (2. Teil)', *SAK* 5: 131–74.

— 1978. *Das Ende der Amarnazeit* (Hildesheim: Gerstenberg).

— 1997. 'Untersuchungen zu König Amenmesse: Nachträge', *SAK* 24: 161–84.

— 2000. *Moïse le Pharaon* (Paris: Éditions du Rocher).

KUHLMANN, K.P. 1981. 'Ptolemais – Queen of Nectanebo I. Notes on the inscription of an unknown princess of the XXXth Dynasty', *MDAIK* 37: 267–79.

KUHRT, A. 1995. *The Ancient Near East c. 3000–330 BC* (London and New York: Routledge).

LABROUSSE, A. 1994. 'Les reines de Teti, Khouit et Ipout I, recherches architecturales', *Homm. Leclant*: 231–44.

— 1997. 'Un bloc décoré du temple funéraire de la mère royale Néferhetepès', *Études Lauer*: 263–70.

— 1999. *Les Pyramides des Reines. Une Nouvelle Nécropole à Saqqâra* (Paris: Hazen).

LAUER, J.-Ph. 1976. *Saqqara, Royal Necropolis of Memphis* (London: Thames & Hudson).

LEAHY, A. 1984. 'Tanutamon, son of Shabako?', *GM* 83: 43–5.

— 1990. 'Abydos in the Libyan Period', in A. Leahy (ed.), *Libya and Egypt c. 1300–750 BC* (London: SOAS): 155–200.

— 1994. 'Kushite monuments at Abydos', *U. Reed*: 171–92.

— 1996. 'The adoption of Ankhnes-neferibre', *JEA* 82: 145–65.

LEBLANC, C. 1988. 'L'identification de la tombe de Henout-mi-Re'', *BIFAO* 88: 131–46.

— 1989a. *Ta Set Neferou: Une Nécropole de Thebes-Ouest et son Histoire* I (Cairo: Nubar).

— 1989b. 'Architecture et evolution chronologique des tombes de la Vallée de Reines', *BIFAO* 89: 227–48.

LECLANT, J. 1961. *Montouemhat, Quatrième Prophète d'Amuon, Prince de la Ville* (Cairo: IFAO).

— 1965. *Recherches sur les Monuments Thébains de la XXVe Dynastie dite Éthiopienne* (Cairo: IFAO).

LECUYOT, G. 2000. 'The Valley of the Queens: a brief history of its excavations', *KMT* 11/2: 42–55.

LECUYOT, G. et al. 1990. 'Une nécropole sacerdotale au Ramesseum', *Les Dossiers d'Archéologie* 149–50: 88 ff.

LEHNER, M. 1985. *The Pyramid Tomb of Hetep-heres and the Satellite Pyramid of Khufu* (Mainz: Philipp von Zabern).

— 1997. *The Complete Pyramids* (London and New York: Thames & Hudson).

LEPSIUS, C.R. 1849–59. *Denkmaeler aus Aegypten und Aethiopien*, 6vv (Berlin/Leipzig: Nicolaische Buchhandlung).

— 1897. *Denkmaeler aus Aegypten und Aethiopien, Text* (ed. E. Naville, L. Borchardt and K. Sethe) (Leipzig: J.C. Hinrichs).

LESKO, B.S. 1998. 'Queen Khamerernebty II and her sculpture', in L.H. Lesko (ed.), *Ancient Egyptian and Mediterranean Studies in Memory of William A. Ward* (Providence: Brown University): 149–62.

LICHTHEIM, M. 1973. *Ancient Egyptian Literature*, 3vv (Berkeley: University of California Press).

LILYQUIST, C. 2003, 2004. *The Tomb of Three Foreign Wives of Tuthmosis III* (New York: MMA).

LINDSAY, J. 1971. *Cleopatra* (London: Constable).

LLOYD, A.B. 1982. 'The inscription of Udjahorresnet: a collaborator's testament', *JEA* 68: 166–80.

— 2002. 'The Egyptian Elite in the Early Ptolemaic Period: some hieroglyphic evidence', in D. Ogden (ed.), *The Hellenistic World: new perspectives* (Swansea: Classical

Press of Wales and Duckworth): 117–36.

LOAT, W.S. 1905. *Gurob* (London: ERA).

MACADAM, M.F. 1951. 'A royal family of the Thirteenth Dynasty', *JEA* 37: 20–28.

MACE, A.C. 1914. 'Excavations at the north pyramid of Lisht', *BMMA* 9: 207–22.

— 1921. 'Excavations at Lisht', *BMMA* November 1921, Part II: 5–19.

— 1922. 'Excavations at Lisht', *BMMA* December 1922, Part II: 4–18.

MACE, A.C. and H.E. WINLOCK 1916. *The Tomb of Senebtisi at Lisht* (New York: MMA).

MACIVER, D.R. and A.C. MACE 1902. *El Amrah and Abydos* (London: ERA).

MACURDY, G.H. 1932. *Hellenistic Queens: A Study of Woman-Power in Macedonia, Seleucid, Syria, and Ptolemaic Egypt* (Baltimore: Johns Hopkins Press).

MALEK, J. 1980. 'Princess Inti, the companion of Horus', *JSSEA* 10/3: 229–41.

MANUELIAN, P. DER 1987. *Studies in the Reign of Amenophis II* (Hildesheim: Gerstenberg Verlag).

MARAGIOGLIO, V. and C.A. RINALDI 1964–77, *L'architettura delle Piramidi Menfite*, III–VII (Rapallo: Officine Grafische Canessa).

MARIETTE, A. 1857. *Le Sérapeum de Memphis* (Paris: Gide).

— 1869–80. *Abydos*, 2vv (Paris: Franck).

— 1882. *Le Sérapeum de Memphis*, I (Paris: F. Vieweg).

— 1884–85. *Les Mastabas de l'Ancien Empire* (Paris: F. Vieweg).

MARTIN, G.T. 1974, 1989. *The Royal Tomb at El-'Amarna* I, II (London: EES).

— 1982. 'Queen Mutnodjmet at Memphis and El-'Amarna', *L'Égyptologie en 1979: Axes Prioritaires de Recherches* (Paris), II: 275–78.

— 1991. *The Hidden Tombs of Memphis* (London and New York: Thames & Hudson).

— 1997. *The Tomb of Tia and Tia: A Royal Monument of the Ramesside Period in the Memphite Necropolis* (London: EES).

MARTIN, G.T. and H.D. SCHNEIDER 1989, 1996. *The Memphite Tomb of Horemheb, Commander-in-Chief of Tutankhamun*, 2vv (London: EES).

MASPERO, G. 1889. *Les Momies Royales de Déir el-Baharî* (Cairo: IFAO).

— 1901. *The Dawn of Civilization: Egypt and Chaldea*⁴ (London: Society for Promoting Christian Knowledge).

MASPERO, G. and E. BRUGSCH 1881. *La Trouvaille de Deir el-Bahari* (Cairo: F. Mourès & Cie.).

MATHIESON, I., E. BETTLES, S. DAVIES and H.S. SMITH 1995. 'A stela of the Persian Period from Saqqara', *JEA* 81: 23–41.

MAYSTRE, C. 1948. 'Un stele d'un Grand Prêtre Memphite', *ASAE* 48: 449–55.

MCDONALD, J. 1996. *House of Eternity: The Tomb of Nefertari* (London: Thames & Hudson).

MERTZ, B. 1978a. *Temples, Tombs and Hieroglyphs* (London: Michael O'Mara).

— 1978b. *Red Land, Black Land: Daily Life in Ancient Egypt* (New York: Dodd, Mead & Co.).

METROPOLITAN MUSEUM OF ART 1999. *Egyptian Art in the Age of the Pyramids* (New York: MMA).

MEYER, C. 1984. 'Zum Titel "*hmt njswt*" bei den Töchtern Amenophis' III. und IV. und Ramses' II', *SAK* 11: 253–63.

MONTET, P. 1947–60. *La Nécropole Royale de Tanis*, 3vv (Paris).

MOOREN, L. 1988. 'The wives and children of Ptolemy VIII Euergetes II', in B.G. Mandilaras (ed.), *Proceedings of the XVIII International Congress of Papyrology, Athens, 1986* (Athens: Greek Papyrological Society): II, 435–44.

MORKOT, R. 1986. 'Violent images of queenship & the royal cult', *Wepwawet* 2: 1–9.

— 1999. 'Kingship and kinship in the Empire of Kush', in S. Wenig (ed.), *Studien zum antiken Sudan: Akten der 7. Internationalen Tagung für meroitische Forschungen vom 14. bis 19. September 1992 in Gosen/bei Berlin* (Wiesbaden: Otto Harrassowitz): 179–229.

— 2000. *The Black Pharaohs* (London: Rubicon).

MOURSI, M.I. 1972. *Die Hohenpriester des Sonnengottes von der Frühzeit bis zum Ende des Neuen Reiches* (Munich: Deutscher Kunstverlag).

MUNRO, P. 1993. *Der Unas-Friedhof Nord-West* I (Mainz: Philipp von Zabern).

NAVILLE, E. 1891. *Bubastis (1887–1889)* (London: EEF).

— 1892. *The Festival-Hall of Osorkon II in the Great Temple of Bubastis (1887–1889)* (London: EEF).

— 1894–1908. *The Temple of Deir el Bahari*, 7vv (London: EEF).

— 1910. *The XIth Dynasty Temple at Deir el-Bahari* II (London: EEF).

NEWBERRY, P.E. 1928. 'The sons of Tuthmosis IV', *JEA* 14: 82–85.

— 1936. 'On the parentage of the Intef kings of the Eleventh Dynasty', *ZÄS* 72: 118–20.

NIWINSKI, A. 1979. 'Problems in the chronology and genealogy of the XXIst Dynasty. New proposals for their interpretation', *JARCE* 16: 49–68.

— 1988. 'The wives of Pinudjem II – a topic for discussion', *JEA* 74: 226–30.

O'CONNOR, D. and E.H. CLINE (eds.) 1998. *Amenhotep III: Perspectives on his Reign* (Ann Arbor: University of Michigan Press).

OGDEN, D. 1999. *Polygamy, Prostitutes and Death* (London: Duckworth).

PARDEY, E. 2001. 'Provincial administration', *OEAE* I: 16–20.

PARKINSON, R. and S. QUIRKE 1992. 'The coffin of Prince Herunefer and the early history of the *Book of the Dead*', in Alan B. Lloyd (ed.) *Studies in Pharaonic Religion and Society in Honour of J. Gwyn Griffiths* (London: EES): 37–51.

PEDEN, A.J. 1994. *The Reign of Ramesses IV* (Warminster: Aris and Phillips).

PERDU, O. 1977. 'Khnemet-Nefer-Hedjet: une princesse et deux reines du Moyen Empire', *RdE* 29: 68–85.

PETERSON, B.J. 1967. 'Djedptahefanch, Sohn des Takeloth II', *ZÄS* 94: 128–29.

PETRIE, W.M.F. 1890. *Kahun, Gurob and Hawara* (London: Kegan Paul, Trench, Trübner).

— 1891. *Illahun, Kahun and Gurob 1889–90* (London: D. Nutt).

— 1892. *Medum* (London: D. Nutt).

— 1902. *Abydos Part I, 1902.* (London: EEF).

— 1905. *A History of Egypt* III (London: Methuen).

— 1897. *Six Temples at Thebes 1896* (London: B. Quartitch).

— 1909. *Qurneh* (London: ERA).

— 1910. *Meydum and Memphis III* (London: ERA).

PETRIE, W.M.F, G. BRUNTON and M.A. MURRAY 1923. *Lahun* II (London: BSAE).

POLZ, D. 1986. 'Die Särge des (Pa-)Ramessu', *MDAIK* 42: 145–66.

— 1995. 'The location of the tomb of Amenhotep I: a reconsideration', in R.H. Wilkinson (ed.), *Valley of the Sun Kings: New Explorations in the Tombs of the Pharaohs* (Tucson: University of Arizona Egyptian Expedition): 8–21.

PORTER, B. and R.B. MOSS 1960; 1972; 1974–81; 1934; 1937; 1939; 1952, 1999. *Topographical Bibliography of Ancient Egyptian Hieroglyphic Texts, Reliefs and Paintings*: I², *The Theban Necropolis*; II², *Theban Temples*; III², *Memphis*; IV, *Lower and Middle Egypt*; V, *Upper Egypt: Sites*; VI, *Upper Egypt: Chief Temples (excl. Thebes)*; VII, *Nubia, Deserts, and Outside Egypt*; VIII, *Objects of Provenance Not Known* (by J. Malek) (Oxford: Clarendon Press/Griffith Institute).

POSENER-KRIÉGER, P. 1976. *Les Archives du Temple de Néferirkarê-Kakai (Les Papyrus d'Abusir)* II (Cairo: IFAO).

PRAG, J. and R. NEAVE 1997. *Making Faces: Using Forensic and Archaeological Evidence* (London: British Museum Press).

PRISSE D'AVENNES, E. 1868–79. *Atlas d'Histoire de l'Art Égyptien* (Paris: Bertrand).

QUAEGEBEUR, J. 1971. 'Ptolémée II en adoration devant Arsinoé II divinisée', *BIFAO* 69: 191–217.

— 1978. 'Reines ptolémaïques et traditions égyptiennes', in H. Maehler and V.M. Strocka (eds.), *Das ptolemäische Ägypten: Akten des internationalen Symposions 27–29. September 1976 in Berlin* (Mainz: Philipp von Zabern): 245–62.

— 1980. 'The genealogy of the Memphite High Priest family in the Hellenistic Period', in D.J. Crawford et al. (eds.), *Studies in Ptolemaic Memphis* (Louvain: Peeters): 47–81.

QUIBELL, J.E. 1898. *The Ramesseum* (London: ERA).

— 1909. *Excavations at Saqqara 1907–1908* (Cairo: IFAO).

— 1912. *Excavations at Saqqara 1908–1910* (Cairo: IFAO).

— 1923. *Excavations at Saqqara 1912–1914* (Cairo: IFAO).

QUIRKE, S. 2001. 'State administration', *OEAE* I: 13–16.

RADWAN, A. 1969. *Die Darstellungen des regierenden Königs und seiner Familienangehörörigen in den Privatgräbern der 18. Dynastie* (Berlin: Verlag Bruno Hessling).

RANKE, H. 1953. 'The statue of a Ptolemaic Στρατηγος of the Mendesian Nome in the Cleveland Museum of Art', *JAOS* 73: 193–98.

RAVEN, M.J. 1994. 'A sarcophagus for Queen Tiye and other fragments from the Royal Tomb at El-Amarna', *OMRO* 74: 7–20.

RAY, J.D. 1988. 'Egypt 525–404 BC', *CAH* IV²: 254–86.

— 2001. 'Late Period: Thirtieth Dynasty', *OEAE* II: 275–76.

REDFORD, D.B. 1965. 'The coregency of Tuthmosis III and Amenophis II', *JEA* 51: 107–22.

— 1984. *Akhenaten, the Heretic King* (Princeton: Princeton UP).

REDFORD, S. 2002. *The Harem Conspiracy: The Murder of Ramesses III* (Chicago: Illinois UP).

READER, C.D. 2001. 'A geomorphological study of the Giza necropolis, with implications for the development of the site', *Archaeometry* 43/1: 149–59.

REEVES, C.N. 1988. 'New light on Kiya from texts in the British Museum', *JEA* 74: 91–101.

— 1990a. *Valley of the Kings: The Decline of a Royal Necropolis* (London: Kegan Paul International).

— 1990b. *The Complete Tutankhamun* (London and New York: Thames & Hudson).

— 2001. *Akhenaten: Egypt's False Prophet* (London and New York: Thames & Hudson).

REEVES, C.N. and R. WILKINSON 1996. *The Complete Valley of the Kings* (London and New York: Thames & Hudson).

REINACH, A.J. 1907. 'Bulletin épigraphique: Grèce du Nord', *REG* 20: 46 ff.

REISNER, G.A. 1931. *Mycerinus: The Temples of the Third Pyramid* (Cambridge, MA: Harvard UP).

— 1942. *A History of the Giza Necropolis*, I (Cambridge, MA: Harvard UP).

REISNER, G.A. and W.S. SMITH 1955. *A History of the Giza Necropolis*, II (Cambridge, MA: Harvard UP).

REYMOND, E.A.E. 1981. *From the Records of a Priestly Family from Memphis* I (Wiesbaden: Otto Harrassowitz).

RHIND, A.H. 1862. *Thebes: Its Tombs and their Tenants* (London: John Murray).

ROBINS, G. 1978. 'Amenhotep I and the child Amenemhat', *GM* 30 (1978), 71–75.

— 1982. 'Meritamun, daughter of Ahmose, and Meritamun, daughter of Thutmose III', *GM* 56: 82–83.

— 1983. 'A critical examination of the theory that the right to the throne of ancient Egypt passed through the female line in the 18th Dynasty', *GM* 62: 68–69.

— 1986. 'The role of the royal family in the 18th Dynasty up to the end of the reign of Amenhotep III: 1. Queens', *Wepwawet* 2: 10–14.

— 1999. 'An unusual statue of a royal mother-in-law and grandmother', *Stud. Smith*: 255–59.

ROEDER, G. 1969. *Amarna-Reliefs aus Hermopolis* (Hildesheim: Gebr. Gerstenberg).

ROMER, J. 1976. 'Royal tombs of the early Eighteenth Dynasty', *MDAIK* 32: 191–206.

ROSE, J. 2000. *Tomb KV 39: A Double Archaeological Enigma* (Bristol: Western Academic & Specialist Press).

ROTH, S. 2001. *Die Koenigsmuetter des Alten Aegypten von der Fruehzeit bis zum Ende der 12. Dynastie* (Wiesbaden: Otto Harrassowitz).

RUFER-BACH, K. 1991–92. 'A mastaba in Chicago?', *KMT* 2/4: 28–33.

RUFFER, M.A. 1921. *Studies in the Palaeopathology of Egypt* (Chicago: Chicago UP).

RYHOLT, K.S.B. 1997. *The Political Situation in Egypt During the Second Intermediate Period, c. 1800–1550 BC* (Copenhagen: Museum Tusculanum Press).

SAAD, Z.Y. 1957. *Ceiling Stelae in the Second Dynasty Tombs from the Excavations at Helwan* (Cairo: IFAO).

SABBAHY, L.K. 1993. 'Evidence for the titulary of the queen from Dynasty One', *GM* 135: 81–87.

— 1998. 'The king's mother in the Old Kingdom, with special reference to the title *s3t-nṯr*', *SAK* 25: 305–10.

— 2003. 'The female family of Amenemhat

II: a review of the evidence', in N. Grimal, A. Kamel and C. May-Sheikholeslami, *Hommages Fayza Haikel* (Cairo: IFAO): 239–44.

SAMUEL, A.E. 1962. *Ptolemaic Chronology* (Munich: Beck).

SCHADEN, O. 1982. *The God's Father Ay* (Ann Arbor: UMI).

SCHADEN, O.J. and E.R. ERTMAN 1998. 'The tomb of Amenmesse (KV 10): the first season'. *ASAE* 73: 116–55.

SCHAFER, B.E. (ed.) 1997. *Temples of Ancient Egypt* (London and New York: I.B. Tauris).

SCHIAPARELLI, E. 1924. *Esplorazione della 'Valle delle Regine' nella necropoli di Tebe* (Turin: Regio Museo di Antichitá).

SCHMIDT, H.C. and J. WILLEITNER 1994. *Nefertari: Gemahlin Ramses' II* (Mainz: Philipp von Zabern).

SCHMITZ, B. 1976. *Untersuchungen zum Titel S3-njswt 'Königssohn'* (Bonn: Rudolf Habelt Verlag).

SCHULZ, R. and M. SEIDEL (eds.) 1998. *Egypt: The World of the Pharaohs* (Cologne: Könemann).

SCHWEINFURTH, G. 1886. *Alte Baureste und hieroglyphische Inschriften im Uadi Gasus* (Berlin: Königlich Preussische Akadmei der Wissenschaften).

SEIPEL, W. 1980. *Untersuchungen zu den ägyptische Königinnen der Frühzeit und der Alten Reiches* (Hamburg: np).

SHAW, I. 1991. *Egyptian Weapons and Warfare* (Princes Risborough: Shire).

— (ed.) 1999. *The Oxford History of Ancient Egypt* (Oxford: OUP).

SILIOTTI, A. and C. LEBLANC 1993. *Nefertari e la Valle delle Regine* (Florence: Giunti).

SIMPSON, W.K. (ed.) 1973. *The Literature of Ancient Egypt: An Anthology of Stories, Instructions and Poetry* (New Haven and London: Yale UP).

SIMPSON, W.K. 1978. *The Mastabas of Kawab, Khafkhufu I and II. G 7110–20, 7130–40 and 7150 and Subsidiary Mastabas of Street 7100* (Boston: MFA).

SKEAT, T.C. 1969. *The Reigns of the Ptolemies²* (Munich: Beck).

SMITH, R.W. and D.B. REDFORD 1977. *The Akhenaten Temple Project* I (Warminster: Aris and Phillips).

SMITH, G.E. 1912. *The Royal Mummies (CCG)* (Cairo: IFAO).

SMITH, W.S. 1946. *History of Egyptian Sculpture and Painting in the Old Kingdom* (London: OUP).

SNAPE, S.R. 1985. 'Ramose restored: a royal prince and his mortuary cult', *JEA* 71: 180–83.

SOUROUZIAN, H. 1983. 'Honout-mi-rê, fille de Ramsès II et grande épouse du roi',

ASAE 69: 365–71.

——— 1989. *Les Monuments du Roi Merenptah* (Mainz: Philipp von Zabern).

STADELMANN, R. 1984. 'Khaefkhufu = Chephren. Beiträge zur Geschichte der 4. Dynastie', *SAK* 11: 165–72.

— 1994. 'König Teti und der Beginn der 6. Dynastie', *Homm. Leclant* I: 327–35.

STRONARCH, D. and A. ZOURNATZI 1997. 'Bisitun', in *OEANE* I: 330–31.

STRUDWICK, N. 1982. 'Notes on the mastaba of *3ḫt-ḥtp; ḥmi* and *nb-k3w-ḥr; idw* at Saqqara', *GM* 56: 89–94.

— 1985. *The Administration of Egypt in the Old Kingdom* (London: Kegan Paul International).

TAYLOR, J.H. 1998. 'Nodjmet, Payankh and Herihor: the end of the New Kingdom reconsidered', *P7ICE*: 1143–55.

TEETER, E. 1990/1. 'Kaemwaset: prince, priest, Egyptologist', *KMT* 1/4: 40–45, 62–64.

THIJS, A. 1998. 'Two books for one lady. The mother of Herihor rediscovered', *GM* 163: 101–110.

THOMAS, E. 1966. *The Royal Necropoleis of Thebes* (Princeton: privately printed).

THOMAS, E. 1980. 'The tomb of Queen Ahmose(?) Merytamen, Theban Tomb 320', *Serapis* 6: 171–81.

THOMPSON, D.J. 1988. *Memphis Under the Ptolemies* (Princeton: Princeton UP).

THÜR, H. 1990. 'Arsinoe IV, eine Schwester Kleopatras VII, Grabinhaberin des Oktagons von Ephesos? Ein Vorschlag', *JOAI* 60: 43–56.

TOMLINSON, R.A. 1987. 'The architectural context of the Macedonian vaulted tombs', *BSA* 82: 305–12.

TRAUNECKER, C. 1979. 'Essai sur l'histoire de la XXIXᵉ Dynastie', *BIFAO* 79: 395–436.

TRESSON, P. 1935–38. 'L'inscription de Chechanq Iᵉʳ, au Musée du Caire: un frippant example d'impôt progressif en matière religieuse', in *MelMasp* I: 817–40.

TRIGGER, B.G., B.J. KEMP, D. O'CONNOR and A.B. LLOYD 1983. *Ancient Egypt: A Social History* (Cambridge: CUP).

TROY, L. 1986. *Patterns of Queenship in Ancient Egyptian Myth and History* (Uppsala: Acta Universitatis Upsalensis).

TUNNY, J.A. 2000. 'Ptolemy "the son" reconsidered: are there too many Ptolemies?', *ZPE* 131: 83–92.

TYLOR, J.J. and F.Ll. GRIFFITH 1894. *The Tomb of Paheri at El-Kab* (London: EEF).

UPHILL, E. 1992. 'Where were the funerary temples of the New Kingdom queens?', *A6CIE*, I: 613–18.

VALOGGIA, M. 1969. 'Amenemhet IV et sa corégence avec Amenemhet III', *CdE* 21: 102–33.

VAN DE WALLE, B. 1968. 'La princesse Isis,

fille et épouse d'Aménophis III', *CdE* 43/85: 36–54.

VAN DEN BOORN, G.F. 1988. *The Duties of the Vizier: Civil Administration in the Early New Kingdom* (London: Kegan Paul International).

VAN SICLEN, C.C. 1974. 'A Ramesside ostracon of Queen Isis', *JNES* 33: 150–53.

— 1995. 'Queen Meryetre-Hatshepsut and the edifice of Amenhotep II at Karnak', in C.J. Eyre (ed.), *Seventh International Congress of Egyptologists, Cambridge, 3–9 September 1995. Abstracts of Papers* (Oxford: Oxbow): 167–68.

VELIKOVSKY, I. 1960. *Oedipus and Akhenaten: Myth and History* (London: Sidgwick and Jackson).

VERNER, M. 1978. 'Excavations at Abusir. Season 1976', *ZÄS* 105: 155–59.

— 1980. 'Excavations at Abusir. Season 1978/1979 – preliminary report', *ZÄS* 107: 158–69.

— 1982. 'The false-door of Khekeretnebty', *ZÄS* 109: 72–75.

— 1988. 'Excavations at Abusir. Season 1987 – preliminary report', *ZÄS* 115: 163–71.

— 1994. *Forgotten Pharaohs, Lost Pyramids* (Prague: Akademia/Skodaexport).

— 1995. *Abusir* III. *The Pyramid Complex of Khentkaous* (Prague: Karolinum Press).

— 1997. 'Excavations at Abusir. Season on 1994/95 and 1995/96', *ZÄS* 124: 71–85.

VERNER, M. and G. CALLENDER 1997. 'Image and reflection: two Old Kingdom queens named Khentkaus', *KMT* 8/3: 28–35.

VERNUS, P. 1976. 'Inscriptions de la Troisième Période Intermédiare (II)', *BIFAO* 75: 67–72.

VIREY, P. 1891. *Sept Tombeaux Thébains de la XVIIIe Dynastie* (Cairo: IFAO).

VIKENTIEV, V. 1954. 'Les divines adorices de Wadi Gasus' *ASAE* 52: 151–59.

VITTMANN, G. 1974a. 'Zwei Königinnen der Spätzeit namens Chedebnitjerbone', *CdE* 49: 43–51.

— 1974b. 'Was there a coregency of Ahmose and Amenophis I?', *JEA* 60: 250–51.

— 1975. ''Dir Familie der saitischen Köninge', *Orientalia* 44: 375–87.

VON BECKERATH, J. 1966. 'Die Dynastie der Herakleopoliten (9./10. Dynastie', *ZÄS* 93: 13–20.

WARBURTON, D.A. 2001. 'Officials', *OEAE* II: 576–83.

WEEKS, K.R. 1998. *The Lost Tomb: The Greatest Discovery in the Valley of the Kings since Tutankhamun* (London: Weidenfeld and Nicolson).

— 2000. *KV5: A Preliminary Report* (Cairo: AUC Press).

— (ed.) 2001. *Valley of the Kings* (Vercelli: White Star).

WEILL, R. 1911. 'Un temple de Noutirkha-Zosir à Heliopolis', *Sphinx* 15: 9–26.

— 1912. *Les Décrets Royaux de l'Ancien Empire Égyptien* (Paris: P. Geuthner).

WHITEHORNE, J.E.G. 1994. *Cleopatras* (London: Routledge).

WILKINSON, T.A.H. 1999. *Early Dynastic Egypt* (London: Routledge).

— 2000. *Royal Annals of Ancient Egypt: The Palermo Stone and its Associated Fragments* (London: Kegan Paul International).

WINLOCK, H.E. 1924. 'The tombs of the kings of the Seventeenth Dynasty at Thebes', *JEA* 10: 217–77.

— 1929. 'Notes on the reburial of Tuthmosis I', *JEA* 15: 59–67.

— 1932. *The Tomb of Queen Meryet-Amun at Thebes* (New York: MMA).

— 1942. *Excavations at Deir el Bahri 1911–1931* (New York: Macmillan).

— 1943. 'The eleventh Egyptian Dynasty', *JNES* 2: 249–83.

— 1947. *The Rise and Fall of the Middle Kingdom at Thebes* (New York: Macmillan).

— 1948. *The Treasure of Three Egyptian Princesses* (New York: MMA).

WOOD, M. 1997. *In the Footsteps of Alexander the Great* (London: BBC Books).

WYSOCKI, Z. 1984. 'The results of research, architectonic studies and of protective work over the North Portico of the Middle Courtyard in the Hatshepsut Temple at Deir el Bahari', *MDAIK* 40: 329–49.

YOYOTTE, J. 1960. 'Le talisman de la victoire d'Osorkon, prince du Sais et autres lieux', *BSFE* 31: 13–22.

— 1972. 'Les adoratrices de la Troisième Période Intermédiare', *BSFE* 64: 31–52.

— 1982–83. 'Un souhait de Bonne Année en faveur du Prince Nechao', *RdE* 34: 142–45.

YURCO, F.J. 1978. 'Merenptah's Palestinian campaign', *JSSEA* 8: 70.

— 1979. 'Six statues at Karnak', *MMJ* 14: 15–31.

ZIVIE, C.M. 1976. *Giza au Deuxiéme Millénaire* (Cairo: IFAO).

ZIVIE-COCHE, C.M. 1991. *Giza au Premier Millenaire, autour du Temple d'Isis, Dame des Pyramides* (Boston: Museum of Fine Arts).

ZIEGLER, C. 1994. 'Notes sur la reine Tiy', *Homm. Leclant* I: 531–48.

— (ed.) 2002. *The Pharaohs* (London: Thames & Hudson).

Addenda

To p. 141:

Unplaced during first half of 18th Dynasty

Amenhotep R (KSon)
Buried in QV82, alongside Minemhat.

Baki (KSon)
Buried in QV72, alongside Hatneferet A; a vase bearing the prince's name in hieratic was found in the tomb.

Hatneferet (KD)
Buried in QV72, alongside Baki.

Hori Q (KSon)
Buried in QV8, alongside [...]18S.

Meryetre B (KD)
Buried in QV17, alongside Wermeryotes.

Meryetre C (KD)
Buried in QV76.

Minemhat (KSon)
Buried in QV82, alongside Amenhotep R.

Wermeryotes (KD)
Buried in QV17, alongside Meryetre B; a canopic jar of the princess was found in the tomb.

[...]18S (KD)
Buried in QV8, alongside Hori Q.

To p. 205:

Djedptahiufankh A (3PA)
Probable husband of Nesitanebetashru A; his mummy was found in TT320.

To p. 247:

Meryetnebes (KD, Adoratrix of Arsaphes)
Daughter of Psametik II, mentioned on a naophorus statue and a *shabti*.

Sources of Illustrations

Unless otherwise listed, all photographs and line drawings are by Aidan Dodson and Dyan Hilton respectively. The authors also hold copyright to all the genealogical tables.

AMP Ägyptisches Museum und Papyrussammlung, Staatliche Museen zu Berlin; BM British Museum, London; CM Egyptian Museum, Cairo; EES Egypt Exploration Society; JR John Ross; MD Michael Duigan; MFA Museum of Fine Arts, Boston; MMA Metropolitan Museum of Art, New York; PC Peter Clayton; RMS Royal Museum of Scotland, Edinburgh.

a above; b below; l left; r right; m middle

Frontispiece CM; 10 JR; 13a Derek Welsby; 13b Derek Welsby; 14a MD; 14b after Brunner 1966; 15 RMS; 21 JR; 22 JR; 24 MD; 26r MD; 27 MD; 29a CM; 30 AMP; 36 De Morgan, Bouriant, Legrain, Jéquier & Barsanti 1894; 37 Chicago, The Field Museum of Natural History; 38 Hervé Champollion; 43 Kate Spence; 44 BM; 46b Brooklyn Museum of Art; 47 Albert Shoucair; 48a Schäfer & Andrae 1925; 49bm Museo Egizio di Torino; 49br after Saad 1957; 51l JR; 54–55 Musée de Louvre, Paris; 57bl Roemer-und-Pelizaeus-Museum, Hildesheim; 57br MFA; 59al Heidi Grassley; 60l after Smith 1946; 60r CM; 61l Lepsius 1849–59; 61r MD; 66a Borchardt 1910–13: II, pl.33; 68a Mariette 1884–85; 68b Albert Shoucair; 69al after Posener-Kriéger 1976: 531, fig.34; 69ar Mariette 1884–85: 183; 74a Jéquier 1933: 55; 74b Brooklyn Museum of Art, Charles Edwin Wilbour Fund; 75 Albert Shoucair; 76 Jéquier 1933: 53; 79 JR; 82 MD; 84a after Lepsius; 86–87 PC; 87 JR; 88b PC; 89al Photo Marburg; 88ar BM; 89b MD; 90 MMA; 91b MD; 95l *The Graphic* 1895; 96 De Morgan 1903: fig.128; 97 CM;

99l MMA; 99r PC; 103a Jürgen Liepe; 105 after W.J. Bankes; 112l PC; 112r PC; 114 BM; 120 Weigall in Petrie 1902: pl.LVII; 121 Andrea Jemolo; 122 Brooklyn Museum of Art; 123a CM; 123b Lepsius 1849–59: III, 2[d]; 124l MD; 124r RMS; 125l CM; 126 MD; 128 Araldo de Luca/Archivio White Star; 131l RMS; 131r MD; 132 MMA; 133b BM; 136 JR; 137 Virey 1891: 368; 139bl CM; 142 Jürgen Liepe; 143 CM; 145a AMP; 145bl PC; 147l AMP; 147r CM; 148a EES; 149b CM; 150b JR; 151br CM; 152 CM; 153 Museo Egizio di Torino; 154al Hayes 1951: fig.27 [KK]; 154ar Sotheby's; 155a MMA; 156a Ashmolean Museum, Oxford; 156b Heidi Grassley; 157al MD; 157b MMA, gift of Edward S. Harkness; 159a MMA; 162b K.A. Kitchen; 163 MD; 166al MD; 167 Cyril Aldred; 169a MD; 169b Quibell 1912: pl.LXX; 170 Roger Wood; 172 Andrea Jemolo; 175l Kunsthistorisches Museum, Vienna; 175r CM; 181a Albert Shoucair; 182a Neville 1891: pl.XXXVI; 182b De Morgan, Bouriant, Legrain, Jéquier & Barsanti 1894; 183a Davis et al. 1908; 185 MD; 190 Petrie 1905: fig.73; 193a Lepsius 1897: 101; 193b Araldo de Luca/Archivio White Star; 195 Jürgen Liepe; 199a&b MD; 202 Emile Brugsch; 203 Albert Shoucair; 204 MD; 206a CM; 206b Smith 1912; 207 Emile Brugsch; 208l PC; 208m&r Smith 1912; 216 BM; 217a Neville 1892: pl.VI; 220 MD; 231 Loat 1905: pl.XIX; 234 Jürgen Liepe; 235 Photo Hirmer; 236 CM; 239l CM; 242 Schweinfurth 1886: pl.II; 245 BM; 246l Mariette 1884–85: 555; 246r Kunsthistorisches Museum, Vienna; 249 BM; 252 Roger Wood; 254 Musée de Louvre, Paris; 255 AMP; 257a CM; 265 Roger-Viollet; 270l&r Royal Ontario Museum, Toronto; 271 MMA, gift of Mrs John D. Rockefeller, Jr, 1938; 272a AMP; 274 AMP; 278 PC.

Index

Names in **BOLD UPPER CASE** are those of kings of Egypt, UPPER CASE those of foreign rulers; *italics* indicate a female; **bold numbers** signify Brief Lives and genealogical trees containing the individual; *italic numbers* signify depiction in an illustration, or mention in the caption thereof.